THE DEMOCRATIC REVOLUTION IN LATIN AMERICA

THE DEMOCRATIC REVOLUTION IN LATIN AMERICA

History, Politics, and U.S. Policy

Howard J. Wiarda

A Twentieth Century Fund Book

HOLMES & MEIER
New York / London

Published in the United States of America 1990 by
Holmes & Meier Publishers, Inc.
30 Irving Place   New York, NY 10003

Copyright © 1990 by the Twentieth Century Fund

Book design by Marilyn Marcus

The paper used in this publication meets the requirements of the American National Standard for Permanence of Paper for Printed Library Materials, Z39.48-1984.

Library of Congress Cataloging-in-Publication Data

Wiarda, Howard J., 1939–
    The democratic revolution in Latin America / Howard J. Wiarda.
       p.   cm.
    Includes bibliographical references, index.
    ISBN 0-8419-1276-9 (alk. paper).—ISBN 0-8419-1277-7 (pbk. : alk. paper)
       1. Latin America—Politics and government—1980–
    2. Representative government and representation—Latin America—History—20th Century.   3. Latin America—Foreign relations—United States.   4. United States—Foreign relations—Latin America.
    I. Title.
    F1414.2.W49   1990
    320.98—dc20
                                                                    90-31311
                                                                    CIP

Manufactured in the United States of America

Contents

Foreword

Latin America experienced a democratic resurgence in the mid-1980s after two decades of growing military-authoritarian rule. The movement toward democracy, along with the debt crisis that has engulfed the entire region, has renewed public interest in this area of the world. The question facing the United States is what effects these changes will have on U.S.-Latin American relations.

The average American would be surprised to learn that there is any serious debate in this country over whether or not our foreign policy should favor human rights and democracy in Latin America. There is a prevailing sense that gunboat diplomacy is a policy stored in some back room, tucked behind the Monroe Doctrine. And even specialists probably feel we have absorbed the bitter lessons learned from supporting almost any government as long as it is anti-Communist. The reality is, of course, more complicated.

Howard Wiarda, professor of political science at the University of Massachusetts, provides an extensive analysis of these issues in this important contribution to the public discussion of American foreign policy. He rightly is concerned with the impact of domestic political trends on our attitudes about what is best for other nations in the hemisphere. In Latin America, after all, democratic principles are embodied in different institutions, derived from individual national histories. Understanding and accepting those differences is, Wiarda argues, the key to developing strong and lasting ties to democratic movements in the region.

The Fund has long had a special interest in Latin America, supporting a number of studies on political and economic affairs in the region since the late 1950s. Here Wiarda looks at the turn toward democracy in Latin

America in the context of the region's social institutions and political traditions, and offers policymakers critical insights into the political transformations that are under way. The Fund is grateful to him for his efforts.

Richard C. Leone, Director
The Twentieth Century Fund
January 1990

Preface

In the past decade Latin America has gone through a profound, sometimes wrenching, but enormously heartening transition to democracy. Seventeen of the twenty countries, and over 90 percent of the population, can now be said to live under democratic governments. More of Latin America is now democratic, or tending in a democratic direction, than at any time in the previous 160-year independent history of the continent going back to the struggle for separation from Spain and, in the Brazilian case, Portugal, in the 1820s.

These new democratic openings carry immense and generally encouraging (the qualifier is explained at length in the book) implications for Latin America. But they also carry major implications for U.S. foreign policy. For, as we shall see in the analysis that follows, democracy is no panacea for improving U.S. policy or relations with Latin America.

The current democratic trend in Latin America raises many questions. Just how democratic is Latin America, and how democratic does it want to be? Is the trend a permanent and lasting one, or is it merely cyclical, another of those democratic waves that periodically sweep over Latin America and then recede? Do the United States and Latin America mean the same things by "democracy" and "human rights"? How successful has the United States been and how successful can it be in exporting its form of democracy to Latin America? What if the new democratic regimes in Latin America define their interests in different ways than does the United States, or if they pursue policies vis-à-vis Cuba or Central America that are at odds with U.S. policy toward the area? If this new wave of democracy is reversed, what should be our response? Are the present domestic and international currents in the United States and in Latin America harmonious and reconcilable, or are they fundamentally so far apart as to be incompatible? These are among the questions explored in this volume.

*   *   *

This project was carried out with the assistance of numerous groups and individuals. Foremost among these are the Center for International Affairs at Harvard University, with which the author has been associated on an on-again-off-again basis since 1979; the American Enterprise Institute for Public Policy Research in Washington, D.C., where he served as resident scholar and director of the Center for Hemispheric Affairs, 1981–87; the Foreign Policy Research Institute, which named him the Thornton D. Hooper Fellow in International Security Affairs for 1987–88; and the Department of Political Science at the University of Massachusetts at Amherst, which has served as home for many years and has also been exceedingly generous with leave. The Twentieth Century Fund supported this project, and its late director Murray Rossant and then its acting director Marcia Bystryn, as well as program officers Scott McConnell and Nina Massen, offered valued advice and guidance. Louise Skillings proved to be the best secretary ever, and, as usual, Dr. Iêda Siqueira Wiarda has given enormously of her time, her professional knowledge, and her research and editorial skills—so much so that if she herself did not object, it would be appropriate to list her as co-author.

These acknowledgments notwithstanding, the book and its conclusions remain the author's own. The debts are many but the final product—and the responsibility—is mine alone.

Introduction

The Trend toward Democracy in Latin America: Opportunities and Problems

Only a few short years ago democracy in Latin America seemed everywhere to be dead, dying, or under siege.[1] In the spring of 1978 twelve of the twenty Latin American countries (and the vast majority of the Latin American population) were governed by military regimes. The list included Argentina, Bolivia, Brazil, Chile, Ecuador, El Salvador, Guatemala, Honduras, Panama, Paraguay, Peru, and Uruguay. In five others—Cuba, the Dominican Republic, Haiti, Mexico, and Nicaragua—either a system of authoritarianism if not (in one or two cases) full-scale totalitarianism was ensconced, or else the military was so close to the surface of power, so much a part of a superficially civilian government, that the familiar distinction between civilian and military regimes was rendered meaningless.

It had become commonplace, in the scholarly literature as well as at the policy level, to emphasize—and lament—the decline of civilian democracy and the rule of law throughout the continent; the rash of military coups since the early 1960s; the rise of brutal, authoritarian, and repressive regimes in such formerly democratic nations as Chile and Uruguay; the widespread use of torture and officially sanctioned murder in such civilized countries as Argentina and Brazil; and the widespread violations of human rights throughout the hemisphere. Meanwhile the number of genuinely democratic regimes had shrunk to a mere handful: Colombia, Costa Rica, and Venezuela. Even these were often categorized as elite-directed democracies (Colombia and Costa Rica)[2] or else were the product of such fortuitous circumstances (the fact that Venezuela almost floats on oil) that their example and experience were unlikely to be repeated elsewhere.

Democracy in Latin America was threatened and under siege not only by the wave of military coups that swept the area in the 1960s and 1970s, but also by a whole new body of literature (which the author had a hand in fashioning) that questioned whether democracy was the goal toward which Latin America aspired or if the "struggle" for it (as in the titles of so many books on the subject) was the correct and most appropriate approach for the area. The problem was not just the rising tide of military-authoritarian rule but a growing corpus of academic studies that saw authoritarianism, corporatism, elitism, and clientelism as essential, almost "natural" (and therefore probably permanent) elements of the Latin American tradition and political culture.[3]

Democracy and its usual accompanying institutions (elections, checks and balances, a free press, separation of powers, and the like) were often viewed in the newer interpretations as foreign and inappropriate Anglo-American imports artificially imposed on a culture and society where they did not fit. In some of the overly deterministic expressions of this argument (from which the author disassociated himself),[4] attempts at democratic reformism were viewed as futile, since, if Latin America is inherently elitist and authoritarian, no amount of democratic reform–mongering (the phrase is Albert Hirschman's)[5] was likely to succeed. Democracy was therefore in trouble in Latin America not just because of spreading militarism but because a whole new school and generation of Latin American historians and social scientists had given up on it, or thought it not important, or pronounced it irrelevant to or outside the main currents of the Latin American tradition. Sometimes these new interpretations, by rationalizing authoritarianism, corporatism, and other nondemocratic features in Latin America, also provided—most often unintentionally—a strong justification and legitimacy for military authoritarianism and some not very democratic practices.

Such a deterministic view is almost certainly wrong. Latin America does have some powerful corporatist, authoritarian, and nondemocratic features that are deeply ingrained in the culture, society, politics, education, religion, and economic life of the region. That strain was the dominant one up to independence, and in many respects even beyond, persisting in altered forms through the nineteenth century and on into the twentieth. Many of these nondemocratic features are still present today. But from the eighteenth-century Enlightenment on, and certainly after independence was achieved early in the nineteenth century, there grew up alongside the older authoritarian tradition, and often coexisting with it, a second framework of social and political organization that was liberal, democratic, and egalitarian. The liberal tradition was not always the dominant or even majority strain, and it was frequently submerged under authoritarianism and abused and repressed by authoritarianism's ruling representatives. But the liberal strain remained alive and vibrant, resurfacing from time to time and even growing gradually in strength, although such growth was frequently disguised by the continuing strength and power of authoritarianism. As the author wrote a decade ago (1978) at the height of authoritarian-corporate rule in Latin America:

> And yet, throughout the hemisphere, the democratic mythos remains very much alive, the struggle for democratic participation and freer societies still goes on, and the aspiration for democratic development continues to constitute a major societal goal. Democracy is under attack, but it is certainly too early to sound its death-knell; and a group of younger scholars has recently sought to revive the democratic dream by arguing that while democracy as North Americans envision it may be fading throughout Latin America, the efforts by Latin Americans to devise democratic structures more in keeping with their own history and cultures constitute both a hopeful and a progressive sign.[6]

Those are precisely the issues we face today. The democratic ethos and institutions that were always present in Latin America have resurfaced; and the authoritarian tradition, while still existent, is currently in headlong retreat—discredited, corrupt, inefficient, thoroughly despised. If one includes Mexico, Panama, Chile, and Haiti in the democratic or evolving-toward-democracy category, only Cuba and Nicaragua on the left and Paraguay on the right (and even there some political openings are present) are outside the democratic camp. The transition to democracy in so many countries in such a short time (ten years) is nothing short of remarkable; indeed, it is one of the epochal and most heartening trends of the late twentieth century. How did such a remarkable transition to democracy in Latin America come about? Is the basis for it more solid than in the past? These, and the implications of the democratic transformations, both for Latin America itself and for U.S. policy, are issues this study addresses.[7]

The Problem

The United States has always waxed hot and cold on Latin America. For the most part we have tended to ignore and often disparage the area until a crisis—Guatemala in 1954, the Cuban Revolution in the late 1950s, the

Dominican Revolution of 1965, Chile under Allende, and Central America today—forces it onto our television screens if not into our consciousness. In terms of a policy response we have usually alternated between "benign neglect" of Latin America and highly charged military interventions. Never have we developed the coherent, sustained policy toward the area that we require.

It is not entirely clear why we have not developed as mature and normal a relationship with Latin America as we have with Western Europe. The book explores some of the reasons for this. They include, in general terms, strongly ingrained biases in the United States toward the foundations of Latin American culture and civilization, ethnocentrism and lack of empathy, asymmetries of size and power between the United States and Latin America, racial prejudice, intellectual attitudes in the United States that have often denigrated Latin America's worth and importance, jealousies in Latin America over the accomplishments and wealth of the United States, and a strong sense of superiority in the United States regarding its successes and what are perceived as Latin America's failures. We will return to some of these themes later; here let it simply be said that at a fundamental level attitudes such as these have not served as a basis for strong, stable, close, or sympathetic relations between the two parts of the Americas.

Now a series of democratic "openings" or "transitions" in Latin America, some of which the United States had a hand in assisting, offers us again the opportunity—perhaps for the last time—to put our relations on a sounder and more consistent basis. The impression is growing stronger, in the United States as well as in Latin America, that this may finally be democracy's moment in the Western Hemisphere. The social, economic, and political conditions now seem to be quite different from those of the early 1960s, when we and Latin America previously attempted—largely unsuccessfully—to build democracy through the Alliance for Progress, the Peace Corps, and other innovative policies of the Kennedy era. Latin America is more developed, the middle class is larger, its political institutions are firmer, affluence is greater and more widespread, and a great deal of modernization has occurred. Castroism seems to have lost its appeal, and extreme right-wing forces are in retreat. It may even be (although one should not be wildly optimistic) that the United States has learned something about Latin America, and Latin America about the United States, in the intervening quarter-century. There are many hopeful signs.

The evidence is growing that not only has Latin America embarked on a democratic course after decades and even centuries marked by the absence of very much democratic growth, but that the recent evolution toward democracy in Latin America may be long-lasting and even permanent.

Sociologically and politically Latin America has changed immensely in the past twenty years. The image of instability we have of the area as conveyed by newspaper headlines recording the latest coup or the stereotypes of comic-opera politics portrayed in numerous cartoons no longer reflects the facts, if it ever did. The new trends in Latin America are major and important, deserving of serious attention and with profound implications for U.S. foreign policy. But in our enthusiasm for democracy in Latin America and for changes in the U.S. policy, we need to keep in mind some cautions and warning signals, for the new trends toward democracy in Latin America need to be more than celebrated. They also need to be analyzed carefully and their foreign policy implications thoroughly explored.

The problem for policy—and the main theme of this book—is whether the United States can adjust and refashion its foreign policy in prudent and appropriate ways so as to take account of these changes in Latin America and the new democratic openings, in order to better secure and cement its relations with the continent. We need to support democracy in Latin America, while simultaneously recognizing that there are limits to what the United States can do in aiding democratic growth there; that democracy is not the sole interest of the United States in Latin America; and that being in favor of democracy will not necessarily or automatically lead to better relations with the individual countries. We need to build a longer-term and a more mature relationship with Latin America, and the new democratic openings there offer a unique opportunity to do so. But we should not lose sight of the complex realities of Latin America or of our now more circumscribed capacity to influence events there.

We need, for example, to stop disparaging the area, to stop dealing with it in a condescending manner, neglecting and ignoring it—only until the next crisis forces us to react. We need to begin understanding Latin America on its own terms, in its own context. This includes Latin America's own sometimes distinctive meanings of democracy, which will also be stressed in the course of this book. In addition, based on these new and deeper understandings, we need to develop a more enlightened, consistent, and "normal" relationship with the Latin American countries. The fact is that the new democratic openings in Latin America offer not only opportunities to U.S. foreign policy but also potential difficulties for it that are far less often discussed. Whether we can comprehend these new currents in the area and appropriately seize the opportunities available remains very much an open question.

Several related themes, which can also be seen as working hypotheses, run through this analysis, giving coherence to the study and helping tie it together:

1. We are often ignorant about Latin American history. Many of our students seem to believe Latin America either has no history or else that its history began in 1979 with the Nicaraguan revolution. We need to know the roots and background of Latin America, why the weight of history and the past remains so heavy there, and why it has been so difficult to establish democracy in the region. We must therefore study not just Latin America's recent politics but its origins in medieval Iberia and in the system Spain and Portugal transferred to the New World.

2. We need to understand the relations between economics and politics in Latin America. In the United States we assume our democratic political institutions are permanent—independent of economic downturns, but in Latin America that assumption cannot be taken for granted. Economics and politics are intimately related. When the Latin American economies go into a tailspin, the political system often topples shortly thereafter. Will that happen again in today's difficult economic circumstances?

3. We need to know the implications of the United States' history of disdainful treatment of Latin America and its tradition of generally ignoring the area. We need to understand the history of U.S.–Latin American relations and why it will be difficult for the United States to shape current developments there. We need to understand the roots of anti-Americanism in the area. We need to know the history of U.S. interventions in such countries as Guatemala, Cuba, Nicaragua, the Dominican Republic, and Chile. The United States does not have entirely clean hands in these affairs, and there is a legacy of U.S. actions in the area that limits our capacity to influence current developments. We need not be deterministic about this spotty past, or fall into the trap of blaming all of the region's ills on the United States, but we do need to know that there is a long history involved that cannot simply be erased.

4. We need to know about the new democratic trends in Latin America, their dynamics, and how permanent they are likely to be. We need to know both the elements of historical Latin American political culture that operate in favor of a democratic transition and those that continue to impede it. We must understand as well the

contemporary social movements and institutions that support democracy and how (if at all) these are stronger and better institutionalized now than in earlier epochs when Latin America has tried democracy, without notable success.

5. We need to know what form or forms democracy will take in Latin America, and whether it will be in accord with U.S. understandings of democracy or even compatible with them. My own earlier research leads me to suggest the new Latin American democracies will likely represent a mix of U.S.–and European-inspired institutions combined with indigenous and traditional Latin American patterns.[8] We will need to adjust to and accommodate these often distinctive forms of democracy, both intellectually and in a policy sense.

This study will thus be concerned with what Latin America means by democracy, how and where that diverges from the U.S. conception as well as where it accords with it, and what are the foreign policy implications that stem from our coming to grips realistically with these distinct interpretations. The broader ramifications of Latin America's new democratic openings, the "new realities" in both Latin America and in U.S.–Latin American relations, and the implications of these for U.S. foreign policy will be examined. The question of whether the United States can now seize the opportunities present in the current context to assist democracy in Latin America while also advancing U.S. policy interests will be assessed. A major concern is whether these goals (Latin American democracy and U.S. policy interests) prove ultimately to be incompatible. Another is whether the United States will recognize the possibilities it now has in Latin America to enhance its relations and put them on a more mature basis, or whether it will revert to its traditional neglect of the area, allow the democracies to founder, and later on have to face the unhappy alternatives of Marxist-Leninist guerrillas or a reassertion of repressive regimes. In short, this research explores the difficulties as well as the possibilities that the new democratic openings in Latin America imply for U.S. policy.

Discussion

Democracy has not always fared well in Latin America. The area has a long and continuing tradition of authoritarian politics. In the 1950s and early 1960s a number of Latin America's longest-lived tyrants passed from the scene, and for a time it appeared that with U.S. assistance under the Alliance for Progress democracy might flourish.[9] But in the mid- to late 1960s and continuing into the 1970s a new wave of "bureaucratic authoritarians,"[10] as they were then called, seized power, intending not just to stage temporary coups but to stay in power sufficiently long to restructure national politics.

Between 1978 and 1988 the situation was dramatically reversed. In South America (Guyana, Suriname, and French Guiana are not included in this study) all the countries except Chile and Paraguay (and even here there was significant movement toward a more open society), and in the Caribbean Basin all except Cuba and Nicaragua, either have democratic governments or have governments committed to democracy. Argentina, Uruguay, Brazil, Bolivia, Ecuador, and Peru have all made dramatic returns to democratic rule in the South American continent. In Central America and the Caribbean the transition to democracy in the Dominican Republic, El Salvador, Honduras, and Guatemala has been similarly inspiring. Haiti is now rid of the Duvaliers and may be moving toward democracy; Mexico may be beginning a transition from a civilian form of organic authoritarianism ("democracy" according to Rousseau's model) to a more genuinely liberal form.

At this time the vast majority of the Latin American countries and people live under the rule of law and a system of government that, with only a little stretching, can be called democratic. The elected leaders of the area as of 1988—Sarney in Brazil, Alfonsín in Argentina, Sanguinetti in Uruguay, García in Peru, Febres and Borja in Ecuador, Duarte in El Salvador, Cerezo in Guatemala, Balaguer in the Dominican Republic, Lusinchi in Venezuela, Arías in Costa Rica, Azcona in Honduras, de la Madrid and Salinas in Mexico, Barco in Colombia, Paz in Bolivia—tend to be pragmatists and moderates, in both their domestic and foreign policies. Hence the opportunities exist not only for a new democratic era in Latin America but also for the United States to cement its relations with a whole new generation of centrist democrats.

The cementing of such a new relationship with Latin America on the basis of the commonality of democratic norms and aspirations will not be easy. On the one hand Latin America retains many practices, institutions, and ways of thinking that are not particularly democratic and that could well come back to power in quite a few countries. On the other hand one cannot assume that a commonality of norms and aspirations will automatically lead to better relations. On the contrary, democracy in Latin America may well lead these countries to conclude that their interests lie in *not* maintaining such close ties to the United States, for many of the new democracies have such strong nationalistic aspirations that they are bound almost by definition to be strongly anti-American or at least quite independent.

These diverse possibilities mean that we need to understand the broad sweep and common ingredients of Latin American history, sociology, and politics as well as the particularities of the individual countries, their policy concerns, and their relations with the United States. This book analyzes the elements from Latin America's long history and its political culture—the *hacienda,* the oligarchy, the older belief system, the traditional class structure, the mercantilist economy—that have in the past retarded democracy. At the same time, it seeks to analyze the newer forces—political parties, new leaders, the middle class, trade unions, technocrats, organized peasant and religious movements—that have recently propelled Latin America in the direction of democracy. The book discusses the key issues in the democratization process as well as the leading case studies. It analyzes those pressures pulling Latin America and the United States together as well as those pushing them apart. The study suggests what policies the United States should pursue to encourage Latin American democratic transitions, what we can realistically do to assist Latin American democratization and its further consolidation, and what kinds of political developments in the region we and the Latin Americans can reasonably hope for. In this sense the book is both analytical and policy-oriented.

Democratization is a significant topic of critical importance to Latin America and to U.S. foreign policy, especially at the present time. As a nation we have been in the process of discovering over the past few years that Latin America is of vital importance to us, but we are still casting about for an appropriate foreign policy response. We have hit upon the democracy theme as a key pillar on which to build our foreign policy, but we have not thought through fully the meaning of what is occurring in Latin America or what the foreign policy implications for the United States are likely to be.

A first-order priority is to be clear about what Latin Americans have in mind when they speak of democracy and whether or how that corresponds to U.S. or more commonly accepted definitions. Abundant scholarship suggests that while there are common beliefs and institutions undergirding both U.S. and Latin American democracy, there are important differences as well.[11] Such key terms as popular sovereignty, representative government, the popular will, participation, rights, even democracy itself often mean something different in Latin America, or they carry distinct nuances and emphases, or they occupy different priorities. Latin America, as we shall see, has historically been closer to the Thomistic and, later, Rousseauean conceptions of these terms than to the Lockean-liberal understandings;[12] and while this is now changing increasingly toward a Lockean viewpoint, the echoes of the past and of other interpretations are still powerful. The Latin American conception of democracy, for example, has often been close to Rousseau's notion of the general will, which is intuitively known through the person of an all-powerful leader or "man on horseback"; it has not historically been based on popular suffrage and one-man-one-vote. In Latin America this notion descended from Rousseau is being gradually supplanted by a system of regular competitive democratic elections, but the legacy from that earlier tradition is still present. Similarly, Latin America's conceptions of representation and pluralism have often taken organic and corporative forms distinct from the individualism of the United States and its unbridled, freewheeling, almost anarchic pluralism.[13]

For a more effective foreign policy we need to know the practical consequences that stem from these distinct meanings of democracy's key terms. Before we put all our foreign policy eggs in the democracy basket, therefore, we had better be quite clear as to what basket we are putting them in. Is Mexico's single-party system democratic? If not or only partially so, and if we push too hard or the wrong way for greater democratization, do we not run the risk (as Alan Riding's excellent recent book on Mexico suggests)[14] of destabilizing the very nation we want above all to keep stable? Are we wise enough to adjust to and accept different conceptions of democracy in Latin America and the implications that follow from these differences for policy? This study explores those issues in detail.

First it is necessary briefly to take up one of the thornier issues here. It involves the compatibility of two of the central arguments of the book. On the one hand we argue here for a more attentive and consistent U.S. foreign policy toward Latin America, on the other for understanding Latin American democracy on its own terms. For this last point we further develop the theme of a U.S. policy often characterized by ethnocentrism and other ills. The two arguments, the strategic and the moral, do not necessarily rest comfortably with each other. While they are not always contradictory, in the world of realpolitik there may be—and frequently is—a tension between the two.

Under what circumstances, for example, can seeing Latin America on its own terms be compatible with U.S. policy interests? What if the two conflict? Is it realistic or wrong to hold that, when push comes to shove, Latin American "terms" will have to give way to U.S. "terms"—that is, power? Or, on the other hand, is it possible to see a learning process under way among U.S. officials, a growth in understanding of Latin America, so that U.S. policy will be based more on enlightened self-interest rather than simply the big stick? Can these changes be nurtured and encouraged? In short, can we resolve this fundamental tension in ways that allow Latin America to go forward with democratic development and U.S. interests to be served at the same time? The author believes that such resolutions of this dilemma are available, and they center on the fashioning of a foreign policy that includes the encouragement of democracy as one of its components. It is a theme to which we return in the conclusion.

A second difficult issue is whether Latin America wants democracy at all or wants it all that much. On the answer to that question hang different interpretations of the area held by professional Latin Americanists, with profound implications for policy. If we believe Latin America is clamoring for democracy, then certain policy recommendations favoring a strong pro-democracy stance would follow. But if Latin America is itself ambivalent about these goals, or if its authoritarian inclinations remain—as historically they have been—as important as its democratic ones, then a more restrained and hands-off policy would likely follow on the part of the United States. Latin America scholars have come down on all sides of this issue, and we need to sort out carefully the facts of the situation.

The answers provided in this book are complex. Yes, Latin America does, in general, want democracy, but with some important qualifications. In Latin American political thought and practice, there have in fact been two dominant traditions: a liberal-democratic one and an authoritarian one. Unlike the United States, where the overwhelmingly dominant tradition has been Lockean liberalism, Latin America has historicaly alternated between two main philosophies and ways of doing things: a democratic way and a Caesarist or Bonapartist way. Even today, although democracy enjoys overwhelming legitimacy, its efficacy in times of crisis in weak and strife-torn countries is still open to question, and most Latin Americans hold in reserve a possible authoritarian or "strong-government" solution if democracy fails to work, proves chaotic, or results in paralysis.[15] In this book, four measures are used to gauge the degree of Latin American support (or the lack thereof) for democracy: public opinion surveys, which tend to show that Latin America wants democracy but is not entirely convinced democracy works very well in the Latin American context, or that it should be in exact accord with U.S. understandings of democracy's workings and institutions; the constitutional tradition(s) where both democratic and authoritarian principles are enshrined, although the balance between these is shifting over time; election results, which similarly continue to emit mixed signals; and actual political institutions and practices, which frequently show crazy-quilt patterns of democracy and authoritarianism. Based on the conclusions reached about Latin American democracy after a careful weighing of these conflicting currents, a more balanced foreign policy approach may be reached.

A third difficulty involves letting our wishes for the area get in the way of hard analysis. We want so much—scholars as well as U.S. policymakers—for democracy to succeed in Latin America that we are often blind to other currents and forces. What we might call "wishful political sociology" or "wishful political science" frequently prevents us from understanding those movements and ideological traditions in Latin America (support for Pinochet in Chile or the Arena party in El Salvador) that are not particularly democratic and may even be antidemocratic. These forces as well as the democratic ones need to be thoroughly analyzed if we are to understand the area and if foreign policy is to be based on realities.

Fourth, we need to weigh Latin American democracy in its broader dimensions. These include, for example, the social structure and class relations of the region, the economic situation, and the international context. Take, for example, the economic downturn through which Latin America has been going as well as the debt crisis, which have devastated the region's economies and threaten to do the same to its political systems. Through 1988 the U.S. response to the crisis was largely a traditional one: that the economic crisis is up to Latin America to overcome, that the debt must be paid and the parties affected (banks and Latin American governments) must resolve it, that Latin America should continue following the austerity package of the International Monetary Fund, that this is an economic and not a political issue, and therefore that apart from some moral suasion to have the Congress augment the resources of the international lending banks, the U.S. government should not get directly involved.

But the issue *is* a political as much as an economic one. Historically, when the bottom has dropped out of the Latin American economies, the foundations of the region's political systems have usually suffered as well. If the Latin American economies continue in their depressed state, we are likely to see soon a new wave of coups d'état and probably more revolutionary challenges as well. The democratic regimes of the area are likely to be toppled. That will give added impetus to extremist groups and to subversive elements inside and outside Latin America who have a vested interest in seeing instability spread. Additionally, the severe damage that would ensue for the banks (primarily U.S.) and the international financial system would have major political and foreign policy implications.[16] Hence we need to begin looking at Latin America's economic and debt crisis as preeminently a political and foreign policy crisis as well as an economic one, and to begin exploring new ways of resolving it before we—and the new Latin American democracies—are overwhelmed by it.

Fifth, we need to think through very carefully the contradictory implications of a too strong or unidimensional pro-democracy position. This is not to say that we should not favor democracy as an aspect of our policy, only that we should recognize the likely results and possible constraints such a stand imposes. Democracy is not a panacea for Latin America's ills, nor will it likely result in significantly improved relations with Latin America. For one thing, it is quite possible that in a number of countries the current trend toward democracy could well be reversed; the United States needs to be prepared for that contingency. For example, if the elected government were to be overthrown or replaced in El Salvador, the implications for U.S. policy would be considerable, and we would likely find ourselves back in the same divisive policy debate as in the early 1980s.

Another related dilemma is that the United States has other strong interests (economic, strategic, political, diplomatic) in Latin America besides democracy, and we may find ourselves in a position in which, for strategic or other reasons, we must maintain good relations with some not very democratic regimes. In addition, quite a number of Latin America's new democratic regimes think of themselves as representing a more "progressive" and "advanced" form of democracy and are not especially friendly toward the United States. While the U.S. strongly supported the restoration of democracy in Argentina, for instance, democratic president Raúl Alfonsín had staked out a quasi-neutralist position on foreign affairs that denies that there is an East-West dimension in Latin America or that the United States has any legitimate strategic interest there[17]—a position that is clearly unacceptable from the U.S. point of view. We should not assume that the welcome trend toward democracy in Latin America will ipso facto make our relations with such proud and increasingly nationalistic countries as Peru, Brazil, or Argentina any more harmonious. In short, Latin America's recent democratic transitions imply problems as well as opportunities, and we need to evaluate carefully these conflicting crosscurrents and their implications for policy.

Sixth, and implied above, we need to distinguish carefully between and among the Latin American countries. The diverse Latin American nations cannot all be lumped together in the same category. They have different histories, traditions, institutions, and levels of development. Not all of them are of equal importance to the United States. In some countries the U.S. influence is greater; in others the United States has special responsibilities and obligations that require particular attention; and in some countries the need as well as the possibilities for assisting democracy are greater than in others. In this book we treat broad, hemispheric-wide themes, but we need to distinguish among the Latin American countries and we clearly cannot cast them all together in the same mold or sketch the same democratic projection for all of them.

Overall what seems to be required is a pragmatic, not a romantic, approach to the Latin American change and democratization processes and to the new requirements of policy that these imply. There are many strong, often partisan feelings "out there" with regard to Latin America but little in-depth knowledge or understanding on the part of either opinion leaders or policymakers. This study seeks to fill that void in our comprehension while arguing the need to put U.S.–Latin American relations on a more stable, mature, and long-term basis than has heretofore been the case. The new democratic openings in Latin America offer us a renewed opportunity to do so.

*   *   *

The Book: A Look Ahead

So far we have introduced the broad issues involved in the trend toward democracy in Latin America.

Part I focuses on the background—Latin American history, political culture, and current realities. Chapter 1 traces the troubled history of democracy in Latin America: the authoritarian origins of Iberian and Latin American society, the emergence of liberalism and democracy in the nineteenth century, and the subsequent alternations between authoritarianism and liberalism. Chapter 2 examines the political culture of the region and wrestles with those difficult questions of just how democratic Latin America really is and how strongly it desires to be democratic. In Chapter 3 the contemporary social, cultural, political, and international forces that are pushing Latin America toward democracy and democratic possibilities are examined.

Part II concentrates on U.S. foreign policy in Latin America and the U.S. responses to changes in the area. Chapter 4 analyzes the earlier, generally spotty, and unsuccessful record of U.S. efforts to export democracy to Latin America. In Chapter 5 the concentration is on human rights, U.S. human-rights policy as it has been applied in Latin America, and the problems and conundrums to which the policy has given rise. Chapter 6 deals with current U.S. efforts to promote democracy in Latin America, particularly the fashioning of the Reagan administration's "Project Democracy" and the National Endowment for Democracy, as well as the results of these efforts. Chapter 7 examines the relationship in Latin America between economics and politics and the implications of the current economic downturn and the debt crisis for the development and consolidation of democracy in Latin America. Chapter 8 shifts direction somewhat by assessing U.S. relations with nondemocratic regimes as well as U.S. efforts to push those regimes in a more democratic direction.

Having considered the multiple aspects of the democracy issues, the study moves in its final section to an assessment. First, in Chapter 9 the current condition of Latin American democracy is evaluated—both the forces that seem to augur well for its continuation as well as those that may undermine it. Chapter 10 wrestles with the difficult dilemmas that policymakers face when attempting to promote democracy in the region. The concern is with the degree to which policymakers can push democracy without interfering—despite the often noble intentions—in another country's internal affairs. A related dilemma is how the policymaker balances concern for democracy with other important interests in a given country. This chapter explores the instruments or levers—foreign aid, diplomacy, military pressures, covert activities, economic influence—the United States has available to it to help nudge countries toward democracy. The dilemma is this: if we push to overthrow an entrenched military regime, can we be sure that what we get instead might not be worse from the point of U.S. interests? In countries with weak democratic political institutions, our pressures might not produce democracy but only chaos or an opportunistic Marxist-Leninist regime. Can we really promote our conception of democracy in countries where the traditions may be different from our own? What do we do if a country (let us say Haiti) has virtually no democratic institutions on which to build? Are we really equipped to construct such institutions and to ensure the success of the transition? Should we send military forces, as Woodrow Wilson did, to "teach" Latin America about democracy? These are tough issues implying difficult choices; this chapter shows just how difficult and often limited the policy options are.

The author is strongly in favor of the United States pursuing a vigorous and energetic human-rights and pro-democracy policy in Latin America. But we need to be concerned about the highly emotional and polarized nature of the debate over these issues and about the lack of knowledge in the United States regarding Latin America and what the United States can and cannot do realistically in promoting democracy.

This book helps elucidate the special conditions, meanings, and institutional arrangements of democracy in Latin America as well as what the United States can reasonably expect to accomplish in the area. The analysis points to the pitfalls as well as the possibilities in a strategy aimed at assisting Latin American democracy. Overall, the book argues for a prudent, balanced, restrained, and ultimately somewhat modest agenda in the areas of human rights and democracy, in contrast to doing nothing or, alternatively, to the strident and sometimes self-defeating missionary campaigns in which the United States as a nation has sometimes engaged.

This conclusion, set forth in Chapter 10, complements another conclusion with regard to general U.S. policy in the area: the need for a prudent, comprehensive, realistic, and mature overall policy toward Latin America. Rather than alternating between benign neglect and responding to crises as we have done in the past, the United States needs to put its relations with Latin America on a more regular, sustained, and normal basis. Such a shift—and there have been important steps in this direction—would not only reflect the new importance of several of the Latin American countries and the area as a whole, but would also do wonders to improve U.S.–Latin American relations. The democracy agenda is therefore good, not only for its own sake, but also as a handle to accomplish these other important foreign policy goals. We should neither neglect the recent changes in Latin America and the opportunities the new democratic openings provide for a better U.S. foreign policy, nor so romanticize them that we lose sight of some of the harsher and often nondemocratic realities of the area. These conclusions are incorporated into a series of concrete policy recommendations with which the book ends.

Research Methodology

The research for this book involves a combination of original interviewing and fieldwork in Latin America, library research, and a review of the existing and current literature and work on the subject. The book is based on original materials drawn in part from my own work and research in this area; but for a wider audience of informed opinion leaders, policymakers, and others, it needs also to bring together the writings and findings of other scholars working on the subject.[18] It draws heavily on Latin American sources and authors, which are seldom used in policy writing but which constitute a rich storehouse of ideas, concepts, and data often quite different from our own. The book also uses the products of Latin America's own growing polling industry, which are almost entirely unknown in the United States. There is now, in addition, a growing literature on the transition to democracy in Latin America and—a further step—on how Latin American democracy may be consolidated.[19] This study brings both new materials and insights to the study of Latin America's democratic transitions and seeks to bridge the gap between academic research on the subject and U.S. foreign policy, which are often miles apart.

The research methodology is historical, political-cultural, and social-scientific. The study draws upon the growing published literature on this subject as well as the papers coming out of the think tanks and research institutes that have organized symposia on these themes. This material is supplemented by fieldwork and interviews carried out in Iberia and Latin America during a number of extensive recent research trips to the area. The analysis draws upon my academic, library, and archival research in Amherst, New York, Philadelphia, Cambridge, New Haven, and Washington, D.C.; interviews conducted in New York, Washington, D.C., and Latin America; and my research position in Washington, D.C., which has made me a frequent participant in and participant-observer of the U.S. foreign policymaking process over the past ten years.[20]

Notes

1. See the analysis in Howard J. Wiarda, ed., *The Continuing Struggle for Democracy in Latin America* (Boulder, Colo.: Westview Press, 1980).
2. Harvey F. Kline, *Colombia: Portrait of Unity and Disunity* (Boulder, Colo.: Westview Press, 1983); Charles F. Denton, *Patterns of Costa Rican Politics* (Boston: Allyn and Bacon, 1971); and John A. Peeler, *Latin American Democracy: Colombia, Costa Rica, Venezuela* (Chapel Hill, N.C.: University of North Carolina Press, 1985).
3. See Guillermo O'Donnell, *Modernization and Bureaucratic-Authoritarianism* (Berkeley, Calif.: Institute of International Studies, University of California, 1973); James Malloy, ed., *Authoritarianism and Corporatism in Latin America* (Pittsburgh: University of Pittsburgh Press, 1977); Frederick B. Pike and Thomas Stritch, eds., *The New Corporatism* (Notre Dame, Ind.: University of Notre Dame Press, 1973); and Howard J. Wiarda, *Corporatism and National Development in Latin America* (Boulder, Colo.: Westview Press, 1981).
4. The parenthetical statement is made necessary by the author's involvement in this important debate and by the fact that some of his earlier writings on corporatism and authoritarianism have been interpreted as arguing for the "normalcy" of repressive regimes in Latin America and, by extension, for the acceptance of such governments by U.S. policy. Such an interpretation is a misreading of my views, as I assumed a careful reading of my earlier writings made clear and as the present book should make clearer still.
5. Albert O. Hirschman, *Journeys Toward Progress: Studies of Economic Policy-Making in Latin America* (New York: Doubleday/Anchor, 1965).

xxviii / *Introduction*

6. Wiarda, *Continuing Struggle for Democracy*, p. xiii.
7. For elaboration of the themes discussed here, see Howard J. Wiarda, *In Search of Policy: The United States and Latin America* (Washington, D.C.: American Enterprise Institute, 1984).
8. Howard J. Wiarda, ed., *Politics and Social Change in Latin America: The Distinct Tradition*, 2d rev. ed. (Amherst, Mass.: University of Massachusetts Press, 1982).
9. Tad Szulc, *Twilight of the Tyrants* (New York: Holt, 1959).
10. See O'Donnell, *Modernization and Bureaucratic-Authoritarianism*, as well as numerous subsequent writings by that author on the subject.
11. For example, Glen Dealy, *The Public Man: An Interpretation of Latin America and Other Catholic Countries* (Amherst, Mass.: University of Massachusetts Press, 1977); Richard Morse, "The Heritage of Latin America," in Louis Hartz, ed., *The Founding of New Societies* (New York: Harcourt Brace Jovanovich, 1964); Howard J. Wiarda, "Systems of Interest Representation in Latin America: The Dialectic between Corporatist and Liberal Forms," Paper prepared for the Seminar on "Partidos Políticos y Factores de Poder: Su Inserción en un Sistema Democrático," The Tinker Foundation and the University of Massachusetts/Amherst, Buenos Aires, June 16–18, 1986; published as Chapter 4 in my book *Finding Our Way? Toward Maturity in U.S.–Latin American Relations* (Washington, D.C.: American Enterprise Institute and University Press of America, 1987).
12. For the contrast, see Louis Hartz, *The Liberal Tradition in America* (New York: Harcourt, Brace and World, 1955), as well as *The Founding of New Societies*.
13. Richard Morse, "The Challenge of Ideology in Latin America," *Foreign Policy and Defense Review* 5, no. 3 (Winter 1985): 14–23.
14. Alan Riding, *Distant Neighbors: A Portrait of the Mexicans* (New York: Knopf, 1985).
15. See the survey data reported in Natalio R. Botana, "New Trends in Argentine Politics," Paper presented at the Southern Cone Seminar, Argentine-American Forum, Washington, D.C., June 5–6, 1983; these findings are discussed in more detail in Chapter 3.
16. Howard J. Wiarda, *Latin America at the Crossroads: Debt, Development, and the Future* (Boulder, Colo.: Westview Press; Washington, D.C.: American Enterprise Institute, 1987).
17. Raúl Alfonsín, "Address by the President of Argentina" (University of Massachusetts at Amherst, November 20, 1986).
18. For some summaries of work on the subject see Richard Sholk, "Comparative Aspects of the Transition from Authoritarian Rule" (Washington, D.C.: Woodrow Wilson International Center for Scholars, Latin American Program, Working Paper No. 114, 1982); Kevin Middlebrook, "Prospects for Democracy: Regime Transformations and Transitions from Authoritarian Rule—A Rapporteur's Report" (Washington, D.C.: Woodrow Wilson International Center for Scholars, Latin American Program, Working Paper No. 62, 1980); and Middlebrook, "Notes on Transitions from Authoritarian Rule in Latin America and Latin Europe: A Rapporteur's Report" (Washington,

D.C.: Woodrow Wilson International Center for Scholars, Latin American Program, Working Paper No. 82, 1981).

19. For a preliminary report, see Scott Manwaring, "The Consolidation of Democracy in Latin America: A Rapporteur's Report" (Notre Dame, Ind.: University of Notre Dame, The Helen Kellogg Institute for International Studies, Working Paper No. 73, July 1986).

20. For a companion volume focused on the Washington experience and the domestic side of U.S. foreign policymaking, see Howard J. Wiarda, *Foreign Policy Without Illusion: How Foreign Policy Works and Fails to Work in the United States* (Chicago: Scott Foresman/Little, Brown, 1990).

THE DEMOCRATIC REVOLUTION IN LATIN AMERICA

PART ONE

HISTORICAL BACKGROUND

1

The Latin American Political Tradition: A Difficult Legacy of Democracy

Democracy in Latin America has never rested on very firm foundations. There are many socioeconomic problems: poverty, illiteracy, malnutrition, a rigid and inflexible class structure, a lack of resources, underdeveloped transportation and communications networks, inadequate housing, short life expectancy, a small middle class, lack of affluence, a dependency on outside markets. These are not, a vast literature suggests, conditions exactly conducive to the flowering of democracy.[1]

However, it is not just socioeconomic conditions that have retarded Latin American democracy. We now know, contrary to some earlier explanations, that there is no necessary, automatic, or causative relationship between socioeconomic development and democracy. There are statistical correlations, to be sure, between high socioeconomic levels and democracy but no cause-and-effect relationship.[2] Some scholars as well as many activists in the development-assistance fields have tended to assume that all that was necessary for democracy to flourish was for the United States to pour in social and economic assistance to the developing nations.[3] When nations reached a certain level of development, according to conventional wisdom, democracy was supposed to be established. But no mention is made in these statistical studies of how exactly this process worked: of how democracy came about and how, once established, it was institutionalized and sustained.

Further, it is now clear that rather than the two correlating closely or automatically, socioeconomic development may in fact be disruptive of

3

democracy.[4] Alternatively, socioeconomic development may lead to the strengthening and hardening of authoritarian and totalitarian regimes, rather than necessarily paving the way to democracy. On the whole, however, if one wishes democracy to succeed and become stabilized, the chances for this are better in an affluent country than in an underdeveloped one. Whether it is applied to nations or to individuals, Pearl Bailey's celebrated comment is generally accurate: "I've been rich and I've been poor. Rich is better." But keep in mind that the correlation is a purely statistical one; it reveals nothing about the processes involved in specific countries or the causative relationships. Rich may generally be better, but to use the title of one of the songs sung by Ms. Bailey, "It Ain't Necessarily So"—either for individuals or for the fate of democracy.

Hence it is necessary to focus on the political traditions, history, and institutional arrangements in Latin America as well as on the socioeconomic conditions, for the fact is that the present democratic upsurge throughout the continent is something new. In the past, Latin America— even in its most developed countries, as measured by socioeconomic criteria—has seldom been governed democratically. Periods of democratic government have been sporadic, brief, and confined to a few countries: Uruguay intermittently (one would now have to say), Chile (but not under Pinochet), Costa Rica (at least since the revolt of 1948), maybe Venezuela, and one or two others. Not only has Latin America a weak and still tenuous democratic tradition (as we see in the present chapter), but it is still not entirely sure that it wants democracy or wants it all that much (as discussed in Chapter 2). These controversial comments cry out for further explanation.

In the United States, as the research of Harvard professor Louis Hartz and countless others has shown,[5] the dominant tradition is a liberal and a democratic one. That is, we all believe (or at least 95 percent of us, the polls show—a higher percentage than in any other country of the world) in the fundamental precepts and institutions of representative, democratic government. Virtually unanimously we believe in a government based on fair and competitive elections, a two-party system, separation of powers, representative rule, basic freedom, liberty, and so forth. In that sense almost all Americans are "liberals" in the classic (and Hartzian) sense of that term—John Foster Dulles as well as Adlai Stevenson, Richard Nixon as well as John F. Kennedy, Ronald Reagan as well as Jimmy Carter.

In Latin America, in contrast, no such consensus on democracy or liberalism exists. Liberalism has not been the dominant tradition. Democracy is often weak and tenuous. Democracy has not always worked well or as intended. It has long been a minority strain, not as in the United States the overwhelmingly majoritarian one. Democracy in Latin America has seldom "delivered" in the way of goods and services. The basic institutions and practices of democracy—political parties, representative bodies, constitutionalism, and the like—are not always or consistently widely admired. Latin Americans in fact have their own strong traditions and practices, many of which are emphatically not democratic.[6]

Hence it is important to understand not only the often difficult history and trajectory of democracy in Latin America but also the alternative authoritarian and elitist traditions that make the establishment of democracy so problematic. In this chapter, we trace the roots, origins, and evolution both of Latin American democracy and of democracy's alternatives, as well as the changing balance of power over time between these contrasting traditions.

Historical Legacies

Latin America is, for the most part, Western in its thinking and formal institutions. That is, Latin America's intellectual categories and historical tradition, including its political culture, derive mainly from the same Greco-Roman and Judeo-Christian roots as do those of the United States. Scholars have nonetheless long had a difficult time classifying Latin America because it does not conform to many of their favorite categories. Latin America does have a powerful indigenous Indian heritage which we shall discuss in a moment. But it must here be made clear what Latin America is not: it is not "non-Western" in the sense in which that term is often used to describe Asia, Africa, the Middle East, and other "Third World" areas. Nor are the Latin American countries, with their approximately 160 years of independence, to be counted among the "new nations." Latin America can be categorized as among the developing regions, but within that category its origins are definitely Western.[7]

However, Latin America represents, within the Western tradition, a particular and often distinctive branch. After completing his monumental and path-breaking work on what he called *The Liberal Tradition in America*,[8] Louis Hartz did a follow-up volume on what he termed the "fragments" of European civilization—the United States, Canada, South Africa, Latin America, Australia, and New Zealand—that were settled by Europeans at different historical points in time and under different social and geographic circumstances, and whose subsequent development was therefore often at variance both from that of their mother countries and from that of "the West."[9] Latin America is one such fragment, Western to be sure but within the Western tradition representing a unique variant, a product of Iberia and not of England or France, representing a particular "time warp" (circa 1500) with a religion, a culture, a psychology, a politics, and ways of doing things that are often distinctly its own.

If Latin America is "Western," how then is it also different from the West? Four distinct aspects or features of Latin America's borrowings from, and roots in, the prevailing Western tradition may be identified. First, although Latin America's origins, like those of the United States, lie deep in the Judeo-Christian and Greco-Roman traditions, Latin America has selectively emphasized or culled out of that tradition emphases such as elitism, hierarchy, and authority, that other parts of the West have either chosen not to stress, or that they have superseded. Second, the Hispanic "Reconquest" of the Iberian Peninsula from the Moors, involving a five-century effort and constituting, according to many historians, *the* distinctive formative feature of Spanish history, gave to Spanish feudalism and the country's early modern period unique features not present anywhere else in Europe. Third, the special character of Spanish Catholicism, along with and related to the particular processes and institutions of Spain's consolidation as a modern nation-state in the fifteenth and sixteenth centuries (here termed the "Hapsburgian model"), also gave to Spain features that made that country quite different from England and Holland during the same time. Finally, the transfer of these sixteenth-century Hapsburgian institutions to the New World, their interaction with and reinforcement by native Indian institutions (similarly hierarchical and authoritarian), the isolation within which these institutions not only developed but were perpetuated from the sixteenth century on, and hence the absence within Latin America of any of those great movements that are associated with the modern world (the Protestant Reformation, the Industrial Revolution)—all contributed to the growth in Latin America of a political culture that, while Western, had also some distinct features of its own.

THE JUDEO-CHRISTIAN TRADITION

With over 90 percent of its population at least nominally Catholic, Latin America is indubitably a part of the Western and Judeo-Christian tradition. Yet within that tradition Latin America has emphasized elements that other parts of the West have not.

To begin, Latin America is often more Old Testament–oriented than New Testament–oriented. It is preoccupied with suffering, disaster, disorder, and sin; and, unlike the Protestant tradition, it gives little attention to hope, improvement, salvation, and redemption. As with Isaiah, Ezekiel, and Jeremiah, the weight of past history and of present foreboding hangs heavily over Latin America. There is a tragic sense of life. Chaos and breakdown seem always to be right around the corner—understandable given Latin America's unhappy history. Latin America has not had historically the same optimistic, hopeful, take-charge, and get-ahead ethos as has the United States.[10]

When Latin America does turn to the New Testament the emphases are also distinct. Latin America focuses more on Jesus' suffering than on His resurrection, thus reinforcing the gloom and doom of the Old Testament. Great stress is placed on God's immutable will as opposed to man's ability to lift himself up. "If God wishes" ("si Dios quiere")—not if man wishes—is the leitmotiv of Latin American history. The political order that is admired is the one set forth by St. Paul in I Corinthians 12: a tightly knit organic and corporate entity, where all the parts are closely tied together to form an immutable whole, where the relations of authority and subordination are determined beforehand and remain unchanged, where each part of the body politic knows and, more than that, accepts its place in the system, and where offending members are punished or simply lopped off.[11]

Thus out of its Christian and Augustinian-Thomistic tradition Latin America draws quite different lessons than would the Dutch, French, or English colonies in the New World. These include an overriding emphasis on (some would say preoccupation with) order, authority, hierarchy, rank, place, position, organicism, corporatism, top-down decision making, and acceptance of one's station in life. None of these values would be conducive to the growth of democracy in Latin America.[12]

THE GRECO-ROMAN LEGACY

Most Western Europeans and North Americans look back on ancient Greece and Rome as providing the philosophy and rationale for democratic and, later, republican forms of government. In Plato and Aristotle the logic and advantages of democratic rule (as well as of other forms of government) are set forth; in Cicero one finds perhaps the clearest statement ever presented for a republic.

Latin America of course knows these traditions in Greco-Roman thought and from time to time has found inspiration in them. But it has inherited other legacies from Greece and Rome that are not particularly conducive to democratic rule. From Aristotle, for example, Latin America has taken not so much his empirical arguments for democracy as his system of deductive logic and reasoning, which was subsequently used by Saint Thomas to construct a particularly authoritative (if not authoritarian) edifice for an unyielding Catholic faith. To deal with the Indians discovered in Latin America, Spain resurrected Aristotle's notion of a "natural" slave class, predetermined to do the manual labor and to remain subservient to its Spanish "betters." From Plato, Latin America has taken the emphasis on top-down rule by enlightened philosopher-kings and the emphasis on oligarchy, as opposed to the threat of mob rule implied in democracy.[13]

From both Greece and Rome, in addition, Latin America has taken the notion of a hierarchy of classes, each knowing and secure in its place. The hierarchy begins with God, then angels and archangels, and eventually men—but only certain kinds of men: those who receive their land, power, and authority directly from God. There is no presumption here of the equality ("one man/one vote") that is so necessary for democracy; rather the emphasis is on the natural *inequalities* among men and between men and women. Society and polity on earth are hence also to be organized, proceeding from the heavenly ordering, on the basis of a hierarchy of classes, with some having a seemingly inherent, God-given, or *natural* right to rule. It does not require great imagination to see how this system could be made to harmonize quite nicely with the organic, corporate, and hierarchical view derived from the Old Testament and from I Corinthians. It is no accident that Francisco Franco in Spain was the *Caudillo por la gracia de Dios*—"ruler by the grace of God,"—not of the people or of the democratic process.

From Rome also Latin America took the idea not of republicanism but of *imperium*. Iberia, after all, was a Roman colony for over six hundred years, from about 200 B.C. until the disintegration of the West Roman empire in the fifth century A.D. Iberia derived its language, its law, its religion, its culture, and its form of political organization from Rome; it also supplied Rome with some of its best-known emperors. Iberia was often thought of as more Roman than Rome itself. And of course it was Rome's imperial system that Spain and Portugal a thousand years later used as a model for their empires in the Americas.

In all these ways Latin America is a child of the Bible and of Greece and Rome, as we are. But while founded on the same Judeo-Christian and Western Greco-Roman traditions, Latin America clearly emphasized traits from these traditions quite at variance from those that, say, the Anglo-American nations of the north emphasized. The traits out of this Western tradition that became integral to Latin America included authority, hierarchy, class structure, discipline, order, and the "natural" inequalities among men. None of these traits could serve as a firm foundation for democracy.

When Rome, in 476, succumbed both to internal tensions and to outside pressures emanating chiefly from Germanic tribes, Iberia too fell prey to Germanic invaders. The most important of these were the Visigoths. Having earlier invaded and even settled in Italy, the Visigoths were already Christian when they came to Spain. Their main enduring contribution to Iberia during a two-hundred-year interlude between the Roman and Moorish occupations was the establishment of an official state church and of an official state religion. The binding of church and state in a mutually reinforcing relationship, in which each serves as an arm of the other, would remain a feature of Iberian and Latin American life up to modern times.[14]

In 711 A.D., taking advantage of a weakened Visigoth leadership as well as their own aggressive and expansionist religious fervor, Moors from North Africa came across the Strait of Gibraltar and invaded Iberia. The Moors were not, as Shakespeare in *Othello* would have us believe, blacks from south of the Sahara; rather they were Berbers from North Africa, of Semitic origins. Moorish rule in Iberia lasted from 711 to 1492, when the last Moorish stronghold, the Alhambra, fell. These seven-plus centuries of Moorish rule are a fascinating period, not least because of the tolerance exhibited by the Moors and because during that era known in the rest of Europe as the Dark Ages, Moorish Spain was an island of culture, philosophy, and *civilization*.

The Moors, however, ruled as overlords and masters rather than as *conquistadores;* they seldom mixed or intermarried with the local population and did not attempt systematically to impose their religion and ways on the Iberians. Therefore, their lasting impact on Iberia was never so great as that of Rome, even though the time periods of these two occupations were roughly equivalent. The Moorish influence was strong in terms of the architecture, particularly of southern Spain, in the language (practically all words that begin with "al" are of Moorish extraction), and, some would say, in the Spanish attitudes toward women, the glorification of the warrior, and the emphasis on "tribe," clan, or clique. But for our purposes, in seeking out the permanent and lasting features of Iberia and their ultimate impact on Latin American democracy, it is the Reconquest of the peninsula from the Moors, more than the Moorish influence per se, that is truly significant.

The Reconquest, many historians believe, is one of the major distinguishing features of Iberian history—maybe *the* distinguishing feature.[15] It began in the north of Spain as a rebellion against Moorish rule and an effort, which continued on and off over the next five centuries, to drive the Moors south and out of the peninsula. This was not just a nascent nationalistic uprising, however; it was also a religious crusade, for Spain considered itself Christian—indeed the most Christian of the former Roman territories—while the Moors were followers of Islam. The Reconquest shaped and determined some of the basic institutions of Iberian life.

First of all, the Reconquest was decentralized. It was not the product of any one single large army, in the modern sense, but of scores of smaller "armies"—chiefly marauding, unprofessional, "peasant gendarmes." This helped give rise to the earliest stirrings of Spanish regionalism that would later be such a powerful and often destabilizing influence, and to the emphasis on the *patria chica* as the center of all life, the "small [local] country" as opposed to the larger one.

Second, the Reconquest was territorial and "feudal," not just military. Those who conquered lands from the Moors had a right not just to the lands they had secured but also to the labor of those living in the captured territories. Each overlord (individual, military order, or religious order) was supreme in the territories conquered. That is what helped give Spanish feudalism, if it can be called such, its distinctive and often militaristic flavor. Conquest, land, and power went intimately together. Within the conquered lands, military, political, social, economic, sometimes even religious power were closely fused—as they would be in Latin America.

The religious character of the Reconquest imparted further characteristics. The Reconquest was a religious crusade and therefore, as with all crusades, was especially bloody, intolerant, and brutal. It paved the way for the Inquisition, for the particularly intolerant and unyielding form of later Spanish Catholicism, and for the absence of religious and, by extension, political pluralism in Iberia. These features also would be carried over to the New World.

Finally, the Reconquest gave rise to some of the dominant institutions of Spanish and subsequently Latin American national life. The local, self-sufficient *hacienda,* virtually a separate sovereignty, was one of these. From the Reconquest came the Spanish emphasis on localism and regionalism, often at the expense of strong and viable national institutions. Out of the Reconquest came Spain's dominant religious orders, which would prove so powerful, as well as its quasi-religious military fighting orders (Santiago, Calatrava, Hospitalers) from which Spanish militarism and the notion of the army as a separate and superior institution, above mere man-made law and constitution and with special rights and obligations, would emerge.[16]

The Reconquest, which culminated in 1492, the same year as the discovery of the Americas, was a determining influence in Iberian history. The conquest of Latin America could even be viewed as a further extension and continuation of the Reconquest of the peninsula from the Moors.

SPANISH CATHOLICISM AND THE HAPSBURGIAN MODEL

As Spain and Portugal began to emerge as modern nation-states in the period from the twelfth through the fifteenth centuries, a period that corresponded to their reconquest of the peninsula from the Moors and to the growth of the institutional arrangements described above, they acquired an ideology and "model" of national development uniquely their own. This neoclassical ideology, grounded on the Catholic-scholastic writings of Saint Thomas Aquinas, provided a justification for more modern, state-building royal authority in the work of a remarkable group of Spanish Jesuits in the sixteenth century, principally Francisco Suárez. With its justification of strong, even absolutist government, this ideology was to Iberia and Latin America what the doctrines of limited government and representative rule as found in the writings of Locke, Jefferson, Madison, and the Anglo-American tradition are to the United States.[17]

Aquinas favored a well-ordered society that served the common good. But in his notion of a well-ordered society could be found abundant justification for a society based on rank, hierarchy, discipline, and order—all concepts that could be used to rationalize elitism, authoritarianism, and absolutism. Moreover, the type of society that Saint Thomas favored was immutable and unchanging, in accord with God's divine will for the universe. If God had ordained such a social order, it was man's obligation to accept it, not question it and certainly not rebel against it. Aquinas' philosophy, while based on a considerable sense of freedom and social justice, served both to rationalize and to lock in place a paternalistic, top-down political order that was prone to abuse.

In actual practice it was the authoritarian, paternalistic, and top-down features that predominated, not the Thomistic notions of justice and freedom. Over the next three centuries, culminating in the rule of Ferdinand and Isabella (1479–1516) and continuing under the Hapsburg monarchy, Spain's largely decentralized administration—based on the rights of the towns, the rights of the several military and religious orders, the rule of law, and the rights of other independent corporate units—was gradually sacrificed in favor of royal absolutism. The wily Ferdinand (one of the models for Machiavelli's unscrupulous prince) and Isabella stripped the nobility of their lands and castles by luring them into the royal court, ignored the provincial *cortes* or parliaments by refusing to call them, deprived the towns of their independent authority, and curtailed the rights of those groups that had maintained some earlier independence from the crown. During the rule of Charles I (Charles V of the Holy Roman Empire) the *comunero* revolt was crushed, and under his successor, Philip II, the bureaucratic-authoritarian character of the regime was further consolidated. By the time of the first Hapsburgs in the sixteenth century, and continuing for at least two centuries thereafter, the independent corporate rights and tendencies that had existed in Spain in the Middle Ages had been entirely eliminated in favor of a system of royal absolutism.[18]

It was this absolutist, hierarchical, and top-down system, what we have called the Hapsburgian model, that was imposed on Latin America. Because this model was not only all-pervasive but remarkably long-lasting, it is important to know more about it. Politically, the model implied a hierarchy of despotism, from king to viceroy to local landlord or *hacendado,* all absolute in their respective domains and ruling in an authoritarian fashion, with neither societal nor constitutional checks and balances. Economically the system was similarly state-directed and mercantilist; a closed, etatist, and authoritarian economic structure was closely related to a closed, authoritarian, and bureaucratic political structure. Socially the system was rigid, unyielding, hierarchical, oligarchic, and two-class; never was an entrepreneurial middle class allowed to develop. Religiously, the system was similarly absolutist, hierarchical, and unchanging; in these regards the state and the church concepts were mutually reinforcing. Intellectually, the system was scholastic, deductive, based on rote memorization; there was no concept of empiricism, scientific method, or inductive reasoning. And legally and administratively, the system was again highly centralized, bureaucratic, and absolutist.[19]

These features constitute the Hapsburgian model of Iberian and Latin American sociopolitical organization in the sixteenth century. What is impressive is the strength of these institutions in shaping social and political life. But at least as remarkable is their durability: they lasted for three centuries of colonial rule and on into the independent period of the nineteenth century. Many analysts argue they are still present in numerous Latin American regimes and institutions today. What is also striking is how much at variance all these institutions are with the institutions that the British and Dutch settlers brought with them to North America. On every dimension the contrast is remarkable. For essentially the Hapsburgian model as brought to the Spanish and Portuguese parts of the Americas in the sixteenth century represented an extension of neo-feudalism and of the Middle Ages. In contrast, the North American colonies, founded a century later, were grounded on a set of institutions based on what has come to be called the modern (and more democratic) era, when the hold of medieval institutions had begun to be broken in the north of Europe, if not yet in Spain, Portugal, and their New World colonies.[20]

THE CONFRONTATIONS WITH INDIGENOUS CULTURES

At the time of the Spanish and Portuguese conquests, the native Indian population of Latin America was estimated at approximately thirty million. This stands in marked contrast to the situation in North America, where the total indigenous population was only about three million. Moreover, in Latin America the Spanish *conquistadores* encountered large-scale Indian civilizations (Aztec, Maya, Inca) with populations of six or seven million each, not small-scale tribal units as in North America. The difference between three million and thirty million was one of kind, not of degree, and carried with it the necessity for different kinds of Indian policies. Whereas in the North we dealt with our "Indian problem" by killing or subduing the native Americans, or gathering them onto isolated reservations, in Latin America the sheer numbers involved made those strategies impossible. In Latin America the strategy was not to shove them aside but to control the Indian populations by substituting Spanish authority for the local chiefdoms, to subordinate the Indians, to coexist with them, and gradually to assimilate them into Hispanic ways and customs.[21] For this task, authority and authoritarianism would be required.

The numbers of Indians involved, at least in some countries, call into question just how "Western" Latin America is. If the United States has had a problem integrating the 14–18 percent of its population that is nonwhite into the mainstreams of American life, imagine what the problem is like in Guatemala, where 70–80 percent of the population is Indian and still only weakly integrated into the modern society. Guatemala's problem of integration makes our own difficult problem of integration seem insignificant by comparison. These comments are not meant to say that Latin America is not "Western," but it is to say that in the so-called Indian countries of Latin America—Guatemala, Ecuador, Peru, Bolivia, Paraguay, perhaps even Mexico—Western civilization sometimes represents a very thin veneer that may yet be submerged or swept into the sea.

To submerge or sweep it away is certainly the goal of the mysterious *Sendero Luminoso* ("Shining Path") movement in Peru (members of which, in a "refreshingly" even-handed way, recently bombed the Soviet embassy in Lima as well as the U.S. embassy), and is one of the great themes of Peruvian history (and of the other Indian countries). A small, white, Catholic, Hispanic, capitalist, Western culture has established itself in the coastal city of Lima and has for a long time succeeded in subordinating the eight or nine million Indians who live in the mountains.

But everyone knows (and has known for five hundred years) that someday that dormant Indian population may rise up and, unless the pace of change for them is quickened, push the thin veneer of Western civilization into the Pacific. Already, that is happening in part, in terms of the mass migration of the rural population into Lima and the changing character of that city, a change that immensely frightens the historic white ruling element. There is no need to wax apocalyptic about these dire possibilities, and in fact over the centuries the authorities in Lima have been remarkably successful in preventing them from happening. But these comments do serve to remind us why, while we consider Latin America part of the Western world, we must also bear in mind how fragile Western institutions are in fully one-third of the countries of the area.

Equally important for this discussion of democracy's prospects in Latin America are the kinds of institutions the Spaniards encountered among the Indian populations of Latin America. In the major Indian civilizations the structure of power and society was remarkably similar to that which the Spaniards brought. Indian society was also hierarchical, absolutist, theocratic, top-down, and corporately or sectorally organized.[22] That is, there was a ruling class, a priestly caste, a warrior caste, a bureaucratic class, a laborer class—parallel in some ways to the organizational structure in Spain itself. Indeed, recognizing these similarities, the Spaniards designed their conquering and imperial strategies accordingly. Rather than entirely destroying Indian civilization as the North American settlers did, the Spanish lopped off its heads (Montezuma, Atahualpa), substituted themselves as the ruling groups, and meanwhile kept intact the rest of Indian structure, through which the Spaniards now ruled. Not only was this strategy interesting in its own right as a ruling principle, but the implications for democracy were also powerful. It means that neither in the Spanish nor in the indigenous civilizations in the Americas were there any structure or seeds of democratic development. Rather, both Spanish and indigenous societies were based on absolutist, hierarchical, theocratic, and authoritarian principles and institutions that permitted no room for democracy.

The isolation of Latin America from the mainstreams of evolving Western civilization over the next three centuries served to reinforce, harden, and perpetuate these traditional and nondemocratic forms. Because of its early colonization (that is, before the Protestant Reformation, before the movement toward representative government, before the emergence of a middle class, before the nascent growth of capitalism, before the scientific revolution), and then the cutting off of the region due to Spain's and Portugal's mercantilist and exclusionary policies, Latin America was cast in the sixteenth-century medieval, premodern, and Hapsburgian mold. It could not evolve or develop itself in the same way the North American colonies, founded a century later and on a modern basis, could. Latin America remained locked in place, a semifeudal and peripheral area whose organization and founding principles were grounded in the medieval, not the modern era. For the next three hundred years and more Latin America's history was marked by the absence of any modernizing movements of any sort. That is why Hegel said the area had "no history" and why Marx was at least as disparaging. The modern age would begin in Latin America only at the end of the nineteenth century—and even then it was only partial and incomplete.[23]

The Colonial Era

The conquest of America by Spain and Portugal beginning in 1492 started a process of Europeanization and Westernization of the globe that would eventually spread to all non-Western areas. But recall that in the Latin American case, first of all, the two colonizing powers represented a distinct, quasi-feudal fragment that they implanted in the New World and, second, that the authoritarian and hierarchical institutions they brought were reinforced by similar attributes prevailing in the indigenous civilizations.

Spain and Portugal transferred an essentially Hapsburgian model to Latin America in all its dimensions: political, social, economic, legal, religious, intellectual. In Latin America, what had been essentially dying and medieval institutions in the rest of Europe not only thrived but received a new lease on life. They persisted through three centuries of colonial rule and on into the independence period. Many aspects of this colonial legacy persist today, and it is precisely that legacy that Latin America is trying to overcome or modify as it seeks to achieve democratic rule.

The legacy is strong, for the hand of history and tradition hangs heavily over Latin America. Since this Hapsburgian model remained so strong, it merits more elaboration than previously given it—even at the risk of some repetition. In the political sphere, as has been seen, the Hapsburgian model meant absolute, top-down authority, with no training whatsoever in local, representative, grass-roots, or democratic government. Sociologically the system was similarly rigid and hierarchical, with a small, white Spanish or Portuguese elite at the top, a large mass of undifferentiated Indians or imported slaves from Africa at the bottom, and almost no one—no independent middle class—in between. Economically the system was also autarchic and monopolistic, oriented toward milking the colonies dry for the sake of enriching the mother countries, and not at all toward developing the local Latin American economies. Latin America is, in fact, a particularly compelling case of how excessive statism and authoritarianism in the political sphere are intimately related to etatism and mercantilism in the economic sphere, and how deadly both of these combined can be for the growth of democracy.[24]

Religiously, the Catholic Church at that time, particularly in Iberia and Latin America, exhibited an absolutism that rivaled yet often reinforced the state concept, again to the detriment of democracy. The legal basis was similarly deductive and absolutist, providing abundant rationalization for dictatorial rule. And educationally and intellectually the Spanish and Portuguese systems were also deductive, based on rote memorization derived from biblical injunctions and the teachings of the church fathers, and nonscientific—really, prescientific.

These essentially feudal and medieval institutions in all their multiple facets were transferred by Spain and Portugal to the New World. They cast Latin America, in contrast to North America, in a premodern mold. Moreover, the whole of these institutions, the full *system* of the Hapsburgian model, was considerably greater than the sum of the individual parts. The system powerfully inhibited any future development in democratic directions, which helps explain why Latin America is still struggling to overcome or somehow come to grips with this heavy past.

The Independence Period

The first strong stirrings of revolt against Spanish and Portuguese colonialism took place in the early nineteenth century. By 1824 all of Latin America with the exception of Cuba and Puerto Rico, which remained Spanish colonies until 1898, had achieved independence.

The Latin American wars of independence were fundamentally different from the struggle for independence in the United States. They were not aimed at securing liberty and democracy as North Americans know these. Rather the "wars of separation" (a more accurate term) in Latin America were fundamentally conservative movements. They were aimed at restoring a status quo ante. They sought to preserve the structure of conservative institutions and ideology that was threatened by the Napoleonic invasion of the Iberian Peninsula, to secure and hold the crown for the conservative monarch ousted by Napoleon, Ferdinand VII. And it was only when Ferdinand returned to power after Napoleon's ouster and was obliged himself to adopt a constitution providing for limited monarchy and some of the classic nineteenth-century freedoms that the even more conservative colonies in the New World broke away.

Hence the movements in Latin America to separate themselves from Spain and Portugal should not be looked on as also social revolutions. That they emphatically were not. No thought was given to making Indians and peasants equal to their Hispanic overlords. After independence the vote was severely restricted to literates and landowners—no more than 1–2 percent of the population. The conservative hierarchy and class barriers of the old society were kept in place. In those few places (Mexico, Peru) where independence was accompanied by an outbreak of social revolution, it was brutally put down. The wars of independence largely substituted one ruling elite for another. Colonial officialdom and the crown were driven out; in its place were substituted the *criollo,* or native elites. Of the fact of the continuation of an elitist and nondemocratic society there can be no doubt.

It is important to be careful, therefore, when judging early Latin American independence history a "failure" for its supposed inability to live up to the republican ideals inscribed in its laws and constitutions. In most cases these constitutions were, in part, patterned on the U.S. model; in several cases the U.S. Constitution was simply translated into Spanish and the French Declaration of the Rights of Man and the Citizen tacked on. There were the usual separation of powers, fundamental freedoms, provision for elections. But these precepts were never meant to be lived up to; rather, and in keeping with a long Latin American tradition that is still frequently followed, they were meant for the rest of the world to see and admire, meant to show that Latin America on the surface was just as "civilized" as other nations. It was the intention of Latin America's founding fathers to provide the appearance of democracy and republicanism but not its substance.[25]

Seen in this light, the men who wrote these early laws and constitutions in Latin America were not the naive and unintelligent persons they are often pictured to have been. They were intelligent, experienced, and sophisticated—at least as much so as our Founding Fathers. They had a complex juggling act to perform, as did our founders. On the one hand they wanted to give the appearance—largely for foreign consumption—of democracy and republicanism. On the other, as practical men of affairs, they recognized fully that Latin America had no training, no experience, no background, no institutional base for democratic rule. Hence they built into their constitutions some decidedly undemocratic features—features that did, however, reflect existing Latin American realities.

These nondemocratic features included broad powers given to the executive, which thereafter provided authoritarianism and Caesarism with a considerable measure of constitutional legitimacy. They included vast emergency powers to suspend liberties and rule by decree, to prorogue and send home the Congress. Little power was given to local government, and there was practically no judicial review. The Hapsburgian model, one could say, thus lived on into the independence period with only limited modifications to make it acceptable in the republican context of the nineteenth century. Latin America thus acquired a liberal and republican veneer, but its essence was certainly not liberal or democratic.

It was not just the hierarchical and authoritarian features that were perpetuated, but the organic and corporatist ones as well. In these new constitutions, for example, the armed forces were given special duties and obligations, as the guarantor of the constitution or the defender of public order, that elevated the military into almost a fourth branch of government. The armed forces were entrusted with what was called the "moderative power" formerly exercised by the crown, so that when the other branches of government were at loggerheads or paralyzed, the military could step in and "moderate," or resolve, the dispute. The Catholic Church and the Catholic religion were similarly given a special place in the system as the officially established church and religion, with vast privileges, lands, and a virtual monopoly (state-supported) in education and social services. Even after church and state were later formally separated, their close but now more informal working alliance continued. The landholding class was similarly given special privileges and perpetuated its hold on social, economic, and political power. In these ways corporate privilege continued into the era of independence and republicanism.[26]

Actually, there were good reasons for Latin America to retain these authoritarian and corporatist features. The case was best presented by Simón Bolívar, the "Latin American George Washington" and its great independence leader. Bolívar fully understood the absence of a democratic base or institutions in Latin America's past. He was perfectly aware of Latin America's *"falta de civilización,"* by which he meant its absence of groups, political parties, or associations of the sort that Alexis de Tocqueville found so abundant in the United States. He recognized the lack of "living together" (which is how Tocqueville defined associability) in Latin America's past and the powerful centrifugal and disintegrative forces alive in Latin American society. Hence Bolívar opted for an artful compromise: democratic norms as found in the laws and constitutions as an aspiration, but strong government as a way to hold society together. It was Bolívar who lobbied for a strong executive, a president chosen for life, and thus a kind of democratic Caesarism. In this he was not altogether different from France's Charles de Gaulle in 1958, who, cognizant of the disintegrative forces in his country then at work, also enacted a constitution with strong executive power and a comparatively weak parliament.[27]

Two models hence competed and continued to coexist during much of the rest of the nineteenth century, often alternating in power. On the one side was the Hapsburgian model, now updated with a republican veneer, implying strong central authority, a corporatist-organic order, and the defense of the status quo. The social base of this model was among the traditional elites, in strongly Catholic and rural regions, on the *hacienda* and among the conservative peasants, and in the armed forces and the church. On the other side was the nascent liberal model, weakly organized, lacking an institutional base in terms of strong political parties or interest groups, without much history or tradition in Latin America, and representing still in the nineteenth century a distinctly minority view. Many of its advocates, when pressed to respond to the question of what liberalism and republicanism meant to them, answered: "strong government"—not a very different aim from that of Bolívar or from their Hapsburgian ancestors. For the fact is that in the past century there were almost as many liberal *caudillos* (strong men, men on horseback) as there were conservative ones. The social base of liberalism included urban and more educated elements, the professional classes and students, and the emerging bourgeoisie who desired greater freedom of markets—all very small in number.

While liberalism remained a minority strain in the nineteenth century, it gradually grew and in some countries (Argentina, Chile, Uruguay) even became ascendant. Among liberal *caudillos* the base of their popular support was generally broader than that of the older men on horseback. The franchise was ever so slowly expanded to encompass, by the end of the century, perhaps 7–8 percent of the population rather than just 1–2 percent. Associational life multiplied. Literacy increased and so did the participatory nation. In a handful of countries liberal and democratic regimes, of a certain kind, came to power. The change process accelerated as the economies of the area began to take off. As the social base of Latin American liberalism expanded, so did liberalism itself.[28]

Even as liberalism emerged more definitively in Latin America as a self-conscious philosophy and ideology, and as more liberal regimes came and sometimes consolidated themselves in power, liberalism retained a decid-edly non–U.S. form. The roots of Latin liberalism in the nineteenth century were Rousseauean, not Lockean. That is, Latin American liber-alism placed heavy emphasis on the "general will" (translated from Thomas Aquinas's "common good"), it stressed strong leadership by a person who intuitively (as distinct from through electoral processes) "knows" the general will, it continued to stress the organic and corporate unity of society, and it carried strong authoritarian (if not totalitarian) impulses.[29] In these ways, even as Latin America became more "demo-cratic," what it meant by democracy was considerably at variance from the Lockean-Madisonian-Jeffersonian democracy of the United States.

The contrasts between Rousseau and Locke are striking and get to the heart of the political differences between the United States and Latin America. Whereas Rousseau emphasized the need for strong government and inspired leadership, Locke stressed limited government. Rousseau wanted an integrated and coherent regime, while Locke, and Madison, preferred checks and balances. While Rousseau favored a sectoral or corporately organized polity with all the diverse interests coordinated with and subordinate to the central authority, Locke and more explicitly Madison favored a genuinely pluralist system. Rousseau stressed the *ends* of government, which to him and countless followers since were great and glorious (provided the right ruler was in power). Locke, in contrast, was more prosaic, stressing the *procedures* of democracy as opposed to some final product. Rousseau presented a vision for poets and visionaries that all too often in Latin America ended up in dictatorship, while Locke pro-vided a formula for a "second-best" regime that, while not spectacular, has long served the test of time for true democrats. Locke's version also had the advantage of not ending up in totalitarianism, as the Rousseauean vision has so often done.

These differences continue today and help explain the profound dif-ferences between U.S. and Latin American democracy—and the lack of understanding in each area for the other. They also help explain why the authoritarian tradition and impulse in Latin America remain so powerful and so omnipresent, even in the new democratic era. For even within Rousseau-style "democracy" itself in Latin America, as well as in the older Hapsburgian tradition, there are some powerful tendencies that are not only not conducive to democracy but that can easily result in total-itarianism of either the left or the right, of a Fidel Castro or an Augusto Pinochet.[30]

It is now easier to understand why Rousseau is so important in the Latin American political tradition. Latin America is far less authoritarian now than it was historically. At the same time, the nations of the area have long feared what the consequences of unfettered liberalism would mean in their context of an uninstitutionalized and fragmented society that is prone to breakdown. Far too often it has meant chaos and anarchy. Rousseau's brand of democracy was therefore a compromise. It enabled Latin America to look, sound, and act democratic. But with its organic, corporatist, and top-down features, it also enabled Latin America to keep a tight rein on its centrifugal forces, to avoid the chaos that it feared from Lockean liberalism and Madisonian pluralism, and to prevent social breakdown during the difficult period of the transition to modernity. By now, in quite a number of Latin American countries—not without considerable trepidation—a full-fledged transition to genuinely liberal and pluralistic democracy has occurred; but in others the half-way houses of the Rousseauean forms are still in place; and even in the first group the top-down features are still often held in reserve—just in case.

Liberalism's popularity in Latin America, therefore, should not be exaggerated. Even at the turn of the century liberalism lacked majority support in all but a few countries. Moreover, liberalism and democracy often continued to mean quite different things in Latin America as compared with the United States. The countries that proclaimed themselves liberal republics, such as Brazil, Chile, Peru, and Argentina, were still governed by their oligarchic elites. The vast mass of the population was still excluded from participation in the national economic and political life. Moreover, Latin America's "liberalism" was not always very liberal: it was infused with Thomistic concepts, it was top-down and nonegalitarian, and it was enormously attracted and often wedded not just to Rousseau but to the emerging nineteenth-century philosophy of positivism, which was similarly holistic, deductive, elitist, and undemocratic.[31] As Maier and Weatherhead conclude, the end of the nineteenth and the beginning of the twentieth centuries in Latin America showed little progression toward— let alone the inevitability of—democracy. The period was rather "the twilight of the middle ages."[32]

Social Change and Alternative Models

By the first decades of the twentieth century, democracy still had not developed very successfully in Latin America. Instability was still rampant, men on horseback often prevailed, very few people participated in the political process, social reform was nonexistent, there had been precious little economic development. The "democracies" that did exist were limited to the elites. Even the openings toward liberalism of the late nineteenth century and the more liberal regimes that came to power early in the twentieth century crumbled under the impact of the great market crash of the early 1930s. The worldwide depression knocked the bottom out from under not only the Latin American economies but their political systems as well. Between 1930 and 1934 fourteen of the twenty Latin American countries had major, revolutionary changes in power. The depression seemed to confirm what many Latin Americans had long believed, that liberalism could not survive.[33]

But if liberalism had failed, what would take its place? There ensued an agonizing, sometimes frantic search for new alternatives. Socialism was one of these. In the 1920s and 1930s new Socialist and Communist parties were organized in nearly all the Latin American countries. Socialism's base, then as now, was chiefly in the trade unions and among students and young, often unemployed, professionals. Few Latin Americans were attracted to Bolshevism because of its harshness, its antireligiosity, and the bloody excesses of Stalinism. But many were attracted to intellectual Marxism because it offered a rational and seemingly quite accurate analysis for their own situation (feudalism mixed with exploitative capitalism), because it painted an apparently attractive picture of the future (especially given Latin America's disastrous past), and because its holistic philosophy was in many respects similar to Latin America's earlier holistic philosophy, Thomism.[34]

Nowhere in Latin America did socialism even come close to enjoying majority support, however, and through the 1950s the various Socialist and Communist parties remained weak and divided.[35] Nonetheless, from the 1930s on socialism represented a major alternative, a third structure of power and society growing up alongside the other two, Hapsburgian authoritarianism and liberalism. With the triumph of the revolutions in Cuba and Nicaragua and the emerging Soviet presence in the area, to say nothing of rising nationalism and accelerating social, political, and economic problems, Marxism in contemporary Latin America has become a major force. In its parliamentary forms, of course, socialism can be compatible with and even complementary to democracy; but in its Castroite and totalitarian forms it is antithetical to democracy and is, in fact, democracy's sworn enemy. United States policy can get along perfectly well with the former kind and has and does in all kinds of circumstances; it is the latter kind that threatens both Latin American democracy and U.S. interests there.

The other major alternative emerging in the 1930s was (and remains) corporatism.[36] Although it is difficult for North Americans, with their solidly liberal-Lockean philosophy and institutions, to comprehend this, corporatism was enormously popular in Europe and Latin America in the period between World War I and World War II. Liberalism seemed bankrupt (quite literally so, after the Great Depression); Stalinism was unacceptable; thus corporatism seemed the only alternative. Corporatism in Latin America generally implied the following:

1. Strong control and direction of the economy by the state.
2. A Catholic, organic, unified view of man and society.
3. Society organized in terms of its major sectoral or corporate units: for example, the church, the armed forces, commerce, labor, agriculture.
4. "Harmonious" labor and industrial relations, enforced by the state, with both labor and employers guaranteed representation in various state agencies and an obligatory system of arbitration and adjudication.
5. Political representation based on society's "natural" groupings: first the family, then neighborhoods and communities, religious bodies, economic activities, and other functional groups.

Several features stand out from this list. One is the continuity or presumed continuity between corporatism and earlier Thomism, as well as with the ideas of Rousseau, with their similar stress upon good order, discipline, and the proper structure of society. A second is that corporatism could be accommodated to Latin America's preferred and traditional ways of doing things—that is, it provided for a gradual adjustment to change (recognizing the rising influence of trade unions, for example) but change that was evolutionary, did not get out of hand, and enabled the elites (now expanded to include the emerging business groups and eventually the middle class) to maintain themselves in power. It must also be noted that corporatism in Latin America was seldom accepted completely. Rather the regimes that adopted corporatist forms (Vargas's Brazil, Perón's Argentina, Mexico and its Party of Revolutionary Institutions [PRI], virtually *all* Latin American regimes in the 1930s and 1940s) did so only partially, incorporating some features of a corporatist system but retaining liberal and representative institutions as well, seeking to blend and reconcile the two frequently in hodgepodge crazy-quilt arrangements. Corporatism seldom triumphed definitively in Latin America as it did in Salazar's Portugal or Dolfuss's Austria, but of the fact its influence was great—and that the influence was not always democratic—there can be no doubt.

In the meantime, while all the Great Debate over these alternative systems—liberalism, socialism, and corporatism—was going on, social change in Latin America was going forward inexorably, eventually rendering some of this debate irrelevant and gradually paving the way for the emergence of a more liberal, pluralist, and democratic polity.

Social change was sparked by the economic "takeoff" that occurred in Latin America beginning in the late nineteenth century. By that time some of the earlier problems that were legacies of the independence struggles had been resolved, a new generation of "order and progress" (positivism's theme) *caudillos* and oligarchies took power, investment began to increase, the population grew, new lands came under cultivation, and Latin America began producing for a new world (capitalist) market. Stimulated by these changes, a new business and commercial elite grew up alongside, and often intermarried with, the older landed and oligarchic elite. In the larger and more prosperous countries (Argentina, Brazil, Chile, Mexico, Uruguay) and eventually in the less developed ones as well, a middle class began to grow that often challenged the elite for political power and provided a social base for moderate, middle-of-the-road, democratic rule. By the 1920s and 1930s a sizable trade union movement had also emerged, one that would continue to grow in strength in the post–World War II period and on into the present. And finally, peasant and Indian elements began to be organized, politicized, and incorporated into the larger national system. Women, domestics, and other traditionally ignored and forgotten elements were, eventually, similarly organized.[37]

These changes opened up new social escalators in Latin America (the universities, business, the military) and helped make the society more open and flexible. The vast social changes under way also opened up the possibilities for social mobilization and new political movements. At the same time, the traditional wielders of power, the economic elites and the armed forces, remained powerful; and the frequent clash between the older and newer groups produced an increasingly conflict-prone society. It is also important to remember that these changes occurred unevenly and varied greatly from society to society. There were far greater social differentiation, pluralism, and societal and political openings in the more advanced, more developed countries of the Southern Cone, Venezuela, and Mexico than in the less developed and only weakly institutionalized countries of Central America.

In the long run these vast social changes provided a broader and stronger base for liberal democratic rule. But in the short run, despite the wildly optimistic predictions of many social scientists and their models, things did not work out that way.

Democratic Openings—and Closures

The 1930s and 1940s in Latin America were decades of change and experimentation with new forms: new ideologies, new social movements, new political institutions. These were also decades of industrialization and import substitution—the replacement of formerly imported goods with the same goods manufactured locally. The old social order dominated by the oligarchy, the church, the *hacienda*, and the traditional military came under increased challenge from new sociopolitical groups: the middle class, business-commercial elements, organized labor. Various forms of populism and reformism were in the air. It was a time of conflict, of social unraveling, of desperate efforts by the elites to hang on to their wealth and power, and by the new groups to garner some for themselves. Social and political conditions were unstable and uncertain.

In a handful of countries (Chile, Costa Rica, Uruguay) democratic breakthroughs occurred. In others more open and reformist regimes alternated in power with military regimes. But the dominant pattern was a profusion of right-wing dictatorships that took power in the unsettled economic conditions of the 1930s amidst the societal disintegration that seemed to be going on all about them. They sought to hold society together by using harsh and repressive means or to reconstruct society on a new and refashioned corporatist-authoritarian basis. These included Batista in Cuba, Hernández in El Salvador, Ubico in Guatemala, Carías in Honduras, Trujillo in the Dominican Republic, Ibañez in Chile, Gómez and Pérez in Venezuela, Velasco in Ecuador, Laureano Gómez and Rojas Pinilla in Colombia, Stroessner in Paraguay, Somoza in Nicaragua, Perón in Argentina, and Vargas in Brazil. The creation of the sectorally organized PRI in Mexico could also be said to fit, with qualifications, into this corporatist mold.[38]

But by the 1950s this particular generation of authoritarian regimes and leaders appeared to have run its course. The Bolivian revolution occurred in 1952, Vargas committed suicide in 1954, and Perón was ousted in 1955. Pérez Jiménez fell in 1958, Castro's revolution in Cuba succeeded in defeating Batista that same year. Trujillo was assassinated in 1961. A popular book of the time proclaimed "the twilight of the tyrants."[39]

The demise of all these strongmen corresponded with a dramatic shift in United States policy toward the region. Heretofore the United States had usually made its accommodations with Latin American dictators since they protected U.S. interests and were staunch anticommunists. But now with the drama of Batista's fall and the consolidation of Castro's Marxist-Leninist regime vividly before them, U.S. officials began to conclude that right-wing dictators, rather than protecting against communism, may in fact provide the conditions in which communism will thrive. Hence in the last two years of the Eisenhower administration and even more forcefully under Kennedy's Alliance for Progress, the United States began to reorient its policy to aid the democratic forces. But note the goals of policy—stability, markets, security interests, and anticommunism—remain the same; only the means to achieve those goals were altered.[40]

The reasons why this and other U.S. efforts to export and promote democracy in Latin America failed so ingloriously are dealt with in detail in Chapter 4. Here it is important to indicate only briefly that the democratic forces in Latin America were very weakly organized; the democratic leadership was very thin (often insufficient even to staff a cabinet, let alone all the other necessary positions); the financial situation was precarious; the traditional elites remained intransigently opposed; the middle class was still small; public opinion was inchoate and divided; the Castroite threat loomed large; and the armed forces—beginning with Argentina and Peru in 1962, the Dominican Republic and Honduras in 1963, Brazil in 1964, and so on—quickly stepped into power. On the U.S. side it needs also to be said that the administration of the Alliance program to assist these fledgling democracies was terribly faulty, that we in the United States never really understood the culture and the social and political processes at work in Latin America very well, and that many of the key assumptions of the Alliance—such as the possibilities to professionalize the Latin American militaries in a U.S.–style nonpolitical mold or to create a stable middle-class society that looked just like our own—were exceedingly ethnocentric and proved downright wrong.[41] We shall have more to say on these themes later in the discussion.

The trend toward a new or renewed form of authoritarianism in Latin America continued, eventually encompassing countries like Chile and Uruguay, which were once assumed to be safely in the democratic camp. These were not just the *juntas* or strongmen familiar from Latin America's past history, however, who step into power to resolve some problem and then quickly leave. Rather the new military or civilian cum military regimes that came to power in the 1960s and 1970s were long-term, including among their goals a reconstruction and reorientation of the national political life. Moreover, these were not just personal dictatorships in most cases but bureaucratic-authoritarian regimes that reflected the greater complexity and modernity of the Latin American societies themselves.[42] By the mid-1970s the military was in power in twelve of the twenty-one republics; in three or four others the military was so close to the surface of power, as I have noted, as to make the line between civilian and military all but indistinguishable.

Beginning in the late 1970s, however, and continuing to the present, a new movement or transition to democracy began in Latin America. It is this most recent evolution toward democracy that is the main focus here. The turnaround was dramatic, reversing the figures for authoritarianism cited in the previous paragraph. Seventeen of the twenty-one countries, with the exception of Chile (now also changing) and Paraguay (also emerging from dictatorship) on the right and Cuba and Nicaragua on the left, now have democratically elected governments or are en route to democracy. The list thus includes Haiti, Mexico, Panama, and other of what might be called "mixed" or "transitional" systems. Later in the discussion we will wrestle with the questions of how and if these can truly be called democratic regimes.

Despite these reservations in some cases, there can be no doubt that a dramatic shift toward democracy has occurred in Latin America. Even if the marginal cases are not counted, more countries and more people are being governed democratically and under the rule of law and democratic constitution than ever before in any period of Latin American history. That is a remarkable accomplishment and a remarkable turnabout. The questions we must ask are: Is this new democratic opening likely to be permanent? Has Latin America now finally overcome or transcended its past history? Are the conditions now different than in the early 1960s when the last great effort to bring democracy to Latin America was launched? And what (if anything) can or should the United States do to assist Latin American democratization?

Several lessons stand out from this survey of Latin American history and of the place of democracy in that history. These are themes and points of debate that are also woven into the discussion that follows.

1. Latin America's experience with democracy viewed historically has been relatively brief and not altogether happy; there must be important reasons for those facts.

2. Latin America has often defined democracy differently than the United States does, and these differences in definition have important implications for analysis and policy.

3. There has not been in Latin America's history an inevitable, auto-

matic, and progressive march toward democracy; rather the process has been by fits and starts, with frequent interruptions and reverses, which may well occur again.

4. Latin America's political evolution has not typically meant the definitive triumph of democracy; instead the political process has usually involved the reconciliation and accommodation of certain democratic features with various authoritarian, organicist, corporatist, and nondemocratic ones.

5. Latin American democracy has not consistently followed or been exactly correlated with social and economic development; indeed, socioeconomic development in the hemisphere has as often been disruptive of democracy as it has been supportive of it.

6. Democracy has not always or consistently been the preferred form of governance in Latin America, and we must ask whether currently the political culture has been sufficiently altered that it is now supportive of democratic rule.

It is important to see how these often disturbing aspects of Latin American democracy, or the lack thereof, now manifest themselves and how great the changes have been. We will begin with a discussion of Latin American political culture.

Notes

1. See, for example, William P. Glade, *The Latin American Economies* (New York: Van Nostrand, 1969); John P. Powelson, *Latin America: Today's Economic and Social Revolution* (New York: McGraw-Hill, 1964); Inter-American Development Bank, *Economic and Social Progress in Latin America* (Washington: IDB, yearly); F. H. Cardoso and E. Faletto, *Dependency and Development in Latin America* (Berkeley, Calif.: University of California Press, 1978).
2. For elaboration, see Howard J. Wiarda, "Development and Democracy: Their Relation to Peace and Security," Paper presented at a Workshop on Regional Cooperation for Development and the Peruvian Center for International Studies, Lima, October 27–29, 1986; also Robert Packenham, *Liberal America and the Third World* (Princeton, N.J.: Princeton University Press, 1973).
3. Especially, W. W. Rostow, *The Stages of Economic Growth* (Cambridge: Cambridge University Press, 1960).
4. Samuel P. Huntington, *Political Order in Changing Societies* (New Haven, Conn.: Yale University Press, 1968).
5. Louis Hartz, *The Liberal Tradition in America* (New York: Harcourt, Brace and World, 1955).

6. See Howard J. Wiarda, ed., *The Continuing Struggle for Democracy in Latin America* (Boulder, Colo.: Westview Press, 1980); Claudio Veliz, *The Centralist Tradition in Latin America* (Princeton, N.J.: Princeton University Press, 1980).

7. John Martz, "The Place of Latin America in the Study of Comparative Politics," *Journal of Politics* 28 (February 1966): 57–80.

8. Hartz, *Liberal Tradition.*

9. Louis Hartz, *The Founding of New Societies* (New York: Harcourt Brace Jovanovich, 1964).

10. Miguel de Unamuno, *The Tragic Sense of Life in Men and Nations* (Princeton, N.J.: Princeton University Press, 1972); Octavio Paz, *The Other Mexico: Critique of the Pyramid* (New York: Grove Press, 1972).

11. I Corinthians 12:12–31.

12. Howard J. Wiarda, *Rift and Revolution: The Central American Imbroglio* (Washington, D.C.: American Enterprise Institute, 1984); also Glen Dealy, *The Public Man: An Interpretation of Latin American and Other Catholic Countries* (Amherst, Mass.: University of Massachusetts Press, 1977).

13. Ernest Barker, *Greek Political Theory* (London: Methuen, 1918).

14. Such a hierarchical organization is of course found in Dante as well as Saint Thomas.

15. C. Sánchez Albornoz, *La España Musulmana* (Buenos Aires: Ed. Sudamericana, 1946).

16. John Crow, *Spain: The Root and the Flower,* 3rd ed. (Berkeley, Calif.: University of California Press, 1985); also Américo Castro, *The Structure of Spanish History* (Princeton, N.J.: Princeton University Press, 1954).

17. J. B. Trend, *The Civilization of Spain* (London: Oxford University Press, 1958).

18. Especially Richard M. Morse, "The Heritage of Latin America," in Hartz, *Founding of New Societies.*

19. Crow, *Spain.*

20. R. Trevor Davies, *The Golden Century of Spain, 1501–1621* (New York: Harper & Row, 1965). The author has described the model as "organic," "patrimonialist," and "corporatist"; see Howard J. Wiarda, "Toward a Framework for the Study of Political Change in the Iberic-Latin Tradition: The Corporative Model," *World Politics* 25 (January 1973): 206–35.

21. A more extended discussion is in Howard J. Wiarda and Harvey F. Kline, *Latin American Politics and Development* (Boulder, Colo.: Westview Press, 1985), chap. 2.

22. Magnus Morner, *Race and Class in the Americas* (New York: Columbia University Press, 1970).

23. On Latin American Indian institutions, see Alfred Metraux, *The History of the Incas* (New York: Random House, 1969).

24. For an extended discussion, see Peter Berger, *The Capitalist Revolution* (New York: Basic Books, 1986).

25. Jorge Domínguez, *Insurrection or Loyalty? The Breakdown of the Spanish American Empire* (Cambridge, Mass.: Harvard University Press, 1980).

26. Glen Dealy, "Prolegomena on the Spanish American Political Tradition," *Hispanic American Historical Review* 48 (1968): 37–58.
27. On Bolívar, see Mario Laserna, *Bolívar: Un Euro-americano frente a la Ilustración* (Bogotá: Ed. Tercer Mundo, 1986).
28. Charles Hale, *Mexican Liberalism in the Age of Mora* (New Haven, Conn.: Yale University Press, 1968).
29. See John J. Johnson, *Political Change in Latin America: The Emergence of the Middle Sectors* (Stanford, Calif.: Stanford University Press, 1958).
30. On this Rousseauean form, see Richard M. Morse, "The Challenge of Ideology in Latin America," *Foreign Policy and Defense Review* 5, no. 3 (Winter 1985): 14–23.
31. Leopoldo Zea, *The Latin American Mind* (Norman, Okla.: University of Oklahoma Press, 1963).
32. J. Maier and R. W. Weatherhead, *The Politics of Change in Latin America* (New York: Praeger, 1964).
33. See the discussion of this period in Howard J. Wiarda, *Critical Elections and Critical Coups: State, Society, and the Military in the Processes of Latin American Development* (Athens, Ohio: Ohio University, Center for International Studies, 1979).
34. A. Luís Aguilar, *Marxism in Latin America* (New York: Knopf, 1968).
35. For a general discussion, see Luís Mercier Vega, *Roads to Power in Latin America* (New York: Praeger, 1969).
36. See Howard J. Wiarda, *Corporatism and National Development in Latin America* (Boulder, Colo.: Westview Press, 1981); also F. Pike and T. Stritch, eds., *The New Corporatism* (Notre Dame, Ind.: Notre Dame University Press, 1974).
37. For elaboration, Wiarda and Kline, *Latin American Politics and Development*, chap. 3; Johnson, *Political Change*.
38. James Malloy, ed., *Authoritarianism and Corporatism in Latin America* (Pittsburgh, Penn.: University of Pittsburgh Press, 1977).
39. Tad Szulc, *Twilight of the Tyrants* (New York: Holt, 1959).
40. Milton Eisenhower, *The Wine Is Bitter: The United States and Latin America* (New York: Doubleday, 1963); J. W. Nystom and N. A. Haverstock, *The Alliance for Progress* (New York: Van Nostrand, 1966).
41. Howard J. Wiarda, "Did the Alliance for Progress Lose Its Way? Or Were the Assumptions all Wrong to Begin With? And Are Those Assumptions Still with Us Today?" in Ronald Scheman, ed., *The Alliance for Progress* (New York: Praeger, 1988).
42. Guillermo O'Donnell, *Modernization and Bureaucratic-Authoritarianism* (Berkeley, Calif.: Institute of International Studies, University of California, 1973).

2

The Political Culture(s) of Latin America

A popular image of Latin America in the United States is that it is a continent seething under the tyranny of seemingly endemic oligarchies and repressive military dictatorships. If only these dictatorships and the repressive institutions that support them (the list usually includes the Catholic Church, the armed forces, the oligarchy, the bourgeoisie, and the U.S. embassy) can be removed or eliminated, the argument runs, then the presumably natural democratic inclinations of Latin America that have long been suppressed will bloom into full flower. This view is happy, optimistic, positive, and soul satisfying, in the sense that it enables us easily to separate the bad guys from the good guys and to identify with moral right. But because such a view does not always or closely reflect Latin American institutions, practices, and beliefs, it lies more in the realms of poetry and romance than of reality. Moreover, the policy consequences that flow from such a view—based as it is on some fundamental misreadings of Latin American culture and society—are likely to lead us astray as well and into some wrong choices.

The fact that the U.S. focus is on democracy and the struggle for democratic ideals does not necessarily mean that Latin America—or the rest of the world for that matter—clamors for the same thing or in the same form or with exactly the same priorities. In the United States we often assume that if other peoples had a choice, they would certainly opt for a political order that looks just like our own. But we seldom bother to examine the evidence, which provides a far more ambiguous picture of

Latin America's presumed desire for democracy than we ordinarily assume. The question of whether Latin American political culture is democratic—and whether its people wish to have a democracy that looks just like the North American one—is by no means settled. Certainly the historical record is not an encouraging one for democracy; the real question is how much have things changed in the contemporary context and to what degree has Latin America now overcome—or perhaps learned to work around, through, or over—the non- or even antidemocratic legacy of the past that has long been so powerful. And the fact is, there *have* been some very significant alterations in Latin American political culture in recent decades.

Political culture as here used refers to the basic values, ideas, beliefs, preferred institutional arrangements, and practices by which a society organizes its political life.[1] The last chapter focused on the Latin American historical record, which has not been particularly supportive of or conducive to democracy. This chapter uses four measures to gauge Latin American political culture and the strength of democracy in the contemporary context: constitutionalism and the constitutional tradition, survey research designed to probe public opinion on the issue of democracy, voting returns, and patterns of political action and legitimacy.

Constitutionalism and the Constitutional Tradition

Immediately after independence in the early nineteenth century, all of the Latin American countries adopted new constitutions. It is important to examine the origins of these new constitutions. Many of the Latin American constitutions used a structure, organization, and sometimes even language that is close to the U.S. Constitution; however, the content, meaning, and intent of these basic laws were fundamentally different from those of the United States. Nor was the British constitution, with its common-law tradition and unwritten rules, attractive to the Latin American founding fathers. Rather, a close examination of these constitutions reveals that the models Latin American constitution writers turned to were the legal and constitutional codifications of Napoleon Bonaparte and the Spanish Constitution of 1820. The earliest Latin American constitutions were thus products of certain currents of the French Enlightenment and of Rousseau more than of the Anglo-American experience. They were liberal but not Lockean.[2] Therein would lie one of Latin America's great problems, not only in perpetuating great misunderstanding about the area in the United States, but also in inhibiting the area's democratic political development.

Rousseau's influence led in these new constitutions to strong power being concentrated in the executive branch and not the legislative, to an emphasis on group rights (the church, the army, the corporate agency) over individual rights, to too strong a reliance on a powerful leader (Fidel Castro or Alfredo Stroessner?) who intuitively *knows* the general will and does not have to bother checking with the electorate, and to an emphasis on organic unity in society as distinct from free-wheeling, often chaotic pluralism.[3] There are of course strong echoes of St. Thomas Aquinas as well as of Rousseau in these precepts, thus enabling the Latin Americans to blend and accommodate two main currents in their historical tradition. In the best of circumstances the Rousseauean principles could serve as the basis for an executive-centered democracy—what we in the United States have sometimes termed an "imperial presidency." But there is also in Rousseau what Peter Berger has called a "totalitarian impulse,"[4] implying a crossing of that fine line between an imperial presidency and a full-fledged Caesarist or Bonapartist regime. In fact, most of the Latin American countries have gone back and forth across this line numerous times in their histories.

We have noted that the wars of independence that led to the separation of Latin America from the mother countries, Spain and Portugal, were actually quite conservative movements. They were aimed at holding the Iberian colonies for the rightful Spanish king, Ferdinand VII, who had been deprived of his throne when Napoleon's troops occupied the peninsula. But when Ferdinand was forced in 1820 to adopt the liberal constitution of Cádiz (which was not really very liberal), the conservative *criollos* in the New World made their final break. By 1824 virtually all of Latin America (except Cuba and Puerto Rico, which remained Spanish colonies) had severed their ties to Spain and Portugal and had become separate countries.

From this point on, and reflecting the political and social currents discussed in the previous chapter, Latin America would have two quite distinct constitutional and legal traditions. There was no one single liberal and democratic tradition that was dominant and had majority support as in the United States. Instead two currents, both politically and constitutionally, have consistently been present, existing side by side and often alternating in power. The first tradition is liberal, democratic, and representative, and it found expression both in the politics of the rising urban intellectuals of nineteenth-century Latin America and in the laws and constitutions that they wrote. It was based on the ideas of Montesquieu as well as Rousseau, on the notion of limited government as found in the 1820 Spanish Constitution, and to a lesser extent on the example of the young democracy in North America. The often idealistic precepts incorporated into some of these early liberal constitutions in Latin America, however, were usually viewed as aims to strive for, not necessarily as a reflection of—let alone as norms by which to regulate—actual operating realities. Indeed, within a few years of independence, whatever notions of republicanism had existed at the beginning gave way to a wave of repressive military men on horseback: Rosas in Argentina, Santa Anna in Mexico, Báez and Santana in the Dominican Republic, and numerous others. These new dictators abrogated the earlier liberal constitutions and put into practice and into the basic laws of the land more authoritarian precepts.[5]

Hence there arose a second tradition inscribed in the laws and constitutions as well as in actual governance. It derived from the colonial experience, from the Hapsburgian model. This tradition was authoritarian, hierarchical, and nondemocratic. It is reflected in the extensive and virtually de jure dictatorial powers afforded the executive, the power of the president to defy both courts and legislature (or to send them home), the limits on rights, the vast emergency powers, the special privileges given to the church, the elevation of the army into a separate branch of government, the limits on the suffrage, the constitutionally privileged power of land and wealth. This more elitist and top-down emphasis derived from Iberian and Latin American history as well as from nineteenth-century conservatism.

Much of Latin America's history in the nineteenth century could be written in terms of the alternation in power between these liberal and conservative currents and movements, and of the constitutions that reflected these alternative principles. Several of the Latin American countries have had upward of twenty or even thirty constitutions in their independent histories, but these large numbers actually reflect variations on the two basic models, the one more liberal and the other more authoritarian. Moreover it must be said that far from being divorced from actual operating practice as some writers have alleged, these constitutions in their various forms often reflected rather closely Latin American realities—however undemocratic these frequently were.[6]

But in this process of alternation, Latin American constitutions and constitutionalism have often evolved over time in important ways as well.[7] Three areas of change particularly command our attention. The first is the really quite remarkable efforts by Latin American constitution writers to resolve the problem of the army. Recall that in one constitutional tradition the army constitutes a fourth branch of government; in the other it is apolitical, subservient to civilian authority, and "nondeliberative." How to deal with this problem realistically? On the one hand the army in Latin America could not at this time be entirely divorced from politics; on the other, for democracy to succeed the army could not be permitted to rule indefinitely either. Latin America's answer—and its political genius—was in some constitutions to give the army special power in times of emergency to preserve domestic tranquility, to guarantee public order, and to protect national sovereignty. In this way democracy could be maintained and the army kept from power in noncrisis times, but in emergency situations the army still had a special place and responsibilities. In the Brazilian constitution (and some others) the army was given what was called the "moderating power"—that is, in times of crisis it was empowered to moderate between the contending political factions or branches of government to ensure continuity and prevent breakdown.[8] These provisions would certainly not be acceptable to a democratic purist, but they did respond to the realities of power in many Latin American countries, and they did enable these countries oftentimes to slide through a crisis with only a temporary interruption of democracy rather than provoking a long-term and full-scale military takeover, the only other alternative. All in all, such compromises were not a bad trade-off, and they enabled democracy to survive in many instances when it would not otherwise have done so.

Second, a number of Latin America's constitutional problems were basically solved over the course of the nineteenth century. In most countries the church came to be, more or less, officially separated from the state. The issue of federalism versus centralism was similarly resolved, more or less, in an evolutionary fashion. The suffrage became less restrictive, paving the way for greater democracy. Various constitutional gimmicks were introduced to try to limit executive authority and thus reduce the possibilities for dictatorship. These included limits on the emergency powers of the president, various provisions to force the executive to consult with the legislature, provisions for British-style cabinet responsibility, and the like. Overall, during the course of the nineteenth century and on into the twentieth, constitutionalism in Latin America became both more stable and more democratic.

Third, new efforts—again often ingenious—were made in several countries to blend and, if possible, reconcile democratic and authoritarian constitutional traditions. For example, the executive was given broad powers, but efforts were concomitantly made to increase the power of the

Congress, the courts, and local government. Group rights continued to be emphasized, but individual rights achieved greater importance. The army still had special responsibilities, but efforts were made to limit and contain them. Functional representation, under which the elite groups had a preponderance of power, was combined with more popular forms of representation. In these ways and others, the Caesarist principles incorporated in one tradition of Latin American constitutionalism came to be combined with the democratic and republican aspirations contained in another body of constitutions. Once again, Rousseau's legacy was present.

The second decade of the twentieth century ushered in some major new constitutional innovations. The Sáenz-Peña law in Argentina provided for near-universal manhood suffrage and paved the way for the first truly democratic elections in the nation's history. The influence of Sáenz-Peña then spread to many other countries. The new century had also ushered in a series of constitutions influenced by positivism, such as the Uruguayan Constitution of 1918, which through its social welfare articles helped provide for a considerable measure of modernization. But the outstanding example of constitutional engineering in this period was the Mexican Constitution of 1917 (still in effect) with its powerful stress on agrarian reform, nationalism, labor rights, and social justice. Despite these innovations, however, it is noteworthy that even the Mexican constitution continued to vest virtually unlimited power in the executive (except for the prohibition against reelection) and to emphasize group or social rights over individual rights.[9]

After World War II a series of new Latin American constitutions reaffirmed the hemisphere's belief in democratic ideals. These included the Brazilian Constitution of 1946, which followed the forced stepping down of the dictator Getulio Vargas, and the Venezuelan Constitution of 1947, which paved the way for a brief democratic interlude. Others, such as the Bolivian Constitution of 1952, were the direct result of revolutionary conditions. In the late 1950s and early 1960s, when democracy in Latin America seemed again about to bud, most countries wrote new democratic constitutions.

The later 1960s and 1970s saw a rewriting of many of the constitutions of the area to mirror the military takeovers and the new restrictions on democracy. Once again the armed forces were given special privileges and obligations, civil liberties were curtailed, emergency powers were expanded, political authority was again concentrated in the executive, and group rights were emphasized over individual rights. The constitutions of this period reflected the needs of what came to be called the "national security state."[10] The Caesarist, or Bonapartist, tradition was back in power.

But by the late 1970s and early 1980s, mirroring the political transformations back again to democracy, a fresh breeze of new constitutions and of constitution writing again blew through the area. A precursor of these new basic laws was the Venezuelan Constitution of 1961, which followed the overthrow of the Pérez Jiménez dictatorship and which served as a model for many other Latin American countries as they later undertook similar democratic transitions. Hence recently in such key countries as Argentina, Brazil, Bolivia, and Peru, as well as many smaller ones, constituent assemblies have been or are being called into session and new constitutions promulgated. Whether these will prove more durable than the hundreds of others issued in the past remains of course an open question.

Although they are often difficult to detect, there are sometimes signs of progress in these periodic oscillations between constitutional forms. On the negative side, most of the Latin American constitutions—including those currently being enacted in the new democratic era—are symbols rather than necessarily evolving from experience as in the United States or Great Britain. The Latin American constitutions are *logical* (stemming from a code law tradition), *anticipatory* (preceding reality rather than reflecting it), and *idealistic,* in the sense of presenting goals to aspire to rather than reflecting actual existing circumstances. They are still extremely detailed in their efforts, seemingly, to engineer and almost wish democracy into existence rather than come to grips realistically with their own national circumstances. The president (and the executive branch) is still extremely powerful; and even where there is the constitutional possibility of having elected governors, these are usually appointed by the president. There is no belief in or even comprehension of coequal branches, except perhaps in Costa Rica. Local government is weakly provided for, and the reality is a system of strict centralization. *Personalismo*—whether in the capitalist countries or in socialist Cuba or Nicaragua—remains the dominant tradition regardless of what the constitutions say.[11]

Moreover, none of the new constitutions has dealt adequately with the role of the military or with other difficult problems. Now that government is back in the hands of the civilians, they naturally wish to exclude the military entirely from politics. The operative constitutional phrases are once more that the armed forces are to be entirely "apolitical" and "nondeliberative." But that represents wishful thinking and hardly reflects a realistic appraisal of the role the military has played and will likely continue to play in Latin American politics. What to do about the armed forces is one of the key issues facing Latin America's new civilian governments—one, among several, that has not so far in the new constitutions been addressed at all realistically.[12] Hence the familiar search for an "ideal" (if not entirely congruent with reality) constitution continues, seeming almost to invite, and certainly to pave the way for, future seizures of power by extraconstitutional means. If the military's role is not formally recognized in the constitution, so the familiar scenario goes, then one day it will have to be informally asserted, most likely by the armed forces themselves. Adding to these oversights and inadequacies even in Latin America's newest constitutions, therefore, is the woefully inadequate machinery to enforce the constitutions or even to ensure that they stay in effect.

Nevertheless, there has been progress: the expanded suffrage, now encompassing women as well as men; the resolution of many earlier constitutional issues; the detailed provisions for human rights and social justice; the decrease in the sheer numbers of constitutions since 1945; and the greater efforts to ensure stability. These changes provide some measure of hope for the future.

Earlier there were signs of hope also in the imaginative efforts by Latin American politicians and constitution writers to blend and reconcile those workable features from Latin America's liberal and democratic tradition with the realities of its authoritarian one. But now those hopes are fading, for in the new constitutions the motive seems too often to be revenge, not reconciliation.

Indeed, there may be too much dichotomous thinking both in the United States and in Latin America: *either* dictatorship *or* democracy. Insufficient attention is being paid to various "halfway houses," as in Guatemala or Honduras, compromises between dictatorship and democracy that may enable democracy to survive even if its form is not entirely acceptable to purists. Such compromises would not only allow democracy to live but provide room for growth and development in more democratic directions. Instead, in many of the new constitutions the military and other antidemocratic forces are to be purged and totally excluded from politics. There is an ideological point that these new constitutions and the new political elites that write them are making, one that may be quite unrealistic: The point is to be exactly the same as Western Europe, or perhaps the United States, where the military is totally subordinated to civilian authority. But that is not Latin American political reality. Not only does this represent wishful thinking, but by excluding the military from all power the new democratic governments invite bitterness and hostility on the part of the military and may be issuing an open invitation to the armed forces to come back to power later on and again exclude those who have excluded them. Hence, while there has been some closing of the gap in Latin American constitutions between the theory and the reality, in this area there may not be enough and, as compared with the earlier efforts at compromise, there may even be regression. At this stage, therefore, it is impossible to be certain that Latin American constitutions and constitutionalism have progressed much from earlier times or whether, as feared, as may be in for another cycle of alternation between civilian-democratic and military-authoritarian regimes.[13]

Public Opinion

Public opinion surveys provide a second gauge of Latin American political culture. Once again, the evidence reveals far more ambiguities than democrats should feel comfortable with.

On the other hand, numerous surveys carried out by the United States Information Agency (USIA) as well as a great variety of private researchers, in virtually all countries and over a long time period, conclude that Latin America desires a democratic and representative form of government.[14] If you ask Latin Americans what kind of institutions they prefer, the answer is, overwhelmingly, democratic ones. Answers to additional questions in these surveys indicate that Latin Americans prefer checks and balances, an independent legislature and judiciary, a free press, human rights, elections, a military that does not beat them up and abuse them, and so forth. These responses lend support to the thesis that democracy is not alien to Latin American culture, that Latin Americans are not "natural" authoritarians, and that the political arrangements Latin Americans prefer are much like those found in the United States.[15]

However, if one probes more deeply, if one asks a series of questions that the USIA surveys seldom ask, then the responses are less clear-cut. For example, while Latin Americans favor democracy, they also tend to favor strong executive leadership—the Rousseau principle—which may come at the expense of an independent legislature and court system and which may verge on Caesarism. There is considerable sympathy in situations of crisis for limiting press freedom and other basic rights. Church and state may be legally separated, but in overwhelmingly Catholic Latin America few really believe that this is entirely feasible or realistic. The military is still widely believed to have a special role in the defense of the nation. Group or social rights still take precedence over individual human rights, although this is now changing. There is widespread belief that in circumstances of national crisis and paralysis the armed forces may have a right—even an obligation—to step in and set matters straight.[16]

These traditional beliefs and attitudes—all of which are now undergoing alteration—have a strong basis in Latin American history. It is necessary to understand that history in order to comprehend why such beliefs are still as strongly held as they are. Latin American history, as noted, has long been dominated by chaos, violence, instability, and fragmentation. Latin America has historically lacked the web of civic, social, political, and commercial associations and associability that has long been the hallmark of U.S. society. If democracy is, as Tocqueville put it, the "art of living together," Latin America has historically been deficient in that art and in the fundamental, grass-roots associational life that are both its basis and its training schools.[17]

Hence, while Latin Americans express admiration for democracy in the abstract, they are not entirely sure that it will work in their countries. Considerable skepticism about democracy's possibilities in Latin America pops up in a large number of surveys. In the face of the endemic violence, conflict, breakdowns, weak civic institutions, and powerful centrifugal forces that from time to time tear the Latin American nations apart, many Latin Americans are unsure that democracy works very well—or that it works very well in their countries in its Anglo-American forms. Latin America has a phrase—the *falta de civilización* ("absence of civilization")—that is often used to describe the area's condition. By this Latin Americans do not mean that they are "uncivilized"; rather what they mean is that they lack the necessary social and political infrastructure—organizations, political parties, civic associations, and the like—to make democracy work. In the absence of such infrastructure, what has sometimes passed for democracy in Latin America has often verged on chaos, anarchy, and total national breakdown.

Hence, to save the nation and to prevent a threatened slide into the abyss, Latin America has often opted for a "savior," who by charisma and force can hold the threatened nation together. Considerable sympathy therefore has long existed in Latin America for an authoritative if not authoritarian leader and type of rule, particularly in times of stress and so long as a mild form of authoritarianism does not degenerate into tyranny as in the cases of Batista, Trujillo, and the last Somoza.[18] If one understands the wrenching, chaotic, disorganized history of Latin America—and how democracy there has traditionally degenerated into chaos—then one can comprehend why Latin America remains suspicious of democracy's viability and why Bonapartism has frequently been seen as the only way out.

More recently these traditional attitudes of skepticism about democracy have begun to change. Newer surveys indicate that not only does Latin America continue to exhibit strong and growing support for democracy but that the reservations about it that once loomed so large are fading as well. Two principal causes seem to be involved. First, Latin America has in general been developing in recent decades the organizational infrastructure on which a more stable democracy can be based. The historic fear concerning the *falta de civilización* and the political consequences of lacking this web of associability necessary for democracy—that is, preference for authoritarian solutions in times of crisis—is now less than it once was. Second, Latin Americans have discovered that authoritarianism does not solve the problem and may make it worse. Rather than providing for order, stability, and cohesion, a Batista, a Somoza, or the El Salvadoran colonels may provoke just the instability, breakdown, civil war, and violence that Latin America seeks to avoid. Rather than providing peace, the military in Argentina, Chile, or Uruguay may provoke chiefly terror, torture, and bloodshed. Instead of providing the setting for sustained national economic growth, military regimes seem as corrupt, inefficient, and ruinous as the civilians they replaced. And instead of preventing communism and guerrilla movements, right-wing dictatorships may in fact provide the conditions in which extremism can flourish. The experience with "bureaucratic-authoritarian" regimes in Latin America in the past twenty years has had a profound negative effect on Latin American public opinion regarding military dictatorships.

Nonetheless, the best public opinion survey literature available, even with the changes of recent years, still provides a quite mixed picture. Two examples of many available illustrate the point: Venezuela and Argentina. Both countries have strong and diversified economies, are among the most developed of the Latin American nations, have an involved and participatory political culture, and, by Latin American standards, have strong political institutions. If democracy cannot survive and thrive in these two countries, it cannot be expected to thrive elsewhere in the continent. And yet in neither country is democracy quite as solidly institutionalized as we would prefer.

Venezuela has been described as an elite-directed, or "tutelary," democracy.[19] It has now been governed democratically for over thirty years. But the question remains how successful the Venezuelan reformers at the top have been in making converts to the democratic alternative among the mass public. To what degree has the mass public internalized democratic values? The answers are mixed. On the one hand the Venezuelan electorate is strongly opposed to military coups (73 percent), supportive of elections as *the* route to power (67 percent), and opposed to one-party rule (65 percent).[20] But one worries about that one-third of the electorate who still do not see elections as the only route to power and who are not opposed to one-party rule. At the same time, more than half of the Venezuelan electorate (53 percent) were disappointed in the democratic government's performance and thought it was not doing enough. The lower strata of the population was especially critical and cynical and tended more than the middle strata to favor rightist solutions and a strong, perhaps even authoritarian government. Forty percent would favor a socialist remodeling of the economy and society—without specifying what form of socialism that would be.

Hence, although Venezuela is often touted as a model of democracy in Latin America, it is probable that democracy in Venezuela is less secure than we are prone to think, that the democratic preference has shrunk as the country has faced severe economic crisis, and that fully one-third to two-fifths of the population prefer not just another president or government but an entirely different, and not necessarily democratic, system of rule. Many Venezuelans are "success democrats": supportive of democracy when the economy is doing well but perhaps ready to abandon it when things turn sour. As the economy has in fact soured in recent years, the causes for worry about Venezuelan democracy have grown. It is easy to see, for example, how a strong, charismatic, and demagogic political leader (a Venezuelan version of Perón, for example) could capitalize on the lower class's preference for strong, authoritative leadership coupled with the 40 percent who want socialism to erect some form of a populist, state-socialist, nationalistic system that would have the effect of undermining or destroying democracy.

There are comparable and equally disturbing data available for Argentina. The return of such a key country as Argentina to democracy and the 1983 election that brought shrewd Raúl Alfonsín to the presidency have been justly celebrated. But such celebrations should not cloud our understanding of Argentina's more complex realities. For example, in the weeks before the 1983 election a nationwide opinion survey showed 86 percent of the Argentines favoring democratic, representative government. That is not unexpected, given the discrediting of the outgoing military regime and the euphoria of Argentina's democratic moment. Nevertheless, only 36 percent of those surveyed supported political parties—any political parties—and less than 30 percent held a favorable opinion of trade unions. When asked the follow-up question that the USIA surveys never do—what they meant by democracy or what form of democracy they preferred—84 percent (about the same percentage as those preferring democracy itself) said "strong government."[21]

These responses clearly reveal a double loyalty: support for democracy but also for its Bonapartist forms. These are in fact the two "forks in the trail" (as they were labeled by the Argentine social scientist Natalio Botana, who conducted the survey) open to the country: broad support for a democratic opening, but widespread concern and skepticism about the disintegrative forces that democracy may unleash and therefore a strong preference for strong government. These results are similar to those found in Venezuela and could easily produce a new form of nationalism and state socialism that may not be supportive of democracy. In point of fact there are some profoundly un- and antidemocratic forces operating in Argentina. Argentines currently prefer democracy but in an organic and orderly form. If democracy should prove chaotic or unworkable, the authoritarian solution might reappear as what Botana called a "wicked necessity." Botana concludes: "There is conflict between two trends and, perhaps, two traditions. Neither has been able to assert itself definitely in Argentina."[22]

These two countries, Venezuela and Argentina, have been used as illustrations because among the Latin American countries they have the strongest sociopolitical underpinnings and prerequisites for democracy: a large middle class, affluence, widespread literacy, high levels of urbanization, and so forth. Yet even in these two countries the support for democracy seems thin, and alternative nondemocratic systems of rule are waiting in the wings. Unfortunately, much the same situation exists in the other Latin American countries, whose democratic prospects are made even more precarious by the lack or weakness of the foundations that Venezuela and Argentina have.

If we conclude, therefore, that public opinion and the political culture are still only incompletely supportive of democracy in Argentina and Venezuela, we have even fewer reasons to be optimistic about some of the other countries. For example, in Central America, while the public overwhelmingly (85–90 percent) agrees with the abstract statement that democracy is the best form of government, they are less convinced that it is right for them. When asked, in a 1987 survey, whether the people of Central America are best off when they live under democratic rule, only 27 percent of the Guatemalans and 47 percent of the El Salvadorans strongly agreed. This contrasted sharply to the situation in solidly democratic Costa Rica, where 83 percent strongly agreed. The results support our earlier argument that, while Central Americans favor democracy in the abstract, they are not at all sure that it works in their countries.

When we ask, now in the Southern Cone, what people mean by democracy, we get a wide variety of answers. In Uruguay the answers are related to social welfare, in Argentina to political expression and freedom, in Brazil to economic equality. But in Brazil fully 50 percent of those surveyed could not provide any definition of democracy, whereas in Argentina and Uruguay only 30 percent could not give an answer. In Brazil, democracy was also widely equated with patronage, with asking public officials for favors—a quite traditional Brazilian practice but one that bears little relationship to any previously known definition of democracy.

In the fall of 1985 an important survey in each of these same countries (Argentina, Brazil, Uruguay) measured degrees of confidence in democratic institutions (see Table 2.1). A score of 5 indicated a great deal of confidence, a score of 3 a fair amount, 2 meant little confidence, 1 was given for no answer, and 0 meant no confidence at all. A total score of 150–200 for each of the institutions evaluated meant a bare plurality (but not a majority) had a favorable view toward that national institution; under 150 indicated little confidence in the institution; and a score of under 100 meant no confidence at all in the institution. Now let us look at the scores for the three countries and their main institutions.

Several features are striking about these figures. The first is the low

TABLE 2.1
Confidence in Main National Institutions

	Argentina	Brazil	Uruguay
Presidency	184	84	151
Congress	184	136	160
Judiciary	179	102	166
Political Parties	151	60	143
Educational System	204	170	205
Civil Service	125	101	115
Police	160	83	126
Armed Forces	118	141	61
Labor Unions	123	108	146
Press	151	121	138
Private Industry	133	90	80
Catholic Church	175	170	95
Neighborhood Organizations	164	135	95

SOURCE: United States Information Agency.

level of confidence in, or legitimacy of, *all* institutions in all three countries. Very few institutions have even a plurality of support, most have very little support, and quite a large number of these institutions have virtually nonexistent support. It is also striking—and worrisome—that in Brazil the armed forces inspire more confidence than does any civilian democratic institution. Equally impressive in a negative way is the remarkable lack of or low confidence in Brazil, even in comparison with these other countries, in any national institution. We have seen that in Argentina and Venezuela democratic institutions were far less firmly established than many think; but the figures for Brazil are really quite remarkable, implying immense difficulties for all democratic governments in the future. And again, for all three countries, it is possible to conclude that, while support for democracy is firm in the abstract, support for democracy's necessary institutional infrastructure—Congress, parties, press, labor unions—is remarkably weak.

The responses to other questions included in this survey also do not augur well for democracy's future. For example, there is an old rationalization for authoritarian rule that says only affluent countries can afford democracy. When asked if democracy was only suitable to a country that is developed economically, 56 percent of the respondents in both Argentina and Uruguay disagreed with the statement. But in Brazil 56 percent agreed with the statement.

When asked whether democracy would be strengthened in the future or authoritarian government would return, 65 percent in Argentina said democracy would be strengthened and only 20 percent said authoritarianism would return. In Brazil the figures were 40 percent and 35 percent, respectively. Uruguay was evenly divided; 45 percent said democracy would last, while the same number indicated authoritarianism was likely to return.

A similar question probed democracy's viability in times of crisis. When respondents were asked to react to this statement: "Some people think military coups are never justified; others think a coup may be justified under certain circumstances," two-thirds of the Argentines said "never" and 15 percent said "sometimes." But in Brazil and Uruguay an equal number, 45 percent, replied "under certain circumstances" and gave the answer "never."

These data are stunning—and potentially explosive if publicized in the countries surveyed. They indicate that democracy—even in such advanced and relatively developed countries as Argentina, Brazil, Uruguay, Venezuela, and perhaps Colombia—is not at all as firm and institutionalized as we would like. But at least democracy has been established, and there is some, still limited, civic consciousness and the democratic institutions to go along with it. How long democracy can last given this weak support for its main institutions is an open question. In Central America, Brazil, and probably Bolivia, Ecuador, and Peru, there are strong doubts about the viability and permanence of democracy, almost no democratic institutions that inspire confidence, and very few accepted and internalized rules that would restrain non- or antidemocratic actions. Uruguay, a traditionally democratic country until 1973, occupies an intermediary position, exhibiting some institutional restraints on undemocratic behavior but a lot of cynicism about the democratic process and about democracy's institutions.

None of this public opinion data is very encouraging for the cause of democracy in Latin America, even in a country that we think of as solidly democratic (Venezuela) or ones that are at the higher reaches of the socioeconomic scales in the area (Argentina, Uruguay). In the other countries (including immense and strategically important Brazil, but perhaps excluding Costa Rica) democracy seems to be still at severe risk. The data help explain the continuing attraction of Rousseauean top-down forms or even of Bonapartist solutions in case of a slide toward chaos.

Election Results

Election results in Latin America during most of the 1980s have been extremely heartening. Never before has such a parade of, for the most part, moderate, centrist, pragmatic, democratic leaders been elected to the presidencies of so many Latin American countries. In presidents Alfonsín of Argentina, Sarney of Brazil, García of Peru, Sanguinetti of Uruguay, Febres of Ecuador, Lusinchi of Venezuela, Barco of Colombia, Paz in Bolivia, Jorge and Balaguer in the Dominican Republic, Cerezo in Guatemala, Duarte in El Salvador, Arias in Costa Rica, and Azcona in Honduras, Latin America had probably a more able group of presidents than at any previous time in the area's history. Moreover, in general (although one should not overstate or romanticize the point), they were democratic presidents with whom the United States could work. It is heartening, both for Latin America and the United States, that in its recent transitions to democracy Latin America has at the polls roundly rejected both the extreme left and the extreme right.[23]

But that hopeful sign should not serve to disguise the many problems that exist. For one thing, the parties and electoral coalitions that helped bring many of these democratic leaders to power are very fragile. In some cases—Argentina, Ecuador, Peru, Brazil, El Salvador, Bolivia—these governing parties and coalitions have already begun to fragment, raising serious questions about the possibilities for continuity of these democratic regimes. The first wave of prudent, centrist, democratic leaders may well be replaced by populists and demagogues who, in a familiar fashion, mismanage the economy and antagonize major political groups in ways that may almost invite the military back into power.

A second problem concerns the parties and party systems themselves. Most remain weak and uninstitutionalized. Few of the parties have long or deep roots within the society. Their labor, peasant, and middle-sector bases are not well organized. The party leadership is terribly thin, and once one drops below the cabinet level there is in virtually all the countries of the region a shortage of trained democratic leaders to handle the reins of government. The parties are often personalist organizations; several of the countries have sixty to seventy of them, making for a weak, fragmented, and potentially unstable party system.[24]

Third is the lack of legitimacy for the parties, as reflected in public opinion. Recall the Argentine data that showed only one-third of the population with a favorable view of political parties—any party. Parties are often viewed as purely private or perhaps patronage agencies, and their functions as agencies of public policy essential to the conduct of democracy are not always appreciated. But the problem, again reflected in the Argentine surveys, is that not only is democracy in Latin America precarious but there seems to be very little support for what most of us would think as democracy's necessary supporting organizations: trade unions or political parties.

Still a fourth problem has to do with what political parties, democracy, and elections mean in Latin America. Once more, troubling problems of definition and conceptualization arise. Political parties are often viewed as essentially spoils organizations—as extensions of the older pattern of clan and family rivalries, whose purpose was to control the public treasury for private rather than public purposes. Such patrimonialist functions have now been disguised and covered over with the language of modern party politics and ideologies, but not necessarily their substance. So long as such a private, self-interested view prevails, it is unlikely the parties will acquire legitimacy as agencies of public and general purposes. This attitude and situation are changing as modern mass-based parties have grown in the area; but to the extent the older attitudes remain, political parties, and with them democracy, are not going to have solid roots in Latin America.[25]

"Democracy" in Latin America is often seen, not according to the U.S.

definition of having regular, competitive elections,[26] but as a system of government that provides for the common good and stays off the backs of its people. A democratic leader must rule in the public interest, but that does not preclude his coming to power through other than democratic elections. Similarly "elections" themselves have historically been viewed in Latin America not necessarily as providing a meaningful choice among alternative parties and candidates but as an opportunity to vote yes or no on a government in power. In this sense elections are often plebiscitary devices, opportunities to ratify an existing government (as in Mexico traditionally) rather than necessarily to choose between it and some other alternative. Once again the parallel with France under Charles de Gaulle comes to mind. Currently these attitudes about democracy and elections are changing in Latin America; the more recent survey evidence shows signs that the Latin American conception of democracy and its institutional underpinnings, and of elections that imply real choice, is coming closer to resembling that of the United States. But again, to the degree the historic conceptions of these terms still hold sway, democracy's prospects continue to be problematic.

Finally, some of the recent electoral results themselves deserve scrutiny because they indicate sometimes rather ominous possibilities for antidemocratic outcomes. The fact is that in Argentina in 1983 Alfonsín was not the favorite; favored to win were the *Peronistas,* who did receive 40.2 percent of the vote and who in fact came back (following the growing disillusionment with Alfonsín) to win the 1989 election. Here we have the situation of a party whose commitment to democracy is widely questioned by Argentines and outside observers alike winning power in a democratic election and then possibly using that power to subvert democracy itself.

Another example is El Salvador. Although José Napoleón Duarte of the centrist Christian Democratic Party won El Salvador's presidential election in 1984, the winner could easily have been major Roberto D'Aubuisson, whom even the former U.S. ambassador in El Salvador had once denounced as a murderer and fascist. What is remarkable is not so much that D'Aubuisson lost; what is remarkable is that he got 44 percent of the vote and would probably have won were it not for U.S. pressures and manipulation. Be that as it may, the support for D'Aubuisson cannot easily be dismissed or forgotten: it was not the result of "false consciousness" on the part of the El Salvadorans, and, since the United States favored Duarte, it was certainly not the result of some U.S. conspiracy. Surely it is nothing short of incredible—and very difficult for North Americans to understand—that such a man, who is blatantly antidemocratic, should get 44 percent of the vote. If nothing else, that should tell us just how fragile democracy is in El Salvador—and maybe in Central America more generally; indeed, it also tells us that antidemocratic sentiment is also still a major force to be reckoned with.[27] Later on, D'Aubuisson's party, ARENA, did win the presidency, but under new leadership and with the pledge to respect the democratic process.

A similar story unfolded in the Dominican Republic. There a left-of-center political party, the Dominican Revolutionary Party, which had governed for the preceding eight years, saw its candidate for the presidency in 1986 lose to Joaquín Balaguer, an aging crony of the late tyrant Rafael Trujillo. Balaguer's previous tenure in the presidency was best characterized as "civilian authoritarianism," a regime that governed formally under democratic ground rules but frequently went beyond any democratic and constitutional provisions to sanction thuggery, human rights abuses, and political murder.[28] It may be that Balaguer has been "civilized" and "democratized" in the intervening years, but one should not be too surprised if the anti- or extrademocratic proclivities are still present. After all, this is the same country in which the author recently watched a presidential candidate give a stump speech in which he got up, waved an electric cattle prod in the air, and said: "I need authority for my cattle and I will need authority for my people"—and no one in the audience even blanched!

Actual Political Practices

In the United States elections are the only legitimate route to political power. Not so in Latin America, at least historically. There, elections are but one route to power; other routes are also open. These may include a skillfully executed coup d'état done with precise planning and finesse, a heroic guerrilla movement such as Castro's that holds out against all odds and finally seizes power, a well-planned protest movement that grabs national and maybe international attention, a general strike or street demonstration that succeeds in toppling a minister or perhaps even a government. Actions such as these are not only widely admired—particularly if they succeed, of course—but they also provide an indication of the means by which a regime that comes to power through nonelectoral methods may achieve the legitimacy it may initially lack. If such a government promotes peace and stability, rules for the general good, and is seen to be popular despite its nondemocratic origins—once more, the Rousseauean vision—it may nonetheless achieve democratic legitimacy. The "populist" regimes of Omar Torrijos in Panama or René Barrientos in

Bolivia are cases in point. Democratic elections offer one route to power and legitimacy; but there are other means to achieve these goals as well as "democracy Latin American style."[29]

Latin American politics in these senses are more informal and open-ended than U.S. politics. There are more routes to power open (coups, revolutions, demonstrations, *and* elections), as well as a greater variety of means to achieve those power goals—including the use of violence along with or in conjunction with or in opposition to electoral processes. By violence I mean not just what most Americans think of when they think of violence—terrorism and bombings—but the use of structured violence by such agencies as labor unions, student groups, or the military. That is, violent means are used at times to seize and hold power, as in the case of the military, or to demonstrate a power capability (and therefore the necessity to be taken seriously as a political force) through street demonstrations and marches that involve the purposeful provocation of violence.[30] This is not to say, of course, that Latin American politics are inherently violent and those of the United States peaceful; but it is to say that Latin America affords a higher degree of legitimacy to violence, as one among several routes to power, than does the United States. This is changing, particularly in the larger and more institutionalized countries of South America; but in Central America and the Caribbean violence remains an important power factor in politics. And a prime agency of the use of violence for political purposes remains the armed forces.

We need to understand this special role of the military in Latin American politics as well as the use of violence as a legitimate facet of the political process, and the implications of this for the future of democracy. First, a vignette. In Santa Cruz del Quiche, Guatemala, Colonel Byron Disraeli Lima, the district military commander, is listening to the news from the capital where the 1985 election campaign is drawing to a close. "All politicians are liars," snorts Colonel Lima. "There's a civilian wave in Latin America now," he says. "But that doesn't mean that military men will lose their ultimate power. Latins take commands from men in uniform," he states with remarkable candor.[31]

Colonel Lima says that it "will take generations" before the army retires to the barracks permanently. His heroes are Napoleon, Hitler, and the Israelis—all "conquerors and warriors," he says. He does not look kindly on civilian politicians. "If a cabinet doesn't work," he states, "I prefer a coup." Even if the new government does work, he and the army will continue to play a major and watchful role. They had already told the civilian presidential candidates in Guatemala in 1985 that their power would be limited. For example, it was made clear that no officer could be tried for any past human rights violations. And, if they wish to remain in office, no civilian politicians would do anything more than contemplate any basic alterations in the military command.

Such attitudes ensconce Colonel Lima and the Guatemalan military in the mainstreams of history and politics in the Central American countries and in some South American countries as well. The military has long been, and remains, one of the dominant institutions in the area. No amount of democratic wishful thinking will alter that fact. Of course there are ways a clever civilian democratic government can deal with its own military: through changes in budget priorities, by reassigning officers within the country and breaking up cliques, by payoffs, by appointing officers loyal to it to key positions, by postings abroad of recalcitrant officers, and through munificence showered upon the army. But all these are risky undertakings that, if handled badly, may result in the overthrow of the civilian government.

Like many top military men in the region, Colonel Lima and his brother officers are, for now, supporting his country's return to civilian government. His reasons are cynical and opportunistic, however, and do not augur well for democratic stability. In his view, the reasons for a return to democracy lie chiefly in appearances. First, he hopes an election will improve Guatemala's tarnished international image enough to attract badly needed capital from international lending agencies. Second, he is counting on a civilian leader winning renewed U.S. military assistance for Guatemala to buy new equipment and to augment the meager military salaries. And third, he is tired of the army taking all the blame for the country's mounting economic problems and its image abroad as a human rights abuser. These may be perfectly rational reasons in the Guatemalan context for restoring civilian government, but they do not serve as a very firm basis for a long-lasting democracy.

Turning from this vignette to a consideration of the region as a whole, a clearer picture emerges of the complex nature of civil-military relations and of democracy's continuing difficulties in the face of the compromises that need to be reached.[32] The dilemma, of course, is that the military has long been one of the key sources of power in the region. Elected civilian presidents do not receive automatic or permanent tenure and legitimacy on the basis of electoral returns alone. Rather they must bargain with the military to share some of the power in some areas of public policy. The activities of the armed forces and their internal "politics" (promotions and the like) are generally off limits to the civilians. The military decides what is good for itself and for the country. Only sometimes are these considerations balanced against what the civilians want or what the U.S. embassy desires.

The problem for a civilian government is not whether it can govern effectively on the basis of its electoral mandate (although that also helps) but whether it can expand its authority without running afoul of the army. This is a constant bargaining process; it is not something that accrues automatically from victory at the polls. Moreover, the relative balance between the civilian and military spheres is subject to continuous change. For a time an equilibrium may be established between the two spheres, but this is not necessarily permanent. And because this balance between two contending power structures, civilian and military, is under constant renegotiation, elections by themselves are not enough to ensure democracy in the region. While democracy is often portrayed as a fact in the United States once elections have taken place, it remains still only a hope in Latin America.

An examination of the relations between civil and military structures in the Central American countries underscores the differences between the appearance of civilian democratic rule and the reality. In Panama Nicolás Ardito Barletta, a moderate whom the military thought it could control, was the choice of General Manuel Antonio Noriega, commander of the Panamanian Defense Force, for Panama's presidency. Ardito Barletta, who was also favored by the United States, won the presidency in an election widely considered to be fraudulent, rigged by the Defense Force. But when he failed to manage either the economy or the polity well, and above all when he failed to contain a scandal involving the Defense Force chief himself, Ardito Barletta was summoned by the military and told to resign. Power then passed to the civilian vice president, by which means the appearance of democracy and constitutionalism were for a time maintained; but it is clear that the Defense Force and Noriega remained the real power behind the throne.

In Honduras the military has similarly preferred in recent years to remain in the background, allowing a civilian president to govern so long as he does so capably and does not involve himself in security issues or in internal military affairs. In this way the civilian democratic government appears to be in charge—and is actually in charge in many public policy areas. But in the spring of 1985, when then-president Roberto Suazo ordered some legislative leaders out of the country as part of a major political maneuver, the military intervened to cancel the expulsion and told the president he was going too far. Constitutional government was thus preserved, but it was the army that proved to be the ultimate arbiter of the basic law.

In Guatemala a parallel situation exists: an elected civilian power structure on the one hand but a military one coexisting alongside it and, as has been shown, by no means subordinated to civilian authority. Elections have given Guatemala a civilian democratic president, but that does not convey definitive legitimacy or a fixed term of office. Rather, at every step the president must bargain with the military high command for the power to carry out his policies. This is a process of virtually constant negotiations between the military and civilian spheres, not one in which the electoral mandate by itself carries final authority. The military and the civilian power structures will thus continue to coexist, with the relations between them often uneasy and with the officer corps defining the limits and parameters of civilian rule behind the scenes. For example, when the then Guatemalan defense minister, General Oscar Humberto Mejía Victores, was asked if the army would tolerate a civilian government's investigation of past human rights abuses, he replied darkly that "it would be a mistake if they did that." In certain key areas, in short, a civilian government's overreaching could well produce a coup d'état.

El Salvador's José Napoleón Duarte cultivated close relations with his military high command. But in dealing with the guerrilla insurgency Duarte gave the armed forces a virtually free hand, and it is clear that there were limits—in the peace negotiations with the guerrillas, for instance—beyond which Duarte could not go. He also had to tread very carefully in dealing with the military. But his position was enhanced by the enormous amount of military assistance that the United States supplied to El Salvador, which made it financially worthwhile for the army to continue under at least the trappings of civilian rule.

These are the realities of Central American (and some South American) politics: civilian-democratic government on the surface but only weakly institutionalized and with the military continuing to coexist as a parallel power structure by no means subordinated to an elected president. Too often in the United States we tend to assume a democratic regime is in place in Latin America once elections have been held and a number of democratic institutions (political parties and the like) begin functioning. Insufficient attention is paid to the readjustments of the power structure and the negotiations that go on *after* the elections, to the role and activities of the military, and to how the ostensible civilian institutions actually do function, which is often a considerable distance from what the constitution says.

Elections and the installation of a civilian elected president, however, are usually sufficient to qualify a country for U.S. financial assistance. Civilian politicians in the area, recognizing the need for U.S. aid, reluctant to jeopardize their own positions by going too far, and used to operating within the strictures that the military imposes upon them, have tended to accept this situation and to recognize the limits of their positions But we should recognize that this dual power structure does not give Central America true democracy. It does provide the appearance of democracy, the possibility for negotiating more, and the qualification for all-important U.S. assistance. That may not be a bad bargain, and it may be about all that those who favor democracy can expect in the present circumstances. Such a dual power structure of civilian and military spheres does after all reflect the realities of power in Central America and in some Caribbean countries. But it should not lead us to conclude that democracy has been fully established in the region despite the constitutional appearances. Rather it should alert us to just how fragile the democratic flowering in the region really is.

*   *   *

The democratic transitions that have occurred in Latin America since 1978 have been enormously heartening. Nor should one understate the significant accomplishments of many Latin American countries, including those in Central America, in further institutionalizing and consolidating democracy. Major changes *have* occurred in the domestic politics of these countries. But as this chapter has suggested, the changes are still tenuous, uncertain, perhaps reversible in quite a number of countries. An examination of Latin America' s constitutional tradition(s), its attitudes toward democracy and democracy's institutions as expressed in opinion surveys, recent electoral results, and the realities of power and the role of the military in the region indicate far more ambiguity than is comfortable if our goal is to see democracy survive and prosper. The changes of the past decade offer us and Latin America great hope for democracy's future, but a realistic assessment forces us to come to grips with those trends, movements, and institutions in Latin America that are not particularly democratic and that are not likely to become so—or perhaps only marginally— for many years to come. Hence our policy prescriptions regarding democracy or any other issue must similarly face up to these often hard realities of Latin American politics.

This chapter has focused on Latin America's political culture and the impediments it has placed in the way of democracy's growth. But political culture is by no means the only factor that has held back democratic development in Latin America. Other factors—the area's underdeveloped economic situation, the immense social problems, Latin America's position of dependence and subservience internationally—have also been critically important. We deal with these other problems, as well as with the changes under way, later in the book.

It needs also to be stressed that the political-cultural factors here emphasized are similarly undergoing change. Changes in political culture, however, are not just something that happens out of the blue or because of some vague changes in what we might call the "world culture."[33] Rather, changes in political culture are intimately related to socioeconomic modernization. As Latin America develops socially and economically, its political culture is likewise certain to change. Whether those changes will necessarily, automatically, or unilinearly be in a democratic direction[34] remains to be seen. Later in the discussion we examine this theme of Latin America's changing political culture, the relations between socioeconomic change and a different kind of political culture, and whether the direction of these changes is now toward democracy.

Notes

1. Lucian Pye and Sidney Verba, eds., *Political Culture and Political Development* (Princeton, N.J.: Princeton University Press, 1966); and Gabriel A. Almond and Sidney Verba, *The Civic Culture*, rev. ed. (Princeton, N.J.: Princeton University Press, 1963, 1980).
2. Russell Fitzgibbon, *The Constitutions of the Americas* (Chicago: University of Chicago Press, 1948).
3. Richard M. Morse, "The Challenge of Ideology in Latin America," *Foreign Policy and Defense Review* 5, no. 3 (Winter 1985): 14–22.
4. Peter Berger, *The Capitalist Revolution: Fifty Propositions about Prosperity, Equality, and Liberty* (New York: Basic Books, 1986).
5. Howard J. Wiarda, "The Dominican Republic: The Mirror Legacies of Democracy and Authoritarianism," in Larry Diamond, Juan Linz, and Seymour Martin Lipset, eds., *Democracy in Developing Countries* (Boulder, Colo.: Lynne Rienner Publishers, 1989).
6. Glen Dealy, "Prolegomena to the Spanish-American Historical Tradition," *Hispanic American Historical Review* 48 (1968): 37–58.
7. William W. Pierson and Federico G. Gil, *Governments of Latin America* (New York: McGraw-Hill, 1957); Harold Eugene Davis, ed., *Government and Politics in Latin America* (New York: Ronald Press, 1958). The two works cited are studies of Latin America's formal, legal, and institutional structures.
8. Alfred Stepan, *The Military in Politics: Changing Patterns in Brazil* (Princeton, N.J.: Princeton University Press, 1971).

9. Frank Tannenbaum, *Mexico: The Struggle for Peace and Bread* (Westport, Conn.: Greenwood Press, 1950). E. V. Niemyer, Jr., *Revolution at Querétero: The Mexican Constitutional Convention of 1916–1917* (Austin: University of Texas Press, 1974).

10. John Child, *Geopolitics and Conflict in South America: Quarrels Among Neighbors* (New York: Praeger, 1985); see also Howard J. Wiarda and Iêda Siqueira Wiarda, "Revolution and Counter-Revolution in Brazil," *The Massachusetts Review* 8 (Winter 1967): 149–65.

11. Based on an examination and analysis of all the Latin American constitutions written in the past twenty-five years and on the new constitutions in the process of being written and promulgated.

12. Howard J. Wiarda, "Systems of Interest Representation in Latin America: The Dialectic Between Corporatist and Liberal Forms," Paper presented at a Seminar on "Political Parties and Factors of Power: Their Insertion in a Democratic System," The Tinker Foundation and the University of Massachusetts/Amherst, Buenos Aires, June 16–18, 1986; published in *Finding Our Way? Toward Maturity in U.S.–Latin American Relations* (Washington, D.C.: American Enterprise Institute and University Press of America, 1987).

13. See my article, "The Armed Forces and Politics in Latin America: The Role of the Military in the New Democratic Era," *Harvard International Review* 8 (May/June 1986): 4–10.

14. The USIA surveys were provided to me on a not-for-direct-attribution basis.

15. The literature on this point is vast; particularly useful is John A. Booth and Mitchell A. Seligson, eds., *Political Participation in Latin America*, 2 vols. (New York: Holmes & Meier, 1978).

16. The theoretical parameters of this discussion and a preliminary report based on the survey data may be found in Howard J. Wiarda, *Dictatorship, Development, and Disintegration: Politics and Social Change in the Dominican Republic* (Ann Arbor, Mich.: Monographs Series, Xerox University Microfilms for the Committee on Latin American Studies of the University of Massachusetts, 1975).

17. Alexis de Tocqueville, *Democracy in America* (New York: Knopf, 1955).

18. Claudio Veliz, *The Centralist Tradition in Latin America* (Princeton, N.J.: Princeton University Press, 1980), Glen Dealy, *The Public Man: An Interpretation of Latin America and Other Catholic Countries* (Amherst, Mass.: University of Massachusetts Press, 1977).

19. Luis J. Oropeza, *Tutelary Pluralism: A Critical Approach to Venezuelan Democracy* (Cambridge, Mass.: Harvard University Center for International Affairs, 1983).

20. The statistics are taken from Enrique J. Baloyra and John Martz, *Political Attitudes in Venezuela: Societal Cleavages and Political Opinion* (Austin: University of Texas Press, 1979).

21. Natalio R. Botana, "New Trends in Argentina Politics," Paper presented at the Seminar on the Southern Cone, the Argentine-American Forum, Washington, D.C., June 5–6, 1983.

22. Ibid.

23. Alan Riding, "The Latin Left Is Free to Be Unpopular," *New York Times,* December 7, 1986.
24. Wiarda, *Dictatorship, Development, and Disintegration,* chap. 13.
25. Richard M. Morse, "The Heritage of Latin America," in Louis Hartz, ed., *The Founding of New Societies* (New York: Harcourt Brace Jovanovich, 1964).
26. Robert Dahl, *Polyarchy: Participation and Opposition* (New Haven, Conn.: Yale University Press, 1971); also Diamond, Linz, and Lipset, *Democracy in Developing Countries,* vol. 1.
27. See Howard J. Wiarda, *Latin America at the Crossroads: Debt, Development, and the Future* (Boulder, Colo.: Westview Press and American Enterprise Institute, 1987).
28. Howard J. Wiarda and Michael J. Kryzanek, *The Dominican Republic: Caribbean Crucible* (Boulder, Colo.: Westview Press, 1987); see also, by the same authors, "Dominican Dictatorship Revisited: The Caudillo Tradition and the Regimes of Trujillo and Balaguer," *Revista/Review Interamericana* 7 (Fall 1977): 417–35.
29. For a general discussion of these processes, see Howard J. Wiarda, *Critical Elections and Critical Coups: State, Society and the Military in the Processes of Latin American Development* (Athens, Ohio: Center for International Studies, Ohio University, 1979).
30. Merle Kling, "Violence and Politics in Latin America," in Paul Helmos, ed., *The Sociological Review,* Latin American Sociological Studies Monograph 11 (Keele, Staffordshire: University of Keele, 1967), pp. 119–32; William S. Stokes, "Violence as a Power Factor in Latin American Politics," *Western Political Quarterly,* 5 (September 1952): 445–68.
31. See the excellent article by Clifford Krauss in *Wall Street Journal,* October 30, 1985, pp. 1ff. The analysis in this paragraph and the following three are based on this account.
32. The analysis here and in the following paragraphs is derived from Edward Cody, "The Generals Still Run Latin 'Democracies,' " *Washington Post,* November 10, 1985, pp. D1ff.; see also Ronald H. McDonald, "Civil-Military Relations in Central America: The Dilemmas of Political Institutionalization," in Howard J. Wiarda, ed., *Rift and Revolution: The Central American Imbroglio* (Washington, D.C.: American Enterprise Institute, 1984), pp. 129–66; and Jerry L. Weaver, "Political Style of the Guatemalan Military Elite," in Kenneth Fidel, ed., *Militarism in Developing Countries* (New Brunswick, N.J.: Transaction Books, 1975), pp. 59–98.
33. The term is used in Lucian Pye's *Aspects of Political Development* (Boston, Mass.: Little, Brown, 1965).
34. That was the thesis of W. W. Rostow and a whole genre of developmentalist thinking and literature of the 1960s; see his *The Stages of Economic Growth* (Cambridge: Cambridge University Press, 1960).

3

The New Democratic Openings in Latin America

Tﾠhere are numerous myths about Latin America. A persistent one is that it has had no democratic past, no democratic history. The image that many outsiders have about the area is that it remains entirely locked even today in the Middle Ages, that its main institutions are essentially feudal, that there has been no economic development and hence no social or political progress. We assume that it is still (and always!) governed by corrupt military regimes or oligarchies (such as El Salvador's proverbial "fourteen families"), usually in alliance with the Catholic Church, and acting against the wishes and best interests of the peasants, workers, and the poor. We assume that Latin America's past has been static and that even today nothing is being done to deal with the area's problems.

The previous two chapters reveal that the democratic tradition has not in fact always or consistently been the dominant one in Latin American history, and that the political culture of the area is similarly mixed, with both democratic and authoritarian currents present. But that is a long way from saying, as some outsiders would have it, that there has been no democratic current or history at all or that the region has always and rather haplessly been governed only by its armies and oligarchies. Such a view ignores entirely the dynamics of change in Latin America, the longer historical perspective, and the processes of development that have led over the past half-century to greater democratization. If one considers the mobilization, the politicization, the changing political culture, the vast social changes under way, the growing pluralism of social and political groups, and the institutionalization that has occurred in Latin America, then the long-term movement and trends toward democratization are plain, impressive, and cannot be ignored.[1]

The issue has major policy implications. If Latin America neither has had nor presently has any prospects for moderate and democratic change, then only two other options seem possible: authoritarianism on the one hand or Marxism-Leninism on the other. The first option, in the form of strong-arm or military regimes, has sometimes been favored by U.S. administrations in the past as the only alternative to chaos or a communist takeover. The second option, Marxist-Leninist à la Castro's Cuba or Sandinista Nicaragua, has often been favored by the U.S. and European left. Not knowing much about Latin America, holding superficial views, and seeing the area as governed only by rapacious elites and gendarmeries, European intellectuals such as Günter Grass have concluded that only a dynamic and mass-mobilizing Marxist-Leninist regime can solve Latin America's problems.[2] But as Peruvian novelist Mario Vargas Llosa has argued,[3] that is an exceedingly patronizing attitude: it reveals a lack of knowledge about the area, it is contemptuous of the significant strides that Latin America has in fact made toward democracy, and it may even be racist, in the sense that it implies that the area is not "up" to democracy and that therefore only a Stalin-like regime can solve its problems. Sadly, that view of Latin America's "incapacity" for democracy, and hence the hope for a victory by the Marxist-Leninist guerrillas, is very widespread among the U.S. and European left.[4]

In this chapter we discuss the Latin American change and development process and summarize the long-term social transformations and democratization that have been occurring in the area. We then consider the partial reversal of those processes during the era of bureaucratic-authoritarianism from the 1960s until the late 1970s, and analyze the "new forces" that began to emerge even during that era of authoritarianism. Finally, we offer a country-by-country review of the recent Latin American transitions to democracy and the prospects for the continuation and stability of democratic rule.

The Latin American Change Process

Latin America has never been so rigid, monolithic, and unchanging as some of the literature, and quite a number of popular stereotypes, suggest. In fact, given the historic heritage of feudal and semifeudal institutions bequeathed by the Spanish and Portuguese colonizers, as well as the lack of many of the right kinds of natural resources, such as iron ore and coal for smelting it, in close proximity, Latin America has not done altogether badly by normal standards. Its historic institutions have proved to be far more flexible, accommodative, and adaptive than earlier scholars had thought, most often bending to change rather than being overwhelmed by it.[5] And alongside these older institutions there has grown up a host of new ones as the area has sought to modernize and catch up with the rest of the world. Latin America's track record has not been the dismal litany of failures that many on the outside have assumed.

Even historically the record is not altogether negative. After the first thirty years of postindependence disorganization, the area by the 1850s had begun to settle down. A number of reforms provided a better climate for investment, defined more clearly the positions of church and state, provided for greater institutionalization, led to economic take-off and population increase, resulted in the greater professionalization of the armed forces, and stimulated improvements in transportation, communications, and the building of port and shipping facilities. Even the franchise was extended during this period; and in several countries new and liberal regimes gained control of the presidential palace, although often temporarily.[6]

By the 1890s in quite a number of important countries (Argentina, Brazil, Chile, Peru), liberal regimes (although often still dominated by the economic elites) had come to power and ushered in further reforms. In many cases these liberal regimes lasted right up to the beginning of the Great Depression in 1929–30. In other words, they were not just particular, short-lived governments that happened to fall into or inherit power only briefly, but broader *systems* and *regimes* of liberal rule that in several notable cases lasted for three or four decades. The pace of growth in Latin America during this period did not match that of Western Europe or the United States, but it was significant nonetheless.[7] It may be noted that as late as 1920 the per capita income of Argentina was greater than that of the United States.

By the 1920s, therefore, Latin America had changed considerably. The Mexican Revolution had occurred, ushering in a new system of mass mobilization and a new style of populist politics. Considerable economic growth had occurred, paving the way for future, even more accelerated change. In Argentina, Uruguay, and Chile the oligarchy had already been largely shunted aside in favor of more middle-class politics. In other countries the pace of change may have been somewhat slower than in these leaders; but there also, the middle sectors were growing in size, and other social changes were under way. The engines of change began to rev up; the infrastructure began to be put in place for even greater future development.

The period of rapid and accelerating social change in Latin America since the 1930s is the primary focus of this chapter. During these decades Latin America truly modernized. Its social structures became more pluralistic, the economies of the area began a drive toward industrialization and diversification,[8] new political movements (socialist, communist, Christian democratic) came into existence, and the oligarchic regimes were generally eclipsed. Democratization went forward, albeit often by fits and starts. These post-1930 modernizing currents are dealt with in more detail in the following section. But it is clear that after 1930 (even earlier in some countries), it was no longer accurate to describe Latin America as still being locked in the grip of its older landed oligarchies or entirely under the weight of always-repressive militaries. The real situation was far more interesting than that.

Latin America occupies an intermediate position between the "first world" of already developed nations and the "third world" of poor and backward ones. By any index one uses, almost all of Latin America (Haiti is the major exception) ranks considerably higher than the poor nations of Africa and Southeast Asia. At the same time, Latin America ranks considerably behind the developed nations of North America, Europe, and Japan. This intermediary position between developed and underdeveloped has given rise to considerable conceptual and terminological confusion: in some cases and for some reasons (often so as to qualify for foreign aid) Latin America is ranked with the Third World, in other cases and for other reasons it is considered part of "the West," and in still other literature it is given special and separate treatment as almost a "fourth world" of development.[9] Whatever indices one uses, it is clear that Latin America does not rank with the poorest of nations and that its developmental efforts have been at least moderately successful.

Quite a number of Latin American countries (Argentina, Brazil, Chile, Colombia, Mexico, Venezuela) have made it into the category of what the World Bank calls Newly Industrialized Countries, or NICs. These are countries that have broken out of the vicious circles of poverty and underdevelopment in which they were locked and joined the ranks of industrialism and largely self-sustained growth. These countries constitute the dramatic success stories among the developing nations; Brazil has now broken into the ranks of the world's top ten countries as measured by gross national product, and the other larger countries listed are not all that far behind.

But while these are the dramatic successes, the smaller Latin American countries have not done altogether badly. The small and weak economies of Central America, for example, were humming along all through the 1960s and 1970s at growth rates of 3, 4, and 5 percent per year. Even the more authoritarian countries of that area—Nicaragua, Panama, Guatemala, El Salvador—had fairly impressive economic growth until the downturn of 1979–80, even while their political development lagged behind. Indeed, it may be precisely because the economic growth and social change outstripped their political development that these countries began to break down in the late 1970s–early 1980s into revolution and civil war.[10] It was the widening gap between socioeconomic modernization on the one hand and the retardedness, repression, and paralysis of political institutions on the other that was probably the chief factor in fomenting discontent, a discontent that was then further fueled in the 1980s by economic depression.

But that is surely a more complex argument than the one that sees Latin America as having made no progress at all, as being continuously governed by oligarchic and military-authoritarian regimes, as having "no history," in Hegel's terms. There *is* in fact a history in Latin America; there has been extensive social, economic, and political change; the area *has* developed; and it is not nearly so retarded and backward as sometimes portrayed. Moreover, even within the framework of instability that we often ascribe to the politics of the region, there is a *system* of politics and of dealing with change that is regular, recurrent, and not altogether inefficient or dysfunctional. That system and its dynamics are spelled out in more detail in Chapter 8; here let us simply say that in the political as well as the socioeconomic spheres Latin America exhibits far greater regularity, progress, functionality, and development than our popular beliefs about the area seem to indicate.

Social Change since the 1930s

If any period can be said to mark a major turning point in Latin American history, it is the period that followed the market crash and depression of 1929–30. In fourteen of the twenty Latin American countries, major revolutions occurred in the early 1930s—not just the usual barracks revolts but ones signaling profounder social changes. The early 1930s marked the end of an era of monolithic oligarchic rule and the beginning of something new and more complicated, which was not always or neces-

sarily democratic but did involve a definite opening toward modernization. If the 1920s could still be thought of as the twilight of the Middle
Ages in much of Latin America, the 1930s ushered in the modern world.
And thereafter the pace of change only accelerated, for it proved impossible other than temporarily to turn the clock back to an earlier and sleepier
era. These changes of the past sixty years and their cumulative impact can
be thought of as implying a profound and long-term social revolution
throughout much of Latin America.[11] These social changes, in turn,
provided the base for the transitions and openings toward democracy that
we are witnessing today.

I propose to discuss this social revolution in Latin America, which is
long-term, profound, and sometimes "quiet," as distinct from the short-
term and often ephemeral "revolutions" that Latin America is also known
for, under five major headings: changes in the political culture, changes in
economic relations, changes in the social structure, changes in the political
and institutional life, and changes in Latin America's relations with the
outside world.[12]

POLITICAL CULTURE

Modern communications and transportation provide the keys to understanding the massive changes in Latin America's political culture of the
past half-century. Even the most isolated and previously inaccessible areas
of the continent are now linked to the modern world of ideas and
alternatives. New roads, new transportation and communications grids,
new literacy programs, and the cheap transistor radio have broken down
the isolation and parochialism of previously uninvolved Indian and peasant elements and brought them into the twentieth century.[13] It is no
longer possible to convince peasants that they must be poor, must live in
substandard dwellings, that their children must have bloated bellies and
die regularly of diseases and malnutrition because God or St. Thomas or
the church has said that the poor must accept their station in life as
divinely given and immutable.

A host of new ideas—socialism, capitalism, democracy, Christian democracy, and others—are now competing for the minds of the Latin
Americans. New ideas of pluralism, voting, and participation are coming
in. These changes have had a profound effect on the Latin American
consciousness, leading to new ways of thinking and to new conclusions.
Although democracy and development are probably the most attractive in
this kaleidoscope of ideas, the outcome of the new competition of ideas
remains uncertain. In any case, there can be no doubt that the values,

ideas, ways of thinking and acting—in short the whole political culture of Latin America—are changing radically and altering the most basic relationships.[14]

THE ECONOMY

The changes in economic relationships have likewise been immense. These include the basic transformation since the end of the past century from a set of economies that could loosely be called "feudal" or "semi-feudal" to a set of economies that can be called "capitalist"—although perhaps "state capitalist" would be a better designation. Latin America has increasingly been brought into the world economy, making it both dependent on the play of global market forces and interdependent with them.

In the process of these fundamental alternatives in the means and modes of production there has been a long-term economic quickening that has brought new prosperity and affected all areas of national life. It has also had the effects of bringing in large multinational corporations whose wealth and power may be greater than that of the countries in which they invest, of making Latin America dependent on world market forces over which it has little control, of sometimes widening the gap between rich and poor, of converting once self-sufficient peasants into either wage-earners or unemployed persons, of accelerating urbanization and industrialization, of resolving some social problems and exacerbating others.[15] Most of these problems are the inevitable by-products of economic development, a price that so far Latin America has been willing to pay. Meanwhile, growth and development went forward inexorably.

SOCIAL CHANGE

The overall economic development of the past hundred years has given rise to immense social changes, the third aspect of what we have termed the contemporary Latin American revolution. To begin, the older Latin American oligarchies have now been largely supplanted by, or are now intermarried with, newer-rich families whose wealth is based on industry, banking, commerce, finance, import-export transactions, real estate, or the professions (or various combinations of these). There is now far more diversity and pluralism among the wealthy elements than used to be the case. Similarly, a new, larger, and more affluent middle class has grown up, which frequently holds the balance of power in these countries. An urban, organized trade union movement exists in all the countries; there are vast un- or under-employed lumpenproletariats in the major cities; the peasantry is being mobilized and organized; and even previously isolated Indian elements who remained outside the modern, Western money economy and society for most of the previous five hundred years are now being brought in and politicized as they never were before.[16]

The major institutions of national life are similarly being transformed by these vast social changes. The armed forces officer corps no longer comes from the elite families but, virtually to a man, from the ranks of the middle class. As a result, the military can no longer be counted on automatically to side with the oligarchies in all cases. The hierarchy of the Catholic Church similarly no longer comes from the old-rich families but from the middle sectors, a change that is reflected in the new political positions taken by the church. Other changes within the church, both in Rome and in Latin America (liberation theology, the worker-priest movement, the Christian base communities), have shaken this venerable institution to its very foundations. The universities, the bureaucracies, the political parties, the professional associations and interest groups—all tend to be dominated by the new and aspiring middle class.[17] These comments about the class bases of these institutions still tell us little about actual political behavior, a subject we take up shortly, but they do serve to indicate the vast social changes that have been and are under way.

POLITICAL CHANGE

The fourth major area of transformation is in the realm of political institutions. Again, the changes are vast. They include the proliferation of interest groups way beyond the traditional triumvirate of church, army, and oligarchy; the growth of modern, mass-based political parties; the vast expansion in the number of government institutions created to provide programs and services; new attitudes toward and expectations from government itself; and new means of expressing political views, through elections, mobilizations, or even revolution. There remains some doubt as to whether even in this new era many traditional Latin American ways of doing things via patronage, spoils, and *personalismo* have changed all that much; but even here the consensus is growing that alterations have occurred, and certainly the institutional framework for continued change is now in place in many countries.[18]

INTERNATIONAL AFFAIRS

The international arena is the fifth area of transformation. Latin America is now part of a vast web of cultural, economic, political, social, diplomatic, and strategic interrelations with the outside world that are unprecedented in its history. Traditionally an isolated area, cut off from the main currents of international life, Latin America is presently caught up in a complex maze of international dependence and interdependence that has made the area a part of the modern world culture and system as never before. Its economies are tied to international markets; its cultural forces and tastes (rock music, Coca-Cola, and jeans) come from abroad; it has political ties with groups and movements in Europe and the United States; its diplomatic and security ties and alliances link it to outside pressures; and modern means of communications and travel connect Latin America to the outside world in unprecedented ways.[19] A telephone call from Buenos Aires across the estuary of the Río de la Plata to Montevideo, which used to go through a telephone exchange in New York, no longer must go that long and circuitous route—only one of many possible illustrations of Latin America's increased web of interconnections. Greater international dependence and interdependence also imply of course that Latin America is currently caught up in cold-war and other international conflicts over which the area has little control and in which its interests are sometimes forgotten.

These, then, are some of the major areas of change in Latin America in recent decades. The effects of these changes are cumulative; moreover, when the several areas of change here outlined are put together, the whole process is considerably greater than the sum of the several parts. These changes indicate that the Latin American social and political systems have not been nearly so rigid and inflexible as is often thought but have actually provided for a great deal of change, modernization, even democratization. Many problems of poverty, abysmal living conditions, and inequality remain of course, but the cumulated changes add up over the long term to what may justifiably be called a revolution in ideas, economy, society, polity, and international relations. They provide the context and setting in which Latin American democracy has had the chance to emerge and grow. But they also provide a context in which instability, upheaval, and developmental retrogressions may take place.

The Reaction: Dictatorship and Bureaucratic-Authoritarianism

The vast social and other changes already described seemed to be proceeding inexorably in the 1950s and early 1960s. Economic growth helped accelerate social and cultural changes, which in turn were giving rise to greater pluralism and accompanying political changes. A number of Latin America's reigning strongmen gave way, or were forced to give way, to more democratic forces, in Argentina, Bolivia, Brazil, Cuba (although there the revolution was misdirected toward Marxist-Leninist goals), the Dominican Republic, Honduras, Peru, Venezuela. The period seemed not only to give rise to a large body of romantic, even poetic literature about the age of the dictators being over, but also to confirm the Rostowian-Lipsetian thesis that economic, social, and political development or democratization went hand in hand and were inevitable.[20]

But almost before it began, and certainly before the new Latin American democracies had a chance to consolidate themselves, this earlier attempt at democracy was snuffed out and the militaries were back in power. Among the countries of the area only Colombia, Costa Rica, Mexico, and Venezuela escaped the clutches of renewed dictatorship and authoritarianism. Since this was a critical turning point, not only profoundly disappointing to the defenders of Latin American democracy but also seeming to refute the premises of a whole body of development literature, the reasons for the renewed militarism of the 1960s and 1970s need to be examined. They include economic, social, and political factors.

In the economic realm, according to the thesis of Guillermo O'Donnell, this was the period when Latin America's prevailing economic strategy of import substitution had just about run its course. The preferred development strategy for Latin America at least since World War II has been to "substitute" locally produced manufactured goods for those produced on the outside and imported to the area. Under this strategy Latin America sought to industrialize while at the same time reducing its dependency on agriculture and the export of primary products that were then seen as causing long-term disadvantages for Latin America relative to the industrialized countries. Hence Latin America turned heavily to industry and manufactures, a tactic that helped produce significant economic growth through the 1950s. But by the 1960s, O'Donnell argues, the import-substitution strategy was "exhausted," the economies of Latin America were in trouble, and as a result a number of civilian governments were replaced by military regimes.[21]

The second factor is sociological. The economic growth of the 1950s and 1960s and the political openings of that time had given rise to a large number of newly mobilized peasant and worker movements throughout Latin America. These movements, patterned sometimes after the Cuban Revolution but more often organized by radical or left-wing political movements or clerics, and often inspired by ideologies other than those previously thought to be the only legitimate ones for the society, severely threatened the older established groups and the newly ascendant middle class. Frightened by what they perceived as the organization and arming of peasant militias, by growing worker militancy, and by a new generation of left-wing and social democratic presidents (Bosch, Frondizi, Goulart, Villeda; later Allende, Belaúnde, Duarte), the historically more traditional elements in society—the church hierarchy, the armed forces, the economic elites, elements of the middle class—joined to help replace democracy with military authoritarianism. The continued poverty and maldistribution of wealth in Latin America, plus the highly uneven nature of the development that did occur, added to the pressures for change.

The wave of coups demonstrated the at least short-term falsehood of various developmentalist "verities": that social, economic, and political development could all go together in harmony and tandem; that democracy was the near-inevitable by-product of socioeconomic development; and that a growing middle class would automatically serve as the bastion of democracy. Instead, the rash of coups of the 1960s and early 1970s demonstrated the contrary theses of Samuel P. Huntington: that socioeconomic modernization could be disruptive rather than necessarily stabilizing, that such modernization could well undermine democracy rather than contribute to it, and that democracy is not the result of inevitable social and economic processes but requires strong institutions in its own right—political parties, civic associations, bureaucracies, organizational infrastructure of all kinds.[22]

That is precisely the third factor in explaining the resurgence of military regimes during this period. Latin America's political institutions, despite significant growth in recent decades, were still woefully inadequate to cope with the new challenges being thrust upon them. The political parties were still weak and inadequately institutionalized, public opinion was inchoate, the bureaucracies and national armies were only partially professionalized, labor unions were weak and poorly organized, and other interest groups did not form that "web of associability" that Tocqueville and virtually all scholars since then have recognized as essential to democracy.[23] In addition, Latin America's own democratic leaders were often not up to the task of governing effectively and well, and were themselves partially to blame for their own overthrows.[24]

The result was a decade or decade and a half of military authoritarianism and frequently brutal repression in the 1960s and 1970s. These were no longer simple, men-on-horseback military regimes as in the past, stepping into power briefly, making some short-term correction such as holding a new election, and then stepping quickly out again. Rather, these were for the most part military regimes determined to stay in power, to wipe out "leftist" influences, and to restructure the entire fabric and direction of the national political society. They were administrative-bureaucratic military regimes in which the *institution* of the armed forces exercised authority, not just one man. Moreover, as in Brazil, these new military regimes often governed in alliance with civilian elements to promote—in contrast to the past—an orderly, structured road to development.

These administrative or bureaucratic-authoritarian regimes often abolished the existing political parties, snuffed out the trade unions and peasant leagues, and sometimes used violent methods to get rid of those opposed to them. They were quite successful—for a time—in wiping out the institutional apparatus of democracy, but they were far less successful in creating any viable substitutes to replace them. Moreover, the economic policies they pursued were not very successful either, and over time the opposition to the military's continuance in power began to mount.

It is important to understand, therefore, the reasons for the military's withdrawal from power beginning in the late 1970s, as well as for the growth or rebirth of new and reconsolidated democratic institutions during that same period that seemed to offer a more solid base than earlier for Latin American democracy to survive and thrive. First we survey the general forces undergirding this new democratic resurgence, and then go on to provide a country-by-country analysis.

The Military's Withdrawal from Politics—and the "New Forces"

There have been literally hundreds of studies of how and why the military gets involved and intervenes in politics in Third World countries, but almost no systematic and comparative studies of the causes and processes of armed forces' withdrawals from politics.[25] Here we analyze the causes of military withdrawal in terms of four main sets of factors: factors having to do with the military itself, factors having to do with civil society outside and often in opposition to the military institution, contextual factors, and external factors.

The armed forces had come into power in many Latin American countries in the 1960s fresh from their military academies and war colleges and with new concepts of professionalism and training. It was not Napoleonic tactics that were being taught any more at these war colleges but modern administration, development theory, management, finance, international trade, and international relations—all subjects that equipped the new Latin American militaries to run large-scale organizations, such as their own countries![26] Moreover, in observing the widespread incompetence of the civilian politicians, the officers concluded—with considerable reason—that they could run their countries better than could the civilians. Furthermore, the discrediting of these civilian-democratic regimes, the perceived threats posed by left-wing movements and mass organizations, and the fears and encouragement of the elites and middle classes made it easy and attractive for the military to seize power—and either to be welcomed as saviors of the nation by the civilian population or to be greeted with apathy as a result of the mistakes and misdirection of the earlier and now generally discredited democratic regimes.

But once the military was in power the problems it faced proved as intractable as for the civilians. Soon it was the vaunted armed forces who, even with all their new training, were now accused of inefficiency, corruption, and incompetence. The military was no more able to deal with Latin America's pressing social and economic problems than the democrats had been. As they used more and more repression to keep themselves in power and to quell the rising opposition, the armed forces were even more discredited. The residue of good will or at least indifference toward the military gradually evaporated. Internal dissent within the military institution itself began to surface more and more.

In the end it was chiefly political combined with professional considerations that drove the military out of power. The armed forces had been discredited as managers and governors, the institution of the military came under strong attack, the military's political coalition began to break up until in virtually all countries it was left with only a handful of diehard supporters, and the military had lost almost all legitimacy. Faced with such widespread opposition that it threatened not only continued military rule but the integrity of the military profession and institution, the military prudently began to move toward finding a way to extract itself from power—it hoped in a manner that would enable it to survive and not be entirely discredited.[27]

As military rule proved weak and even vulnerable, civilian institutions that had been either snuffed out or in abeyance for many years began to stage a comeback. The resurgence of civilian institutions was fueled by the general discontent with the military. People were simply fed up with military bumbling, corruption, cruelty, and arrogance. As the popular apathy gave way to popular mobilization, the political parties, trade unions, and other groups that had been illegalized, suppressed, underground, or inactive began again to play a role. The two forces played upon and reinforced each other: as the military was more and more discredited, the civilian institutions were more and more emboldened; and as the civilian institutions became resurgent, the military came under ever stronger attack.[28]

Of particular importance during this early phase of the transition were the so-called new forces that had grown up during the 1970s. These included the new community base movements organized by the church and other agencies, a variety of new grass-roots political movements, human rights organizations and offices, religious groups that took on a political orientation, and so on. Eventually these newer mass organizations would be largely submerged in the major political parties and movements, and their importance would decline as democracy became more strongly institutionalized; but in the beginning—and perhaps on into the future—these new forces played a significant role.[29]

As usual in Latin America, however, it was chiefly the elites who led the movement for change, not the masses. Their opting for democracy was purely a pragmatic action and did not necessarily derive from any great love of democracy per se. The elites saw which way the wind was blowing, that military rule was discredited, that the U.S. government also favored democracy and that was where the aid would come from, and that any other alternative—Castroism or *Sandinismo,* for example—was entirely unacceptable. Hence the elites chose democracy.[30] But if their actions were thoroughly pragmatic, and not driven by any firm or lasting commitment to democracy, then at some future point they may equally pragmatically choose to abandon democracy in favor of something else.

The third main set of factors helping to explain the resurgence of democracy in Latin America may be termed contextual. First, by this term we have in mind fad and fashion. The fact is, although the evidence is mainly impressionistic, that by the late 1970s military and authoritarian regimes, and the social-science explanations that went with and occasionally justified them—bureaucratic-authoritarianism, corporatism, and organic-statism—were no longer fashionable.[31] The democratic opening in Spain in 1975 and the democratic revolution in Portugal in 1974 demonstrated that democracy was possible even in those Iberian "mother countries" where authoritarianism and corporatism had long been powerful, and which presumably constituted the models for Latin America. Now authoritarianism was "out" and democracy was "in." In Latin America, which has always paid very close attention to European and North American fads, intellectual and otherwise, that meant simply that the existing military regimes had to go and democracy had to emerge. It was as simple as that: the military was out of date and would no longer "do"; democracy was the wave of the future. Once this massive shift in popular consciousness had taken place in Latin America, there was simply no longer any question of what had to occur.[32]

The other, somewhat "fuzzy" factor that needs consideration under the contextual heading is what could be called the "demonstration effect." Once one country or a group of countries had begun the transition to democracy, then others had to follow suit. There is a considerable basis for this contention in Latin American history, for in the past both coups as well as moves toward democracy have come in waves. The explanation lies in the rivalries and jealousies, as well as the common economic and social features, among and between the Latin American countries. If Brazil gets an aircraft carrier, Argentina must have one too. Likewise with democracy. If Argentina opens up toward democracy, so must Brazil. If Argentina and Brazil become democratic, Uruguay has little choice in the matter. Chile also, eventually, must follow Argentina's and Brazil's lead. If the Southern Cone becomes democratic, so must Peru. And if Peru and Colombia are democratic, Ecuador must go along. This of course is not to say that any of these states are simply pale imitators of their neighbors; each country had internal dynamics of its own that led to a democratic transition. Nor is to give a weight to this factor that it may not deserve. But there is a demonstration or ripple effect that operates in Latin America, and that certainly had an effect in this era on the transition to democracy.[33]

The fourth and last factor is external influences on the emerging transitions to democracy in Latin America. There are several forces operating here that merit brief attention. The first is that usually amorphous concept called "world public opinion." By the late 1970s the European and North American criticisms of Latin American military regimes, and particularly of their human rights abuses, had become a loud chorus. Latin America, which has always sought to present its best face to the rest of the world, was affected by the criticism and the ostracism that went with it. Although the relationships will always be imprecise, there is no doubt that world public opinion had an effect on pushing the armed forces out of power. If nothing else, it helped change the national mood, which left rule by the military with almost no remaining popular support and therefore no real reason to stay in power. Few of Latin America's military regimes, after all, were actually *driven* from power; rather they left, for the most part, peacefully and quietly. It was simply acknowledged, by the armed forces as by everyone else, that their time had come and gone.

The second force was that of the world market. The mid-1970s had been boom years for quite a number of Latin American countries, even "miracle" years in some. But by the late 1970s the two great oil shocks of that decade had hit, prices were down for Latin America's exports, and the boom years were over. Latin America went into an economic downturn that only deepened and worsened in the depression years of the early 1980s. The relations between economics, politics, and democracy in Latin America are treated in more detail in Chapter 7. Here let us simply say that historically, when the bottom drops out of the Latin American economies, the political structure and regime in power often disintegrate shortly thereafter. The late 1970s and early 1980s were no exception to this rule. To the already existent charges of political and administrative incompetence directed at the military regimes was now added the charge of economic mismanagement and incompetence, though previously the economy had been among the areas in which the military had claimed its greatest competence and successes. Even military regimes proved unable to cope with the region's pressing economic problems, and as that became clearer they removed themselves from power.[34]

Finally, but not least important, there is the U.S. role. Jimmy Carter's emphasis on human rights, however maladroitly the policy was managed, undoubtedly helped legitimize the struggle of the Latin Americans for democracy and human rights and mobilize popular opposition to authoritarian regimes. But it must be said that in the early moves of the major South American countries toward democracy, the United States at the beginning was often caught unawares and unprepared for these democratic transitions. The openings toward democracy in Latin America were almost exclusively and autonomously a Latin American operation. The United States eventually went along with and encouraged these moves even though it did not initiate them. Only when the U.S. government began to see the political advantages to be gained domestically and in terms of securing the support of its allies for other foreign policy goals did the United States begin to get on the democracy bandwagon. For the United States to take credit for the movement toward democracy in most South American countries would be akin to the rooster taking credit for the dawn.[35]

The situation in the Caribbean and Central America was different. In these small countries within the United States' sphere of influence and where the U.S. has considerable strategic interests, right from the start the United States was a major actor in the effort to achieve or restore democracy. In the Dominican Republic in 1978, it was U.S. pressure that forced an honest counting of the electoral ballots, thereby ensuring the defeat of the authoritarian regime of Joaquín Balaguer and ushering in a new democratic period under the Dominican Revolutionary Party.[36] In El Salvador in the early 1980s it was the United States that sought to push for alternatives other than the guerrilla left or the repressive military and that helped launch that country on the road to elections and democracy. The United States put immense pressure on the Salvadoran right to force a democratic opening, helped arrange for fair and honest elections, read the riot act to the Salvadoran military to improve the human rights situation, and massively aided the democratic government of José Napoleón Duarte that was eventually elected. In Grenada in 1983 the U.S. militarily intervened to restore a measure of peace and order to a small country torn asunder by internecine leftist rivalries and conflict, and to restore a climate for the practice of Westminster-style democracy.[37] In Guatemala, Honduras, and Ecuador, the United States took forceful action both to usher in transitions to democracy and to maintain democracy when it was threatened.[38]

The democratic successes in Central America, especially in El Salvador, led some U.S. officials to an exaggerated sense of their own accomplishments and to the idea that they could export the El Salvador "model" to other countries. But Brazil is not El Salvador, not only in terms of its size and resources but also in terms of its nationalism, pride, and strong sense that it could not learn anything from the El Salvador experience. The Salvadoran model was used in Guatemala and Honduras, but not in the larger countries of the area.

The overall result was considerably greater balance, some modesty, and even growing sophistication in U.S. policy toward Latin America.[39] The United States continued to monitor closely the internal as well as the international affairs of the smaller and institutionally weaker states of the Caribbean and Central America, sometimes nudging and pushing, sometimes playing a proconsular role, and sometimes recognizing the need to back off. With regard to South America, the U.S. role was more limited: we certainly encouraged democracy and supported it strongly; but in general we allowed the institutionally stronger states of that region to work out their own problems. In the two countries where the United States did attempt a larger role in getting rid of authoritarian regimes and opening up to democracy—Chile and Paraguay—the results were by no means uniformly successful, at least in the short run. The longer term looks better, however.

These distinctions and differentiations between countries, as well as greater sophistication in recognizing what the United States can and cannot accomplish in the Latin American part of the world, represented signs of growth and maturity in U.S. policy toward that region. They indicated some encouraging steps toward putting our relations with Latin America on the same normal and regular basis that we have long maintained with Western Europe. They also indicated growth in our thinking and greater maturity as to what the United States can do to aid democracy in Latin America and what the limitations are of our efforts to implant democracy there.

Country Case Histories

While there have been general patterns of change in Latin America in recent years that apply to the continent as a whole and that help provide an overall context for a return to democracy, there are also individual circumstances that are unique to each country. Argentina is very different from Peru, and Ecuador from Honduras. By treating all the countries together we miss a great deal about their special circumstances, and we perpetuate our misunderstandings of the area. In the end knowledge of both the area-wide patterns and of the distinctiveness of the individual cases is necessary. Detailed case studies cannot be provided here, but we can provide brief summaries of the events and forces in the key countries (the remaining authoritarian regimes are treated in Chapter 8).[40]

ARGENTINA

Argentina remains an enigma in Latin America and the world, a country of vast human and material resources that has never quite lived up to its potential. Why it has not done so is the great Argentine national preoccupation and the source of numerous frustrations and national complexes.

Argentina has had on-again, off-again military rule since the early 1930s. Neither Perón nor the military nor the intermittent civilian governments were able to solve the national malaise or to govern effectively. There was widespread strife at the time of Perón's death in 1974; his second wife, Isabel, succeeded to the presidency but proved unable to administer the country. The armed forces again took power in 1976 with widespread support from civilian elements and with the aim of eliminating the armed guerrilla opposition.

But the military's political and economic problems soon mounted, its policies alienated virtually all groups in the society, and there was factionalism and dissatisfaction among the officers themselves. With the elimination of the left, the raison d'être for military rule no longer existed; the economic slump revealed that the military was no more able to rule effectively than were the civilians it replaced. The catastrophic defeat of the armed forces in the Falklands/Malvinas war with Great Britain in 1982 was the last straw, revealing the generals' weakness and ineptitude even in their own, presumably, undisputed area of expertise.

Argentina's most recent return to democracy began with a record-breaking turnout of fifteen million voters in the 1983 election that swept Raúl Alfonsín into the presidency over his Peronist rival. Despite waves of terrorist bombings on one side and a threatened coup on the other,

Argentine democracy continued in power, and Argentina in the mid-1980s was perhaps more calm, peaceful, and tranquil than at any other time in the past sixty years. Later, however, the tensions began to mount once again, the economy proved to be a disaster area, and the future of Argentine democracy was uncertain. How Argentine democracy survives under Peronist leader Carlos Menem, elected in 1989, will likely provide for close watching.

BOLIVIA

Few countries in the world can match Bolivia's instability, with two hundred presidents in a little over a century and a half of independent life. Unlike Argentina, Bolivia is a very poor country, with vast social and economic problems and little institutional or associational infrastructure to deal with them.

After eighteen years of military rule, Bolivia returned to democratic government in October 1982. Elected President Hernán Siles Zuazo, facing a chaotic economic situation that included inflation of 20,000 percent, social upheaval, the threat of both military coups and revolutionary challenges, and possibly the incapacitation of his government, called for new elections in 1985, a year ahead of schedule. Since no candidate won an absolute majority in the first round, the congress then chose Victor Paz Estenssoro president.

Paz, who had served as president before, imposed stringent economic reforms and sought to deal with disruptive social elements. Challenges to his rule came from all political directions. Whether Paz could survive the minefields that stemmed from Bolivia's drug exports, its political machinations, the country's economic and political uncertainties, and its long history of instability remained very much an open question. Although democratic government in Bolivia had lasted longer than most observers expected (Paz did succeed in serving out his term), the continuation of democracy is by no means assured. Among the Latin American countries that have embarked on a course of democracy in recent years, the outcome of this process in Bolivia is among the least predictable.

BRAZIL

After two decades of military rule that began in 1964 with an effective and honest administration, presiding over a period of unprecedented economic growth in this vast nation, and ending with weak and ineffective leadership, Brazil returned to democracy in January 1985. Military rule in Brazil, which was never so brutal or repressive as in Argentina or Chile, nevertheless proved less and less popular over time; the consensus grew that the military's time in power had run its course.

The elections held were indirect, through an electoral college. But president-elect Tancredo Neves, who had built a political coalition out of diverse groups of the center and center-left, fell ill on the eve of his inauguration and died without taking office. Vice president—elect José Sarney, a political unknown without Neves's skills or charisma, became president.

Sarney emerged gradually as a major political figure in his own right. He benefited from the national euphoria over the return to democracy, and for a time his economic plans seemed to be working as well. But by 1987 inflation was again at triple-digit rates, exports were slumping, and Brazil announced that it would suspend interest payments on its huge foreign debt. The economic failures undermined Sarney's political support, which had never been firm to begin with, and led to increased pressures on him to shorten his term of office and hold new elections since he had not been popularly elected.

Brazil is such a large, important, dynamic country that its progress will likely not be held back for long.[41] But in 1989 the country was facing a severe economic crisis that was spilling over into the political arena and had the potential to upset Brazil's new and none too stable democracy.

DOMINICAN REPUBLIC

The case of the Dominican Republic is somewhat different from the others here considered in that it evolved in the late 1970s not from a military-dominated regime to democracy but from a regime that was civilian-led, albeit authoritarian, caudillistic, and paternalist, to a more genuinely democratic regime.

The Dominican Republic's long-time dictator, Rafael Trujillo, had been assassinated in 1961. There followed in quick succession several transitional regimes, an elected democratic government under Juan Bosch, a coup against Bosch, another conservative and transitional regime, a revolution launched by the pro-Bosch elements, U.S. military intervention, another transitional regime, and then the election of Joaquín Balaguer in 1966. Balaguer ruled as a kind of civilian man on horseback for the next twelve years, regularly returning to office in plebiscites in which he was the only candidate.

But by 1978 his popularity had waned and there was a serious challenge from the democratic opposition. As the ballots from the election were being counted and began to show the opposition had won, Balaguer and the army stepped in and seized the ballot boxes. Intense pressure from the United States forced the ballot count to be resumed and resulted in Antonio Guzmán being elected president. Eight years of government by the Dominican Revolutionary Party ensued (1978–86), after which the aging Balaguer was returned to the presidency, this time in a fair election.[42]

ECUADOR

Ecuador returned to civilian democratic rule in 1979 after seven years of military government. However, its elected president, Jaime Roldós, was killed in a plane crash in 1981. Vice President Osvaldo Hurtado then took power in an orderly transition, even though he belonged to a different party.

In 1984 León Febres Cordero was elected president, marking one of the few times in Ecuadoran history that one democratic government had succeeded another. Febres, a conservative businessman, was a favorite of the Reagan administration. But his rule proved more and more tempestuous as the opposition mounted a vigorous campaign against him, and Febres's own confrontational style alienated many voters.

In 1986 a disgruntled air force general, Frank Vargas, launched two unsuccessful uprisings against the government. In January 1987, rebellious air force troops briefly detained the president himself and thereby secured Vargas' release. There were new coup rumors and calls for Febres to resign. But, backed by the United States, he declared his intention to serve out his constitutional term until 1988. Rodrigo Borja, a man of the left, was elected to succeed Febres.

Democracy is still alive. But the coup attempts and rumors, the instability of the country, and the tactics of the opposition seemed to indicate that the political culture of Ecuador may not have changed all that much.[43]

EL SALVADOR

A more or less moderate military regime that had governed El Salvador in the 1960s gave way in the 1970s to one that was increasingly repressive. The corruption and brutality of that military regime helped spark the guerrilla uprising that by the late 1970s represented a serious challenge. Conflict escalated between the left and the right, resulting in accelerating violence and civil strife.

A more moderate, even reformist, military faction seized power in 1979 and formed a *junta* that included three civilians. It was faced with the immediate opposition of both extreme left and right groups. The *junta* swung to the right for a time and then back to the center as José Napoleón Duarte and his Christian Democrats were brought in.

In 1982 elections for a constituent assembly were held in which none of the parties received a majority. The assembly elected Alvaro Magana to serve as interim president. In 1984 presidential elections were held, which resulted in Duarte defeating the rightist candidate, Major Roberto D'Aubuisson, in a runoff. During all this time, it is important to remember, a civil war was being fought, the guerrillas were seeking to undermine all these painfully slow steps toward democratization, and strenuous efforts were being made to reform El Salvador's major institutions, including the land system, the judiciary, and the armed forces. The hand of the United States in all these matters was sometimes so heavy that it amounted to proconsularism.

As Duarte's term wore on, so did the conflict. The peace talks with the guerrillas remained deadlocked, the economy continued to decline, and for the first time popular discontent against Duarte was manifested. The discontent was reflected in the victory of the opposition ARENA party, now led by Alberto Cristiani, in the 1989 election. The strength of the guerrilla challenge had slowly ebbed under military pressure, but that did not necessarily translate into any greater devotion to democracy by the armed forces. Meanwhile, the "internationalization" of El Salvador's conflict, the fact that all groups look abroad for support, and the ongoing violence and corruption raise the question of whether El Salvador can make democracy work or whether it will in the long term be torn asunder rather like Lebanon.

GUATEMALA

This country, like Bolivia and Ecuador, has had a particularly troubled history. From 1944 to 1954 a revolutionary regime was in power that, in its later years, invited communists into the government and that was overthrown in a coup supported by the U.S. Central Intelligence Agency. Thereafter the country was dominated by the armed forces with (rather like El Salvador) more or less moderate military or military-cum-civilian regimes in the 1960s and increasingly repressive ones in the 1970s. The earlier centrist regimes were strongly attacked by both the extreme left and the extreme right, thus undermining any hope for Guatemala to develop in a democratic direction.

In 1982 a change-oriented military officer, General Efraín Ríos Montt, took power. This began Guatemala's transition to democracy. Although Ríos Montt was overthrown in 1983, his successor, General César Mejía Victores, promised to hold elections that would pave the way for a return to civilian government. A constituent assembly election was held in 1984, in 1985 there were elections for the National Assembly and the presidency, and in 1986 Christian Democrat Mario Vinicio Cerezo was inaugurated.

Guatemala faces deep social and racial divisions dating back to the sixteenth-century Spanish conquest, immense social and economic problems, a long tradition of harsh authoritarianism, and a military that is the most powerful institution in the nation's life. There are still widespread human rights abuses, lingering guerrilla challenges, and an unstable and only weakly institutionalized democratic government. The civilian president cannot be perceived as undermining the military, ruling without them or, worse, putting them on trial for past human rights abuses, or his days will be numbered.

HAITI

"President-for-Life" Jean-Claude Duvalier's removal from the presidency (ushered onto a plane provided by the United States) in 1986 terminated an almost three-decade autocratic rule by the Duvalier family and initiated Haiti's hoped-for transition to democracy. "Baby Doc" left behind a bankrupt treasury, a nation with the lowest per capita income in the Western Hemisphere, and a country not only unschooled in democracy but with almost none of the social, economic, and political infrastructure on which a functioning democracy could be built.

A National Governing Council under General Henri Namphy was set up as a transitional government. The new government promulgated a calendar for elections, ended some of the most repressive practices of the old regime, provided a new climate of freedom, and began the process of helping or enabling new institutions to grow. Constituent assembly elections were held in October 1986, the new constitution was approved in March 1987, and in January 1988 (after the first scheduled election ended in a bloody massacre) political scientist Leslie Manigat was elected president. Rather like in Guatemala, the new civilian leadership and the dominant military continued to coexist in an often uncomfortable arrangement—until later in 1988 when Manigat was ousted and the military returned to full power.

Haiti remains a real problem area for the democracy campaign. The country is virtually without topsoil, its economy is all but hopeless, and it lacks almost totally the social and political institutions on which democracy might be established. Only massive and continued infusions of U.S. assistance will keep Haiti afloat. Having gotten rid of the Duvaliers (the easy part), the United States now faces the far more difficult task of building democratic institutions where none had existed before. So far the effort has not been successful.

HONDURAS

Honduras is, rather like Guatemala and Haiti, a country with dual power structures continuing uneasily to coexist side by side. The one is military and authoritarian and the other civilian and democratic; the process of negotiation (or confrontation), accommodation, and adjustment in their relative power is virtually constant.

The military in Honduras had been in power for nearly eighteen years prior to the calling of constituent assembly elections in April 1980. In 1981 Roberto Suazo Córdova was elected president. However, this transition to democracy was achieved only by mortgaging the new government to an "iron circle" of military hardliners headed by Gustavo Alvárez. The jockeying between the military and the civilian arms of the government (and its opposition) led to a constitutional crisis of major proportions in which the country's supreme court was sent packing.

In November 1985, new elections were held in which José Azcona Hoyo was chosen as president. Since then, Honduran democracy has continued to limp along, burdened by severe economic problems and sometimes overshadowed by the military. Honduras is also caught between, and entangled in, the civil wars in both El Salvador and Nicaragua. Honduran democracy must similarly survive the pushes, pulls, blandishments, as well as help provided by the U.S. Embassy, which, here as elsewhere in Central America, sometimes plays a too heavy-handed or proconsular role and thus puts an added burden on an already fragile system. The tightrope that Honduran democracy must walk and the juggling act a skilled president must perform on an almost daily basis leave little room for mistakes or maneuver.

PANAMA

The Panamanian National Guard—now known as the National Defense Forces (NDF)—has long been close to the surface of power if not actually in power. General Omar Torrijos seized the reigns of government in 1968 and ruled for the next thirteen years until his death in a plane crash. He was succeeded for a time by other military men, but in 1983 a series of constitutional amendments paved the way for the restoration of democratic government.

Although the Defense Forces remained the dominant institution in the country, military rule in Panama has generally been freer and more open than most, has often followed constitutional norms, and has not been so overtly repressive. But even when democratically elected presidents are in power, the military's involvement in governmental affairs is pervasive.

In the 1984 election Nicolás Ardito Barletta, favored by the United States, was elevated to the presidency in a balloting contest that was widely viewed as fraudulent. Ardito Barletta, who had been a World Bank vice president and was not an experienced politician, was viewed as weak by the military, was not able to deal with the country's severe economic troubles, and continued to be seen both as a leader whose democratic legitimacy was questionable and as a puppet of the United States. When he failed to protect the National Defense Forces, especially their commander General Manuel Antonio Noriega, from being implicated in a plot involving the murder of a leading Panamanian leftist, Ardito Barletta was forced to resign. He was succeeded by the vice president, Eric Arturo Delvalle.

The fall of Ardito Barletta was the first military-inspired coup in Latin America since the hemispheric-wide movement toward democracy began. The coup was terribly embarrassing to the United States, which had instigated the democracy campaign, and potentially even more disastrous for U.S. policy if the coup plague spread. Hence the United States put enormous pressures on the Panamanian NDF not to seize power fully for itself but to allow Vice President Delvalle to continue in power and thus preserve constitutional government. In this way Panama could still be included in the "democratic" camp, even though that claim represented a rather thin facade and the military remained the power behind the throne.

Delvalle continued for a time as an ineffective leader, but Noriega was obviously the main authority in the country. His regime was revealed to be more and more corrupt as well as repressive, and popular pressure mounted for Noriega to step aside. The United States added its weight to the pressure, and a grand jury indicted Noriega for drug trafficking. But Noriega fought back and tried to rally nationalistic sentiment in support of his regime. He cancelled the results of an election that repudiated him and continued to rule in an autocratic fashion.

PERU

Of all the military regimes that came to power in Latin America in recent decades, the one in Peru beginning in 1968 attracted the most favorable outside commentary. Its program was nationalistic and revolutionary and seemed to offer a new model of "Nasserist" modernization.[44] But in failing health and unable to deliver on his many promises, the revolution's leader, General Juan Velasco Alvarado, stepped aside in 1975; thereafter most of the wind went out of the "revolution." Velasco was succeeded by another general, Francisco Morales Bermúdez, who brought the regime back to a centrist orientation, ended the revolution, and presided over "just another" corrupt and inefficient military government. The country was now in economic crisis, and the regime had almost no public support.

After a new constitution was promulgated in 1979, elections were held in 1980 that were won by Fernando Belaúnde Terry, whom the armed forces had ousted back in 1968. But by now Belaúnde was old and tired and ruled ineffectively. New elections held in 1985 were won by the American Popular Revolutionary Alliance Party (APRA) and its leader Alan García.

García faced severe problems: a huge national debt, a bankrupt economy, accelerating social change that threatened to get out of hand, the challenge of a Khmer Rouge–like guerrilla movement (the mysterious *Sendero Luminoso*), and a restive military deeply suspicious of García and his party. García managed to survive, but he did so in part by antagonizing the United States and scaring off needed capital investment.

Democracy is alive in Peru, but it is very precarious. In addition to the possibility of a military coup, there is little organized center or conservative opposition to the government (except novelist Mario Vargas Llosa), leaving the communists as the most visible present alternative. That is not a very comfortable prospect from the U.S. point of view. Moreover, the vast social changes now occurring in Peru have given rise to a great fear among Peruvians that their country may be becoming "another Bolivia"—with all the portents for disintegration and political instability implied in that term.

URUGUAY

Uruguay, like Chile, had one of the longest and strongest traditions of civilian democratic rule and institutions in Latin America. In 1973, however, faced with evidence of widespread incompetence and corruption among the civilian leadership, a serious problem of terrorism and insurgency by the *Tupamaros,* and long-term economic decline that revealed the country to be living way beyond its means, the armed forces took power in what has been called a "creeping coup." That is, rather than seizing power all at once, the military first imposed restrictions on some civil liberties, then dissolved Congress, prohibited political parties, and continued to govern through a civilian figurehead president—until he too was eventually removed from office.

The period of military government is seen by almost all Uruguayans as an anomaly in the country's democratic tradition. However, that may be an overstatement. Most studies of Uruguay have concentrated on its democratic institutions, thus neglecting or glossing over a whole range of institutions that are not particularly democratic. These include the armed forces, many social institutions, the landholding system, the patronage network, and so forth. It may be that Uruguayan history is due for a reexamination that fairly assesses both its democratic and its more authoritarian tendencies.

By the 1980s, however, the Uruguayan military had been discredited just as armed forces' rule in its two giant neighbors, Argentina and Brazil, had been. Elections were held in 1984 and a new democratic government under Julio María Sanguinetti was inaugurated in 1985. Uruguay had thus returned to the democratic camp. Some analysts will say that is where it naturally belongs, unlike some of the other Latin American countries with stronger authoritarian traditions. But Uruguay's similarties (including militarism) to the other Latin American countries may be as impressive as the differences from them; moreover, the economic problems have not been solved and the tendency toward political fragmentation has reasserted itself. The fate of Uruguayan democracy is uncertain, as are democracy's prospects in these other countries.

*   *   *

Latin America, everyone agrees, has made some remarkable and impressive strides toward democracy during this past decade. The transition to democracy has been facilitated by general trends at work in the region as well as shaped by individual circumstances and conditions in each country.

While the movement toward democracy has been enormously heartening, not only to the Latin Americans but also to outside observers and to U.S. foreign policy, one is also struck by the immensity of the problems remaining, highlighted by the brief country-by-country analysis here and discussed at greater length later in the book.

The main problems include:

1. The immense and continuing social and economic problems faced, in different degrees and in differing ways, by all of the countries of the area.

2. The absence or weakness of viable democratic institutions in so many countries of the region.

3. The continued coexistence of democratic and authoritarian practices and institutions in quite a number of the countries.

4. The tentativeness and precariousness of democracy, democratic leaders, and democratic regimes even now.

5. The ever-present possibilities for setbacks and reversals of the areas' democratic trends.

6. The degree to which the United States must still intervene to prop up or save democracy in so many of the weaker countries, which is complicated by the decline of U.S. influence in many of these countries and by decreased U.S. assistance funds, which also give us diminished leverage.

Notes

1. Martin C. Needler, *Political Development in Latin America* (New York: Random House, 1967); Edward J. Williams and Freeman J. Wright, *Latin America: A Developmental Approach* (Palo Alto, Calif.: Mayfield Publishing, 1975).
2. Günter Grass was quoted as saying that the countries of Latin America could not solve their problems until they followed "the Cuban example."
3. Mario Vargas Llosa, "A Media Stereotype: Intellectuals Who Advocate a Cuban Solution for Latin America Employ a Double Standard," *Atlantic* 253 (February 1984): 20ff.
4. On this whole subject of Iberia's and Latin America's supposed "incapacity" for democracy, see Richard M. Nuccio, "The Family as Political Metaphor in Authoritarian-Conservative Regimes: The Case of Spain," Program in Latin American Studies, Occasional Papers Series No. 9 (University of Massachusetts, 1978).
5. A theoretical framework for studying this Latin American change process has been presented in Howard J. Wiarda, "Toward a Framework for the Study of Sociopolitical Change in the Iberic-Latin Tradition," *World Politics* 25 (January 1973): 206–35; book-length treatment by the same author may be found in *Corporatism and National Development in Latin America* (Boulder, Colo.: Westview Press, 1981).
6. Roberto Cortés Conde, *The First Stages of Modernization in Spanish America* (New York: Harper and Row, 1974); Richard Graham, *Britain and the Onset of Modernization in Brazil, 1850–1914* (London: Cambridge University Press, 1968); H. Hoetink, *The Dominican People, 1850–1900: Notes for a Historical Sociology* (Baltimore: Johns Hopkins University Press, 1982).
7. See David Scott Palmer, *Peru* (New York: Praeger, 1980); David Rock, *Politics in Argentina, 1890–1930* (London: Cambridge University Press, 1975).
8. W. W. Rostow, *The Stages of Economic Growth* (Cambridge: Cambridge University Press, 1960).
9. See the discussion in J. D. B. Miller, *The Politics of the Third World* (London: Oxford University Press, 1967).

10. Howard J. Wiarda, ed., *Rift and Revolution: The Central American Imbroglio* (Washington, D.C.: American Enterprise Institute, 1984).

11. Richard N. Adams, et al., *Social Change in Latin America Today* (New York: Vintage, 1961); Charles W. Anderson, *Politics and Economic Change in Latin America* (New York: Van Nostrand, 1967).

12. A more detailed treatment of these themes may be found in Howard J. Wiarda and Harvey F. Kline, *Latin American Politics and Development* (Boulder, Colo.: Westview Press, 1985), Part 1.

13. Richard Adams and Dwight Heath, eds., *Contemporary Cultures and Societies of Latin America* (New York: Random House, 1965).

14. Leopoldo Zea, *The Latin American Mind* (Norman: University of Oklahoma Press, 1963).

15. William P. Glade, *The Latin American Economies: A Study of Their Institutional Evolution* (New York: Van Nostrand, 1969).

16. Charles Wagley, *The Latin American Tradition* (New York: Columbia University Press, 1968).

17. John J. Johnson, *The Military and Society in Latin America* (Stanford, Calif.: Stanford University Press, 1964); Henry A. Landsberger, ed., *The Church and Social Change in Latin America* (Notre Dame: Notre Dame University Press, 1970).

18. Douglas A. Chalmers, ed., *Changing Latin America* (New York: Academy of Political Science, Columbia University, 1972).

19. One can identify these dependency features without necessarily being identified with the ideological positions of the so-called dependency school; see Howard J. Wiarda, *Dictatorship, Development, and Disintegration: Politics and Social Change in the Dominican Republic* (Ann Arbor, Mich.: Monograph Series of University Microfilms, 1975), chaps. 11, 12.

20. Rostow, *Stages of Economic Growth;* S. M. Lipset, *Political Man: The Social Bases of Politics* (Garden City, N.Y.: Doubleday, 1960).

21. Guillermo O'Donnell, *Modernization and Bureaucratic-Authoritarianism* (Berkeley: Institute of International Studies, University of California, 1973). The problems with this explanation are numerous: (1) It doesn't apply very well to the small countries of the region; (2) it may not apply to the bigger ones either from which the model was derived; (3) it doesn't explain why import substitution then continued under the military regimes that took power and remained the dominant strategy as they, in turn, were replaced by democratic governments. The crisis of import substitution as an explanation for the demise of democracy and the rise of bureaucratic-authoritarianism elevates a useful but still partial explanation into a single and all-encompassing one, and in its efforts to find an economic cause for the wave of coups in the 1960s ignores fundamental political and sociological causes. For more extensive critiques, see David Collier, ed., *The New Authoritarianism in Latin America* (Princeton: Princeton University Press, 1979).

22. Samuel P. Huntington, *Political Order in Changing Societies* (New Haven: Yale University Press, 1968); Edwin Lieuwen, *Neo-Militarism in Latin America* (New York: Praeger, 1964).

23. Alexis de Tocqueville, *Democracy in America* (Garden City, N.Y.: Doubleday, 1969).
24. Lee Fennel, "Leadership and the Failure of Democracy," in Howard J. Wiarda, ed., *The Continuing Struggle for Democracy in Latin America* (Boulder, Colo.: Westview, 1983), pp. 201–14.
25. Talukder Maniruzzaman, *Military Withdrawal from Politics: A Comparative Study* (Cambridge, Mass.: Ballinger, 1987).
26. Lyle N. McAlister et al., *The Military in Latin American Sociopolitical Evolution* (Washington, D.C.: Center for Research in Social Systems, 1970).
27. Maniruzzaman, *Military Withdrawal.*
28. See Guillermo O'Donnell et al., *Transitions from Authoritarian Rule: Prospects for Democracy* (Baltimore, Md.: Johns Hopkins University Press, 1986).
29. Margaret E. Crahan, personal communication to the author, February 9, 1983.
30. Douglas A. Chalmers and Craig H. Robinson, "Why Power Contenders Choose Liberalization: Perspectives from Latin America," Paper presented at the Annual Meeting of the American Political Science Association, Washington, D.C., August 28–31, 1980.
31. For a discussion, see Howard J. Wiarda, "Interpreting Iberian–Latin American Relations: Paradigm Consensus and Conflict," in Wiarda, ed., *The Iberian–Latin American Connection: Implications for U.S. Foreign Policy* (Boulder, Colo.: Westview Press, 1986), pp. 209–49.
32. Fad and fashion may be viewed as a not very strong or, in social science terms, entirely satisfactory explanation. Nonetheless, in the Latin American context it was an important contributing factor in explaining the continent-wide move toward democracy. But obviously with such tough strong-arm men as Stroessner and Pinochet, the existence of such a fad was, at least for a time, insufficient.
33. This factor is discussed in O'Donnell et al., *Transitions.*
34. For a full discussion, see Howard J. Wiarda, *Latin America at the Crossroads: Debt, Development, and the Future* (Boulder, Colo.: Westview, 1987).
35. See the discussion in Kevin Middlebrook and Carlos Rico, eds., *The United States and Latin America in the 1980s* (Pittsburgh: University of Pittsburgh Press, 1986), Introduction and Part III.
36. Michael J. Kryzanek, "The 1978 Election in the Dominican Republic: Opposition Politics, Intervention, and the Carter Administration," *Caribbean Studies* 19 (April–July 1979).
37. Jiri Valenta and Herbert Ellison, eds., *Grenada and Soviet/Cuban Policy* (Boulder, Colo.: Westview Press, 1986).
38. Based on extensive interviews with U.S. officials and officials of the countries mentioned.
39. On this see Howard J. Wiarda, *Finding Our Way: Toward Maturity in U.S.–Latin American Relations* (Washington, D.C.: American Enterprise Institute and University Press of America, 1987).
40. For the background I have relied on the country case studies in Wiarda and Kline, *Latin American Politics.* The magazine *Current History* provides useful

summaries of events in each country on a yearly basis. Extensive case studies of
the individual countries are also included in Larry Diamond, S. M. Lipset, and
Juan Linz, eds., *Democracy in Developing Countries,* 4 vols. (Boulder, Colo.:
Lynne Rienner Publishers, 1987–89). Dr. Iêda Siqueira Wiarda compiled the
notes and wrote a first draft of the materials for each country; I have also relied
on *Democracy in Latin America and the Caribbean: The Promise and the Challenge* (Washington, D.C.: Department of State, Bureau of Public Affairs,
Special Report No. 153, March 1987).

41. An especially good interpretive account is Robert Harvey, "Brazil: Unstoppable," *The Economist,* April 25, 1987, pp. 3–26.
42. Michael J. Kryzanek and Howard J. Wiarda, *The Politics of External Influence in the Dominican Republic* (Stanford, Calif.: Hoover Institution, 1988).
43. John Samuel Fitch, *The Military Coup d'Etat as a Political Process: Ecuador, 1948–1966* (Baltimore, Md.: Johns Hopkins University Press, 1977).
44. Howard J. Wiarda, "The Latin American Development Process and the New Developmental Alternatives: Military 'Nasserism' and 'Dictatorship with Popular Support,'" *Western Political Quarterly* 25 (September 1972): 646–90.

PART TWO

U.S. POLICY INITIATIVES

4

Earlier U.S. Efforts to Establish Democracy in Latin America

The United States has a long, albeit sporadic, inconsistent, and sometimes half-hearted history of trying to establish and assist democracy in Latin America. At times the furtherance of democracy has been the dominant motif in our foreign policy; more often than not, however, democracy has been subordinated to a hard-headed defense of the national interest. But in almost every U.S. administration the advance of democracy in Latin America has been considered one of the goals, sincerely believed or merely rhetorically stated, that should be pursued. Seldom, however, in all the two hundred years of the North American Republic, has the lofty ideal of bringing democracy to Latin America been successfully realized, a fact that should serve as a check on the excessive enthusiasm for the cause that some U.S. officials harbor even today.[1]

Of course, democracy in Latin America, as noted earlier, has never had very solid foundations. The history and political culture of the region have not been supportive of democracy, and the social and economic conditions of poverty and backwardness mitigate against the kind of solid base that democracy needs if it is to thrive. In addition, the U.S. efforts to promote democracy in the region have run into trouble because our goals have often been mixed or ambiguous. The U.S. enthusiasm to bring democracy to Latin America has by no means been consistent. Moreover, because we have not understood Latin America very well, we have often foisted inappropriate institutions on the region, and the implementation of our Fourth-of-July statements in favor of democracy has lagged far behind the rhetoric. Finally, if Latin America's own history, political culture, and socioeconomic conditions have not provided a strong foundation for democracy, then it is reasonable to ask how the United States could conceivably have expected to overcome such obstacles and succeed in bringing democracy to the region.

These problems may not have been entirely overcome in the current campaign to bring democracy to Latin America. A review of U.S. policy in the region and our efforts to encourage democracy may provide useful lessons for today's policymakers who need to keep in mind that U.S. foreign policy toward Latin America is fraught with inappropriate and failed attempts to foster democracy there, and that in the present campaign to export democracy we run the risk of repeating all the mistakes of the past.

The Colonial Period

The earliest concrete ties between the Thirteen Colonies and Hispanic America were commercial. In the seventeenth century, New England merchants and shippers began to explore the commercial possibilities in the Spanish Caribbean. In the famous "triangular trade" New England ships carried molasses, trinkets, and manufactured goods to Africa, where they were bartered for slaves. The slaves were brought to the Antilles, where they were sold; the profits were used to purchase sugar, tobacco, and hardwoods that were then shipped back to New England, thus completing the triangle. Additionally, fish from the New England coast was traded directly with the Caribbean. All the parties in these transactions, in the Thirteen Colonies and in the Caribbean, were in direct violation of the trade monopolies that both mother countries, England and Spain, had sought to impose. But as historian Edwin Lieuwen remarks, "the New World colonists apparently had few scruples where economic advantage might be gained."[2]

But alongside, and sometimes above and beyond, these commerical ties were moral, ethical, and political considerations. The Protestant and Calvinist colonists in New England had already begun to think of themselves as a special people with a missionary and civilizing mission to perform. The missionary attitude was both religious and secular, with the two frequently joined together. The New Englanders thought of themselves as God's specially chosen people. They despised the Papists of the Spanish colonies, whom they remembered as having burned at the stake their compatriots and ancestors in the Netherlands during the Dutch struggles to achieve independence from Spain. They felt it was their obligation, missionary style, to try to infuse the Caribbean with Puritan ways and beliefs and to check the papal legions.[3]

These religious sentiments carried over into the political sphere from which, in those days, they were inseparable. The New Englanders not only despised the Spaniards' Catholicism but also assumed, from the beginning, that North American political, social, and economic institutions were far superior. They believed that they had the responsibility for bringing the blessings of Protestantism to Latin America—and at the same time U.S. habits, behavior, and institutions—especially capitalism and democracy.[4] The paternalism, condescension, and ethnocentrism implied in such attitudes would repeatedly resurface in the subsequent history of U.S.–Latin American relations, and they remain strongly with us today.

Latin American Independence

"The Latin American policy of the United States," historian Samuel Flagg Bemis wrote, "has reflected constantly the vital necessities of national security and the idealism of the American people." Of these two elements, he went on to say, national security has always been uppermost. He states, "It is natural and understandable that this should be so, for without national security there could be no American idealism, no so-called 'American mission.'"[5]

The conflict between idealism and security concerns has loomed repeatedly in U.S. relations with Latin America, at least since the time of the Latin American independence struggles. During these struggles the United States made some gestures of support to the Latin American independence leaders; sent representatives to observe conditions in some key South American countries; and clearly sympathized with the revolutionaries in their rebellion against Spain, which was frequently likened to the U.S. war of independence against England. Prudence dictated a more cautious, even neutral, official position, however, because the United States was at that time negotiating with Spain over the acquisition of Florida, did not want to antagonize the Latin American mother country, and did not want to anger Great Britain either, which was then allied with Spain and had similar ambitions with regard to Florida. Official neutrality, however, did not deter numerous private individuals in the United States from aiding the Latin American revolutionaries.[6]

Henry Clay, one of the earliest champions of giving quick recognition to the Latin Americans struggling for independence, spent nearly ten years advancing their cause in Congress. He was opposed by Secretary of State John Quincy Adams, who was against early recognition and wanted, practically, to remain neutral until it was clear who would win the war. Their contrasting attitudes on the prospects for democracy and development in the Latin American region are strikingly similar to the debate one hears today.

> CLAY: [The nations of Latin America would be] animated by an American feeling and guided by an American policy. They would obey the laws of the system of the New World, of which they would comprise a part in contradistinction to that of Europe. . . . At the present moment the patriots of the south are fighting for liberty and independence—for precisely what we fought for.[7]

> ADAMS: I have not yet seen and do not now see any prospect that they will establish free or liberal institutions of government. . . . They have not the first elements of good or free government. . . . We shall derive no improvement to our own institutions by any communion with theirs. Nor is there any disposition in them to take any political lessons from us.[8]

That debate was resolved by the march of events: as the balance in the war swung away from Spain and toward the independence-seeking rebels, the United States ratified these realities by recognizing the new Latin American republics. The United States in fact was the first country to do so. But the issues raised by the Clay-Adams debate remain with us to the present.

The Monroe Doctrine

"The Monroe Doctrine," political scientist Michael J. Kryzanek has written, "brought the United States into the mainstreams of international power politics." By publicly declaring its intention to protect the Western Hemisphere from outside interference, the United States went on record as saying it wanted to be recognized as a growing world power. The fact that the United States could not effectively back up the moral injunctions contained in the doctrine by military force, and that the doctrine was frequently violated until the time that the United States became a serious world power later in the nineteenth century, is in Kryzanek's view perhaps less important than the fact the United States was taking its first steps toward playing a more ambitious international role. "From this point onward," Kryzanek writes, "the United States sought to control events by declaring itself the dominant force in the hemisphere."[9]

The Monroe Doctrine was a response to threats to the hemisphere from czarist Russia, which then owned Alaska and was expanding its claims southward into the Pacific Northwest; from the Holy Alliance of Russia, Austria, Prussia, and France—all monarchies that feared the rising tide of representative government; and from rumors of a combined French-Spanish fleet that would sail to the New World and recapture the newly independent countries and restore them to colonial status and the monarchical cause. This is the stuff of realpolitik.

But also imbedded in the Monroe Doctrine was the familiar idealism and missionary zeal of the United States—and not just as post hoc rationalizations. There is no doubt, then as now, that the United States genuinely wanted Latin America to grow, prosper, and become democratic. To that end, the doctrine sharply contrasted the monarchical systems of the Old World to the representative ones (or aspiring thereto) of the New. "The political system of the [European] allied powers," the doctrine declared, "is essentially different from that of America." The United States was "more immediately connected with the republics than with the monarchies." The United States opposed any effort by the European powers to extend "their system" to any portion of the Western Hemisphere. "But with the governments who have declared their independence and maintain it," the doctrine said in its key passage, "and whose independence we have, on great consideration and on just principles, acknowledged, we could not view any interposition for the purpose of oppressing them, or controlling in any manner their destiny, by any European power, in any other light than as the manifestation of an unfriendly disposition toward the United States."[10]

The doctrine was full of such lofty idealism, which both complemented and provided an additional moral dimension to its strategic intentions. But not only was the doctrine largely unenforced and unenforceable for the next seventy years; often, in the name of the doctrine, we did some quite nasty things in Latin America that could be justified as advancing the cause of democracy and representative government there only by a strong leap of imagination.

Manifest Destiny

The period between the proclamation of the Monroe Doctrine and the Civil War is known as the era of Manifest Destiny. Defining the period is difficult. It may have started earlier, since the Monroe Doctrine itself was in part a product of popular sentiment for the United States to play a more ambitious role; and it lasted longer, for U.S. ambitions for expansion into the Caribbean and Central America did not abruptly end with the Civil War. It was a period when a restless, expansionist, and even aggressive spirit infused both the people of the United States and their government. It was a time of new national striving and optimism, of ambition, and of national confidence that was virtually unbounded.[11]

During this period numerous outspoken public figures, doubtless reflecting the views of their constituents, argued that it was the destiny of the United States to expand. Expansion would be westward to the Pacific Ocean and, in the view of some, northward into Canada and southerly toward Mexico, Central America, and the Caribbean. The compromise settlement with Great Britain in 1846 checked the northerly expansionism; but the westerly one involved us in a war with Mexico that deprived our southern neighbor of one-third of its national territory; and the southerly one brought us deeply into the internal affairs of the Caribbean Basin nations for the next hundred years and led to numerous interventions.

In the early decades of the nineteenth century, cotton production had expanded rapidly along the Gulf of Mexico from Florida toward the West. In 1823, the year of the Monroe Doctrine, the newly independent Mexican government gave permission to U.S. citizens and their slaves to settle in Texas. The results are familiar to anyone acquainted with U.S. history. More and more U.S. citizens soon flocked into Texas; these new settlers maintained a strong attachment to the United States and proved unwilling to submit to Mexican law and authority, and independence sentiment grew. When Mexico sent troops into Texas in 1835 to enforce its law, the colonists prevailed, and in 1836 Texas became an independent nation. In 1845 Texas was annexed to the United States, and the following year the United States and Mexico were at war. Mexico's defeat resulted in the annexation, after the payment of fees that now seem modest, of even more former Mexican territory: California, New Mexico, Arizona, parts of other states, and a disputed area of Texas that made the Rio Grande our southernmost border. The United States now stretched from the Atlantic to the Pacific.

The spirit of Manifest Destiny subsequently turned further south. Cuba was coveted not only because of its strategic location but also as a potential additional slave state. In 1846, during the Mexican War, the United States acquired a toehold on the Isthmus of Panama. The Clayton-Bulwer Treaty of 1850 gave the United States transit rights across Nicaragua. There were, additionally, various schemes afoot, some private, some official, some mixed, to annex Puerto Rico, Hispaniola, and other

Central American countries and Caribbean islands. The notorious fil-ibusterer William Walker sought to "liberate" lower California from Mexican rule. When that effort failed, he moved to conquer Nicaragua, had himself elected president, and concocted a plan to seize all of Central America. These efforts ultimately failed as well, and Walker himself was executed by a Honduran firing squad. But his were only the most dramatic of hundreds of often harebrained and often self-serving schemes to draw the entire region into the U.S. orbit. And the dreams of annexation, protectorates, and colonization certainly did not die with Walker.[12]

While many of these schemes were selfish and self-serving, there is little doubt that their proponents and supporters were usually sincere in their belief that they were also liberating those lands from the yoke of oppression (Spanish, Mexican, Catholic) and bringing them the benefits of Christian, Protestant, democratic civilization. In fact, all these territories did prove, by virtually any measure used, to be far better off under U.S. rule than under Mexican sovereignty. But while the intentions in some cases were good and the results quite favorable, depriving Mexico of 35 percent of its territory (thereby earning us the lasting resentment of that nation), intervening repeatedly in the internal affairs of the Caribbean and Central American nations, and assuming a strongly patronizing and condescending attitude toward all things Hispanic were not convincing ways to bring democracy to Latin America.

There is a powerful thesis[13] that only by such "radical Westernization" as in the case of Japan, can true and irreversible modernization be brought to the Third World. And certainly the present-day citizens of the southwestern United States are content that they have been under U.S. and not Mexican rule for the past 140 years. Still, if our goal, even partially, was to bring democracy to Latin America, the era of Manifest Destiny was not an example of how to do so. In fact, a very strong case can be made that such ethnocentrism and heavy-handedness are self-defeating when it comes to the expansion of democracy: they forever poisoned our relations with Mexico and the nations of Central America and the Caribbean.

Interventionism and Dollar Diplomacy

During the first thirty years following the Civil War, the United States did not pay much serious attention to Latin America. The United States was preoccupied with its own dynamic, booming economy and the filling and settling of the immense internal territories. There was, during this period, a feeble effort to annex the Dominican Republic, jingoistic but sporadic concern with the Cuban revolution against Spain, and the beginning of what would soon become major economic investment in Central America. But until the mid-1890s the United States generally stayed out of Latin American issues, acquiring no new territories there. Meanwhile, based on the industrialization and unprecedented economic development that was occurring in the post–Civil War period, the United States had become a major world power, with the economic and military might to back up the bold but heretofore unenforceable provisions of the Monroe Doctrine.

In 1896 the United States, on the basis of the Monroe Doctrine, became involved in a border dispute between Venezuela and British Guayana in which the other principal protagonist was Great Britain. It was during this event that U.S. Secretary of State Richard Olney issued his famous doctrine, "The United States is practically sovereign in this continent and its fiat is law upon the subjects to which it confines its interposition." No more sweeping expression of U.S. power—and arrogance—has ever been issued.[14]

A much more important demonstration of U.S. power—and our willingness to use it—occurred in Cuba, which had been struggling for independence from Spain for decades. When that process was nearly completed in 1898, the United States declared war on Spain, sent its forces to Cuba, and thus guaranteed that the final independence of Cuba would come only under U.S. auspices. By the terms of the Treaty of Paris that settled the war, the United States forced Spain to cede Puerto Rico and the Pacific island of Guam to the United States, to sell the Philippine Islands for $20 million, and to grant independence to Cuba. But independence came only after the Cubans agreed to attach the infamous Platt Amendment to their constitution. This gave the United States virtual carte blanche to intervene in internal Cuban affairs for almost any reason whatsoever, a provision that led to numerous U.S. interventions between 1898 and 1933 when the amendment was finally abrogated.

With Theodore Roosevelt in the presidency and Admiral Alfred Thayer Mahan serving as his apostle of expansionism and global sea power,[15] the United States moved further toward controlling and even acquiring that ring of Caribbean islands that stretches from Florida to Venezuela. There and in Central America we acquired bases, listening posts, tracking stations, and port facilities. We bought the Virgin Islands from Denmark, used Hispaniola's bay and peninsula of Samaná as a port and naval tracking station, and kept Guantánamo as a base even after giving independence to Cuba. In Central America, we used a number of the small islands along the Mosquito Coast, closely protected our transit rights over the isthmus, and monitored carefully the domestic political affairs of such countries as Nicaragua and Guatemala. These bases and outposts took on far greater importance once we had acquired the Panama Canal Zone and built the transoceanic waterway, after encouraging and assisting the breakaway province of Panama to secede from the nation of Colombia.

In 1905 we sent U.S. customs agents to the Dominican Republic to administer the collection of taxes and to help pay off that country's foreign debt, and within two years we had to send a contingent of troops (which later became an occupation force) to help protect the customs agents. From 1905 to 1909 we also occupied Cuba militarily. This was Roosevelt's "big-stick" diplomacy in the Caribbean, justified by the president in the following sweeping terms: "Chronic wrongdoing, or an impotence which results in a general loosening of the ties of civilized society, may in America, as elsewhere, ultimately require intervention by some civilized nation, and in the Western Hemisphere the adherence of the United States to the Monroe Doctrine may force the United States, however reluctantly . . . to the exercise of an international police power."[16]

In 1908 William Howard Taft entered the White House and continued the interventionist tactics of his predecessor. Taft, however, carried the process a step further. A leading Latin America scholar, Federico Gil, characterized Taft's efforts as "the promotion and expansion of United States financial and banking interests."[17] These efforts to advance U.S. banking interests in Haiti, Cuba, and the Dominican Republic, combined with Taft's active and aggressive encouragement of U.S. investment throughout the region and his attempt to use U.S. commercial interests to ward off European competition, became known as "dollar diplomacy."[18] The United States sent customs agents to Nicaragua who were under the direct control of the U.S. secretary of state, a move that was preceded by a more traditional form of intervention: diplomatic efforts and favoritism toward a rebel group that was seeking to overthrow anti-American dictator José Santos Zelaya.

But it was under President Woodrow Wilson (1913–21) that the urge to intervene was combined most strongly with a now-secularized Calvinistic vision of the United States as a "redeemer nation" with a special destiny and proselytizing mission. Known as the "Presbyterian of the Potomac," Wilson wanted both to advance U.S. interests and to bring the blessings of democracy to "our little brown and black brothers" (the words are quoted advisedly to indicate the paternalism involved) in the Caribbean and Central America. To this end (and doubtless worried also, as World War I loomed, about the possibilities of European powers taking advantage of the chronic instability to establish beachheads in the Caribbean) Wilson sent U.S. troops to Haiti, Cuba, Nicaragua, the Dominican Republic, and Mexico. These were not just brief interventions, as before, to correct some problem of the moment, but were full-scale military occupations (except in the Mexican case) that lasted for eight, ten, twelve, or more years.

The legacies of these interventions were numerous and often nefarious. The U.S. occupation forces brought chewing gum and baseball to the Caribbean (it is no accident that the three countries in Latin America in which baseball and not soccer is the national sport are Cuba, the Dominican Republic, and Nicaragua). The Marines and army troops also built roads, put in telephone and telegraph systems, improved port facilities, modernized the land cadastral system (principally to the advantage of U.S. investors), and installed sewer systems—all the things that the U.S. military forces and the Corps of Engineers are good at doing.

But they did not advance democracy. Indeed a very strong case can be made that Wilson's often well-intentioned efforts "to make the world safe for democracy" were destructive of the tender shoots of democracy that existed in the Caribbean, rather than helping them grow. The U.S. forces, in installing military-run, occupation governments, largely eliminated the fledgling local political institutions that did exist. The occupations shunted aside or rode roughshod over a whole generation of local civilian politicians. The occupations ruled out any practice in self-government, set back the learning process of democracy, and impeded the natural, indigenous political evolution and institutionalization of the Caribbean Basin states. By its high-handed ways—our racism toward the darker-skinned peoples of the Caribbean, the occasional brutality of the occupation forces, and the ruthlessness by which we hunted down the native irregulars who resisted or took up arms against the U.S. forces but were viewed as great patriots by their own peoples—the United States stimulated only hostility and anti-Americanism.[19]

Furthermore, by establishing national constabularies designed unrealistically to be an apolitical police force to keep the peace after the occupation forces left, the United States created the avenues by which such bloody tyrants as Somoza and Trujillo could rise and seize power. Thus many Latin Americans hold the United States responsible for the bloody excesses, persecutions, and abuse of democratic developments of the entire Somoza and Trujillo eras.[20] One can even argue that it is precisely because of these dictatorial regimes that went way beyond the pale even by Latin America standards, which as we saw earlier allowed a certain tolerance for authoritarian regimes, that Marxist-Leninist regimes were brought to power in Cuba and Nicaragua, and almost, in the U.S. view, in the Dominican Republic. In any case, it is undoubtedly true that Wilson's missionary zealotry and good intentions did little to aid the cause of democracy in Central America and the Caribbean and in fact set back democracy many decades.

The Good Neighbor Policy

The process of withdrawing the U.S. occupation forces from the Caribbean began under the succession of Republican presidents in the 1920s, and many of the ideas that were later incorporated into Franklin Delano Roosevelt's Good Neighbor Policy actually originated in the policies of President Herbert Hoover.[21]

The Good Neighbor Policy, nevertheless, did represent a break with the past. President Roosevelt revoked the Platt Amendment under which we had repeatedly intervened in Cuba and suspended the humiliating intrusions into Latin America that had been common earlier in the century. The president won the goodwill of the entire continent, without committing a dime of foreign aid, by announcing that his policy would be based on the revered Latin American principle of nonintervention. As the president stated in his 1933 inaugural address: "In the field of world policy, I would dedicate this nation to the policy of the good neighbor— the neighbor who resolutely respects himself and, because he does so, respects the rights of others—the neighbor who respects the sanctity of his agreements in and with a world of neighbors."[22]

But under the Good Neighbor Policy the United States was interested primarily in the political status quo, not necessarily in democracy. Essentially the policy was a strategy of what would later be called "benign neglect." It led—until World War II forced us into a more active stance— to a U.S. withdrawal of interest from Latin America and enabled the United States to reap political and even moral advantage from its policy of noninterference. It did not obligate the United States to do anything *for* Latin America—at a time when Latin America was facing the worst economic depression in its history.

Moreover, the lofty rhetoric of the Good Neighbor Policy ignored the fact of U.S. indifference to such "good neighbors" as dictators Rafael Trujillo in the Dominican Republic, Fulgencio Batista in Cuba, or Anastasio Somoza in Nicaragua. It implied U.S. acquiescence in—and as World War II approached even support for—such authoritarian regimes as those then existing in Brazil, Peru, Argentina, and Mexico, among others. It was, after all, at the height of the Good Neighbor Policy that Roosevelt coined his famous aphorism, the subject of which has been variously identified as either Somoza or Trujillo, that "he may be an SOB but at least he's *our* SOB."

Most of the New Dealers had little enthusiasm for such dictators, but that in no way made the Good Neighbor Policy a crusade for democracy.[23] Indeed, a strong case can be made that had the United States paid more attention to these dictators then, pressuring them to move toward democracy or even to step aside, we would not face the problems that we now face in the region. It is no accident that the three most critical "problem countries," which the United States would have to deal with in later years often in unhappy ways, were precisely the three ruled by strong-arm dictators whom the Roosevelt administration chose to ignore: Cuba, the Dominican Republic, and Nicaragua.

Postwar Containment

In the immediate post–World War II years, there was a brief spurt of interest by the United States in Latin American democratization. Ambassador Adolph Berle helped push the dictator Getulio Vargas to resign in Brazil, U.S. Ambassador to Argentina Spruille Braden tried—futilely as it turned out—to influence the outcome of the Argentina elections of 1946 by denouncing Juan Perón, and in such smaller countries as the Dominican Republic there were efforts to get the reigning dictators to reform their regimes and liberalize.[24]

But these efforts were short-lived and sporadic. Moreover, the liberalization that the United States advocated was often aimed more at economic liberalization than at democratization. The United States wanted the Latin American countries to liberalize their restrictions on trade and commerce to provide an opportunity for U.S. investors and markets more than it wanted political liberalization. Furthermore, as the postwar ambience of "good feeling" degenerated into the cold war in 1947–49, the United States became even less concerned with democracy in Latin America and more preoccupied with stability, the status quo and anticommunism, even if that meant propping up some of the region's most notorious dictatorships.[25]

U.S. policy, in Latin America as elsewhere, came to be based on the doctrine of containment, that is, taking all possible steps to prevent the spread of communism in the area. It implied the signing of military assistance programs and mutual defense pacts with the area's bloodiest dictators (who, to take advantage of the U.S. largesse and preoccupation with this issue, often posed as the "foremost anticommunists of the hemisphere").[26] It meant the strengthening of the military, the one institution in Latin America that hardly needed strengthening and which had a long history of opposition to any form of democratization. And it meant U.S. assistance to some pretty nefarious regimes in Latin America, a posture that also helped produce a new wave of military-authoritarian governments in the late 1940s and 1950s that snuffed out the earlier stirrings of democracy.

The Truman and Eisenhower administrations generally continued Roosevelt's policy of nonintervention, except of course in those instances where a genuine communist threat loomed imminent, or seemed to, such as Guatemala in 1954 and Cuba in 1961. There was a significant shift in the approach of the Eisenhower administration, however, during its last two years. The change was precipitated by Vice President Richard Nixon's trip to Latin America in 1958, during which he was spat upon, widely booed, and put in physical danger; and by the report on Latin America that Milton Eisenhower prepared for his brother.[27]

It was becoming clear that U.S. indifference to Latin America had broadly alienated the population, and that our policy of support of dictators, rather than holding back the forces of communism, provided the conditions under which communism thrived. Hence policy in the late 1950s began to shift direction. The shift, which began under Dwight D. Eisenhower in much the same way that FDR's Good Neighbor Policy began under his predecessors, flowered in John F. Kennedy's Alliance for Progress.

This historical record of U.S. foreign policy efforts to encourage democracy in Latin America is not very encouraging. Many would argue that democracy was not our purpose, rather that spreading "democracy" was only the cover for less unselfish U.S. motives, including expansionism, hegemony, and exploitation. Our record in the region hangs heavily over U.S. policy today, casting suspicions on our current efforts to aid democracy because of past machinations and raising doubts about U.S. purposes. It serves as an impediment to present attempts to assist democracy in the region.

But in the 1960s, with the Peace Corps and the Alliance for Progress, a new policy and a new era began in U.S.–Latin American relations. Or were they really new? Depending on one's point of view, they represented either a sharp break with the past record already surveyed or a continuation of it under new language and with new rationalizations. Hence this period and policy merit some detailed considerations.

The Alliance for Progress

We should be clear from the beginning what the Alliance for Progress was and what it was not. It was not just a romantic foreign aid giveaway program, nor was it entirely a wishful and unrealistic crusade for Latin American democracy. Rather it was a quite hard-headed attempt to frustrate communism and advance U.S. interests in Latin America, but using means other than those employed in the past. Building on the later Eisenhower approach, the alliance sought to bolster the traditional U.S. interests of stability and anticommunism in Latin America, but not by aid to dictators. Rather, the policy was to assist democratization in Latin America through socioeconomic aid and thus inhibit the spread of communism. The basic U.S. goals of promoting stability and anticommunism did not change, only the best means to achieve these goals.[28]

There are many things that can be said about the alliance, though it is not our intention to review the entire history of the program here.[29] First, the alliance was not so sharp a break with the past as is often thought. Not only were the goals of the program—stability and anticommunism— closely in keeping with U.S. strategic policy going back many decades, but many of the means—for example, support of the Latin American militaries—were the same as well.[30] Second, President Kennedy was not so committed to democracy in Latin America that he was willing to take a stand against dictatorships—Somoza's and Trujillo's stand out as examples—unless he could be certain first that a Castro-like Marxist-Leninist regime could be kept out of power.[31] Third, the alliance was based on an ethnocentric conception of Third World development, had little to do oftentimes with Latin American realities and operating principles, and represented—at least in some respects—the triumph of "true believers," committed to democracy but often with enthusiasm that outran their good sense or the necessity to base policy on sometimes hard Latin American realities.[32]

The alliance assumed, for example, that the Latin American middle class would be a bastion of stability, progress, and democracy, when the evidence pointed toward a more mixed conclusion.[33] It assumed that the Latin American military could be reformed, professionalized, and recast in the mold of the apolitical U.S. military, despite abundant evidence to the contrary.[34] It placed excessive hope on the Latin American democratic left, despite widespread evidence that this group was no more skilled politically or capable of governing Latin America effectively than any other group.[35] It sought to instigate agrarian reform, and a host of other development-related programs, in the face of vast bodies of sociological and anthropological evidence that the Latin American countries could not be converted overnight into societies of moderate, happy, medium-sized middle-class family farmers, or infused with civic consciousness and democratic beliefs on the model of rural Wisconsin and the New England town meeting. Nor did agrarian reform seem likely to expand sorely needed economic production in the region.[36]

Despite these fatal flaws in the assumptions behind the alliance, assumptions that ultimately guaranteed its failure, the alliance represented one of our most noble policy efforts toward Latin America. Its excessive enthusiasm for some just causes was reminiscent of Woodrow Wilson's missionary campaign to make the world safe for democracy; and its romanticizing about Latin America served as a forerunner of Jimmy Carter's similar campaign, strong on good intentions but weak on implementation and good sense, to bring U.S.–style human rights to the area. Nevertheless, by pouring in vast amounts of economic aid, albeit for programs too often based on erroneous assumptions, and by paying—at least for a time—serious attention to Latin America, the alliance ushered in a new period in U.S.–Latin American relations. It may be that the alliance represented, even with all its flaws, the best that the United States could do; and that, shorn of its mistakes and wrong assumptions, it could stand as a basis for later, more successful efforts. In fact, a good part of the Kissinger Commission's sensible recommendations on Latin America in 1984 reflected and built upon the alliance.

One other subject merits attention in this context: the Kennedy administration's more explicit efforts to bolster and build, where it was lacking, democracy in Latin America. On numerous occasions—Peru in 1962, the Dominican Republic in 1963, Honduras in 1963—the Kennedy administration sought to use diplomatic means, including the cutoff of economic aid, either to bolster democratically elected governments or to restore democracy where it had already been overthrown by coup d'état. In none of these efforts was the United States successful, and in quite a number of cases the U.S. efforts were so naive and divorced from the realities of Latin American political processes that they produced—contrary to the goal of the policy—even stronger anti-Americanism. The policy may also have inadvertently helped produce the wave of authoritarian-bureaucratic regimes in the 1960s and 1970s oriented toward not listening to the United States on any policy matter and toward staying in power for long periods of time in contrast to the usual practice of staging a *golpe,* forming a *junta,* holding new elections, and then leaving power. The new, more institutionalized authoritarian regimes instead remained in power, in part to flout the United States and to teach it that such blatant interventionism in their internal affairs was no longer acceptable. The U.S. policy was not only naive but often self-defeating and downright negative so far as the attainment of U.S. goals was concerned.[37]

The U.S. efforts to build democracy in Latin America had as many false starts and misplaced assumptions as did the diplomatic pressures aimed at maintaining it. These efforts were centered in the Institute for Political Education, which the United States helped found in 1960 in San José, Costa Rica, as part of the Eisenhower administration's new concern and preoccupation with Latin America.[38] The institute aimed to train young Latin American peasant, labor, and party organizers in democratic ideas and methods. Later, after Trujillo was assassinated, the school was transferred to the Dominican Republic. Numerous prominent Latin Americans—Rómulo Betancourt, José Figueres, Juan Bosch—taught there.

The institute was a marvelous idea so far as the cause of the promotion of democracy in Latin America was concerned, but it was implemented in all the wrong ways. First and most important, it was funded by the Central Intelligence Agency (CIA). Given the reputation of that agency in Latin America because of its past interventions, no program in support of democracy can be successful if it is funded by the CIA. Second, institute leadership was all wrong: CIA operatives, a furtive Romanian who many felt worked as a double or triple agent, and a Catholic priest who was an incompetent administrator and had many ideas deemed by his colleagues to be "crazy." Third, the institute was excessively partisan, pursuing one political ideology (social-democratic) and selecting its students from a very narrow range of Latin American young people. These and other problems condemned the institute to failure. Its flaws were such that its demise was destined, but the idea of assisting and training Latin American party, labor, and peasant leaders in democratic ideology and practice was sound—and revived in President Ronald Reagan's National Endowment for Democracy.

Benign Neglect

Following Kennedy's assassination in 1963, the Alliance for Progress was reformulated and eventually put on hold and then abandoned. Every president has his own policy "thing," which his successors may or may not wish to follow; in this case it was clear that neither Presidents Johnson, Nixon, nor Ford had much interest in Latin America. There were some spectacular U.S. interventions in the region during this period (the Dominican Republic in 1965, Chile in 1973) but little in the way of a consistent or sustained policy to support either democracy or any of the other main initiatives of the alliance. The priorities now lay elsewhere (Soviet relations, Vietnam, the Middle East, China); and particularly after the death of Che Guevara in Bolivia and the failure of other Castro-like guerrilla movements, the United States decided that Latin America might not be so ripe for Cuba-style revolutions after all. There were numerous hortatory pronouncements about "new beginnings" or a "new dialogue" with Latin America but very little that was concrete.[39]

The era came to be known as a period of "benign neglect" in U.S. attitudes and programs for Latin America. But we now know that the neglect was not so benign. Problems began to fester, tensions began to build, and yet the United States did nothing about them. Preoccupied with Vietnam, Watergate, and other problem areas that seemed larger, the United States mainly ignored Latin America. In retrospect, such neglect was not only dangerous but again self-defeating from the point of view of U.S. policy goals. Benign neglect proved to be as inappropriate as a basis for U.S. policy as the excessive enthusiasm and well-meaning but hopelessly unrealistic policies of the past.

The year 1972 was a critical turning point in Central America, but the importance of the events there was not sufficiently recognized in the United States. In 1972 the military in El Salvador annulled the democratic election that candidate José Napoleón Duarte had clearly won. They jailed and beat Duarte, sent him into exile, and ushered in the period of extreme repression that not only served as a strong impetus to the growth of the Marxist-Leninist guerrilla movement but that later caused immense problems for U.S. foreign policy toward that country. Also in 1972 an earthquake hit Nicaragua and leveled the capital city of Managua, and international relief assistance was mobilized. Instead of sharing the usual graft that accrues with such windfalls, as his father had done and the norms of Nicaraguan politics heretofore dictated, Somoza Jr. pocketed the assistance money all for himself and turned brutally repressive to protect his power. He thus brought on the chain of events leading to the Sandinista revolution, and the capture of that revolution by Marxist-Leninist elements that has proved so divisive in U.S. foreign policy. These events in Nicaragua were part of an emerging pattern in the early 1970s; in Guatemala, it was also a period of increased military repression that polarized the country and brought it to the brink of civil war.

In all these countries, if the United States had taken action in the early 1970s, ameliorating the oppression and pushing for greater openness, pluralism, and freedom, the foreign policy crisis we had to face in Central America in the 1980s would not have reached the proportions it did. Benign neglect allowed small problems to grow into larger ones that eventually reached the crisis stage. Had the United States been engaged earlier, had we been involved then (the early 1970s) even at some minimum levels, the crisis with which we now must grapple with so much contention would never have become so intense. But at that time President Nixon and Secretary of State Henry Kissinger were so preoccupied with Vietnam and Watergate that when ranking State Department officials went to them and said, "Here is the situation in Nicaragua, in El Salvador, in Guatemala; what should we do about it?" the answer received was, essentially, "Don't bother us with this; we're too busy with other problems."[40] Benign neglect was as disastrous for U.S. foreign policy as the sins of excessive enthusiasm and its accompanying tendency toward interventionism were in past U.S. history.

Conclusions

In this chapter, we have looked at U.S. attitudes toward Latin America from colonial times to the Alliance for Progress and beyond. Throughout this period, U.S. attitudes toward Latin America have always been condescending and patronizing. In earlier times such attitudes stemmed from the presumed superiority of North American Protestant and Calvinist civilization over the Catholic, Latin one. Just as Puritan preacher Cotton Mather questioned when he had a toothache what sin he had committed with his teeth, so Americans have always believed that there are fatal flaws in Latin America that have prevented it from being as successful as we are, and that we can then transform. Nowadays these differences are no longer put in terms of Protestant-Catholic dichotomies but in terms of "developed" versus "developing."

As a developed country we have generally believed we have things to bring and teach to Latin America. Woodrow Wilson used to say that his goal was to "teach Latin America how to elect good men." In a similar way so the architects of the Alliance for Progress assumed that they could bring U.S.–style development to the region; and one can have no doubt that Presidents Polk, McKinley, and Theodore Roosevelt believed that they were doing good in Latin America even while absorbing large chunks of its territory. In all these instances, from Clay and Monroe to Kennedy and

Jimmy Carter, our attitudes have been superior, ethnocentric, and arrogant. We have consistently assumed Latin America (and Latin Americans) to be incompetent and the United States to have the right answers. Condescension and a patronizing attitude have often been combined, or sometimes alternated, with indifference and neglect. These go together: the less we know about a country or region, the more easily we can assume to know what is best for it. Hence the frequently sporadic and episodic history of U.S. policy in Latin America. As we have seen, fits of intervention have alternated with eras of disinterest and neglect, benign or otherwise.

These swings between official concern for Latin America and official indifference, between involvement and nonintervention, or between idealism and *realpolitik,* prevented development of a clear, consistent, and balanced program for the area. We have alternated between such neglect that the region's problems are allowed to mushroom until they got entirely out of hand, and such heavy involvement that we in effect take over these countries and almost literally re-create them in our own image. Never have we achieved the constancy, the consistency, and the comprehensive policy that is clearly necessary. It remains to be seen precisely what such a consistent and multifaceted policy would consist of and whether it has been achieved by either of the previous two administrations—those of Presidents Carter and Reagan.

Notes

1. A good summary is Edward G. McGrath, ed., *Is American Democracy Exportable?* (Beverly Hills, Calif.: Glencoe Press, 1968).
2. Edwin Lieuwen, *U.S. Policy in Latin America* (New York: Praeger, 1968).
3. Charles Gibson, *The Black Legend: Anti-Spanish Attitudes in the Old World and the New* (New York: Knopf, 1971).
4. Robert Freeman Smith, ed., *The United States and the Latin American Sphere of Influence: Vol. I. Era of Caribbean Intervention. 1890–1930* (Malabar, Fla.: Krieger, 1981); see also Herbert Schneider, *The Puritan Mind* (Ann Arbor: University of Michigan Press, 1958); and Michael McGiffert, ed., *Puritanism and the American Experience* (Reading, Mass.: Addison-Wesley, 1969).
5. Samuel Flagg Bemis, *The Latin American Policy of the United States: An Historical Interpretation* (New York: Norton, 1967), p. 384.
6. Arthur P. Whitaker, *The United States and the Independence of Latin America, 1800–1830* (Baltimore: Johns Hopkins University Press, 1941).
7. Calvin Colton, ed., *The Works of Henry Clay* (New York: Federal Edition, 1904) 6:140 (March 14, 1818).

8. Charles Francis Adams, ed., *Memoirs of John Quincy Adams,* 12 vols. (Philadelphia: 1874–77), 4:28; 5:176.
9. Michael J. Kryzanek, *U.S.–Latin American Relations* (New York: Praeger, 1985), p. 10.
10. For the full text, see J. D. Richardson, *Messages and Papers of the Presidents* (New York: Johnson Reprint Corp., 1969), vol. 2: 209. The foremost student of the Monroe Doctrine is Dexter Perkins, in various volumes.
11. Lieuwen, *U.S. Policy,* p. 20; also Albert Katy Weinberg, *Manifest Destiny: A Study of Nationalist Expansionism in American History* (New York: AMS Press, 1979).
12. See Graham H. Stuart, *Latin America and the United States* (New York: Appleton-Century-Crofts, 1966).
13. Contained in a research project being undertaken by Daniel Pipes at the Foreign Policy Research Institute in Philadelphia comparing Turkish and Japanese modernization.
14. Jacqueline Anne Braveboy-Wagner, *The Venezuela-Guyana Border Dispute: Britain's Colonial Legacy in Latin America* (Boulder, Colo.: Westview, 1984).
15. Alfred Thayer Mahan, *The Influence of Sea Power Upon History* (Boston: Little, Brown, 1980); by the same author, *Lessons of the War with Spain* (Boston: Little, Brown, 1989).
16. *Congressional Record,* 58th Congress, 3rd session.
17. Federico Gil, *Latin American–U.S. Relations* (New York: Harcourt Brace Jovanovich, 1971), p. 71.
18. The classic study is by Dana G. Munro, *Intervention and Dollar Diplomacy in the Caribbean, 1900–1921* (Princeton: Princeton University Press, 1964).
19. See especially Bruce J. Calder, *The Impact of Intervention: The Dominican Republic During the U.S. Occupation of 1916–1924* (Austin: University of Texas Press, 1984).
20. Marvin Goldwert, *The Constabulary in the Dominican Republic and Nicaragua* (Gainesville: University of Florida, Center for Latin American Studies, 1958); also Richard Millett, *Guardians of the Dynasty: A History of the U.S.–Created Guardia Nacional de Nicaragua and the Somoza Family* (Markyknoll, N.Y.: Orbis, 1977); and Enrique Apolinar Henríquez, *Episodios Imperialistas* (Ciudad Trujillo: Montalvo, 1958).
21. The best account is Bryce Wood, *The Making of the Good Neighbor Policy* (New York: Columbia University Press, 1961); but see also Irvin Gellman, *Good Neighbor Diplomacy: United States Policies in Latin America 1933–1945* (Baltimore: Johns Hopkins University Press, 1979).
22. Franklin Delano Roosevelt, Inaugural Address, Washington, D.C., March 4, 1933.
23. Donald M. Dozer, *Are We Good Neighbors?* (Gainesville: University of Florida Press, 1961); and Jerome Levinson and Juan de Onis, *The Alliance that Lost Its Way* (Chicago: Quadrangle, 1970), pp. 31–32.
24. Michael Grow, *The Good Neighbor Policy and Authoritarianism in Paraguay: United States Economic Expansion and Great Power Rivalry in Latin America During World War II* (Lawrence: University of Kansas Press, 1981). This

book has important implications that go considerably beyond its case study materials.

25. A fresh look at this period is by Leslie Bethell, "Latin America between World War II and the Cold War (1945–1948): Lost Opportunities," Paper presented at the Woodrow Wilson International Center for Scholars, Washington, D.C., July 29, 1987, reported in *The Wilson Center Reports* (September 1987).

26. Edwin Lieuwen, *Arms and Politics in Latin America* (New York: Praeger, 1961).

27. Published as *The Wine Is Bitter: The United States and Latin America* (New York: Doubleday, 1963).

28. Levinson and de Onis, *The Alliance that Lost Its Way;* and Lincoln Gordon, *A New Deal for Latin America: The Alliance for Progress* (Cambridge, Mass.: Harvard University Press, 1963).

29. The literature is vast; an especially good recent evaluation is Ronald L. Scheman, ed., *The Alliance for Progress: A Retrospective* (New York: Praeger, 1988).

30. See the assessments of the alliance prepared by the staff of the Senate Foreign Relations Committee, *The Alliance for Progress* (Washington, D.C.: Government Printing Office), various volumes dealing with the military, political, and other aspects of the alliance.

31. See the statement by Kennedy quoted approvingly in Arthur M. Schlesinger, Jr., *A Thousand Days: John F. Kennedy in the White House* (Boston: Houghton Mifflin, 1965), p. 652.

32. See the critique in Howard J. Wiarda, "Misreading Latin America—Again," *Foreign Policy* 65 (Winter 1986–87): 135–53.

33. Richard Adams et al., *Social Change in Latin America Today* (New York: Vintage, 1961; Emilio Willems, *Latin American Culture* (New York: Harper and Row, 1975); and Charles Wagley, *The Latin American Tradition* (New York: Columbia University Press, 1968).

34. Lieuwen, *Arms and Politics;* Alfred Stepan, *The Military in Politics: Changing Patterns in Brazil* (Princeton: Princeton University Press, 1971); Also Lyle McAlister, *The "Fuero Militar" in New Spain* (Gainesville: University of Florida Press, 1957).

35. Lee Fennell, "Leadership and the Failure of Democracy," in Howard J. Wiarda, ed., *The Continuing Struggle for Democracy in Latin America* (Boulder, Colo.: Westview, 1980), pp. 201–14; also John Bartlow Martin, *Overtaken by Events* (New York: Doubleday, 1966).

36. Howard J. Wiarda, *Ethnocentrism in American Foreign Policy: Can We Understand the Third World?* (Washington, D.C.: American Enterprise Institute, 1985).

37. Abraham Lowenthal, "Limits of American Power," *Harpers* 229 (June 1964): 87ff.; Edwin Lieuwen, *Generals Versus Presidents: Neomilitarism in Latin America* (New York: Praeger, 1964).

38. The history and activities of the program are recounted in Juan Bosch, *Crisis de la democracía de América en la República Dominicana* (Mexico City: Centro de

Estudios y Documentación Sociales, 1964); Sacha Volman, *La Educación para el Cambio Social* (Mexico: Centro de Estudios y Documentación Sociales, 1964).

39. See Abraham Lowenthal, *Partners in Conflict: The United States and Latin America* (Baltimore: Johns Hopkins University Press, 1987).

40. Based on interviews with the participants involved in the discussions.

5

Toward an Effective Human Rights Policy

Human rights have become one of the pivotal issues of U.S. foreign policy. Congress, the media, various church and human rights lobbies, the White House, and the public at large have in the past fifteen years paid increased attention to human rights issues in formulating judgments and policies about the foreign nations with which we have relations.[1] The change has been so dramatic that the question today is whether human rights should be *the* linchpin of our foreign policy or only one component among many within a broader foreign policy framework designed to enhance U.S. national interests.[2]

The discussion and debate have been so intense because the subject goes to the heart of our concept of ourselves as a nation. Is the United States just another nation cynically pursuing its national interests by whatever means possible? Or are we something special as a nation, a beacon on a hill, a new Jerusalem, destined to serve as a democratic example and inspiration to peoples everywhere? If one believes the former, then human rights would tend to be deemphasized, viewed as one U.S. foreign policy instrument among many aimed at advancing our interests. But if one believes the latter, then presumably human rights and a strong pro-democracy agenda would be the keystone of our foreign policy.

The contemporary dispute over human rights is hence closely related to a larger and older issue in foreign policy: the idealism versus realism debate. The realist position,[3] as exemplified by Hans Morgenthau and, in an earlier incarnation, Henry Kissinger, suggests that in international affairs all nations follow and must follow their national interests rather than such moral or ethical concerns as human rights. The pursuit of the national interest may lead the United States to become allied with some pretty nasty human rights violators—for example, Joseph Stalin's Russia during World War II in the common effort to defeat Nazi Germany. In pursuing a policy of realpolitik, the United States should have, as Eisenhower's Secretary of State John Foster Dulles once allegedly put it, "no friends, only interests."

The idealist position rejects this premise and suggests that the United States is a special case, unlike the Machiavellian countries of Europe whose amoral maneuverings helped give rise to the realpolitik school of thought. To the idealist, the United States is a nation with a special mission, destined to bring the benefits of U.S. accomplishments (including ones in the political and human rights spheres) to the rest of the world. As seen in the previous chapter, this view has a long history and tradition in U.S. political thought and action. It finds contemporary expression in the debate over how much weight in U.S. foreign policy should be accorded human rights—or whether human rights should have any place at all. The apostles of realpolitik have said no to this question, seeing the human rights agenda as often getting in the way of a rigorous defense of the U.S. national interest. To the human rights activist, however, it is inconceivable that the United States, as *the* showcase of freedom in the world, should not take a moral stand against such notorious regimes as Augusto Pinochet's or those of the Argentine or Brazilian generals. The question is whether there is any possibility for a meeting of minds on this issue.

Historical Background

The United States has long had a moral and ethical underpinning to its foreign policy. Even in those instances where morality was not conspicuously present, U.S. presidents have usually felt compelled to rationalize and justify our actions with the language of high moral purpose. We are, or have been, a religious and in many ways a Calvinist nation: we are preoccupied with sin and guilt, we feel we have a calling to do right, and we want to be loved and admired for our noble actions. As a result, we have long, and more or less consistently, had a foreign policy based on human rights—and we began practicing such a policy, as viewed in our own light, long before a manifest human rights policy became fashionable.

In the modern era the initial impetus to incorporating human rights formally into U.S. foreign policy came during the late 1960s as a result of the Vietnam War.[4] As the congressional challenge to the president's exercise of his war powers grew, the larger issue of the place of human rights in overall U.S. foreign policy was also raised, first by liberals and antiwar Democrats, then by a broader liberal–conservative coalition. The liberals, however, were most concerned with human rights abuses in rightist regimes (South Vietnam), while the conservatives focused chiefly on human rights violations in North Vietnam, China, and the Soviet Union. Therein lay one of the earliest dilemmas of human rights policy: consistency and even-handedness.

Providing an impetus to Congress on human rights issues during this period was an amorphous coalition known as the human rights "movement" or "community."[5] Its activities were coordinated by the Human Rights Working Group of the Coalition for a New Foreign and Military Policy, as it came to be called, headed by Jacqui Chagnon, an antiwar activist. Forged during and in the aftermath of the Vietnam War, this movement was especially important in the ground-breaking congressional hearings that led to the first human rights legislation in the mid-1970s. The movement provided information, witnesses, and testimony that sympathetic congressmen were not likely to hear from the White House or the State Department.

Within the movement, including in the innocuous sounding organization called Clergy and Laity Concerned, were a good number of people who genuinely wanted to promote human rights. Others wished to promote human rights while pushing their own, generally left-wing political agenda. Still others, including a number among the leadership of the movement, simply wished to use the human rights issue to advance a political agenda that had little to do with human rights. Among this last group were persons who were openly pro-Hanoi and pro-Soviet and who wished for and applauded the U.S. defeat in Southeast Asia. Others among this group hoped to use the human rights issue to break the bonds of Latin America's "dependency" on the United States, as Cuba had done; or to assist Latin American revolutionary movements such as those in Nicaragua or El Salvador.[6] These "other agendas" of a number of groups that call themselves human rights activists remain a part of the problem of human rights policy today.

The first legislation systematically linking U.S. economic policy to human rights issues was the Jackson-Vanik Amendment to the 1972 trade agreement, which made trade concessions to the Soviet Union contingent on greater opportunities to emigrate for dissident Jews, Christians, and others. The first broad legislative initiative occurred in 1973 when the Subcommittee on International Organizations of the House Foreign Affairs Committee, chaired by Democrat Donald Fraser, conducted hearings on the international protection of human rights. Other strong human rights activists in those early days included Representative Tom Harkin of Iowa and Senators James Abourezk, Alan Cranston, Hubert Humphrey, and Edward Kennedy. Soon an extensive body of legislation was in place making U.S. bilateral assistance conditional on the recipients' human rights performance. An effort, only partially successful, was also made to have these restrictions apply to the main international lending agencies: the World Bank, the International Monetary Fund, and the regional development banks.

The human rights thrust of the Congress was controversial from the beginning. While the Fraser Subcommittee report lamented the fact that human rights were not afforded a higher priority in U.S. foreign policy, the Department of State took the position that human rights were a domestic matter of the countries with which we have relations and in which we ought not to interfere.[7] And while the Congress was calling for a higher priority for human rights as both a "moral imperative and a practical necessity,"[8] Henry Kissinger was expressing strong reservations. At his confirmation hearings in 1973 for the position of secretary of state, Kissinger said: "I believe it is dangerous for us to make the domestic policy of countries around the world a direct objective of American foreign policy. . . . The protection of human rights is a very sensitive aspect of the domestic jurisdiction of . . . governments."[9]

Through the mid-1970s the main initiatives continued to come from Congress. In the Foreign Assistance Act of 1973, for example, human rights became a major consideration. This was the same act that incorporated for the first time a Basic Human Needs approach (which stressed the fundamental needs of the poorest majorities in the poorest countries—as opposed to infrastructure development, for example, or other aid approaches) into U.S. foreign assistance. It sought to deny economic and military assistance and funds for police training to countries that had violated human rights. The act also called on the president to help protect human rights in Chile from the excesses of the Pinochet regime.

In 1974 the Congress added a new section, 502B, to the Foreign Assistance Act that declared, as a "sense of Congress," that "a principal goal of foreign policy shall be to promote the increased observance of internationally recognized human rights by all countries."[10] The criterion used was the following: "The President shall substantially reduce or terminate security assistance to any government which engages in a *consistent pattern of gross violations of internationally recognized human rights.*" [emphasis added]

Reservations emanating from the State Department about the human rights provisos prompted even stronger legislation from the Congress. Section 116, the Harkin Amendment, of the Foreign Assistance Act no longer conveyed simply the "sense of Congress" but actually prohibited assistance to any country that had "a consistent pattern of gross violations." It then added a curious qualifier: "unless such assistance will directly benefit the needy people in such country." The president was now required to submit to Congress an annual report concerning compliance.

In 1976 the Congress extended these restrictions that had previously applied only to U.S. bilateral aid to encompass assistance provided by two regional development banks. Public law 94-302 directed the influential executive directors (U.S.) of the African Development Bank and the Inter-American Development Bank to "vote against any loan, any extension of financial assistance, or any technical assistance" to a country violating its citizens' human rights. These provisions were adopted over the objections of the banks' executives who argued (1) that they were directors of multilateral agencies that had to take into account definitions and criteria other than those of the United States, and (2) that the banks were prohibited by their charters from using political criteria in the determination of loans. That same Congress included additional human rights directives in the International Security Assistance and Arms Export Control Act. This legislation included the creation of a position of Coordinator of Human Rights and Humanitarian Affairs in the Department of State. It also required the secretary of state to submit to the Congress annual reports dealing with human rights practices in each country receiving security assistance.

To this point the initiatives in the human rights field had come all but exclusively from a Congress controlled by Democrats. Neither President Nixon nor Secretary of State Kissinger wished to have human rights criteria occupy a very high priority in American foreign policy consideration. They both had a grand design for U.S. foreign policy involving balance of power, realpolitik, the opening to China, and the establishment of regional power centers (Iran, Brazil), which they felt would only be upset by the too strict application of human rights criteria. The State Department issued a report in late 1975 indicating its preference for "quiet but forceful diplomacy" and outlining its reservations concerning the human rights focus:

Experience demonstrated that the political, social, and cultural problems which cause seemingly intractable human rights abuses to occur need to be resolved *before* real improvements in human rights conditions can apparently take place—with or without bilateral or international pressure.

. . . In view of the widespread nature of human rights violations in the world, we have found no adequately objective way to make distinctions of degree between nations. This fact leads us, therefore, to the conclusion that neither the U.S. security interest nor the human rights cause would be properly served by the public obloquy and impaired relations . . . that would follow the making of inherently subjective . . . determinations that "gross violations" do or do not exist or that a "consistent" pattern of such . . . does or does not exist in such countries.[11]

This report had the opposite effect of that intended, prompting the Congress to enact even tougher human rights requirements. But President Ford was not inclined to accept the more stringent of these requirements, and was flatly opposed to the use of economic sanctions against human rights abusers whom the United States might wish nevertheless to assist on national security grounds. Ford and Kissinger, who had continued as secretary of state in the Ford administration, were particularly against the use of punitive measures that might be employed against such (then) stalwart allies as Iran, Saudi Arabia, and the Philippines, or that might endanger the grand balance-of-power strategic design to lure the People's Republic of China out of the Soviet camp and to use China's numbers and potential threat to the Soviet Union itself as a way of tying down numerous Soviet divisions and worrying the Kremlin leadership.

Nevertheless, the wheel slowly turned. After first vetoing the Arms Export Control Act because of what he considered its intrusion on the executive's foreign policymaking prerogatives, Ford eventually signed it when Congress changed the bill to the extent of requiring a joint resolution in order to terminate aid. And Kissinger himself, notwithstanding his earlier reservations about enforcing human rights standards in foreign policy, responded to the pressures from Congress and came to see the necessity of having American foreign policy legitimated by a strong human rights component. He criticized the actions of the Pinochet government and those of South Africa. At the 1976 meeting of the General Assembly of the Organization of American States (OAS), the secretary devoted his entire speech to the subject of human rights. He said: "One of the most compelling issues of our time, and one which calls for the concerted action of all responsible peoples and nations, is the necessity to protect and extend the fundamental rights of humanity."[12]

The Meaning(s) of Human Rights

As the human rights agenda was articulated and set forth in the mid-1970s, and, particularly as the possibility began to loom larger of sanctions being imposed on human rights abusers, increasing numbers of questions began to be raised about the policy. The first set of questions had to do with the meaning of human rights: Is there a common meaning or understanding of the term *human rights*? Are human rights everywhere the same and universal? Are they relevant in the same sense to all societies in all time periods? And do grounds exist for the hope of exporting human rights standards to other lands and cultures? On the answers to these questions would hang the possibilities for success or failure in the human rights area. How these questions were answered would also help determine the fluctuation of human rights policy over the next decade.[13]

The difficulty is that terms like *democracy, participation, representation, freedom, pluralism, social justice,* and *rights* mean different things, convey different connotations, or enjoy different degrees of respect and legitimacy from society to society. Moreover, even in a single society, including the United States, these human rights concepts may change in meaning or emphasis over time, relating generally to broad cultural, socioeconomic, and political transformations. Human rights are *not* one and the same in every society—if they were, a sound human rights policy would be relatively easy to carry out.

It has been clear for some time that such differences of meaning exist in regard to the so-called peoples' democracies. Marxist-Leninist regimes, while often denying or running roughshod over the individual political and civil rights (by Western standards) of their members, nevertheless proclaim that they provide the most basic human rights by putting an end to class struggle and terminating the exploitation of one class by another. Socioeconomic *group* or *class* rights thus take precedence over individual and political rights. This difference became evident in 1985 in the case of imprisoned American journalist Nicholas Daniloff where it became clear that freedom of the press and individual political rights do not carry the same meaning in the Soviet Union as in the Western democracies. Nor does freedom of religion, or speech, or assembly carry the same importance or legitimacy in the communist countries as in the West.

In the non-Western world, human rights are defined and interpreted in diverse ways depending on the different histories and cultures of the countries and on the level of their political and socioeconomic development.[14] Such Western values as freedom of the press; freedoms of expression, religion, and association; and the right to vote in open elections for government officials compete in many Third World countries with other values and rights based on demands for greater material welfare or on the preservation of traditional laws and mores. Islamic law, for instance, stipulates elaborate rules for personal behavior and defines in great detail the rights and duties of persons in a Moslem society to each other—children to parents, husbands to wives, and the faithful to the hierarchy. Hindu practices similarly define personal status and worth and the interrelations between individuals, groups, and the larger society. The Confucian tradition emphasizes harmony and consensus as distinct from the pluralism and checks and balances of modern Western democracy. These values and the conceptions of human rights that go with them will obviously vary considerably from culture to culture.[15]

Modernization has a major impact on human rights, as the inexorable forces of development give rise to a greater pluralism of social groups, new expectations, and emphasis on merit and both individual achievement and individual rights, as contrasted to claims based on familial or tribal inheritance. Even under the weight of modernization, however, traditional structures and practices often remain strong, bending to change rather than necessarily or automatically giving way or collapsing before it. The result is often mixed and overlapping patterns of traditional and modern, Western and non-Western, which human rights practitioners must take into account if they wish their policies to succeed. Such cultural, philosophical, and socioeconomic determinants of values relating to human rights as well as the differing practice of human rights must be factored into an effective human rights program.

Latin America is a mixed case *par excellence*. Often thought of as Western (perhaps a retarded or "underdeveloped" version thereof), Latin America is thus expected to adhere to Western human rights standards. Latin American elites also like to identify with the West and have taken great pains to imitate Western styles, institutions, and practices. Moreover, from a policy point of view, we tend to use Latin America as a human rights laboratory, almost an experiment station, because (1) we assume that as a "Western" area we will likely have greater success there, and (2) even if the policy fails, little harm will have been done because the security costs in Latin America are assumed to be nowhere near as great as the consequences of a failed human rights policy in, say, Saudi Arabia, China, or the Soviet Union.

But the question of whether Latin America is as Western as we like to believe and as Latin American elites like to proclaim is a bit more complicated. On the one hand we have the problem of the so-called Indian countries of Latin America and whether they are Western or not. For example, Mexican historians are still debating (with profound implications for human rights and human policy) whether that country's authoritarianism, patrimonialism, *caciquismo* (strong, domineering tribal or clan leadership), and violence stem from its Indian or its Spanish past, or maybe a little of both. Moreover, even if Latin America is Western, it is, as noted earlier, a special branch or fragment of the Western tradition,[16] with institutions and practices that are uniquely its own. Given Latin America's origins in a quasi-feudal, semimedieval, particularly *Iberian* part of the West, and its powerful Rousseauean tradition, it should not be surprising if its understanding and practices of human rights are quite a bit different from the U.S. understanding and practice as well.

These issues have been discussed at length in the academic literature;[17] here is presented only a summary of that work. Thus, when Latin America speaks of *rights,* it tends to mean group or corporate rights, not the individual rights of the U.S. polity—although (and this is what makes the issue so difficult) this corporate concept has now been overlaid with a full gamut of individual rights as well. *Pluralism* generally means limited pluralism (eight or nine main groups),[18] not the untrammeled interest group competition of North American pluralism. *Representative government* means a regime that is representative of the nation's main corporate groups, not necessarily a system of elected officials representing their constituencies. *Elections,* we have seen, may mean not a choice between rival candidates but a plebiscitary ratification of an existing regime. *Democracy* is similarly interpreted in a Thomistic sense, updated and given a modern, secular twist by Rousseau, as a government that both reflects and interprets the popular will even though it may not have come to power through electoral means.[19] *Freedom of religion, freedom of the press,* and *separation of church and state* likewise mean somewhat different things in the Latin American as compared with the U.S. conception.

The beginning of wisdom in implementing an effective human rights policy would seem to require an understanding of these differences and an attempt to comprehend Latin America in its own terms and context. But that has not generally been the case. Instead, we have tended to assume that the meanings of human rights terms are universal, or that ours is the most advanced form of Western civilization and that we have both a right and an obligation to bring our understandings of human rights to our poor, misguided neighbors in Latin America and elsewhere. That strategy has not worked well and will not work. What is required is a good dose of both cultural relativism and empathy in our human rights policy.

Note the stress on a "good dose" of cultural relativism, not an absolute commitment to it, for if the argument is carried too far it can lead us to look benignly on a Hitler, Stalin, or Idi Amin, a Pinochet or a Duvalier as simply following the norms of their cultures, societies, and particular times. I reject the cultural relativism argument when carried to such ridiculous extremes. I believe it is necessary both to understand the often distinct political traditions and meanings that Latin America gives to these terms, and to draw moral distinctions and to take a stand—though we must recognize that we may still continue to differ about where precisely to draw the lines. Such uncertainty does not worry me too much; that is why we have lively debate and a vigorous political process.

The other problem with cultural relativism in the human rights area is of course that the dictators and human rights abusers will use the above argument as a rationalization for carrying out some highly nefarious practices. This is a tricky area where some fine distinctions need to be drawn. We need on the one hand to be sensitive to culturally different ways of doing things. On the other, we need not necessarily believe the claims of a Franco, a Pinochet, a Castro, or a Stroessner that he alone is in a position to interpret what his country's cultural tradition is and ought to be. In the region between these two poles is where the debate will continue, and once again it is in the political process (and rightly so) that answers will be worked out. No pat formula or hard-and-fast rules will work, although obviously we do need perimeters, options, and guidelines.

There are other and more subtle approaches, in short, than taking either a completely culturally relativist or a completely universalistic position on human rights.[20] We need to look at human rights in broad, comparative terms, asking such questions as: To what extent, if at all, does a concept of human rights exist in traditional, non-Western cultures and political philosophies? To what extent is Latin America Western or non-Western, and can the Western and non-Western attributes be bridged? Are the non-Western ideals of rights compatible with the classical Western notions of rights? Can the pre-modern and semifeudal concepts of rights that prevailed in an older, more traditional Latin America be made compatible with the newer and more modern conception? Does the traditional Western notion of human rights have universal validity, or are there ways that the Western notions can be appropriately expanded?

These questions in turn lead to a comparison of different conceptions of human rights in terms of the following dimensions:[21]

1. Whether rights claims are based on status as an individual human being or status as a member of some group or community.

2. The extent to which differential treatment of individual persons is permitted on grounds of achievement or ascription.

3. The emphasis on rights as compared with duties or obligations and the extent to which rights and duties are seen as interdependent.

4. The emphasis on so-called economic and social rights compared with the emphasis on civil and political rights (frequently viewed as a difference between the positive rights of governmental obligation to provide economic and social well-being, and the negative rights of governmental obligations to refrain from abridging political and civil rights).

5. The extent to which rights are viewed as absolute or relative.

The boundaries separating these criteria are not absolute. But they do contribute to a framework for comparing distinct cultural and political systems. In general it can be said that the classical Western idea of human rights stresses inviolable political and civil rights, while most non-Western countries emphasize the community or group base of social and economic rights. Further, Marxist-Leninist regimes stress economic rights and duties grounded on the collective ownership of the means of production and distribution.

The considerable cultural and socioeconomic variety that these categories reflect has proved a difficult issue in human rights policy. How can one evaluate human rights practices—and abuses—in the face of such diversity? How can a global framework for human rights and a viable policy be constructed? Can effective human rights instruments be fashioned in the face of such diverse and culturally specific concepts of human rights?

Not surprisingly, human rights analysts have given widely diverging answers to these questions. The answers fall into a pattern that may be divided into four types, which can be the basis for designing a reasonable and effective human rights policy. The four types are:[22]

1. Traditions other than Western liberalism often lack concepts of human rights; therefore, the Western liberal tradition is either the only or the most legitimate concept of human rights.[23] This position has considerable support among democracy and human rights "true believers" in the United States and elsewhere: but it is too ethnocentric, and it will not work for us simply to export our brand of democracy and human rights to other nations. It is possible, however, to urge and nudge non-Western countries in further Westerly directions, including in the human rights area.

2. Non-Western ideas about human rights may not only be compara-

ble but in many areas may be compatible with Western human rights ideals. Examples include the emphasis on group as well as individual rights, the wish to be left alone by abusive government officials, or the condemnation of torture, killing, and undue imprisonment by repressive regimes. Such views are not very far from the Western human rights conception. One should not romanticize these possibilities for compatibility, but there are areas of correspondence and complementarity that can be further nurtured.

3. Non-Western traditions may differ even to the point of incompatibility with the Western notions, but it is still possible to reconcile various views. For example, some non-Western traditions are almost entirely nonindividualistic; nevertheless, areas of compatibility in terms of basic rights may still exist. This point has less relevance to Latin America with its Western or partially Western traditions than it does to other areas where the Western influence has been small if not nonexistent.

4. Human rights concepts not only differ across nations and regions, but cultural relativism means that no particular view can be held more valid than others. This position is often set forth by apologists for the Soviet Union—or for that matter for Pinochet. We need that dose of cultural relativism, but I reject the corollary that follows; it represents a nihilistic and extreme view that I cannot accept and that would paralyze all human rights policy.

An appropriate strategy, it seems to me, would borrow eclectically from all of these categories. Categories 1 and 4 seem to me extreme positions, although I want both a strong dose of the cultural sensitivity and empathy contained in 4 and a notion of progress toward Westernization contained in 1. Let us face it: some ideas *are* better (more humane, more sophisticated, less prone to bloody excesses, more conducive to progress, more in accord with popular desires) than others. Category 3 is of limited relevance in Latin America given its dominant existent Western traditions (even though sometimes weak); but the idea of using cultural awareness (Category 4) to build understanding and achieve reconciliation (3) is doable. Overall, Category 2, invigorated by useful ingredients from these other categories, seems a useful route for building a broader basis for human rights in Latin America, through the notion that different concepts of human rights may not only be compared but may be bridged and even be made compatible.[24]

Let us now see how these criteria have been lived up to by the most recent U.S. administrations, and the dilemmas and problems that U.S. human rights policy has raised.

The Carter Administration

Through the mid-1970s human rights had been viewed as a noble and laudable, if not very practical, policy goal. There had been some congressional initiatives, but most of these were resisted by the White House and the State Department. Human rights had not become an issue of great public resonance. Now that was about to change.

During the 1976 election campaign Jimmy Carter prominently raised the human rights issue. It seemed to evoke some favorable response; furthermore it seemed also to fit in closely with Carter's campaign orientation, which contained heavy doses of moralism and piety. Candidate Carter criticized the Ford administration for its emphasis on national security and neglect of human rights and said that, if elected, he would carry out a vigorous human rights program.[25]

Then, at his swearing-in on January 20, 1977, Carter declared that "our commitment to human rights must be absolute." In subsequent public statements, Carter continued to indicate that human rights would be central to his foreign policy, insisting that the pursuit of human rights was also in the U.S. national interest.

During the next several months, Carter's position was refined and the personnel and bureaucratic machinery put in place for a major human rights effort. The culmination of this early phase was Carter's speech at the University of Notre Dame, where he proclaimed, "America's commitment to human rights is a fundamental tenet of our foreign policy." At Notre Dame, and subsequently, Carter stressed four points:[26]

1. He rejected the argument of his predecessors that concern for human rights represented interference in the internal affairs of other nations. He argued that all the signatories of the UN Charter had pledged themselves to respect the long list of human rights contained therein, and therefore that no UN member could claim that the mistreatment of its citizens was purely its own business. This of course ignores that the signatory nations had quite different ideas about and attached different meanings to these various rights, that the hortatory injunctions contained in the charter and the UN's Universal Declaration of Human Rights represented goals to achieve rather than actual operation reality, that realistically they

could not all possibly be carried out and obeyed by all nations (including the United States), and that the status of these articles as binding international law was open to considerable question.[27]

2. He rejected the "linkage" conception of former Secretary of State Kissinger, who argued that a too vigorous pursuit of the human rights agenda would endanger more fundamental goals of world order and national security. He argued instead these could all be pursued harmoniously and in tandem. This strategy of course proved impossible in actual practice.

3. He declared that the United States must honor its commitments to human rights even if doing so damaged bilateral relations with important countries. That is a dangerous position, which any beginning student of international relations would have recognized as such, and it led, as will be seen, to irreparable harm.

4. He insisted, again, that concern for human rights was in, and would serve, the national interest. That is an arguable proposition; of course, it depends on individual cases and how the policy is implemented.

Carter moved quickly to translate his high-sounding rhetoric into practice. He immediately signed the two UN covenants on human rights, which the United States had not previously agreed to, and sent them on to the Senate for approval. He moved to strengthen, financially and politically, the work of the OAS's Human Rights Commission. He moved to repeal the 1972 Byrd Amendment, which had permitted the United States to import chrome from southern Rhodesia, in conflict with a UN resolution on the issue. And he acted to cut off military aid to such Latin American authoritarian regimes as Argentina and Uruguay.

Meanwhile, the machinery for implementing the human rights agenda was set in place. Carter beefed up the State Department's Office of Human Rights and Humanitarian Affairs, upgraded it to a bureau, and appointed Patricia Derian, who had been an enthusiastic election campaign worker, as its first assistant secretary. Derian had formerly been a civil rights activist in Mississippi and carried the same missionary zeal into the human rights office. She believed it was her (and the United States') right and obligation to extend the U.S. civil rights movement to foreign areas, to bring human rights U.S.–style to other countries whether they wanted them or not and without due regard to whether broader U.S. interests were being served. Derian's staff in the Human Rights Bureau, and her allies in Ambassador Andrew Young's UN mission, were similarly militant, veterans of the U.S. anti-Vietnam movement, persons who had been radicalized in the campus protests of the late 1960s and early 1970s or by the U.S. role in Chile in 1973. They all had a crusading fervor and a mission not only to change the course of events in Latin America but also to radically reconstruct U.S. society at home.[28]

The policy and the excess enthusiasm produced, during the first year and more of the Carter administration, a host of false starts, misfires, and actions contrary to U.S. (and Latin American) interests. For example, Derian would often rave and rant about Argentina as a "fascist country" and a "vicious" human rights abuser as if that entire country and all its people were guilty, thus insulting Argentine nationalistic sensibilities and giving Argentine public opinion no other choice than to rally to the support of the nation and its government. Or she would condemn the *entire* Argentine military, thus undermining the efforts of moderate officers to bring about change and forcing the whole (and very proud) officer corps to rally to the defense of the institution. Such gross, unrefined, and indiscriminating charges were repeated in Brazil and Chile, thus securing for the United States the enmity of three of the most important countries in Latin America, countries that had long been our friends and allies.[29] It is obvious that the human rights situation in these countries needed much improvement and the actions of some elements within these military regimes were far beyond the pale, but Derian's methods were not calculated to solve the problems. Instead, they often made the situation worse by strengthening the hand of the worst elements in these countries' militaries and doing severe damage to long-term U.S. interests in the region.

Another important agency was the Interagency Committee on Human Rights and Foreign Assistance, headed by Deputy Secretary of State Warren Christopher and therefore usually referred to as the Christopher Committee. The committee's purpose was to coordinate policy and to ensure that all the State Department's bureaus were following the human rights program set by the president. The problem had been that the various regional bureaus, including especially that on Latin America where human rights policy was concentrated, complained loudly about Derian's actions and how, as outlined in the previous paragraph, her actions were damaging relations with important Latin American countries. But the Christopher Committee, set up to harmonize and coordinate policy, came down almost always on the side of Derian and against the regional bureaus. U.S. policy therefore continued to follow an abstract and theoretical formula based on ethnocentric assumptions about the rest of the world, and ignored the regional and country expertise found in the geographic bureaus.[30] The result was a loud, controversial and self-defeating policy that in the end produced meager results.

It is not my purpose in these pages to provide a complete history of U.S. human rights policy; that has been admirably done in an excellent book by Joshua Muravchik.[31] Suffice it here to say that the Carter administration's policy, and particularly its style and methods of carrying out human rights policy, provoked a great deal of controversy and renewed the old realist-idealist debate. There is no doubt that as a result of the Carter policy some persons were released from jail, torture was used less often in some countries as an instrument of official policy, and some lives were saved. These are no small accomplishments, especially for the persons affected. In addition, the human rights issue was raised to a level of global consciousness that had not existed before. At the same time, none of the grandiose accomplishments that the policy's ardent supporters sometimes claimed for it came to fruition. Oppression and authoritarianism did not end as a result of the Carter policy (indeed, a strong case for the policy producing the opposite results could be made); democracy did not flower, at least not in the short term, because of Carter; and the lot of the vast bulk of the population did not improve—and may have worsened—as a result of the ineptness of the officials responsible.

Criticism of the Carter human rights policy came from two main schools of thought. One, associated with the traditional realist school, argued that human rights should have no or minimal influence in U.S. policy considerations. Henry Kissinger had once been an apostle of this realpolitik position, but his experience in government had taught him that in the United States a successful foreign policy must be justified in moral and ethical (including human rights) terms and not just on the basis of the national interest. Nevertheless, the realpolitik position and critique remained powerful, as exemplified in the writings of Ernst Haas.[32] Haas argued that a human rights policy could not possibly succeed given the amoralism of international politics and the wide disparity of the world's cultural traditions and political systems. Haas wrote: "A consistent and energetic policy in the human rights field makes impossible the attainment of other, often more important, objectives of American policy. Once this was realized, something had to give. . . . What was understood by previous administrations also became clear to Carter: international politics is not like the politics of the American civil rights movement."

The second line of criticism, while strongly sympathetic to the idea of incorporating a human rights component into U.S. foreign policy considerations, was nevertheless strongly opposed to the particular form this took under President Carter, and to the unenlightened *implementation* by the Carter administration. I associate myself with this viewpoint.[33] The criticism centers on the following features of the Carter approach:

1. The policy was applied inconsistently and sometimes incoherently; there were no agreed-upon criteria. Even the definition of "human rights" was changed several times.

2. The policy represented a double standard: right-wing regimes that were friends of the United States were attacked; left-wing regimes were not. Other variations on the double-standard theme were that small states were picked on more often than larger ones because the U.S. strategic interests there were also small, and that Latin America was a special target because it did not count for much in the world balance of power.

3. The officials charged with carrying out the policy were often incompetent and knew appallingly little about Latin America.

4. The policy was often uninformed, unsophisticated, and undiscriminating; it used too blunt instruments, was unaware of or unsympathetic to national and cultural differences, and was unable to distinguish between the generally milder (and often changeable) forms of abuses of authoritarian regimes and the gross and systematic (and difficult of reform) abuses of communist totalitarianism.

5. The policy was counterproductive. It led frequently, for the reasons already given, to a hardening of attitudes and policies in the offending countries rather than to much reform.

6. The policy was unrealistic. It could not systematically sort out the possible from the merely desirable or even the impossible. It often verged on the romantic and the wishful rather than having a solid base in international realities.

7. The policy was ineffective. It produced few real changes. A few people were helped, but basic policy in the offending countries went unchanged. There was a lot of noise over very little.

From 1978 on, the Carter policy was moderated as the administration went through the same kind of learning process that other U.S. administrations comparatively inexperienced in foreign affairs had gone through. It came to view human rights as one component of foreign policy but not the only or the driving component. It sought to balance human rights concerns with other important U.S. interests. It reined in or got rid of some of the "loose cannons" in the administration. It came eventually (although incompletely) to emphasize strategic policy and vigorous defense of the national interest as the primary bedrocks of U.S. foreign policy. In the process of these changes the Carter administration eventually returned close to the mainstream of U.S. foreign policy. However none of these changes came without a tough internal battle within the administration, and to the end some of the Carter appointees continued to push the romantic and often left-wing line of the human rights "movement."

What then were the accomplishments? They were quite modest: a few prisoners released, some torture prevented, some actions not taken by human rights abusers. In addition, many Latin Americans came to feel that Carter's policies, viewed over a longer term, came to legitimize their own human rights struggles and helped to mobilize popular opposition to authoritarian regimes. When authoritarianism eventually went "out of fashion," the public position of the Carter administration on human rights was partly responsible for that change. In this way the Carter administration not only contributed to the Latin American democratization process but also started a rolling snowball that would eventually oblige his conservative successor to similarly follow a strong human rights and pro-democracy policy.

But concretely and in the short term, not much was accomplished by the Carter human rights campaign, and the negative results of the policy may have outnumbered the positive ones. After all the sound and fury, as Larman C. Wilson's excellent article on the policy concludes, the Carter administration learned how easy it was to make public commitments to human rights in foreign policy and how hard it was to implement these effectively. Under Carter, human rights took center stage chiefly at the rhetorical and hortatory level; the policy was considerably modified after 1978 because it proved harder to translate the rhetoric into practice. As the human rights policy moved from being "at the center" of the administration's actions to being "factored into" overall policy, a good deal of steam and zeal went out of this missionary campaign. Many seasoned foreign policy analysts, as contrasted to the administration's true believers, saw that as a healthy and realistic step.[34]

Human Rights in the Reagan Administration

The 1980 election campaign raised once more the issue of the proper balance in foreign policy between human rights concerns and national security interests. Candidate Ronald Reagan and his advisers suggested strongly that they favored a reemphasis on national security issues. Reagan's campaign came of course on the heels of the Marxist revolutions in Grenada and Nicaragua and the relative decline of U.S. power vis-à-vis the Soviet Union in the 1970s. Reagan too spoke in favor of human rights in other countries. But he was sharply critical of the Carter administration's approach, which he viewed as clumsy and heavy-handed, and of its emphasis, which he viewed as stressing human rights concerns to the detriment of U.S. security interests. During the campaign Reagan attacked Carter for neglecting security interests, emphasized that the Soviet Union and other communist countries were the most grievous violators of human rights, and stressed that in his administration national security would be given primary attention and human rights would receive lower priority—although the precise balance was still left open.

Shortly before the 1980 campaign, Georgetown University professor Jeane Kirkpatrick had published a powerful critique of the Carter policy.[35] While herself strongly in favor of human rights, Kirkpatrick accused Carter of practicing a double standard. The administration, she said, had been critical of abuses of human rights violations in right-wing regimes like Somoza's and sought to undermine them, while remaining silent about left-wing regimes like Cuba's and seeking to establish better relations with them. Professor Kirkpatrick, soon to be named UN ambassador and a key Reagan foreign policy adviser, argued that the Carter policy was misapplied; that authoritarian regimes like Somoza's at least had the possibility of evolving into democratic regimes with U.S. assistance and pressure, whereas left-wing totalitarian regimes were not only worse human rights violators but also showed no evidence of evolving toward democracy. She criticized the Carter human rights policy for losing Nicaragua while at the same time allowing the Somoza government to be replaced by a Marxist-Leninist regime that was not only hostile to the United States but an even worse human rights offender than had been Somoza.

In the first months of the Reagan presidency the human rights issue was very controversial, both within the administration and between it and the defeated opposition. Some within the administration, followers of realpolitik, wished to do away with the human rights emphasis altogether and to concentrate exclusively on security issues. The president's first nominee for the position of assistant secretary of state for human rights and humanitarian affairs, Ernest Lefever, promised that if confirmed by the Senate he intended to phase out the office that he was being considered to head. It was not that Lefever was opposed to human rights, for in his career and writing he had been a strong human rights advocate. But he did not believe human rights should have a strong place in foreign policy. Moreover, he believed the Carter administration's strong enforcement of human rights policy vis-à-vis Argentina, Chile, Iran, and the Republic of Korea had damaged U.S. security interests.[36] This position, actually quite defensible—at least in the abstract—was seized upon by the Democratic opposition, distorted, and used to embarrass the administration. Lefever was forced to withdraw his name from consideration. The experience taught the Reagan administration a lesson: that what is justifiable intellectually is not necessarily smart politics. In the United States it is no longer possible, in terms of domestic politics, to conduct a successful foreign policy without a strong human rights component.

The other position within the Reagan circle of policy advisers was represented by Michael Novak, Richard Schifter, as well as Jeane Kirkpatrick and others. This position was strongly favorable to human rights—as Ambassador Kirkpatrick put it, that was the essence of what the United States stood for—but they felt the policy had been misapplied under Carter. Carter's policy in their view had been fumbling, uninformed, unsophisticated; unaware of or unsympathetic to national and cultural differences; unable to distinguish between the totalitarian behemoth (the Soviet Union and its allies) and the generally milder form of authoritarianism that existed in Latin America and which, in any case, represented no threat to U.S. security as the Soviet Union did. What they supported was not the abolition of a human rights policy but a more refined, informed, sensitive, and even-handed strategy—one that would reestablish a balance between human rights and U.S. security, economic, and diplomatic concerns. Eventually this position became the dominant one in the administration.

Meanwhile, however, the Democratic opposition, aided by the now far more numerous human rights lobby, was using the issue to beat the administration over the head. Ambassador Kirkpatrick's position was regularly, systematically, and often purposely misrepresented, and the administration was criticized as being opposed to human rights. The human rights lobby, whose interests were often not just human rights but the undermining of the Reagan administration, geared up to wage major political battle. Much of the criticism was unfair and inaccurate, but in part the administration had brought the criticism on itself by its early insensitivity and indifference.

Five months into the Reagan administration, Elliott Abrams was appointed to the human rights position in the State Department for which Lefever had earlier been considered and rejected. Smart, tough, and able,

Abrams began to reorganize the human rights office and bring order to it. He generally practiced quiet diplomacy rather than the public denunciations that had so antagonized allies during the Carter term—and was no less effective for following this route. But when quiet diplomacy failed, the administration was not averse to arm-twisting and the use of quite unsubtle tactics—for example, in pressuring Marcos in the Philippines and Duvalier in Haiti to resign and in putting immense pressure on Pinochet in Chile. The Human Rights Bureau was now more fully integrated into foreign policy decision making, but this was done not by riding roughshod over the regional bureaus but by working closely with them. In addition, leftist human rights abusers—Nicaragua, Cuba, and especially Poland and the Soviet Union—came in for at least as much attention as did rightist ones. Although some may differ about the emphases, it is probably fair to say that by this time a prudent, realistic, and balanced human rights concern had become an integral part of U.S. foreign policymaking.

The policy that gradually evolved was true to President Reagan's political beliefs and instincts, while recognizing political realities. It repudiated the Lefever position but did not embrace the Carter position either. The Reagan administration sought the elimination of human rights violations and the furthering of democratic institutions as the surest guarantor of human rights. The Reagan approach was based on a number of beliefs:[37]

1. There is a close relationship between democracy and human rights. Democratic governments are more likely to respect human rights. Therefore a pro-democratic policy (again, as under Carter, the policy was most strongly applied in Latin America) is a pro–human rights policy.

2. There is a close relationship between Soviet expansionism and the loss of human rights. There is similarly a relationship between U.S./ Western influence and the protection of human rights. Therefore, a policy of opposition to Soviet expansionism and of strengthening the United States is a pro–human rights policy.

3. The United States must occasionally work with friendly authoritarian regimes that are resisting communist aggression. Because such regimes can often be nudged toward democracy and because a Marxist-Leninist takeover will surely make the human rights situation worse, that policy is also a pro–human rights policy.

4. There is an important difference between human needs such as food and housing (social and economic "rights") and basic civic or human rights, which can be preserved only if state power is restrained. A state-socialist regime (like Cuba) that provides social and economic improvements while denying basic liberties should not be thought of as a beacon of human rights.

5. Human rights are best preserved by moderate, pragmatic, democratic, middle-of-the-road regimes of neither the extreme left nor the extreme right. Such regimes are also least likely to engage in war, to attack their neighbors, or to interfere in their neighbors' internal affairs. A policy that promotes such centrist regimes is therefore also a pro–human rights policy. Such a policy also serves U.S. interests in maintaining stability and anticommunism.

The evolution of the administration's human rights policy was related to the overall learning process that the administration went through, especially in foreign policy.[38] The early position as articulated by the hardliners that the United States should not pay any attention to human rights, that only considerations of the national interest should govern foreign policy, was seldom heard anymore. The administration had learned a political lesson. The lesson was that the best way to get Congress, public opinion, the press, and our allies to support or at least remain neutral toward controversial foreign policy objectives (as in Central America in the early 1980s) was to have a strong democracy/human rights agenda included within the policy. National interest was no longer sufficient justification by itself. Rather, the policy had to be couched in human rights terms, or else human rights had to be incorporated as an integral part of the policy objectives. That is, in addition to its intrinsic value, why the Reagan administration came so strongly to support the trend toward democracy in Latin America; it is also the reason for its emphasis on human rights. This new consensus on a multifaceted U.S. approach in Latin America, encompassing democracy, human rights, socioeconomic assistance, as well as security interests more narrowly defined, was embodied in the Kissinger Commission report.[39]

The ongoing Central American crisis had added another ingredient to human rights policy: the congressionally mandated requirement of six-month reports on human rights "progress" in key countries like El Salvador. The administration had fought the policy at first, since it took enormous amounts of staff time to prepare the reports and of higher officials' time to testify on the reports before Congress. In addition, the reports were often highly controversial because the Democratic opposition tried to use them to embarrass the administration; and, the fact was, there was often very little human rights "progress" to report. Nonetheless, the administration had to say there was progress or its whole program would be in jeopardy. Eventually, some meeting of the minds emerged out of this conflict. The Congress continued to use the certification requirement to try to score points against a Republican administration, while the administration used the threat of a congressional cutoff of funds as a way to pry some reforms out of an often reluctant El Salvadoran government and military. As a result, both the human rights situation in El Salvador and the Central America policy of the United States improved and became more moderate and centrist.[40]

There continued to be differences over the application of human rights policy in specific circumstances: for example, how, when, and how heavily to apply sanctions on Pinochet's Chile or on *Sandinista* Nicaragua. But the last years of the Reagan administration showed some remarkable achievements: an awareness of human rights issues not present before, the machinery for effective human rights implementation, and a prudent and realistic policy. Nonetheless, there remained serious unresolved issues of human rights policy.

Unresolved Issues of Human Rights

While human rights policy has come a considerable distance since the early days, numerous problems still stand in the way of a more effective policy. Nine such problems are discussed here, which must be grappled with seriously if we are to have an effective human rights policy.

1. *DIVERSE MEANINGS OF KEY HUMAN RIGHTS TERMS*

Other nations and culture areas clearly mean different things than we do by human rights or key human rights terms, or have different priorities. That is true not just of the so-called peoples' democracies but of non-Western or only partially Western (Latin American) culture areas as well. In Latin America, for instance, many of the historic organic, Rousseauean and corporatist forms of democracy are now in the process of being gradually replaced by a Western and modern conception of democracy, competitive elections, civil liberties, pluralism, and the like. That evolution is heartening and provides room for political maneuver and progress in the human rights area; but the more traditional and historic Latin American meanings of *representation, democracy,* and so on, should not be forgotten. Sensitivity, empathy, and understanding of these differences are essential. Serious scholarly research and comprehension of the diverse meanings and shadings of such terms are fundamental to an informed and effective human rights policy.

2. CATEGORIES OF HUMAN RIGHTS

Human rights may be conveniently divided into three types: political and civil rights, social and economic rights, and basic rights affecting the human person (absence of torture, and so forth). In its excess enthusiasm, the Carter administration tried to secure gains in all three areas at once. But the fact is that there is less consensus globally on some of these rights than others, and therefore more probability for success in some areas than in others. Our experience has been that the best chances of success are in the area of rights of the human person (preventing torture, getting people out of jail, securing humane treatment for prisoners) because most of the world shares agreement on this; that there is less consensus and therefore more limited opportunities for success in the area of political and civil rights (guaranteeing freedom of the press, of assembly, of speech, and so on); and that there is very little consensus except perhaps at the rhetorical level on social and economic rights. It would be nice if all three categories could be advanced simultaneously—and none should be ignored—but policymakers need to know that the possibilities for success are stronger in some areas than in others.

3. EVENHANDEDNESS

As it has evolved, U.S. human rights policy is now more evenhanded than it was in the early years. Nevertheless, liberal administrations have tended to be more condemnatory of abuses in right-wing regimes and to pay less attention to abuses in left-wing regimes, while conservative administrations have tended to emphasize the abuses of Marxist-Leninist regimes and to have mixed feelings about criticizing (and thereby potentially destabilizing, with possibly disastrous foreign policy repercussions) right-wing ones. Even more worrisome has been the continuing attitude of some of the major human rights lobbies who are quick to condemn abuses in Chile or El Salvador but are very quiet on abuses in Cuba or Nicaragua. They rationalize this lack of balance by saying they are only concerned with those countries to which the United States provides assistance. But that is of course a terribly weak rationalization and will not do: either one is in favor of human rights or one is not; and if one is in favor, then one must condemn human rights abuses regardless of the ideological coloring of the regime—unless of course the purpose of these lobbies is not human rights but some other agenda (see point 9 below). In general (and there may be valid reasons for certain exceptions under some circumstances), we need to be evenhanded in our approach to human rights, which means concern for the human rights situation in both left-wing and right-wing regimes.

4. INTERVENTION VERSUS NONINTERVENTION

When we pursue a strong human rights policy in another country, we need to face the fact that we are intervening in that country's internal affairs. It may be a "good" (human rights) versus a "bad" (gunboat diplomacy) intervention, but it is still intervention and we need to be aware of the sensitivities involved. It is clear, for example, that some such interventions, often for the best of intentions, on the part of the Carter administration, were deeply resented and counterproductive; and that the U.S. diplomatic intervention in the Dominican Republic in 1978 (to guarantee an honest ballot count, often claimed as the most successful of the Carter capers) reinforced that country's dependence on and subservience to the United States, which was certainly not the intention of those involved.[41] As an intervention in other countries' internal affairs, for however noble a cause, human rights policy requires sensitivity, knowledge, and understanding of the full implications of our action. Riding roughshod over local practices and ways of doing things, blatant interference, wholesale and indiscriminating condemnations of entire countries and their institutions, arrogance, and insensitivity are likely to produce the opposite effects of those intended.

5. WHAT INSTRUMENTS?

How best and most effectively to further human rights? Do we use quiet or public diplomacy? Do sanctions work or not? The answers are complex, subject to change, and they must be redesigned for individual situations. But in general quiet diplomacy works better than the loud kind—until a point is reached (as in the case of Pinochet's Chile) where quiet persuasion has gotten nowhere and policymakers are left with no choice but to go public. As for sanctions, the Carter administration cut off aid to Somoza, but there was so much aid already in the pipelines that the cutoff had no real practical effect. Then the United States tried to rev up the aid to exercise influence over the direction of the *Sandinista* revolution, but that took added time and had little effect as well.[42] In general, sanctions have limited effect except psychologically; moreover, by cutting off aid to a country we lose whatever leverage we might otherwise have had.

6. *BALANCE WITH OTHER U.S. INTERESTS*

The Carter administration, particularly in its early years, put too great a stress on human rights concerns sometimes at the cost of important U.S. political, diplomatic, economic, and strategic interests; the Reagan administration made the mistake in its early months of so downplaying human rights as to give the appearance it was not important in U.S. foreign policy considerations. Both of these approaches were too extreme. The United States needs to have a strong human rights component in its foreign policy, and indeed it seems impossible to have a successful U.S. foreign policy without that component. But the human rights concern cannot be permitted to submerge important strategic and other considerations. Although we will still disagree about specific cases—cases that can appropriately be decided in the political process—I think we have now achieved a fairly good balance between the strategic, the diplomatic, the economic, and the human rights aspects of our policy.

7. *HOW HARD TO PUSH?*

How much pressure do we exert on a country before we do irreparable harm to them and to us? This is a hard question, the answers to which may vary in different contexts. Do we push the white South African regime so hard that we destroy it, producing yet another shoddy Marxist-Leninist regime on the strategic tip of Africa? Does our interest in democracy and human rights in Haiti force us to occupy the country militarily as the best or only way to accomplish that goal? Do we push Saudi Arabia so hard that we eventually face a cutoff of our oil supplies (and probably produce a regime like Khomeini's—hardly a paragon of human rights virtue)? And how far do we push the human rights issue vis-à-vis the Soviet Union, a country with a miserable human rights record, yet having the power to destroy us and all mankind? There are no easy answers to all these questions; they are raised here as illustrations of the complexities involved and to point up the fact that there are limits beyond which any well-meaning human rights policy probably ought not to go.

8. *THE NATIONAL INTEREST*

I believe human rights ought to be a major component of U.S. foreign policy, but it must also be remembered that there will be instances when human rights concerns will have to be subordinated to a more pressing national interest. Take El Salvador, for example. Under José Napoleón Duarte's able democratic leadership, our human rights and our strategic interests (preventing a Marxist-Leninist takeover) were able to go forward in tandem. But if Duarte (or now Cristiani) were to be overthrown and a repressive military regime come to power again in that unfortunate and guerrilla-ravaged country, we might still have to come to that regime's defense because we have an even stronger interest in preventing a communist-guerrilla takeover. We could then work with that regime to improve human rights conditions, but we would also need to support such a regime. In these circumstances we would have returned to the situation in El Salvador that prevailed in the early 1980s—and would have all the possibilities for a renewal of the divisive and nearly paralyzing policy debate that existed then.

9. THE POLITICS OF HUMAN RIGHTS

Human rights are no longer just a moral and ethical interest and a matter of individual conscience in the United States. Rather human rights are now the stuff of major lobbying organizations, of vast amounts of money, of armies of activists and demonstrators, of national mobilization campaigns. Other agendas besides the human rights one (often disguised or hidden) are acted out in the name of human rights. Human rights issues are used in an attempt to undermine or destroy administrations with which some persons may disagree; human rights issues have proved deeply divisive between the White House and the Congress; human rights have been politicized, used by one party to embarrass the other and vice versa. The human rights issue, coupled with the divisive debate over Central America, has the possibility quite literally to paralyze and immobilize the entire foreign policymaking apparatus of the U.S. government—as seemed to be the case in the early to mid-1980s.[43] This point is made not because I believe the discussions of human rights issues can be entirely removed from the political arena, or even that that would be desirable, but to indicate that there frequently are other agendas besides the human rights one involved, that the issue can be extremely divisive and is used purposely so by some groups for their own political purposes, and that such divisiveness can hamstring U.S. foreign policymaking. We need to be alert to these potential dangers.

*   *   *

Now, if all these issues can be resolved—and some of them have been addressed and ameliorated over the years but by no means all—we can have an effective, balanced, viable human rights policy. It is a daunting task. The history recounted here and the nine problem areas discussed show how complex and potentially divisive a human rights policy can be. Of course, not all of these issues need to be resolved now and for all time;

they are—and appropriately so—a part of the U.S. political process, open to further discussion and modification. But we have made impressive progress over the years to the point where human rights are an integral part of U.S. foreign policymaking and a global concern. Carter succeeded in raising the public consciousness about human rights but was not very successful at implementation; after a shaky start, Reagan embedded a strong human rights component into a broader democracy framework. Between the two, we now have a strong and defensible human rights policy that George Bush and other future presidents will also be obligated to follow.

Notes

1. A good history is Lars Schoultz, *Human Rights and United States Policy toward Latin America* (Princeton, N.J.: Princeton University Press, 1981).
2. This argument for the preeminence of human rights may be found in Margaret E. Crahan, ed., *Human Rights and Basic Needs in the Americas* (Washington, D.C.: Georgetown University Press, 1982); and A. Hennelly and J. Langan, eds., *Human Rights in the Americas: The Struggle for Consensus* (Washington, D.C.: Georgetown University Press, 1982).
3. Hans Morgenthau, *In Defense of the National Interest* (New York: Knopf, 1951); Henry Kissinger, *A World Restored: Metternich, Castlereagh and the Problems of Peace* (Boston: Houghton Mifflin, 1973).
4. The analysis here follows the outline provided in the excellent essay by Larman C. Wilson, "Human Rights in United States Foreign Policy: The Rhetoric and the Practice," in Don Piper and Ronald Terchek, eds., *Interaction: Foreign Policy and Public Policy* (Washington, D.C.: American Enterprise Institute, 1983), pp. 178–208.
5. This and the two succeeding paragraphs are based on interviewing of the key persons involved.
6. Adam Garfinkle, *Telltale Hearts: The Vietnam Antiwar Movement Twenty Years After Tet* (Philadelphia: Foreign Policy Research Institute, forthcoming).
7. Library of Congress, Congressional Research Service, *Human Rights and U.S. Foreign Assistance,* Report prepared for the Committee on Foreign Relations, U.S. Senate, 96th Cong., 1st sess. (1979).
8. "Human Rights in the World Community: A Call for U.S. Leadership," 93rd Cong., 2nd sess. (1974), p. 13, quoted in Wilson, "Human Rights," p. 181.
9. Quoted in Roberta Cohen, "Human Rights Decision-Making in the Executive Branch: Some Proposals for a Coordinated Strategy," in D. T. Kommers and G. D. Loescher, eds., *Human Rights and American Foreign Policy* (Notre Dame, Ind.: University of Notre Dame Press, 1979), p. 217.
10. The analysis here follows that of Wilson.
11. Library of Congress, *Human Rights,* p. 18.
12. Quoted in John Martz and Lars Schoultz, *Latin America, the United States,*

and the Inter-American System (Boulder, Colo.: Westview Press, 1980), p. 176.

13. Howard J. Wiarda, "Democracy and Human Rights in Latin America: Toward a New Conceptualization," *Orbis* 22 (Spring 1978): 137–60. The issues raised in this paper had been presented earlier at a colloquium hosted by the Bureau of Inter-American Affairs, Department of State, February 1977.

14. See the discussion in Edward Kolodziej, "The Diffusion of Power within a Decentralized International System: Limits of Soviet Power," in Edward Kolodziej and Roger Kanet, eds., *The Limits of Soviet Power in the Developing World* (London: Macmillan, 1989).

15. An excellent discussion of these differences and their foreign policy implications is Adda B. Bozaman, "American Policy and the Illusion of Congruent Values," *Strategic Review* (Winter 1987): 11–23.

16. Louis Hartz, *The Founding of New Societies* (New York: Harcourt Brace Jovanovich, 1964).

17. Howard J. Wiarda, *Corporatism and National Development in Latin America* (Boulder, Colo.: Westview Press, 1981); also Wiarda and Harvey F. Kline, *Latin American Politics and Development* (Boulder, Colo.: Westview Press, 1984), pt. I.

18. See the discussion in Juan D. Linz, "An Authoritarian Regime: Spain," in E. Allardt and S. Rokkan, eds., *Mass Politics* (New York: Free Press, 1980).

19. On Rousseauean democracy in Latin America see Richard M. Morse, "The Challenge of Ideology in Latin America," *Foreign Policy and Defense Review* (Winter 1985), pp. 14–23.

20. The analysis here follows that of A. D. Renteln, "The Unanswered Challenge of Relativism and the Consequences for Human Rights," *Human Rights Quarterly* 7 (1985): 514–40.

21. The analysis here follows that of M. Glen Johnson, "Human Rights Practices in Divergent Ideological Settings: How Do Political Ideas Influence Policy Choices?" Paper prepared for delivery at the 1986 Annual Meeting of the American Political Science Association, Washington, D.C., August 28–31, 1986; see also James C. Hsiung, ed., *Human Rights in East Asia: A Cultural Perspective* (New York: Paragon Press, 1985).

22. Again, following Johnson.

23. An example of this position is Jack Donnelly, "Human Rights and Human Dignity: An Analytical Critique of Non-Western Conceptions of Human Rights," *American Political Science Review*, 76 (June 1982): 303–16. See also Allan Bloom, *The Closing of the American Mind* (New York: Simon and Schuster, 1987).

24. For a parallel view see R. S. Manglapus, "Human Rights Are Not a Western Discovery," *Worldview* 21 (1979): 4–6. It is perhaps no accident that Manglapus is from the Philippines, another semi-Western country with a strong Hispanic heritage overlaid with U.S. influence.

25. The analysis here follows that of Wilson, "Human Rights," pp. 183ff.

26. Again, following Wilson.

27. See especially Hans Kelsen, *Principles of International Law*, 2nd ed. (New York: Holt, Rinehart and Winston, 1966).

28. The best and most complete discussion is Joshua Muravchik, *The Uncertain Crusade: Jimmy Carter and the Dilemmas of Human Rights Policy* (Lanham, Md.: Hamilton Press, 1986).
29. Based on interviews with current and former U.S. government officials, as well as Argentine scholars.
30. Ibid.
31. For a complete history, see Muravchik, *Uncertain Crusade*.
32. Ernst B. Haas, "Human Rights: To Act or Not to Act," in K. A. Oye, D. Rothchild, and R. L. Lieber, eds., *Eagle Entangled: U.S. Foreign Policy in a Complex World* (New York: Longman, 1979).
33. See Howard J. Wiarda, ed., *Human Rights and U.S. Human Rights Policy* (Washington, D.C.: American Enterprise Institute, 1982).
34. Wilson, "Human Rights," p. 190.
35. Jeane Kirkpatrick, "Dictatorship and Double Standards," *Commentary* 70 (November 1979): 34–45.
36. Ernest Lefever, "The Trivialization of Human Rights," *Policy Review*, no. 3 (Winter 1978).
37. Juliana Geron Pilon, "Human Rights," in S. M. Butler, M. Sanera, and W. B. Weinrod, eds., *Mandate for Leadership II: Continuing the Conservative Revolution* (Washington, D.C.: Heritage Foundation, 1984).
38. Howard J. Wiarda, "The United States and Latin America: Change and Continuity," in A. Adelman and R. Reading, eds., *Confrontation in the Caribbean Basin* (Pittsburgh: Center for Latin American Studies, University of Pittsburgh, 1983), esp. pp. 221–24.
39. The *Report of the President's National Bipartisan Commission on Central America* (New York: Macmillan, 1984); also Howard J. Wiarda, ed., "U.S. Policy in Central America: Consultant Papers for the Kissinger Commission," Special Issue of the *Foreign Policy and Defense Review* 5 (1984).
40. Margaret Daly Hayes, "Not What I Say But What I Do: Latin American Policy in the Reagan Administration," in John Martz, ed., *U.S. Policy in Latin America* (Lincoln, Neb.: University of Nebraska Press, 1986).
41. For elaboration see Howard J. Wiarda and Michael J. Kryzanek, *The Dominican Republic: Caribbean Crucible* (Boulder, Colo.: Westview Press, 1982).
42. For the controversy, see Jiri Valenta and Esperanza Durán, eds., *Conflict in Nicaragua* (Winchester, Mass.: Allen and Unwin, 1987).
43. Howard J. Wiarda, "The Paralysis of Policy: Current Dilemmas of U.S. Foreign Policy Making," *World Affairs* 149 (Summer 1986): 15–21.

6

Project Democracy and the National Endowment for Democracy

Foreign policy panaceas tend to come and go in Washington, almost as frequently as the seasons. Such panaceas as applied to the Third World and especially to Latin America are particuarly prevalent. Moreover, these foreign policy cure-alls have a life and social history of their own: they are born, they grow, they become institutionalized; and then they prove to be unworking or unworkable, and hence they wither on the vine. Unlike the human analogy, however, these panaceas seldom die completely; rather they continue to hang on even after interest in them has waned and usually with a core body of "true believers" committed to carrying out the program. This was the case of agrarian reform in the early 1960s, community development in the mid-1960s, and family planning in the late 1960s and early 1970s. It would be a fascinating project to undertake a comparative social and political history of the rise and decline of each of these panaceas.[1]

In the administration of President Carter, as we saw in the last chapter, human rights became the new panacea, or perhaps the leitmotiv. Under President Reagan "Project Democracy," which included human rights as a key element, became the dominant agenda item. It must be said that there is nothing intrinsically wrong with any of these programs; indeed, they all—agrarian reform, community development, family planning, human rights, democracy—rank high on my own list of policy priorities. What is worrisome, however, is the boom 'n' bust nature of these policy cycles, the fickleness and inconstancy of our commitment to these programs, the ethnocentrism involved, the partisan politics to which they are subject and political uses to which they are put, our missionary reverence and enthusiasm for them one minute and indifference the next—in short the fact that they are seen as panaceas, quick fixes that will solve Latin America's, or our own, problems once and for all.

This chapter will focus on President Reagan's Project Democracy and examine the National Endowment for Democracy (NED), the agency created to administer its programs. The chapter will examine the origins of the democracy initiative and explore the goals of the program, its structure and organization, NED's activities as well as its problems. The chapter focuses on Project Democracy, but of course it should not be thought that this was the first time that the United States sought officially to promote democracy; nor is the NED the only institution the U.S. government and citizens use to try to encourage democracy abroad. The Democracy Initiative, however, offers a way to assess the Reagan administration's foreign policy accomplishments and false starts, just as its human rights initiative provided a key to assessing the Carter administration. At the end, we draw up a balance sheet to assess what is useful and what not so useful in the new democracy program.

Origins

The plans and inspiration for a vast program to assist democratic development as a counter to Soviet totalitarianism were set forth in President Reagan's address to the British Parliament of June 8, 1982: "The objective I propose is quite simple to state: to foster the infrastructure of democracy, the system of a free press, unions, political parties, universities, which allows a free people to choose their own way to develop their own culture and to reconcile their own differences through peaceful means."[2]

The president announced that a bipartisan foundation was studying "how the United States can best contribute as a nation to the global campaign for democracy now gathering force" and said that he intended to use the recommendations of a panel of political leaders he had constituted "in the common task of strengthening democracy throughout the world." That was of course a lofty and ambitious goal and recalled the rhetoric and global vision of John F. Kennedy.

This address, among the most important of the Reagan presidency, was in fact the culmination of a long process during which the administration's democracy agenda was articulated, bargained over, and set forth. The process by which Project Democracy came into existence was at least as interesting as the high-sounding goals it envisioned, and it tells us a great deal about policymaking and why we should maintain a somewhat reserved, maybe even skeptical, view of what the United States can hope to accomplish through this program, the most recent of our nation's long history of such missionary campaigns.

At least seven major influences, not all of them related let alone consistent, came together as part of the democracy campaign.[3] The first emerged from the humiliation of defeat in Vietnam; the momentum of revolution in Grenada, Nicaragua, and El Salvador; the aggressive expansionism of the Soviet Union during the 1970s; and the seeming impotence of the Carter administration to do anything to stem or reverse the tide. Much of the Washington foreign policy establishment—those who attend those endless dinners, seminars, and receptions where in fact a good deal of future U.S. foreign policy is sounded out and winnowed—and by no means only Reaganites, had come to the conclusion that the United States now needed to take the political and ideological offensive.[4] What was needed, the growing consensus said, was something akin to the socialist or communist internationals but with a democratic orientation. Others suggested organizations aimed at promoting democracy similar to the "foundations" maintained by the three main West German political parties, which provide scholarships and political training for Third World student, labor, and political leaders. Such programs would serve the noble purpose of advancing democracy abroad, but they would also advance U.S. foreign policy goals. Of course, many within the foreign policy establishment had reservations about one or another of these activities, and some scoffed entirely at the idea of the United States exporting democracy. But by the late 1970s–early 1980s something of a bipartisan consensus had begun to emerge that the United States should no longer simply stand by and watch Soviet gains but should itself take the initiative.

A second influence on the democracy project grew out of earlier CIA precedents for such activities. In the early and mid-1960s the CIA had clandestinely funded a host of magazines, publishing houses, youth groups, labor groups, political parties, training programs, and so on.[5] Later, revelations concerning the sources of the funds forced many of these activities to cease, and in the mid- to late 1970s—in the aftermath of Vietnam and CIA efforts directed against Salvador Allende in Chile— congressional prohibitions on CIA activities forced even more of these kinds of activities to cease. But with the Soviet ideological and political offensive in the Third World during the 1970s, the sense grew that it was necessary to fund such activities and groups, but under open and non-CIA auspices. The consensus was strong that many of the program activities to aid young labor and party leaders abroad in the early 1960s were positive and useful, only the sponsorship was wrong. Hence sentiment grew to relaunch some of the programs that had previously been terminated, but to do it above the table and not below.

A third major influence was the AFL-CIO and especially its international arm, the American Institute for Free Labor Development (AIFLD). Since World War II, AIFLD had been promoting U.S.–style trade unionism abroad in an effort to combat the communist influence in many foreign labor movements. Operating as almost another arm of the U.S. embassy in many countries, AIFLD ran training programs for upcoming labor leaders, provided funds and orientation to the unions, organized an anticommunist trade union federation, and sought to implant a model of collective bargaining and apolitical trade unionism patterned after a somewhat idealized version of U.S. trade unionism. For these activities AIFLD had received large shots of CIA money. But that funding was cut off about the same time as the CIA's funding of other like activities was terminated, and from that time on the AFL-CIO had been looking for a new source of money.[6]

A fourth influence was the cadre of democracy "true believers" in Washington, supported by intellectual weight in the academic community. These are persons who *really* believe that the United States is a model and exemplar of democracy and as such has an obligation to export it to other lands. Moreover, they believe that the United States model is the only kind of democracy worth supporting. These true believers are often terribly uncomfortable with the notion that there are distinct meanings and nuances of democracy in Latin America (and elsewhere), that democracy there takes Rousseauean as distinct from Lockean forms. In these ways the democracy true believers are much like the human rights true believers.

The true believers tended to dominate in the early months of discussion about the democracy project, and they still have considerable influence on the program even now. The agenda of the true believers is sometimes scary: they wish to export U.S. institutions to Latin America, jettison virtually all Latin American institutions as "traditional" or "backward," and substitute U.S. ones in their place.[7] That radical agenda would of course produce total chaos in Latin America, and it would certainly not lead to greater democracy. On the contrary, it would likely only produce breakdown, chaos, and authoritarianism. Fortunately, as the democracy proposal went forward in the Congress, many of the wilder visions of the true believers were sacrificed and a more pragmatic, realistic, and limited version eventually emerged. That was healthy, but it disillusioned the true believers, a number of whom then dropped out of leadership roles.

A fifth influence was the learning process through which the Reagan administration went. It will be recalled from the previous chapter that although the administration did not seem very much interested in human rights at first, it soon moved to a stronger pro–human rights stand. The same thing happened with democracy. The administration came to realize that democratic regimes are less bellicose, less inclined to intervene in their neighbors' affairs, more pragmatic, and easier to get along with than authoritarians of the left or right. Not only that, but the Congress, the media, public opinion, church and labor groups, to say nothing of our allies, are much more cooperative and supportive when the goals of our policy are presented as "democracy." As the administration absorbed these lessons in its first two years, it came around to a strong pro-democracy position—and began lobbying for its Project Democracy.

The sixth influence was U.S. policy successes in El Salvador. The Reagan administration had inherited in that strife-torn country a situation of civil war, a tottering and repressive military regime, and well-entrenched Marxist-Leninist guerrilla forces aided by Nicaragua and seemingly poised on the verge of success. During the first two years of Reagan's presidency, El Salvador could only be described as a foreign policy disaster waiting to happen, another domino on the verge of toppling, and one of the most divisive, nastiest issues in U.S. foreign and domestic policy. But through a combination of manipulation, arm twisting, coddling, assistance, and outright bribery, the administration—and the Salvadorans—succeeded in turning the situation around. A series of elections was held, José Napoleón Duarte became president, the human rights situation improved, and the guerrillas were forced on the defensive. The turnaround was so dramatic, even inspiring, that some administration officials began talking of applying the El Salvadoran "model" to other countries.[8] To do so required a mechanism like the NED, that could be partially separated from U.S. official policy instruments. Of course, it was preposterous to speak of the "El Salvador model" as applied to an Argentina or a Brazil, where the conditions were entirely different and where national pride resisted the notion that backward, small El Salvador had any lessons to offer to them. But that did not prevent U.S. officials from over-generalizing from the El Salvador case and seeking to use the Salvadoran experience for broader purposes.

The seventh influence was the larger and broader antidictatorial, pro-democratic thrust occurring in Latin America itself, as well as globally. Most of the returns to democracy in Latin America in the past decade have come as a result of Latin American efforts, not those of the United States. The United States helped reestablish democracy in the Dominican Republic, championed democracy in El Salvador, helped preserve a measure of it in Ecuador and other countries, and helped nudge it along in Honduras and Guatemala; but in the rest of the continent it was local forces that presided over the transitions to democracy, not Washington or the local U.S. embassy. But the administration did have the good sense to ratify and get behind these trends once they were under way and to support the fledgling democracies and their leaders as they came to power. It was the Latin American influence that was all-important; with the exceptions already noted, what the United States did was prudently to jump aboard an already moving bandwagon. Then it moved to make the democratic trend the big drum on its own foreign policy bandwagon.[9]

These factors provided the general setting in which the democracy project finally was realized. For a long time the idea had languished. As early as the late 1960s, following the disclosures of CIA financing of many cultural and political activities, Congressman Dante Fascell introduced a bill to create an international institute that would carry out international political activities overtly instead of covertly. The Fascell bill failed, however, to obtain sufficient support, and for a decade the idea got nowhere.

But by the late 1970s the climate had changed. The origins of the democracy project center in a core group of persons, most of whom are still active on the NED's board. These include Congressman Fascell; the AFL-CIO's Lane Kirkland, whose union has a strong political as well as financial interest in the program; William Brock, who was then chairman of the Republican National Committee; and the former chairman of the Democratic National Committee, Charles Manatt. At lower levels the project was supported by Eugenia Kemble of the Free Trade Union Institute and Keith Scheutte, a former aide to Secretary of State Alexander Haig and recently head of the Republican Institute for International Affairs. Also important in these early days in mobilizing scholarly, think tank, government and private sector support for the project were political scientist George Agree, historian Allen Weinstein, and Chamber of Commerce official (and former ambassador) Michael Samuels. None of the latter three is any longer formally associated with the program. Fascell aide Spencer Oliver was instrumental in building political support for the project in Congress and in negotiating its structure among various interested parties.[10]

In 1979 Agree, Brock, and Manatt formed the American Political Foundation. Its purpose was to investigate ways to promote international and democracy-building projects by the two U.S. political parties and to get the United States into the "democracy business." They along with Oliver and others then launched a campaign to promote the democracy plan and to get the think tanks, Congress, the administration, the AFL-CIO, and the Chamber of Commerce behind it. Three years later they had secured the endorsement of the Reagan administration and gotten the Agency for International Development (AID) to put up $400,000 in seed money. Launched in November 1982, the project was known initially as the Democracy Program; and on its board were Agree, Brock, Fascell, Kirkland, Samuels, and several others. Weinstein was named project director, although he was passed over for the presidency when the program was converted into the National Endowment for Democracy. Agree later also resigned when he became disenchanted with how the NED was structured and with its (congressionally mandated) more pragmatic and less ideological program.

Among the first activities of the program was a joint American Enterprise Institute and Department of State–sponsored international conference on free elections.[11] The conference, part of which was held in the White House, brought together over two hundred participants from six continents for three days of discussion on the role of elections in supporting democracy. Especially striking to the U.S. participants in the conference was the variety of forms, institutional arrangements, and definitions of democracy presented. This conference was followed in the spring by another AEI-sponsored international conference on constitutionalism and self-government hosted by the Chief Justice of the Supreme Court.[12] Both of these conferences attracted widespread publicity and offered rich agendas. Both were specifically mentioned by President Reagan in his Parliament speech launching the project. But both also provoked criticism on the grounds that U.S. government funds should not have been channeled to foundations and research institutes identified in the popular mind with conservative causes.

In April 1983, the Democracy Program issued an interim report urging the establishment of an institution to promote democracy abroad. In November, despite being denounced by some congressmen as a "boondoggle," the legislation creating the NED was enacted. Carl Gershman, who had a strong background in labor and social-democratic affairs and had earlier been chosen by Jeane Kirkpatrick as one of her aides at the United Nations, was named president of the new agency.

Goals

The National Endowment for Democracy seeks to strengthen democratic institutions throughout the world through quasi-private, ostensibly nongovernmental efforts.[13] Funded by the Congress, it is nonetheless a privately incorporated, nonprofit organization with a board of directors comprising leading citizens from both the private and the governmental sectors, from both big labor and big business, and from both major political parties. The NED is thus both an agency of the U.S. government and a private agency at the same time, a contradiction that helps explain many of its early problems. It has the advantage of being funded by the federal treasury and is subject to the guidance, oversight, and overall direction of U.S. government policy. But because it is privately chartered, it has a measure of autonomy and independence. Its private status also enables it to deflect criticism from the U.S. government when its policies and programs go awry or prove embarrassing—as they sometimes do.

The NED embodies a broad, bipartisan U.S. commitment to democracy. But what precisely democracy means, or ought to mean, when extended abroad remains quite vague in the NED's enabling legislation and early statements of purpose. Fortunately the NED resisted the idea of stating a definition of democracy that would be an exact reflection of democracy in the United States itself. That was a subject of major controversy in the early days of planning for the NED, and in its statements of purposes both the U.S. definition and a more culturally relativistic conception are set forth. The NED says that it seeks to enlist the energies and talents of private citizens and groups in the United States to work with those abroad who wish to build *for themselves* a democratic future.[14] [Emphasis added]

The NED's avowed objective of strengthening democratic groups and institutions in other countries not only reflects the hopes and ideals of the American people but also is rooted, its backers argue, in universally recognized principles of international law. The UN's Declaration of Human Rights, the conventions of the International Labor Office (important given the central role of the AFL-CIO's AIFLD in the program), and the Helsinki Final Act commit the world's governments to honoring fundamental human rights. These charters are used to justify the NED's activities on behalf of democracy and democratic institutions in other peoples' countries—a considerable leap of logic and interpretation. No attention is paid in the NED's statements to an opposite and equally important principle of international law: noninterference by one nation in the internal affairs of another. Thus far the NED's record has been a mixed one here also: blatant and occasionally stupid and self-defeating interference in some cases and considerable sensitivity in others.

U.S. values and international law, however, are not the only motives at work, for the NED seeks both to strengthen the U.S. foreign policy position abroad and to weaken that of the Soviet Union. Democracies have been found to be more stable, less warlike, and more sympathetic to U.S. goals and initiatives. Therefore, the NED seeks to strengthen those fragile countries where democracy is in danger of perishing (in West Africa, for example) and to bolster democracies that are just getting back on their feet (such as Guatemala or Brazil). Such efforts clearly serve U.S. strategic purposes as well as general humane and humanitarian purposes. But at the same time, NED seeks to water the seeds of democracy that are sprouting in some communist nations, such as the Solidarity movement in Poland. Such programs have the effect of both strengthening ostensibly democratic institutions in some important nations and weakening totalitarian institutions as well as the hold of the Soviet Union over its satellites. In these respects the NED goals are both idealistic as well as, preeminently, focused on the cold war rivalry between the United States and the Soviet Union. The NED's programs therefore are aimed at supporting pro–U.S. groups, at providing an alternative to Castroism and *Sandinismo,* at weakening the Soviet Union, and at giving the United States another overt foreign policy instrument (since covert and CIA activities had been largely ruled out) to use in the larger global struggle between democracy and totalitarianism. These cold war considerations were clearly uppermost in President Reagan's thinking when he launched the Democracy Project and said: "What I am describing now is a plan and a hope for the long term—the march of freedom and democracy which will leave Marxism-Leninism on the ashheap of history as it has left other tyrannies which stifle the freedom and muzzle the self-expression of the people."[15]

In that same speech before the British Parliament, President Reagan spoke to another issue of major concern to this discussion, that of ethnocentrism and cultural imperialism. The objective of the Democracy Project, as we have seen in the president's statement quoted earlier, was to foster democracy's institutional infrastructure, its underlying associational life, its instruments of peaceful reconciliation of divisive issues, its cultural underpinnings. But then the president went on to say:

This is not cultural imperialism, it is providing the means for genuine self-determination and protection for diversity. Democracy already flourishes in countries with very different cultures and historical experiences. It would be cultural condescension, or worse, to say that any people prefer dictatorship to democracy. Who would voluntarily choose not to have the right to vote, decide to purchase government propaganda handouts instead of independent newspapers, prefer government to worker-controlled unions, opt for land to be owned by the state instead of those who till it, want government repression of religious liberty, a single political party instead of a free choice, a rigid cultural orthodoxy instead of democratic tolerance and diversity?[16]

The establishment of the NED and its emphasis on private, voluntary initiatives reflected a sense, widespread in the government since the collapse in the 1960s of CIA funding of many of these same or similar activities, that government action alone was inefficient, unsatisfactory, and incapable of promoting democracy internationally. Indeed, the creation and structure of the NED reflected the view that the U.S. private sector "is both a more appropriate and a more effective vehicle than government for working with groups abroad to advance the democratic cause."[17] The NED's "nongovernmental character" gave it a flexibility as well as a shield from immediate political and governmental considerations and oversight in developing cooperative and partnership arrangements with similar organizations overseas. The NED's semiprivate standing was seen as a way of enhancing U.S. private sector groups, especially organized labor, to assist their counterparts abroad—but using public funds to do so. The private nature of the agency enabled it to make long-term and coordinated commitments, presumably immune from immediate pressures and changing political winds. For these ends the NED was supposed to be oriented toward a consistent, bipartisan, and long-term approach.

The NED seeks to focus on the realm of ideas as well as institutions that are central to democracy. It organized a modest research program as well as an action agenda. Its aim is to nourish an intellectual climate in which democracy can grow and flourish. "Fundamental to the democratic process is a lively competition among points of view, interest groups, and independent institutions." Its goal, it proclaims—again in response to earlier criticism of its missionary zeal—is not to steer other nations toward the adoption of any particular set of policies, but rather to help them evolve into stable and vigorous democratic societies.

The activities supported by the NED are to be guided by the six purposes set forth in its Articles of Incorporation and the National Endowment for Democracy Act passed by the Congress in November 1983.[18] These purposes are:

(1) to encourage free and democratic institutions throughout the world through private sector initiatives, including activities which promote the individual rights and freedoms (including internationally recognized human rights) which are essential to the functioning of democratic institutions;

(2) to facilitate exchanges between United States private sector

groups (especially the two major American political parties, labor, and business) and democratic groups abroad;

(3) to promote United States nongovernmental participation (especially through the two major American political parties, labor, business, and other private sector groups) in democratic training programs and democratic institution-building abroad;

(4) to strengthen democratic electoral processes abroad through timely measures in cooperation with indigenous democratic forces;

(5) to support the participation of the two major American political parties, labor, business, and other United States private sector groups in fostering cooperation with those abroad dedicated to the cultural values, institutions and organizations of democratic pluralism; and,

(6) to encourage the establishment and growth of democratic development in a manner consistent both with the broad concerns of United States national interests and with the specific requirements of the democratic groups in other countries which are aided by programs funded by the Endowment.

In all its efforts to implement these purposes, the NED is to be guided by the following principles:[19]

- that democracy involves the right of the people freely to determine their own destiny;
- that the exercise of this right requires a system that guarantees competitive elections, freedom of expression, belief, and association, respect for the inalienable rights of individuals and minorities, free communications media, and the rule of law;
- that a democratic system may take a variety of forms suited to local needs and traditions, and therefore need not follow the United States or any other particular model (this principle was adopted in response to criticism of the early Democracy Project as excessively ethnocentric);
- that the existence of autonomous economic, political, social, and cultural institutions is the best guarantor of individual rights and freedoms and the foundation of the democratic process;
- that private institutions in free societies can contribute to the development of democracy through assistance to counterparts abroad;

- that such assistance must be responsive to local needs and seek to encourage—but not to control—indigenous efforts to build free and independent institutions; and,

- that the partnership envisaged between those who enjoy the benefits of democracy and those who aspire to a democratic future must be based upon mutual respect, shared values, and a common commitment to work together to extend the frontiers of democracy for present and future generations.

As incorporated in the congressional legislation and in NED's carefully considered statements of principles and objectives (as distinct from the early documents of the Democracy Project, which were excessively ethnocentric and encumbered by missionary zeal), the goals and objectives of the NED seem quite reasonable. In addition to taking account of the cultural and economic diversity of the countries where its programs would be concentrated, the NED intended to adapt its activities to the level of democratic development existing in different countries as well. In countries where democracy exists but is not sufficiently established, the goal would be to enhance the credibility and efficiency of democratic governance and strengthen the institutional and cultural infrastructure of the private sector. In countries in transition to democracy, the plan was to assist in broadening confidence in the democratic process and to reinforce those groups committed to democracy. And in countries where democracy could be only a long-term goal, the aim was to help build such institutions as independent business organizations, free trade unions, a free press, and an independent judiciary. Where even these independent institutions were prohibited, as in the totalitarian societies, the objective was to enlarge whatever possibilities existed for independent thought, expression, and cultural activity. Thus, in the NED's words, while it intended to concentrate the major part of its resources on situations that offered a realistic prospect of achieving progress toward democracy, it would not neglect those that kept alive the flame of freedom in closed societies.

After a considerable discussion over what precise types of activities the NED should support, five substantive areas were decided on: pluralism; democratic governance and political processes; education, culture, and communications; research; and international cooperation. By "pluralism" the NED meant assistance to independent business associations, trade unions, and other private sector institutions such as cooperatives or human rights groups. The business/labor connection in fact was so strong that, as explained in the next section, these two entities were incorporated

within the organizational structure of the NED. By democratic governance and political processes, the NED had in mind aid to political parties,
assistance with elections, aid to foreign think tanks and research centers,
assistance in the administration of justice, and programs to teach democratic values to the military. Under education, culture, and communications, the NED planned support for newspapers and journals, democratic
education, and activities aimed at strengthening the "popular understanding and education of democracy."

Although most of its grants were aimed at support of action-oriented
programs, the NED allocated a small portion of its resources to funding
research. The focus was to be on general comparative studies on the
preconditions and prospects for democracy, studies of the problems of
democracy in particular regions (especially Latin America) or countries
where the NED had particular interest, and evaluations of the effectiveness
of previous and existing efforts to promote democracy. The type of
research the NED aimed at supporting was studies that would aid it in
carrying out its mission and that had considerable interest to a larger
audience. The first recipient of an NED grant was Seymour Martin Lipset
and a group of other scholars, whose project involved a comparative study
of the causes of success and failure of democracy in developing nations.[20]

Finally, the NED focused on efforts to encourage regional and international cooperation for democracy. That involved grants to promote
greater cohesion among existing democracies and to enhance coordination
among democratic forces. For example, the NED sought to coordinate its
activities with those of the West German political party foundations—
which after all had served as one of the key models in fashioning the U.S.
program. The NED tried to enlist the cooperation of private sector
groups in countries that are particularly close politically to the United
States and that have a special relationship with a particular region—for
example, Australia and Japan in Asia and France in Francophone Africa.

The NED recognized that the effort to foster democracy had to be
long-term. Through the efforts described it sought to enhance a sense of
common identity and purpose among democratic groups and nations.
Those purposes would not be achieved through a single election or reform
but required long years of steady, persistent work. The work involved
changing institutions, values, procedures, and habits that themselves have
evolved over time and, it was recognized, according to the needs and
traditions of diverse political cultures. Essentially, the NED sought to
make the democracy idea attractive to ordinary people. It believed that for
"billions of people" democracy had enormous appeal, far more so than
authoritarianism or communism; and it was prepared to launch a global

campaign to assist democracy to flower. It saw these billions as its partners or potential partners. As the NED's statement of principles and objectives put it, "We hope that the Endowment's work will not only help them achieve the blessings of democracy, but will strengthen the bond between them and the people of the United States, a bond based on our common commitment to democracy as a way of life."[21]

Organization and Structure

One of the most curious—and controversial—features of the NED is its organizational structure.[22] Of the NED's rather modest, initial budget of approximately $18 million—a paltry sum given its grandiose goals and objectives—the bulk goes to four core institutes that form a kind of corporately organized structure within the NED. The NED itself has a small staff of fifteen to twenty people; most of its activities, according to the legislation creating the NED, were to be conducted through the four component institutes. These institutes are: The National Republican Institute for International Affairs, the Democratic Institute for International Affairs, the Center for International Private Enterprise, and the Free Trade Union Institute. The NED thus consists of a coalition representing the two major U.S. political parties, an offshoot of the American Chamber of Commerce, and a branch of the AFL-CIO.

First and foremost, therefore, the NED structure reflects the major institutions of U.S. political life. Indeed, it is quintessentially American. Moreover, this structure was the result at least as much of political compromise as it was of any rational or coherent planning. The two U.S. political parties had to be involved or the proposal would never have gotten through Congress. And because the AFL-CIO was involved, so too had to be the Chamber of Commerce. Never mind that the Chamber had almost no prior international experience; or that the AFL-CIO's AIFLD had acquired a reputation over the years of sometimes being as destructive of democratic unionism abroad as contributing to it; or that the U.S. political parties had, as parties, no more experience with international institution building than did the Chamber of Commerce. Rather, these core institutes came into being as the result of a series of political compromises that were undoubtedly rational in a political sense at the time, but may prove disastrous in the long run. This organizational structure is the Achilles' heel of the NED. But, as argued by Congressman Fascell, the core institutes are "vital to the concept," "fundamental to American political life."[23]

The decision to build the NED as a kind of umbrella organization overseeing the four core institutes, which would perform the bulk of the overseas activities, was "not coincidental," according to William Brock; rather, he said, "it is a statement of the importance we attach to free labor, business, and free political parties as fundamental to any free society."[24] NED President Carl Gershman also argued the core institutes were essential because they could relate to parallel groups abroad. And officials of the four institutes themselves, especially the AFL-CIO, contend that they and not the NED have the connection and affinities with overseas organizations to make the program work.

Others dispute these claims and suggest more cynical reasons. The political parties, they say, wanted to create their own international institutes not so much to build democracy but to gain more patronage positions and to help those parties abroad whose ideology is close to their own. Some critics see the NED as a back-door way for the parties to get government funds despite the opposition of the bulk of the U.S. electorate to such public funding. These criticisms were so strong that initially Congress refused to appropriate the funds to support the two party institutes. However, a deal was apparently cut whereby the labor institute agreed to use only a portion of its share of the $18 million (labor's share originally was approximately two-thirds of the budget) and to leave some for the parties, even though they had not been directly funded. In return, the AFL-CIO insisted on having final say in the selection of the NED's president—Gershman. This maneuver, to fund the party institutes under the table, so angered Congress that it came close to abolishing the NED.

The four core institutes have been a continuing source of controversy. Initially the AFL-CIO's Kirkland wanted a single bipartisan organization to promote democratic pluralism abroad, but he was outvoted by the NED's board, on which sit the chairmen of the national parties themselves. A General Accounting Office (GAO) study suggested that entities besides labor, business, and the parties should have been involved in the program. The GAO criticized the staff for being so preoccupied with the legislative maneuvering to establish the NED that it ignored the problems inherent in structuring the NED the way it was. The staff ignored the advice of the American Political Foundation, for example, which had helped launch the Democracy Project; and similarly ignored the questions and recommendations raised by U.S. embassy officials abroad to whom the early proposal had been sent for review.[25]

The participation by the U.S. political parties is especially problematic. The Congress succeeded in eliminating the parties from the annual appropriation in 1984 and 1985, the NED's first two years; but in 1986 and

1987 the two party institutes did receive about $2 million each. Some congressmen feel, however, it is wrong for the parties to receive government money, and Brock acknowledged the fear that the funds would be used for domestic political purposes. The head of the Democratic Party Institute, R. Brian Atwood, a former congressional aide and State Department official, attributed the congressional reluctance to fund the party institutes to fear that they would meddle in other countries' internal politics. Keith Schuette, who directs the Republican Party Institute, indicated that because of the continuing dispute the party institutes have tried scrupulously to avoid controversial activities; but as will be seen in the next section, the strategy has not always been successful.

The party international affairs institutes seek to involve themselves in what they call "party building," a term that is akin to the "nation-building" plan and program of twenty-five years ago.[26] The institutes argue and assume that political parties are essential to the functioning of democracy and that the institutes' role is to provide like-minded foreign parties with advice and assistance. To avoid any hint of controversy, the Democratic Party Institute had refused to finance election-related programs, including educational or registration efforts or poll-monitoring activities, although it did later get involved in such activities in aiding the "no" position in the plebiscite held by dictator Augusto Pinochet of Chile on his rule. The Republican Party Institute, on the other hand, has from the beginning worked with similarly conservative political parties abroad and has funded an institute in Guatemala to train conservative party leaders. The aim is to bring the Latin American right, which has seldom seen the need to organize political parties and has usually employed personal or family contacts or occasionally a military coup to secure and protect its political interests,[27] into the democratic political process. That of course would represent a major transformation in the way things are done in Latin America, requiring almost a sea change of the Latin American political culture, and would likely take a generation or two. Whether the party institutes have the experience, the personnel, and the know-how to effect such a change is open to serious question.

The Chamber of Commerce's Center for International Private Enterprise has taken a very cautious and go-slow approach in its NED-sponsored activities. In part the caution stems from uncertainty as to what precisely the chamber could do in these areas (in contrast to the AFL-CIO, which already had a very clear agenda) and in part from reluctance by many chamber officials to get involved in the program at all. William T. Archery, who is a former official in the Department of Commerce and is both a vice president of the chamber and president of the NED-funded Private Enterprise Center, has said that he came in with very mixed views about the program. The center aims to encourage the development of independent businesses, voluntary trade associations, open market economies, and incentives for economic growth, in those countries where the center feels "some form of private enterprise still exists." The plan is to make business in the Third World a "major component of pluralistic development"—a concept that never received any attention at all in the vast literature on development a quarter century ago.[28] The center seeks to make the case that "democracy and private enterprise go together"—an arguable case,[29] but one that has few intellectual defenders outside of the United States. The center's limited agenda has included seminars to educate students and business leaders about private enterprise and a new magazine, the *Journal of Economic Growth,* containing articles on the same theme.

While the agenda of the Private Enterprise Center has been very modest, it does reflect a growing current in Latin America. Throughout the region there is a trend toward greater private sector activities, destatization, a recognition of Latin America's burgeoning (and essentially capitalistic) informal economy, and individual self-worth. While the Center for Private Enterprise cannot change Latin America's traditional emphasis on a strong state, it can assist those more individualistic and initiative-producing activities in the hemisphere that are already under way.[30]

The situation with the Free Trade Union Institute is the most complex of all. It has been suggested that the whole reason for the NED was to funnel U.S. government funds to AIFLD, that all the rest (the party and free enterprise institutes) are smoke screens. When it was no longer feasible to provide CIA funds to the AFL-CIO for its labor activities abroad, a new mechanism had to be found for the supply of such money, and the mechanism finally fashioned was the NED. Prima facie evidence for such assertions are the appointment of a protégé of AFL-CIO president Lane Kirkland as president of the NED over other candidates, and the fact that over two-thirds of the funds appropriated for the NED so far have gone to the Labor Institute.

The United States does need a mechanism of a quasi-private nature to deal with the foreign policy problem of fascist and communist influence in and subversion of foreign labor movements. The labor movement and the broader industrial relations system are not only a major anvil on which the socioeconomic structure of the modern state and society has been largely forged; they are also critical policy arenas in which fascist, communist, and democratic elements vie for political control. Most labor movements abroad are funded either by the state or by outside powers whose interests are inimical to the United States as well as to our sense of democratic trade unionism. Therefore there is in this crucial battleground a powerful argument for U.S. assistance to the democratic forces.[31]

But the question is whether the AFL-CIO's AIFLD does this wisely or well. The track record is a very mixed one. AIFLD has done a lot to train young union leaders abroad and to provide assistance to fledgling labor movements. But it does not have the corps of efficient and trained leaders necessary to operate effectively abroad; its administrators often do not understand Latin America very well; AIFLD has often proved to be a divisive element in the Latin American labor movement, operating from a political agenda that may not be appropriate there; and the model of labor relations used is the nonpolitical collective bargaining model of the United States, which frequently has little relevance for Latin America.[32] Over the past twenty-five years AIFLD has both contributed to the Latin American labor system and also made such horrendous mistakes as to raise serious questions about its overall program. At the same time, because this is the AFL-CIO and therefore sacrosanct politically, no congressman or agency has been willing to delve very deeply into AIFLD's failures. The AFL-CIO is one of those private groups that in effect carry out their own foreign policy which, although funded by the United States, is not always closely coordinated with broader U.S. policy goals and is almost entirely immune from oversight or serious review.[33]

Nevertheless, change is in the air here as well. For the 1986 fiscal year, Congress put a cap of 25 percent of the NED's total appropriation as the amount that any one single institute within the NED could receive. The AFL-CIO fought this change, and some congressional critics of the program said that a labor refusal to accept such a cap would be the death knell for the NED. In addition, AIFLD has grown somewhat more modest as to what it can reasonably expect to accomplish, as well as less ethnocentric, and it now argues that it does not seek to impose its brand of unionism on other nations where it does not fit. Finally, the death of Jay Lovestone and the retirement of Irving Brown in the early 1980s removed AIFLD's most militant ideologues and paved the way for a younger and more pragmatic leadership that may be more committed to helping Latin American labor movements rather than simply imposing an inappropriate and ill-fitting U.S. labor model on them.

Activities

In its first four years the National Endowment for Democracy undertook a considerable—and growing—range of activities.[34] After all, its charter proclaims that its campaign for democracy is global. And in this world-wide ideological offensive the number of movements, parties, unions, and other groups that could conceivably be supported is vast.

Most of the activities that the NED has supported have been non-controversial. They are activities and movements that most Americans would support. Only a handful of the NED's activities have been controversial. But these of course have received all the headlines. In the fiscal year 1984, the first year of its operation, out of a total budget of $18 million, the NED awarded grants totaling $17,520,000 to over twenty private sector organizations. The lion's share, $11 million, went to the Free Trade Union Institute, which already had a structure and ongoing program, to support a broad range of activities aimed at promoting the development of free and independent democratic trade unions. The National Chamber Foundation, whose program was just getting started, received $1.7 million.

The National Republican Institute for International Affairs received $1.5 million for programs to support the development of democratic political systems and institutions. It hosted a conference of Latin American public policy institutions, ran two voter education and mobilization programs (in Grenada and Guatemala), and held another conference on the alternatives to totalitarianism. The National Democratic Institute, which also received $1.5 million, supported a program of legislative and graduate fellowships, a workshop on democratic development, and a series of consultations with foreign leaders to lay the groundwork for future programs. It sounds like, and was, a very thin agenda—so much so that Congress voted not to fund the party institutes the next fiscal year. Many congressmen (or their constituents) were troubled by the idea of taxpayer money being used to support the two U.S. political parties. In all fairness, it must be said that the limited activities during the first year represent only three months' activities and the need for both party institutes to establish offices, recruit staff, and decide what they were going to do.

In addition to the four institutes, the NED made grants in 1984 to the Afghanistan Relief Committee ($50,000) to open schools in an area controlled by the resistance; the Caribbean/Central American Action ($127,500) to establish an ostensibly nonpartisan studies center in Guatemala; the *Chinese Intellectual* ($200,000), a journal aimed at Chinese students studying in the United States; Columbia University ($100,000) for human rights law student internships; and the Committee in Support of Solidarity ($91,825) to aid Poland's independent trade union movement. Other recipients included the Cuban National Foundation, Freedom House, the Overseas Education Fund, Partners of the

Americas, the Andrei Sakharov Institute, and Stanford University—$100,625 for a comparative study of democracy in developing countries directed by Seymour M. Lipset. There are no radical or left-wing groups listed as recipients. On the other hand, there are no rabid right-wing ones either—although as might be expected of a Reagan administration–created agency, the preponderance of funds have gone to more conservative institutions. On balance, however, the programs supported seem eminently reasonable.

By 1985 a wider range of programs was being supported. Of the $14,079,679 total grants, labor got $11,560,788 and the Chamber of Commerce $1,438,326. No funds went to the party institutes—although NED did get in additional trouble with the Congress for cheating on the spirit of the prohibition against giving to the parties by channeling some fiscal year 1984 funds to them. New recipients in 1985 included Jamaica World Relief, the National Council of Negro Women, two Russian-language journals published by emigré writers, and PRODEMCA (Friends of the Democratic Center in Central America), a nonprofit educational organization that had generally supported Reagan administration positions and that was used as a conduit to funnel newsprint to the threatened *La Prensa* in Nicaragua.

By 1986 the ban had been lifted on providing funds to the party institutes, although the issue remained sensitive in Congress. By mid-1986 the party institutes were actually functioning, recruiting staff, and beginning some programs. The Republican Party Institute funded or aided ex-president Hugo Banzer's private foundation in Bolivia, the New National Party in Grenada, the Conservative Party in Nicaragua (which has historically been quite liberal), the Christian Democratic Party in Portugal, and an institute for training conservative party leaders in Guatemala, as well as several conferences on development and democracy.[35] The Democratic Party Institute sought to avoid such close election-related activities, but it did bring members of the New Korean Democratic Party to Washington to discuss constitutional reform, the transition to democracy, and free elections.

A number of NED's programs got the agency in trouble and added to its woes in Congress, where all during this period its very continued existence was exceedingly precarious. The program for the Korean opposition brought a protest from the U.S. embassy in Seoul, which feared that relations with the government would be damaged during a critical period. The PRODEMCA grant to the Nicaraguan opposition newspaper *La Prensa* became controversial because the U.S.–based organization bought a newspaper ad at the same time supporting the Reagan administration's

Central America policy and, it was alleged, used the grant money to do so. In Panama NED backed the party of Nicolás Ardito Barletta for the presidency, a candidate supported by the military, which brought forth protests from the opposition and the U.S. embassy. Adding further embarrassment was the fact that the elections Ardito won were fraudulent; the irony of the democracy endowment supporting a military puppet was also pointed out. In another celebrated case, the NED provided support to moderate Catholic parties in Northern Ireland but failed to give any to the Protestant ones. Congressman Barney Frank from heavily Irish Massachusetts added to the furor over this kind of bias by asking since when did U.S. public funds have to be used to teach Irishmen about politics anyway.[36]

Controversy was also generated by the AIFLD's activities in Europe. At Irving Brown's urging, funds (more than $500,000) were channeled to the French Union Nationale Inter-Universitaire, a conservative anticommunist student group that used the money to attack President François Mitterand. Another $800,000 was used by AIFLD for a French union group. Questions were raised about the propriety of aiding a group that opposed the president of a democratic ally, and whether the funds should be used in Western Europe at all as distinct from developing nations. The fact that these funds were given secretly, despite the NED's commitment to public disclosure of all its grants, added to the controversy. Given the historic dominance of a large sector of French trade unionism by the communists, few objected strenuously to that grant; but the award to the anti-Mitterand student group was thought to be wholly inappropriate. Part of the problem lay in the lack of supervision of the NED over its core institutes, and in particular the unwillingness of AIFLD to countenance any oversight of its activities or even to tell the NED how it was using the money. Part of the problem also arose out of what Congressman Dan Mica, chairing the House committee that oversees the NED, called the "excessive zealousness" of the NED and its supporters.[37]

A Balance Sheet

The NED is a fine idea. The United States has long been locked in a war of ideas and ideologies as well as of economic systems and weapons with the Soviet Union and its communist allies. For too long the U.S. was wholly on the defensive in this ideological battlefront, content to let Soviet propagandists take the lead and assuming that democracy's merits would emerge, unaided, to the surface. In international forums and elsewhere, the United States had seemed to receive all the blame for the world's troubles, while the Soviet Union and others heaped often unanswered abuse upon us. The existence of NED, as Senator Orrin Hatch has said,[38] sends a powerful message to the world that the United States is a serious participant in the global competition of ideas. The quasi-private NED, in addition, can do things that the more staid and official State Department cannot do. Furthermore, it is much better to have the NED openly and publicly assist these groups and engage in the kind of activities it has than to have the same activities carried out covertly by the CIA.[39]

On the other hand, there are so many problems with the NED that a congressional vote on whether it should be continued could still very easily tip either way. For one thing the NED is very limited in its budget, programs, and impact; it is still an "inside-the-Beltway" phenomenon and is not yet well known outside of it, let alone in foreign countries. Second, it has not been able to exercise sufficient oversight over its core institutes, especially the AIFLD, which brooks no interference at all. Added to that is the fact that none of the institutes is so far performing particularly well. Third, there is a zealousness still present, a missionary spirit—rather like that one finds among some human rights activists—that is both disturbing to political pragmatists and sometimes defeating of the NED's own goals. A fourth problem is the partisan political uses to which the NED is sometimes put and the bias of its grant giving. The NED would in the long run be best off being operated on a nonpartisan basis, much like other semiautonomous agencies such as the Inter-American Foundation (IAF). The IAF has maintained its political independence in ways the NED has not, and hence it is welcomed in countries that welcome neither the NED nor AID.

Perhaps most fundamental is the question with which the chapter opened: do we really know what we're doing in many of these international policy areas? Our case study of the NED, the key agency in President Reagan's Democracy Initiative, sheds light on these problems. In this as in other programs there is a pervasive ethnocentrism in what the United States is attempting, the sense that we will bring the blessings of our style of democracy to our poor, benighted brothers and sisters in the less developed nations (and even, as the aid to the French groups illustrates, to some developed ones) whether they wish it, or wish it all that much, or not. We are not very good (again as in the human rights agenda) at drawing the line between well-meaning assistance to and gross intervention in the internal affairs of other nations. We still get confused over whether the program is designed to advance democracy or thwart communism, or over where and how to combine the two. And as in human rights, the conflict and overlap between our pro-democracy and idealistic goals and our realistic and strategic ones often lead to confusion and programs that are at cross purposes. Perhaps most critical, we are still not sure how precisely to institute change in many of these foreign development and institution-building areas or how to proceed in a policy sense. The European parties and foundations, especially the West German ones after which the NED was in part modeled, are far more experienced than we in the areas of aiding like-minded trade unions, building political parties, assisting cultural groups, and developing institutions. Too often our inexperience in these areas shows, as does our still-present reluctance and hesitation to engage in these activities at all. We feel vaguely uncomfortable in the missionary role, preferring to let our deeds and example speak for themselves, and uncomfortable in the trenches of ideological warfare.

Several years ago, when the Democracy Project was still only a gleam in some advocates' eyes, this author wrote a scathing and quite jaundiced critique suggesting that the U.S. form of democracy was not exportable and that we were ill equipped to engage in most of the activities then envisioned by the program's sponsors.[40] That critique was overstated, underestimating both the U.S. capacity to assist democracy abroad as well as the desire of other countries for representative government. But in part because of that critique and a subsequent paper that suggested a much more modest agenda (limited aid to labor, peasant, and political groups; expanded cultural changes; nudges and pushes toward democracy but no grandiose *campaigns*),[41] the NED, as it was winnowed in the political process and subjected to the pluralist pressures that are American and the scrutiny the Congress gave it, proved to be far less a romantic exercise and far more a prudent and realistic one than at first seemed possible. It has made some mistakes (not all the result of its own miscues), and it has sometimes run to missionary excess. But by and large the NED's programs have been sensible, realistic, modest and prudent; its accomplishments have been limited, but the damage it has done is minor. And in some areas the NED has struck a spark and begun to be effective. Not much more should realistically be expected at this stage. And on that somewhat humble basis (which is not all that bad given the alternatives), the NED— at this moment—deserves our support in a close vote.

The NED is perhaps the most ambitious and far-reaching of the U.S. efforts to assist Latin American democracy. That is not to say that it is necessarily the most important, for as discussed in the next chapter, economic development may be even more important—the sine qua non for Latin American democracy to thrive, prosper, and become consolidated. But the NED is where we have largely placed our democracy marbles for now and where our manifest efforts have been concentrated. In concert with a strong human rights and other programs there are important things the United States can do to assist Latin American democracy—and further its own interests at the same time. The experience of the NED, however, should give us some pause as to what we can hope for and expect in our efforts to promote democracy. We can in some instances contribute to furthering human rights, we can assist some democratic processes, and it may be that by now we have arrived at a consensus—in contrast to attitudes in the 1970s—that both human rights and democracy abroad flow from a strong and prosperous United States and not a weak or impotent one. But the actual gains have so far been very modest indeed, and what we can realistically expect to accomplish in this area is still quite circumscribed. A realization of these limits is not all bad and helps temper some of the excessive zeal we often bring to such endeavors. The experience of the NED therefore should both be sobering and offer us some hope.

Notes

1. The agenda for such a study has been set forth in Howard J. Wiarda, "The Problem of Ethnocentrism in the Study of Political Development: Implications for Foreign Assistance Programs," *Society* (Summer 1986); also published in *Estudios Públicos* (August 1985).
2. President Ronald Reagan, "Address to Members of Parliament, June 8, 1982," *Weekly Compilation of Presidential Documents* 18, no. 23 (June 14, 1982): 764–70.
3. The materials in this section are derived from three sources: the documents and publications of the Democracy Project, interviews with the major participants involved, and participant observation in the early to mid-1980s in quite a number of the meetings and forums described.
4. For some comments on these informal centers of foreign policymaking see I. M. Destler, Leslie H. Gelb, and Anthony Lake, *Our Own Worst Enemy: The Unmaking of American Foreign Policy* (New York: Simon and Schuster, 1984).
5. See especially Irving Louis Horowitz, *The Rise and Fall of Project Camelot: Studies in the Relationship between Social Science and Practical Politics*, rev. ed. (Cambridge, Mass.: MIT Press, 1974).
6. For the background on AIFLD's activities see Sidney Lens, "American Labor Abroad: Lovestone Diplomacy," *The Nation,* July 5, 1965; Howard J. Wiarda, "The Development of the Labor Movement in the Dominican Republic," *Inter-American Economic Affairs* 20 (Summer 1966): 41–64; and Ronald Radosh, *American Labor and U.S. Foreign Policy* (New York: Random House, 1969).
7. My disagreements with this orientation are set forth in Howard J. Wiarda,

Ethnocentrism in American Foreign Policy: Can We Understand the Third World? (Washington, D.C.: American Enterprise Institute, 1985); see also James Gardner, *Legal Imperialism: American Lawyers and Foreign Aid in Latin America* (Madison: University of Wisconsin Press, 1980).

8. Based on interviews with a number of these officials and on their statements in forums organized on a not-for-attribution basis.

9. See the discussion in Kevin Middlebrook and Carlos Rico, eds., *The United States and Latin America in the 1980s* (Pittsburgh: University of Pittsburgh Press, 1986), esp. pt. 3.

10. The best source on the early history is Christopher Madison, "Selling Democracy," *National Journal*, June 28, 1986, pp. 1603–8.

11. "Conference on Free Elections," Department of State and the American Enterprise Institute (Washington, D.C.: November 4–6, 1982), Conference Papers.

12. Robert Goldwin and Arthur Kaufman, eds., *On Constitutionalism by Constitution-Writers* (Washington, D.C.: American Enterprise Institute and University Press of America, 1988).

13. For the major statements see National Endowment for Democracy, *Strengthening Democracy Abroad: The Role of the National Endowment for Democracy—Statement of Principles and Objectives* (Washington, D.C.: Mimeo, December 1984); George Shultz, "Project Democracy," Statement before the Subcommittee on International Operations of the House Foreign Affairs Committee (Washington, D.C.: Department of State, Bureau of Public Affairs, February 23, 1983); *National Endowment for Democracy* (Washington, D.C.: NED, July 1985); "National Endowment for Democracy," The National Endowment for Democracy Act (Washington, D.C.: Acts of the Congress, 1983), pp. 52–60.

14. *Strengthening Democracy Abroad*, p. 3.

15. Reagan, "Address to Members of Parliament," p. 769.

16. Ibid., p. 768. The reference to "cultural imperialism" was a response to the comments of early critics of the program. See Howard J. Wiarda, "Can Democracy Be Exported? The Quest for Democracy in United States Latin American Policy," in Middlebrook and Rico, eds., *The United States and Latin America;* presented earlier in draft form at the Woodrow Wilson International Center for Scholars and at the Department of State.

17. The analysis here is based on materials prepared and distributed by the National Endowment for Democracy.

18. As set forth in the document "Strengthening Democracy Abroad: The Role of the National Endowment for Democracy—Statement of Principles and Objectives."

19. Ibid.

20. See Larry Diamond, Juan Linz, and Seymour Martin Lipset, eds., *Democracy in Developing Countries,* 4 vols. (Boulder, Colo.: Lynne Rienner Publishers, 1988–89).

21. "Strengthening Democracy Abroad."

22. The analysis here follows that of Madison, "Selling Democracy."

23. Quoted in Madison, "Selling Democracy," p. 1606.

24. Quoted in *Ibid.*

25. Many U.S. embassy officials abroad had worries about the NED interfering with their normal state-to-state relations, had doubts about the feasibility of the United States exporting democracy, and were concerned by both the ideological and the programmatic thrusts of the NED.

26. Karl W. Deutsch and William J. Foltz, eds., *Nation-Building* (New York: Atherton Press, 1963).

27. See Luis Mercier Vega, *Roads to Power in Latin America* (New York: Praeger, 1969), chap. 3.

28. If one examines the classic Princeton University Press series on political development, one finds that all subjects—bureaucracy, political parties, communications, and so forth—are treated, except the role of business in development. The same is true for virtually all the literature on development: there is no or little mention of business, private investment, or the role of the private sector.

29. Quoted in Madison, "Selling Democracy," p. 1608.

30. This conclusion emerges from a research project being carried out at the American Enterprise Institute entitled "The State and Economic Development in Latin America."

31. George C. Lodge, *Spearheads of Democracy: Labor in Developing Countries* (New York: Harper and Row, 1962); and Sidney Suffrin, *Unions in Emerging Nations* (Syracuse, N.Y.: Syracuse University Press, 1964).

32. Bruce H. Millin, *The Political Role of Labor in Developing Countries* (Washington, D.C.: Brookings Institution, 1963); also James Payne, *Labor and Politics in Peru* (New Haven: Yale University Press, 1965).

33. Grant McConnell, *Private Power and American Democracy* (New York: Vintage, 1966).

34. The analysis here is based on the annual reports prepared by the National Endowment for Democracy, as well as those of its core institutes.

35. National Republican Institute for International Affairs, "Brief Introduction to the National Republican Institute for International Affairs" (Mimeo, undated); and National Republican Institute for International Affairs, "Summary of Programs for Fiscal Year 1986" (Mimeo, June 11, 1986).

36. Quoted in David Shipler, "Missionaries for Democracy: U.S. Aid for Global Pluralism," *New York Times,* June 1, 1986, pp. 1ff.

37. Quoted in Madison, "Selling Democracy," p. 1607.

38. Orrin Hatch, "Strategy to Help Democracy Thrive," *Washington Times,* February 28, 1985, p. 1D.

39. These materials were incorporated in the author's detailed study of the Dominican Republic entitled *Dictatorship, Development, and Disintegration* (Ann Arbor, Mich.: Monograph Senes, Xerox University Microfilms for the Committee on Latin American Studies of The University of Massachusetts, 1975). My conclusion, then as now, was that it was appropriate and useful for the United States to sponsor such activities, but that the CIA's funding of them was wrong and self-defeating.

40. Wiarda, "Can Democracy Be Exported?"

41. Howard J. Wiarda, "Project Democracy in Latin America: Reservations and Suggestions," Presented at a U.S. Information Agency Conference on Project Democracy, Washington, D.C., June 1983.

7

Economic Crisis and Democracy

Since 1979, Latin America has been going through its worst economic crisis since the world depression of the 1930s. In some countries the current depression is far severer than the one that followed the "great crash." In all the countries of the area gross national product (GNP) dropped, per capita income fell, and living standards plummeted.[1] Some countries' economies fell back to mid-1970s levels, others (the worst hit) dropped to the production levels of the 1960s. Not only have the national economies of the area faltered, but the economic downturn has had a devastating effect on the lives of the Latin American peoples. In many areas nutrition is down, and general health and living standards have gone into a tailspin. The result has been food riots, strikes, bitterness, a widespread sense of loss and frustration, and dashed expectations.

Moreover, the economic crisis has, or threatens to have, a profoundly negative effect on Latin America's new democracies. Democratic legitimacy is already weak in Latin America, and the current economic crisis may undermine it even further. Democratic institutions are similarly frail, and in the present very difficult economic circumstances they may be blamed for the ills which Latin America is suffering. In a context of a stagnant or shrinking economic pie, there are simply fewer pieces to go around, and certainly not enough to satisfy the clamoring new groups and social forces. It is not just a zero-sum game in which for every gain someone else must lose; rather in many countries it is a negative-sum game in which all lose except for the few who are fortunate and well connected.

169

Unfortunately the current crisis is so severe that it threatens to bring down perhaps the finest group of democratic presidents that Latin America has had in years—maybe ever. The severity of the crisis, and especially its effect on democratic institutions, is what makes the downward economic spiral of Latin America in recent years of both immediate and long-term relevance to this study of democracy. As one of the Latin American presidents told the author, "This debt problem may ruin us, both economically and politically."

Economics and Politics in Latin America

In the United States the stability of the political system is taken for granted. Our cities may be in flames, the protesters may be out in the streets, the economy may be on a downward course, and a president may be obliged to resign. But no one would seriously consider that any of these events would cause the U.S. political system to collapse. The U.S. system has been so stable for two hundred years that it is inconceivable that any such event would cause it to collapse, disintegrate, or be overthrown by coup or revolution. Indeed, the very stability of the U.S. political system, and the separation of economic or political performance from the overall stability of the democratic system, makes it extremely difficult for Americans to understand that in other countries the dismal performance of a particular government may result in the overthrow not just of that government but of democracy itself.

That, unfortunately, remains the situation in Latin America. Not only are democratic institutions still quite weak, but the very legitimacy of democracy as a system is also precarious. Not only can a particular regime be overthrown with relatively little provocation, but democratic legitimacy remains so inchoate, so superficial, so incomplete and unconsolidated that the entire system of democracy may be swept away. That is what makes the present economic crisis in Latin America so dangerous, for it has the potential to undermine not only quite a number of existing democratic governments of the area but also the whole system of democratic rule.

The precedents for such a gloomy prognosis are many. Historian Warren Dean has traced the incidence of Latin American *golpes* (coups d'état) and found that over the past 160-plus years they have been intimately associated with downward economic cycles.[2] Whenever there has been a recession or depression in Latin America, the political systems of the area have dissolved into chaos as well, not just particular regimes but whole *systems* of rule. The worst collapse heretofore occurred in the Great Depression of the 1930s, which was a worldwide phenomenon and not just limited to the United States. Within the first four years following the 1929 crash, as the depression deepened, there were no less than fifteen revolutions in the twenty Latin American countries.[3] As the bottom fell out of the sugar industry, the coffee industry, the tin industry, and the banana industry (at that time among the major Latin American exports), the bottom soon dropped out of the political systems of these countries as well. This was a crisis not just of particular regimes (although it was that too) but of a whole system of increasingly liberal and democratic rule. To that point, let us say from the 1880s to 1929, most of Latin America had been governed under a regime that was much more liberal, open, and pluralist than anything that had gone before. The suffrage had been extended, slavery had been abolished, the middle class was playing an increasing role politically, and the continent seemed poised on the threshold of a new era of democratic stability.[4] The world depression of the early 1930s not only ended that hopeful democratic interlude but also brought into power a large number of authoritarian regimes whose leitmotiv was corporatism as a system, not democracy. Not only did these regimes overthrow and destroy the emerging democracy of the region, but they also ushered in a period of authoritarianism and quasi-fascism that carried through World War II and beyond.

The connection between poor economic performance and system instability has been continuous; in the 1960s and 1970s, when the region was also faced with social and economic crisis, the same types of corporatist-authoritarian regimes that had governed in Latin America in the 1930s came back into power. Now Latin America is gravitating away from these kinds of corporatist-authoritarian regimes, but once more there is a severe economic crisis that threatens to destroy all the democratic gains made—and there is again the danger of return to authoritarianism. If U.S. policymakers want to develop policies to prevent that kind of systemic change from taking place, they need to understand the relationship of economics to politics in Latin America.

We have spoken here for purposes of emphasis of a *system* of Latin American politics. Many observers, seeing the instability long characteristic of Latin America, doubt that such a system exists. Instability, they believe, is the hallmark of a polity that lacks system. The best scholarship on Latin America, however, argues exactly the opposite. Coups, revolutions, and instability, when they are so regular, recurrent, almost "normal" as they are in Latin America, are a part of the system, not apart from it. They can be counted, quantified, and explained in systematic terms.[5] The problem, therefore, is not that Latin American politics are unsystematic; rather it is that it is a system of politics that is different from our own and that we only dimly (if at all) comprehend.

As a matter of fact, as Kalman H. Silvert once explained,[6] coups and revolutions are among the most interesting of political phenomena to be analyzed and explained systematically. When they are as frequent and as recurring as they have been in Latin America, then it is time to take such phenomena seriously, as regular and expected parts of the political process. Of course, these are not the only aspects of the Latin American political process. But they are parts of it; moreover, they show the distinctiveness of the Latin American political process and system.[7]

Space limits here rule out a detailed discussion of all the facets of the Latin American political process and system.[8] Suffice it to say that in Latin America the process is somewhat more informal, based more on family, clan, and personalistic ties than it is in the United States. The legitimacy of a government in power in Latin America is generally weaker than that of a government in the United States; at the same time, in Latin America there may be several legitimate routes to power, or routes that are capable of acquiring legitimacy. These include not just elections but a heroic guerrilla struggle, a skillfully executed general strike, or a coup d'état carried out with flair and finesse. In several of these processes violence may be purposely mobilized and employed as an instrument of policy—sometimes far more so than would be deemed appropriate or permitted in the United States. The political process may work not necessarily or always through the regular succession of democratically elected governments; rather there may be alternation between democratic and authoritarian kinds, thus reflecting the two realities, the two pillars, that our earlier analysis of Latin American history showed to be continuously present and to coexist in uneasy relationship there.

In a path-breaking work published some twenty-five years ago, Charles W. Anderson not only described the processes and institutions of Latin American politics but also showed how these systems responded to social change.[9] The process Anderson analyzed demonstrated considerable flexibility and responsiveness, in contrast to our usual stereotypes of Latin America as a region devoid of or conspiring to hold back change. Two conditions were necessary for a new and aspiring social or political group to be admitted to the system: it had to demonstrate its "power capability," that it was numerous and strong enough to damage or destabilize the system if the group continued to be excluded from it; and it had to agree to abide by the prevailing rules of the political game—that is, it would not attempt to monopolize all goods and power for itself but would allow the more traditional "power contenders" to continue to have their share. In this way the newer groups were accommodated in a kind of continuous fusion-absorption process, while older groups were seldom totally discarded as in the Marxist-Leninist revolutionary scenario. By such means Latin America managed to incorporate the rising business elites early in the twentieth century, the rising middle class from 1910 on, and at least some segments of the trade unions beginning in the 1920s. It was a system that both maintained continuity and provided for gradual change. And for a considerable period the system worked not altogether intolerably or undemocratically.

But the system's continuing to function was predicated upon an ever-expanding economic pie. So long as the economic pie was expanding, there were always new pieces to hand out to the clamoring new groups without the old ones having to be deprived. But when the economic pie stopped growing or actually contracted, as it did in the 1930s and during the crisis of import substitution in the 1960s,[10] politics turned increasingly into a zero-sum or, worse, a negative-sum game. In the zero-sum game, for every gain, someone else would have to lose; in the negative-sum one everyone (or most everyone) would have to lose. It proved impossible under these conditions to continue the system of accommodative or, by Latin America's lights, "democratic" politics. In country after country democracy gave way to authoritarianism. As the economic system broke down, the political system came crashing down; a more or less flexible, more or less inclusive, increasingly pluralistic and democratic politics was replaced by a new system of authoritarian-corporative control from the top.

These same conditions of economic crisis and with them the possibilities for another round of political unraveling face Latin America today. Democracy there cannot be taken for granted. The severe depression that has afflicted Latin America during the 1980s has the potential to reverse and destroy the impressive democratic openings and transitions that have occurred there recently, not only to undermine a number of elected governments currently in power, but also to destroy a whole system of flexible, responsive, accommodative, middle-of-the-road politics that both we and the Latin Americans can agree in calling increasingly pluralistic, representative, and democratic. It is incumbent on the United States, from its own foreign policy point of view, to provide the economic assistance to preserve democratic regimes throughout the region. That is a policy that will serve Latin America's interests as well as our own.

Origins of the Current Economic Crisis

Latin America's current economic malaise lies at the root of its spiraling social and political troubles. The causes of this malaise are complex, deep rooted, and long-term,[11] stemming from national and international forces over which Latin America has little control. The economic crisis has been exacerbated by the ongoing debt crisis, which has produced new and ever more serious problems.

Among the long-term problems is the continued dependence in many countries on a single major crop for export earnings. It matters little whether the crop is sugar (Cuba, the Dominican Republic), bananas (Ecuador), coffee (Colombia), tin (Bolivia), or copper (Chile). When a country is a one-crop economy and 40, 50, or 60 percent of its export earnings come from the sale of that primary product, all it takes is a drop of a few cents per pound in the world market price for that product for the bottom to drop out of the national economy. Strenuous efforts at diversification are being made in all these countries, but it takes a long time to change an entire economy—and the particular form of society that goes with it—especially when the economy has been based on the export of a single product for a hundred years or more.

Related to this problem is the issue of the worldwide terms of trade and the price Latin America receives from the sale of its primary products. Over the long term the price that Latin America receives for its exports has not kept pace with the costs it must incur for imports, chiefly manufactured goods. Prices for the latter have multiplied, while prices for the former have gone up only gradually, or in some cases have actually decreased. For over a half century now the terms of trade, while going through ups and downs, have seldom been favorable to Latin America. There is some reason to think that in the present era of presumably scarcer resources, Latin America may again do well as an exporter of primary goods.[12] But so far that turnabout has not occurred.

Then there are changing consumer habits. The United States (and other importers) is consuming less coffee and less sugar on a per capita basis than in the past. We drink "lite" beer instead of sugared beer, diet cola rather than the real thing, saccharin in our coffee instead of sugar, and, for fear of cancer and other maladies, fewer cups of coffee. All of this has undoubtedly been of great benefit to our shapes and sizes, but it has been disastrous for the countries—whether capitalist or socialist, it makes no difference—that export these products.

Technology is also playing a major role. Around the time of World War I a German scientist devised a method to produce nitrate in a laboratory, thereby devastating the Chilean nitrate mining industry, historically the backbone of the economy. Brazil's rubber industry was similarly devastated by the development of synthetic rubber in the 1930s and 1940s. There are now rumored to be ways to produce aluminum by means other than mining, which would be a blow to the critical bauxite industry of Jamaica and Guyana. And more recently it has been announced that it is possible to manufacture so-called left-handed sugar molecules that contain no calories.[13] Other technological breakthroughs may prove equally ruinous to Latin America's primary products exports.

Changing sources of production have similarly hurt Latin America. The world's largest sugar producer is now the Soviet Union; the last thing the U.S.S.R. really needs is to import more Cuban sugar, at subsidized prices. We (and the Soviets) continue to import these unneeded products as a way of keeping the economic (and thereby the political) systems of our respective clients afloat, but at some point the subsidies will have to end, leaving these countries on their own. Meanwhile, U.S. domestic sugar production has nullified our need to import sugar from the Caribbean.

In many product areas, furthermore, the exports of other Third World countries—Indonesia, the Philippines—are competing vigorously with Latin American exports. In many cases these other countries are able to undersell the Latin American ones because, as middle-level developing countries, the Latin American countries face greater costs—particularly labor costs—than do these other, even less developed ones.

To help cope with these potentially devastating production problems, Latin America turned to industrialization. The strategy was called "import substitution"—the substitution of costly imported goods with those made at home. The strategy required the establishment of many state-run companies, which in the long term proved enormously costly and inefficient, as well as high tariff barriers to protect the fledgling native industries from more efficient foreign competition. Import substitution worked for a time and helped get industrialization going in Latin America on a large scale. But during the 1960s the import substitution strategy experienced a crisis that once again contributed to the fall of a number of democratic governments that had come to power during that period.[14]

Declining foreign aid has been a further factor in Latin America's economic troubles. Since the de facto end of the Alliance for Progress in the late 1960s, Latin America has not consistently received the kind of assistance that it needs. In some countries (for example, the Dominican Republic) foreign aid was essential to help keep the economy afloat, and the results of declining assistance hurt badly. Other countries such as

Brazil and Venezuela had graduated to the level of newly industrialized countries (NICs) and thereby were no longer eligible for aid; but the cutoffs still hurt and were particularly devastating for the lower classes.

The twin oil shocks of 1973 and 1979 added further blows. Prices for petroleum and petroleum products, which most of the Latin American countries must import, doubled, doubled, and then doubled again. Oil is not elastic (unlike, say, bananas), and the Latin American countries were forced to pay the new high prices. The result in country after country was that whereas before it took three, four, or five bags of sugar or coffee to buy one barrel of oil, it now costs fifteen or twenty bags for the same barrel. One need not be a professional economist to understand that such price changes wreaked havoc on the Latin American economies.

Even the oil-exporting countries of Latin America—Ecuador, Mexico, Peru, Venezuela—did not fare well. They failed to reap the initial bonanza expected from the hike in oil prices and at the same time overspent and overborrowed in anticipation of becoming better off. When the world market price of oil dipped again, they were forced into cutbacks even more drastic than those of the oil-importing countries. Because of mismanagement, overconfidence, and poor planning, having oil proved to be no more advantageous for such countries than not having it.

In addition, war and revolution, often funded and supported from the outside, have devastated several of the economies of the area. In Nicaragua and El Salvador, the damage from revolution and protracted societal upheaval has been severe. But in addition to these countries, Guatemala, Peru, Ecuador, Colombia, and Bolivia have all been wracked during the decade of the 1980s by externally supported insurgencies. In addition to creating the general mayhem and devastation that result from conflict and war, the express purpose of the guerrilla groups has been to bring these countries to their knees by destroying their economic infrastructure. That means attacks not just on soldiers but on dams, highways, banks, bridges, power stations, buses, export storage facilities, transport, and public buildings and institutions. That is why the GNP in quite a number of these countries has dropped to 1970s or even 1960s levels.[15]

The most crushing external blow to the Latin American economies was the world depression that began in 1979 and deepened in succeeding years. Once again, the bottom dropped out of the markets for Latin America's principal exports, and thereby out of the region's economies. And whereas the United States, which during the period similarly suffered from a severe economic recession and the considerable political and social tension to which it gave rise, began to pull out of its slump by late 1983, Latin America experienced a considerably longer period of decline. It usually takes eighteen months to two years for a U.S. recovery to begin to be felt in the dependent economies in Latin America; it was not until 1985 or 1986 that some of the stronger Latin American economies like Chile or Brazil began to respond, and in many of the Latin American countries there has still been no recovery. Meanwhile, the one key factor that was probably most important in helping Brazil to recover—declining oil prices—now proved to be disastrous for those Latin American countries (Ecuador, Mexico, Peru, Venezuela) that had their own sources of oil and therefore had managed to do more or less tolerably well during the early part of the slump that more strongly affected their neighbors.[16]

These were the principal long-term and *external* factors contributing to Latin America's economic woes. It is necessary to turn to the *internal* factors to see how Latin America contributed to its own problems. Such a balanced view is necessary because in Latin America the tendency is to blame all of its troubles solely on the external forces; in the United States the inclination is to point a finger first at Latin America's own inefficiencies. To understand the Latin American crisis, both external and internal factors must be examined.

Latin America's internal economic problems are really quite easy to describe, although doing anything about them is not at all easy. The main problems are widespread corruption and graft, capital flight on a large scale, incredibly bloated and inefficient public bureaucracies, tremendously wasteful spending policies on the part of a variety of military regimes, enormously extravagant social and economic programs in many countries, inefficient and wasteful state-run corporations that stemmed from the era of import substitution, and fantastic subsidies that provide a vast array of goods and services. The Argentine generals spent hundreds of millions in a futile war to recapture the Falkland/Malvinas Islands from Great Britain, and thereby to keep themselves in power. Other Latin American regimes gambled with their foreign exchange policies in ways that proved unwise. Vast sums seeped away to foreign bank accounts or to subsidize luxurious life-styles. The 1970s was, in general in Latin America, a period of enormous, often "miracle" economic growth that was coupled with fantastic waste, corruption, and extravagance.[17]

It is fairly easy to catalog and describe these wasteful practices but almost impossible to do very much about them. Some of the areas described are amenable to change, but others are not. For example, the widespread subsidization by Latin American governments of basic food items such as rice and beans is what enabled their lower classes to keep from tipping over the always thin line separating subsistence from starvation. The subsidies for the middle class, in the form of extravagant (for any country but especially for Third World countries) social and health programs, credit subsidies, educational subsidies, attractive retirement plans, and the like, were essential to keep this important swing element loyal to the regime in power. The bloated, inefficient, and corrupt state agencies served as vast employment agencies for both the lower and middle classes. Virtually everyone was put on the public payroll so as to fulfill the obligations of clientage that all these systems of patronage politics have. Capital flight can be curtailed, but it does reflect economic realities in Latin America, and to stop it would require giving even more economic power to already heavily statist regimes.

It is easy to lament these practices and the abuses to which they all too often give rise. But the point is to show how many of them are absolutely essential to the survival of the various Latin American regimes in power that the United States is and must be committed to support. These patronage and other functions are as essential today under democratic governments in Latin America as they were earlier under military governments. Their "acts" can be cleaned up a little but not all that much. To do more would surely risk the destabilization of those regimes that U.S. interests demand that we bolster. That is why the demagogic insistence by some U.S. politicians that Latin America radically streamline its public bureaucracies, sell its public sector corporations back to the private sector, eliminate patronage and subsidies, and curtail sinecures and graft is just that: demagogy. Some of these things will change in Latin America and must change. But demagogic insistence on radical reform by U.S. officials clearly will not work, will prove dysfunctional, and will lead to such disruption and chaos as to harm rather than help U.S. interests.[18]

Once the economic crisis of Latin America had set in, through this combination of external and internal causes, it became steadily worse. An understanding of some of the main trends is essential to our understanding of the interrelations of economics and politics in Latin America and their effects on democracy and U.S. foreign policy. First, as the economic depression worsened, foreign investment (chiefly U.S.), fearful of the potential for instability in the region, also began to dry up. Today, with the exception of only the largest countries (Brazil, Mexico), there is practically no new investment going to Latin America, although investment is essential if the area is ever to recover. Indeed, chief executive officers (CEOs) of major U.S. corporations tell us that, with a few notable exceptions, the Latin American countries are not good investment risks and have said that they would have to be "crazy" to invest there.[19] The overwhelming majority of CEOs are assuredly not that.

Second, the U.S. and other foreign investment that was previously in

Latin America began to pull out. In the mid-1980s *not a single* U.S. Fortune 500 company had more than 10 percent of its holdings in Latin America. That stood in marked contrast to earlier eras in which such companies as Grace, United Fruit, International Petroleum, and Gulf and Western sometimes rode roughshod over local sensitivities and local governments alike. For most U.S. companies Latin America is no longer an attractive area for investment. They are fed up with wasted time, excessive paperwork, and graft, and they also have concluded that Western Europe, Japan, the Asian Pacific countries, Canada, and the United States itself are much better investment possibilities than is Latin America.

Third, Latin American capital began to flee the area on a massive scale. There has always been "prudent" investment by Latin American entrepreneurs in the United States or Switzerland, but now the flight of capital has reached staggering proportions. The capital fleeing the area considerably surpasses that entering in the form of either new loans or new investment. Moreover, the capital flight is not just from those countries that one might expect to be potentially unstable in the future but also from such countries as Brazil and Venezuela, with their extensive human and natural resources, whose businessmen had previously had immense faith in the development and potential of their own countries.

If one combines the external and the internal factors contributing to Latin America's economic crisis, with the exacerbating complications of the past several years, the crisis looks very severe indeed. And it is unlikely that the crisis will get better soon. Not only are the depressed conditions continuing in most countries in the region, but the lack of new investment means that Latin America is unlikely to pull out of its economic doldrums anytime in the near future.

The numbers do not, however, make clear the suffering that lies behind the statistics. Malnutrition and malnutrition-related diseases are endemic throughout Latin America. Unemployment may encompass, depending on the country, 20–30 percent of the work force; when combined with underemployment, the figures may go as high as 50–60 percent. Tensions are rising, families are disintegrating, and individual self-worth is increasingly being questioned. The figures available show that in Latin America alcoholism, drug use, wife beating, and church attendance—always accurate albeit unfortunate indicators of troubled times—are all on the rise. Bitterness, violence, and what social scientists call "anomic" (unorganized and scattered as distinct from organized and focused) protest movements are also all on the rise.

None of this augurs well for the future of democracy in Latin America. Some of the early literature on development posited a more or less one-to-one relationship between economic growth and the prospects for democratic stability.[20] That was clearly too rigid a formulation and it was largely discredited, but it is important not to fall into the opposite trap either of assuming that there is no relationship between democracy and development. There is. Particularly in Latin America, the data suggest, when the economy goes into a tailspin, so usually and shortly thereafter does the political regime. Once again it bears repeating that it is not just particular democratic regimes of the moment that are likely to go under—however tragic and problematic that would be both for the countries affected and for U.S. policy—but also an entire framework, model, and system of more or less moderate, more or less centrist, and more or less democratic rule.

The Debt Issue

On top of all these other, long-term downward trends in the Latin American economies has come the debt issue.[21] The debt problem is a result of both the internal and the external economic difficulties previously discussed; it is at the present time the point where these problems and controversies all come together. The debt issue may well be the debilitating force that erodes the Latin American economies and their political systems as well. In that sense the debt may be thought of as having profound implications not only for Latin America but also for U.S. efforts to bolster Latin American democracy. The debt issue and Latin America's ongoing economic crisis relate directly to all the main themes of this study.

The debt issue has the potential to be an absolute disaster for everyone: for the banks that hold the debt, for the Latin American countries that must repay it, for the international financial system that is threatened with collapse if the debt is not paid, and for the United States, which in the long run will probably have to face the possibility of bailing out everyone else: the banks, the Latin American governments, and the international financial system. That is not, understandably, a prospect that politicians and officials in Washington wish to contemplate or talk publicly about.

The sheer size of the Latin American debt is staggering. The total for all the Latin American countries is over $400 *billion,* although no one knows for sure because many Latin American state-owned enterprises have the legal autonomy to negotiate loans on their own and have not always or consistently notified their own central banks when they have done so. Brazil's debt is the largest, at $120 billion; Mexico has accumulated about $100 billion in debt; and Argentina and Venezuela among the larger countries have debts of approximately $60 billion and $40 billion, respectively. Costa Rica has a small total debt compared with these others, but if the debt is put on a per capita basis Costa Rica's is the heaviest burden of all.

Although some interest payments are being met, the unpaid interest on the debt has been adding about $40 billion *yearly* to the total. No one thinks seriously that the full principal of $400 billion will ever be paid off; the only question presently is about the interest payments. Quite a number of Latin American governments cannot pay even the interest, let alone the principal, and that is a major problem for them, the banks, and the United States. Most Latin American governments must pay 30, 40, 50 percent, or more of their export earnings just to "service," or pay interest on, the debt. That high a percentage leaves little for consumption, for investment, or for growth. It is no wonder that many countries, faced with strikes, food riots, and the possibility for violent overthrows, are now balking at, or have stopped, paying those interest charges as well as any principal. The fact that most of those governments under siege are democratic governments makes the issue of particular relevance to this study.

The causes of the great debt crisis are, in retrospect, fairly clear. First, the big international banks, mostly U.S.–based but some in Europe and Japan as well, were flush with money due to the immense influx of dollars earned by the petroleum exporting countries during the boom years of the 1970s. The banks had seemingly limitless funds to loan and were aggressive in pursuing customers, in Latin America and elsewhere, without checking too closely into their creditworthiness. Second, the Latin American countries were eager to borrow—for advanced social programs, military hardware, graft, and other purposes. Since in the 1970s their economies were doing quite well and more loan money seemed always to be available, it appeared unlikely that the bubble would burst. Third, the U.S. government saw such private lending as a substitute for public foreign aid (then being cut back) and thus as a means for the United States to continue its influence in Latin America. In addition, both the lending banks and the borrowing Latin American countries believed, or were led to believe, that the U.S. government would underwrite and ultimately guarantee the loans. (And, although it is not often publicly acknowledged, it is likely that those guarantees are still operative.) In the last analysis, the United States cannot permit the private U.S. banks, or a succession of Latin American governments (especially democratic ones), or the international financial system to "go under."

The global depression that began in 1979–80 was the precipitating factor that turned the debt "situation" into a debt "crisis." The bottom fell out of the demand for Latin America's products, markets and production dried up, and the interest rates on new loans to pay off the debt soared. Latin America could no longer pay, the banks could not collect, and the U.S. government was caught in the middle.

Before proceeding further with the analysis, it is necessary to clear away the underbrush of cant and rhetoric concerning the debt issue and state some unpleasant truths. It is necessary to do this because there are a lot of smoke screens, camouflages, and mirrors surrounding the debt issue that impede a proper understanding of its complex dimensions. With all the optimistic talk about "refinancing," "restructuring," and "renegotiating" the debt, it becomes necessary for the proverbial child to say, "But really, the emperor has no clothes on."

First, the full debt cannot and will not be paid—ever. It is so large that it is inconceivable that Latin America could ultimately pay it back. Some interest payments will continue to be paid, as a way of qualifying for still further loans, but not the principal or the bulk of the interest. That is the message contained in the recent write-downs by many U.S. banks of a sizable share of their Latin American loans and of the deal to trade Mexican debt paper for U.S. Treasury paper, at considerably discounted rates.

In this way it could be said that the major agenda item of the "South" in the so-called North-South dialogue—the massive transfer of resources from North to South—has, in a sense, already been accomplished. The debt is unpaid and unpayable; the resources (the bank loans) have already been transferred and they will not be returned. No one is quite sure what results this exchange will have or whether there will not be more requests for further "transfers," but there is no doubt that a massive and permanent shift in resources to Latin America has occurred.

Second, even though everyone knows that Latin America cannot pay them back, the Latin American countries cannot actually default on these loans. That would stigmatize the Latin American nations as "uncivilized" and "irresponsible," it would make them ineligible for new loans, it would result in the seizure of a number of their assets by the creditors, and it would subject them to a considerable range of international and financial penalties.

Third, even though the banks know these loans to be mainly uncollectible, they cannot write them off as such. That would force their management to have to account to their stockholders as well as to the Securities and Exchange Commission; it would prevent them from collecting even the meager interest that does continue to come in; and in the case of several of the big New York banks whose loan exposure in Latin America represents an especially high percentage of their outstanding loans (and may even be several times greater than their capital), it could actually mean their financial collapse.

And fourth, the U.S. government must also maintain the illusion that the debt someday will be repaid, for if the illusion is not maintained, the political consequences will be terrible. To begin, the U.S. government will have to bail out the commercial banks—not a prospect that politicians are eager to face in this populist age. Then they will have to bail out a succession of Latin American governments—again not a happy prospect for politicians but made necessary by the fact that the United States cannot for strategic reasons allow any Latin American government to go "down the tubes" and risk having it become another base and satellite of the Soviet Union. And finally, the United States would also have to pitch in to save the international financial system, which will be severely threatened if several or only just one of the big banks is forced to write off its Latin American loans as uncollectible. The political consequences of such actions would be terrible.

Hence the need for charade, for facade, for smoke screen. The debt cannot be paid, everyone knows that; and yet the myth must be maintained that it can be or else the entire house of cards will come tumbling down.

But if the debt cannot be paid, and default cannot be admitted, wherein lies the answer? The answer is that the debt can be *managed*. That is why when bank and U.S. government officials talk about solutions to the debt, they talk about its "manageability." Only rarely and as a kind of empty rhetorical flourish does anyone talk of repayment. "Managing" the debt is already a tacit admission that it cannot and will not be paid. And since repayment is viewed as unrealistic and impossible, and since the other alternatives (default on or writing off the debts) are seen as having even worse consequences, management of the debt is viewed as the only possible alternative—however fraught with danger that option is.

"Managing" the debt is therefore a code word for the "lesser evil" among the several alternative ways of dealing with the debt crisis. To the banks, managing the debt means keeping the Latin American loans on the books as potentially collectible, even those that are nonperforming. It means offering all but bankrupt countries new loans so that they can keep a trickle of interest flowing in. It means rescheduling the payments for a later time, renegotiating interest rates and the fees (rather like points in a real estate transaction) that the banks charge, and putting together new packages of assistance for the debtor countries to keep them from going under completely. And it means ignoring the bankruptcies and de facto defaults of small debtors like Bolivia and Peru for the sake of keeping alive the possibility of avoiding default in the "biggies" like Brazil and Mexico.

To the Latin American governments, "managing" the debt means going along with some requirements imposed by the International Monetary Fund (IMF), considerable belt tightening to increase efficiency and exports, and constantly renegotiating the precise terms and schedule of repayments. In this way the Latin American governments demonstrate "good faith," qualify as "creditworthy" and therefore eligible for new loans, continue to pay a small amount of interest or at least promise to do so, but *never* actually pay back any of the principal.

And for the U.S. government, the fact that the debt is being "managed" means that it can continue to treat it as a purely private matter between the banks and the Latin American governments. As long as the debt is being "managed," furthermore, the United States does not have to bail anyone out—at least not yet. Only in genuinely crisis circumstances does the U.S. government intend to step in, such as during the bailout of a bankrupt Mexico in 1982, in the Baker Plan of 1985 when the Treasury Department stepped in to encourage greater private investment in Latin America and an increase of the assistance programs to Latin America from the World Bank and other international lenders, and in the effort again to rescue Mexico in 1987. Managing the debt thus means postponing and avoiding the issue and its dire political consequences, and hoping that when the great crash comes—if it comes at all—it will be on someone else's watch, in some other administration.

Hence all the parties to the debt crisis have a strong interest in maintaining the notion that it is a "manageable" issue that need not necessarily lead to full-scale collapse. At the same time, all the parties to the crisis similarly have a strong interest in continuing the myth that the debt is payable, that the loans and interest will one day be collected, that the banks or the Latin American governments will not collapse, and that the international financial system is stable and secure. All of these assertions are of course very tenuous; they hang by very thin threads. The great hope is that no one will strip the fig leaves away.

The strategy on the part of all the participants in the debt crisis is to play for time, keep postponing the day of reckoning, and hope for the best. That is not an altogether inappropriate basis for meeting the debt crisis, albeit not a very glorious one. It rests on quite a number of assumptions that may yet prove to be unfounded. The hope is that the world economic recovery that began in the United States in 1983 and then spread somewhat dissipatedly to other areas will have a ripple effect on Latin America, enabling the region to *grow* out of the debt crisis.

But what if the "worst-case scenario" actually comes to pass: if the U.S. economy slips into another recession like that of the early 1980s, the markets for Latin America's exports dry up as a result, and the economies of the area go into a renewed tailspin? Then it is clear that not just the Latin American economies but also Latin American democracy will be in deep trouble.

Meanwhile, quite a number of the banks (although often to the displeasure of the bigger ones with a large Latin American exposure) have been converting their Latin American loans to new forms of paper, selling it at discount prices, and thus getting rid of their Latin American debt holdings while simultaneously absorbing a considerable loss—although not so great a loss as they would have to suffer if the debtor countries went bankrupt and they received *zero* cents on the dollar. In this way the banks are getting rid of their poor-performing Latin American loans as soon as possible; at the same time, the Latin American countries can reduce or retire their obligations, since some of the best customers for these discounted loans are the very Latin American governments that are in debt. Meanwhile, the banks continue to look for other formulas that will enable them to absorb some modest losses without having to inform the stockholders fully of their Latin American miscalculations, to increase their profits in other areas to compensate for and disguise these bad loans that are uncollectible, to divert attention from the debt issue until it recedes from the public consciousness and is absorbed through a "quasi-vanishing act,"[22] or even to come up with a scheme to oblige the U.S. government (and ultimately the taxpayer) to assume most of the responsibility for the Latin American debt. In short, the strategy is to wait the crisis out, meanwhile doing a series of small things that will make it less severe (or appear less severe) and hoping that the engine of a strong U.S. economy will also pull the "sidecar" economies of Latin America over the hump. Given the unattractiveness of the alternatives, this play-for-time strategy may be the best available.

If this is the strategy, how is the debt crisis then *managed?* There are a number of key components that have by now become familiar. These include ignoring the bad news that comes from Bolivia, Peru, and other small countries in de facto default, postponing the due dates of payments from the larger debtors, reducing bank charges, renegotiating interest rates, rolling over the debt, and always talking optimistically. At the same time, the banks have insisted that the Latin American debtors conform to a strict austerity program imposed by the IMF, increase their exports, and at least go through the motions (and occasionally more than that) of continuing to honor their debt obligations. The tactics may include "refinancing" of the loans of a debtor unable to pay, pledging assets that may or may not be available, insisting on a house-cleaning (reducing the size of the public service, eliminating corruption, selling state-owned enterprises back into private hands) by the debtors, and talking tough about austerity and going through the motions when everyone knows little will be done. Under this strategy the due dates for payments can be put off indefinitely, new loans can continue to be made available, and very little of a dramatic sort will happen. The banks need never collect and the debtors need never pay. That is called "managing" the debt.

The Latin American governments have also become skillful players in "managing" the debt. Most Latin American governments have not been attracted to the idea set forth by Fidel Castro that the debt is a form of international imperialism and therefore ought to be entirely repudiated. Nor have they taken up the banner of Peru's Alan García, who dramatically announced that his country would pay no more than 10 percent of its export earnings to service the debt, which was actually more than Peru was then paying. While not following the lead of Castro and García, however, most Latin American presidents have seen the usefulness of having these more radical leaders stake out a lead position on the debt problem and serve as "point men," which makes their own positions look positively benign and moderate by comparison. From the perspectives of these more moderate leaders there is a great deal to be gained and not all that much to be lost from following the present course.

After all, these leaders are not being forced actually to pay back their countries' debts. They understand as well as we do that the full debt cannot be paid back—ever. On the other hand, they do not want to repudiate their debts either because that would result in their countries' being labeled as outcasts or pariah states, would call forth severe economic sanctions, and would make them ineligible for new loans for a long time to come. That is why prudent Latin American leaders (as distinct from the demagogues and firebrands) have concluded, like the banks, that it is better to "manage" these accounts than to repudiate them. In that way very little other than some modest interest ever has to be paid back; meanwhile, new loans continue to materialize.

The fly in this ointment is of course the IMF sanctions that force these governments to impose austerity and initiate changes in return for new loans. Typically the austerity measures involve a freeze on wages, sharp restrictions on imports, freezes on government hiring, cutbacks in social programs, and belt tightening principally by the poor and the middle class. The implementation of such unpopular measures especially in a democratic context involves a tricky juggling act whose outcome is uncertain; it also makes the juggling act more precarious, since it is performed on a high wire without much in the way of political safety nets and from which the juggler can easily fall. That is, the prudent Latin American president must walk the tightrope of imposing an austerity that will save and reform his economy in long-range terms, while at the same time not allowing the austerity to be enforced so severely that it costs him his job—and maybe results in the overthrow of democracy as well.

There is no doubt that in some countries presently ruled democratically—the Dominican Republic, Venezuela, Brazil, others—austerity has resulted in severe hardship. It is usually the poorest and least well organized peoples in these countries who bear austerity's hardest burdens—precisely because they are unorganized and unable to resist politically. There have been strikes, food riots, seizures of private lands, and threats of a general shutdown. Opposition politicians have seized on the widespread discontent to rally public opinion, to make demagogic appeals concerning the debt and other issues, and to threaten the stability of the government itself. These are serious disputes over serious issues, and they have put immense pressures on existing governments not to go along with any IMF- (read, U.S.–) imposed austerity. Such pressures may yet force a number of Latin American governments to reject "management" of the debt as outlined here in favor of outright repudiation.

On the other hand, *not a single* Latin American government has yet succumbed to such pressures, nor has a single one (even Cuba) repudiated its debts. Nor have any of the new democracies in the region (so far) been overthrown. In part that stems from the fact that the IMF has been more prudent and sensible than most of its numerous critics would admit, and has learned how far it can push, when it should relax the austerity measures, when to back off.[23] But an even more important factor has been that the Latin American governments themselves have been very clever in imposing—and then backing away from—the austerity. They have learned that austerity can be "managed" just like the debt itself.

The "management" of austerity for those clever and skilled enough to bring it off is handled by the same means as the management of the debt itself—by stealth, smoke screen, and mirrors. For example, in 1985 during one of its periodic budget crises, Mexico "riffed," or fired, fifty thousand public employees as a means to satisfy the creditor banks, the IMF, and the U.S. government. But within a week (after no one was looking) thirty thousand were rehired, and by the end of the year nearly the entire fifty thousand (plus some new employees) were back on the public payroll. The "paring" was done for public, especially external, consumption; but in terms of the reduction in the number of public employees not much changed.

Similarly with the issue of privatization of state-owned enterprises for the sake of introducing greater efficiency and less costs in the governmental bureaucracy. A few of the state-run companies have actually been returned to private hands; but others have simply been sold to other state companies, or have been put in the hands of joint public-private concerns in which very little really changed. For example, six state-owned concerns in Mexico were reorganized into one, and then laudatory public statements put forth showing a reduction by five in the total number of parastatals. Other parastatals in Mexico have been sold to the trade unions that are themselves a part of the state system.

In general it may be said that, once acquired, the Latin American states have been extremely reluctant to divest themselves of the vast economic controls that such a large state sector (roughly 40–70 percent of GNP in most countries) makes available to them. In Argentina, moreover, President Alfonsín discovered that not only was austerity necessary but that it could be turned at least temporarily to political advantage. In Brazil as well as other countries, austerity was imposed, then relaxed long enough for the government to win an election, then imposed again after the election. The Latin American governments, in short, learned that austerity was not always as painful as it seemed, that the banks would not mind too much if they postponed or relaxed the austerity as long as they avoided outright default, and even that austerity could be turned to political advantage. Austerity's bark was far worse than its bite, at least in quite a number of countries of the area.[24]

This strategy of "managing" the debt, which is played by all the parties concerned—the U.S. government, the commercial banks, and the Latin American countries—and which is predicated on the notion that, while the debt cannot be repaid, outright repudiation must be avoided, may prove to be too clever by half. It is a dangerous and a precarious policy, and it hangs by very thin threads. It is based on the assumption of the continued expansion of the economies of the United States and the Organization for Economic Cooperation and Development (OECD), which will in turn enable the Latin American economies to *grow* out of their present doldrums. But what if growth in the United States slows or is lackadaisical, or if OECD growth is only tepid? What if the world economy plunges into another depression as it did in the early 1980s, or continues flat? What if oil prices again fluctuate wildly? What if Argentina or Mexico or Brazil or all the big debtors at once default, or postpone payments indefinitely, or decide not to pay at all? What if populist dema-gogues take power from the present moderate democrats, or force the latter into more extreme positions? What if the stockholders of the com-mercial banks demand an honest accounting of the collectibility of these huge unpaid debts? And what if the U.S. taxpayers, and through them elected officials, sense that, as in the domestic savings and loan crisis, they will be left holding the bag, that they will ultimately—through inflation, higher taxes, higher interest rates, lower stock dividends, tax write-offs for the banks, or a combination of these—be forced to bail out both the banks and the Latin American governments? These and other uncertainties make the debt issue a very precarious one indeed.

So far, therefore, the debt crisis has been "managed," but it has by no means been resolved. The banks, the U.S. government, and the Latin American governments have all learned a great deal about how to live with the crisis, but they have not been able to make it go away. The days of reckoning have been repeatedly postponed, but putting off a solution has meant avoiding the root causes that precipitated the debt crisis in the first place. There is an emerging consensus that since the blame for the crisis must be shared by several parties, so too must the burden; but there is as yet no agreement on a formula for doing so that satisfies all the parties affected.

Meanwhile, the successful management of the crisis continues to de-pend on a host of factors largely outside the control of the main actors: the performance of the world economy, trade patterns, consumer preferences, political explosions, protectionist sentiment, as well as droughts and earth-quakes. It depends on people not talking about it very much, and their not stripping away the fig leaves. Any one of a dozen or more factors could cause this entire and very precarious house of cards to tumble. The whole edifice of debt "management" is based on dissembling and illusion which cannot be sustained indefinitely.

The debt and the interest charges, meantime, continue to pile up. The crisis may be getting worse rather than better. The debt adds a further and very grave dimension to Latin America's already serious and perhaps mortal economic ills. Particularly devastating have been the effects of the debt and the accompanying austerity programs on the region's poor. Although the several parties to the debt issue have been quite adept at managing it so far, the system and process they have devised to do so are haphazard and ad hoc; it cannot be expected that the current stratagems will last forever. There will likely have to be movement toward a general resolution of the crisis, or else we will soon have genuine upheaval, breakdown, and disintegration on our hands, not just of the Latin American economies but also—and that is why it is of particular interest to this study—of Latin America's emerging but still weakly consolidated democratic political systems as well.

Responding to the Crisis: Future Scenarios

The 1980s, as former Mexican finance minister Jesús Silva Herzog remarked, is likely to be viewed in the longer run of Latin American history as the "lost decade."[25] The economies of most of the area have been at a standstill and in some countries, such as El Salvador, have severely contracted. Despite the skills of Latin America's leaders in managing the tricky shoals of the debt issue, the burden of the debt has been heavy. Debt interest and the debt repayments have produced some disastrous social consequences. In the United States the debt has generally been seen purely as an economic issue—"they owe us"; but increasingly in the debtor nations it is seen as a political issue that must be decided on political grounds. That is, a resolution of the debt issue must be the shared responsibility of all the parties. Increasingly it seems apparent that austerity and democracy cannot survive long in tandem. The debt crisis and its accompanying austerity, particularly if continued for a long time, are liable to undermine the democratic political systems that are now emerging in the area and in whose continuation as democracies the United States—to say nothing of Latin America—has a very powerful interest.

Quite a number of the trends analyzed here do not augur well for the future of the region. There is little new investment in Latin America, established companies are pulling out of the area, capital flight is reaching epidemic proportions, payments on the debt are extracting a heavy toll, and it is unlikely that we will soon see any large new foreign assistance programs. Still more debt being piled up to solve the debt problem is not a solution to the debt problem. On the other hand, a handful of Latin American countries are still doing fairly well even in the midst of this severe crisis, and others may follow suit. Chile, Brazil, and Mexico continue to attract new investments, including some very large ones, and all three are now exporters of manufactured goods as well as of primary products. In 1987 Mexico exported more manufactures than oil. The small countries have not done so well, but some of them not altogether badly either.[26] Furthermore, the vast resources of Latin America, the expanding market for manufactured goods, the growing middle class and hence the larger consumer market, the huge and comparatively inexpensive labor force, and the thrust for change and reform throughout the area all but guarantee that over the longer term Latin America will continue to attract capital and investment. The problem, therefore, would seem to lie more in the near- and medium-term time frames—how to recover from the current depression and how to get out from under the debilitating debt burden.

Renewed and continued economic growth is the only real answer to the problem. But the sheer magnitude and the interest burden of the debt may now be viewed as the prime factors impeding growth. To achieve growth Latin America must increase its exports; at the same time, Latin America must reduce its own protectionist barriers to encourage the investment that will stimulate growth. The U.S. government must also not erect further protectionist barriers to keep out Latin American products. The United States, the banks, and Latin America must find a means to break out of this vicious circle of debt, more debt, and continued retarded growth if the region is to begin to recover. The solutions seem clear and obvious on paper: we know what *must happen,* but to make what must happen *actually happen* is an entirely different matter.[27]

One can envision three major options for dealing with the problem. The first is an essentially laissez-faire or hands-off approach: to let the crisis fester until it either resolves itself or produces explosion. The second is ad hocism and muddling through, dealing with the crisis piecemeal and only when it actually does threaten to explode. The third option is a formula that provides a general, all-encompassing resolution of the problem. Of course, various combinations of these three are also possible.

There is a great deal to be said for the early Reagan administration policy of dealing with the crisis, which represents a combination of options one and two. The U.S. government has largely maintained a cautious, hands-off policy with regard to the debt, continuing to insist (at least publicly) that it must be paid, that it is an economic and not a political issue, and that the debtors should follow the guidance of the IMF in order to meet their debt obligations. Only in genuine crisis situations has the U.S. government officially stepped in. Under this policy little of the debt has been paid back; but then default has not occurred either. For their part U.S. officials are very fearful that a stronger U.S. government intervention would let the Latin American countries off the hook of having to pay their debt obligations or of having to reform their inefficient economies, would set a terribly bad precedent for other debtors in future years, might set off a new round of inflation in the United States itself, and would produce deleterious economic consequences that the economic planners did not anticipate.

This policy has not solved Latin America's severe economic problems, nor has it provided any stimulus to growth. Some would say that just the opposite result has been achieved. On the other hand, 1985 and 1986 were fairly good years, and the economies of several Latin American countries improved without a general U.S. intervention.[28] U.S. officials of course argue that that proves the success of their formula. The fact that outright repudiation has not occurred, that most of the Latin American countries are still trying to meet their obligations, that the IMF-imposed austerity is effecting reforms without that toppling any democratic governments, and that the debts have not yet been written off as "uncollect-ible" all point, in the view of the U.S. officials responsible, to the wisdom of continuing—with some adjustments—the present course.

Nor have the Latin American countries managed the crisis altogether badly. Argentina, Brazil, Costa Rica, and Mexico have all become very adept at navigating these treacherous financial shoals. They have learned to manage, in a political sense, not only the international dimensions of the debt but also the administration of austerity, in ways that make them appear to be following the strictures of the IMF (and even actually to do so on an on-again, off-again basis) while not allowing the austerity to become so severe that they lose their domestic political support. It is a risky business, but the Latin American players in this game have their own skills, tricks, and pressure points. They know that in the last analysis the United States for strategic reasons will not allow them to go down the drain, especially Mexico, which shares a two-thousand-mile border with the United States and which Mexican politicians know full well is the last country even the most hard-line privatization and IMF defenders in the United States wish to see destabilized.

The banks too have shown remarkable flexibility. They have done virtually anything to avoid having to write the Latin American debt off as uncollectible. They have forgone payments on the principal, forgone interest payments, lowered the interest charged, forgone fees, and de facto forgiven the loans of some small debtors (Bolivia, Ecuador, Peru) for the sake of clinging to the fiction that they will eventually collect from the larger debtors (Argentina, Brazil, Mexico, Venezuela). Many banks have also converted their debt holdings into equity in the resources of the countries where they hold loans, or have converted their debt holdings into paper and sold it on the open market for whatever they can get: thirty or forty cents on the dollar, sometimes less. That represents a considerable loss for these banks, but it is not so great a loss as would be involved in holding these unpaid debts indefinitely and eventually collecting nothing.[29]

Surprisingly, there are buyers for this Latin American debt paper. The buyers include the subsidiaries of major U.S. companies that may need a sudden influx of local capital to finance a major expansion with pesos bought rather cheaply; speculators who buy one day, sell the next, and can make a profit even in the Latin American debt game; the debtor countries themselves, who see this as a way of retiring part of their foreign debt at discount prices; and private individuals, often nationals of the country affected, who have a political interest in having their own governments in debt to them. Officials of a number of the commercial banks say that, if they have five years' time, they will succeed in selling off virtually their entire Latin American debt portfolio. But these steps do not endear them to some of the big New York banks, a number of whose outstanding Latin American loans are far in excess of their capital and who cannot afford to take thirty to forty cents to the dollar for their Latin American debt holdings or they will be in deep trouble.

No magic solutions exist for the Latin American debt crisis; there are no panaceas. Each country of the area exists under different social, economic, and political conditions, and each will have to devise its own way out of the crisis. The most successful strategies, those used by Brazil and Mexico (who also have, both because of the size of their assets and the size of their debt, the greatest leverage), have employed very pragmatic methods and a combination or package of responses. These include cutbacks in the public service, efforts to increase exports, decreased imports, sales of state-owned firms, and various austerity measures. But while the austerity has sometimes been severe in some countries, the IMF has also been less than draconian in its implementation and the countries themselves have learned to administer austerity in small doses. It has been imposed on an on-again, off-again basis depending on the climate and circumstances, including the electoral climate for the government in power. Austerity is relaxed in the months before elections so as not to antagonize the voters and then turned on again once the returns are in. In this way the austerity medicine can be imposed without the doctor administering it dying in the process.

It is likely that the economic crisis that plagues Latin America and its debt problems can be managed in this way for some time to come. There will be new crises but not total collapse. The debt is not repaid, but default and/or repudiation are avoided. And because of the pressure applied, some structural reforms may even be pried out of the reluctant Latin American governments. Meanwhile, the banks would have time either to divest themselves of their Latin American loans as described above, or to roll up such large profits that when they do actually have to admit that the debt is uncollectible, the losses on the international loans can be absorbed in the profits from other activities and the stockholders will not be overly concerned. To meet the crisis in the short term the banks must further extend the Latin American payments period, forgo more fees, keep lowering interest charges, keep rolling over the loans, provide new loan packages just to keep interest payments coming in, erect some ingenious rescue packages, and above all keep alive the myth that the debt will eventually be repaid.

The strategy is based on prudence, patience, and playing for time. It represents a pragmatic and largely ad hoc way of dealing with the crises. It recognizes that simplistic formulas à la Fidel Castro or Alan García will not resolve the crisis, while at the same time it lays the groundwork for careful, long-term solutions encompassing a variety of necessary steps. It avoids the potential pitfalls and unanticipated consequences that some of the proposed "general solutions" to solving the debt would likely entail. The fact is that bankers, public officials, and economists are often reluctant to reach for some overarching plan or "solution" that almost inevitably ignores some factors, oversimplifies others, and thus produces more complications or outright disasters than it does useful answers.[30] It is oriented to helping the Latin American countries grow out of their economic doldrums while encouraging some limited reforms from within. And since the U.S., European, and Asian economic performance since 1984 has remained strong if not robust, more and more of the debtor countries have begun to recover. There have been and will continue to be ups and downs, but Brazil, Chile, Colombia, and Uruguay all registered impressive gains (in excess of 5 percent) in GNP in 1986. Virtually every other country also registered gains, although not so impressive. Only Bolivia, Haiti, El Salvador, and Mexico registered negative growth in 1986—a remarkable turnaround since the early 1980s when almost all the countries began sliding downhill.[31] In this piecemeal way it had been hoped that Latin America would emerge from its doldrums without some more radical and probably dangerous solution having to be applied. But 1987 was not a good year economically in Latin America and 1988 was even worse, so other solutions will have to be explored.

This first scenario—ad hocism—may well be appropriate and workable in the short run, but in the long term it seems far more questionable. For example, the presidents of such key debtor countries as Argentina, Brazil, and Mexico may not always be reasonable and pragmatic ones. Nor can one necessarily assume that U.S. policy toward the debt issue will remain the same, particularly if the United States' own debt and trade deficits worsen. Even less can we assume that world economic growth, which has begun in the past few years to pull the Latin American economies out of their slump, will continue. Nor can austerity continue forever—even on the on-again, off-again basis that has been described here. For example, it is estimated by many economists that it will take Mexico, even allowing for some very large assumptions about that country, at least until the year 2000 to recover from its present economic downturn. It is inconceivable that austerity or even stop-and-go austerity can be maintained for that long a time. Something will have to give long before the year 2000, or else an explosion in Mexico is virtually inevitable. The same is true for the other Latin American countries; austerity can be maintained for another year or two but not for a decade or more.

That is what the so-called Baker Plan (named after the then–Treasury Secretary James Baker) of 1985 was all about. Secretary Baker took a long step toward recognizing that austerity could not indefinitely be imposed, that the only long-term solution was to help Latin America to grow out of its debt problem, and that the issue not only was an economic one involving debtors and creditors but had profound political and strategic implications as well.[32] The decision was made (actually it had been made as early as 1982 during the first Mexican bailout, but this was the first time it became public) that politically and strategically the United States could not allow Latin America to "go under." Hence Baker put pressure on the commercial banks to come forward with new loan packages for the area, he urged the World Bank and the Inter-American Development Bank (IDB) to increase their loans, he pressured Congress into augmenting the budgets for these agencies, and he gave assurances—elliptically to be sure, for understandable political reasons—that in the last analysis the U.S. government would come to the rescue. This was the "breakthrough," albeit still partial, toward a "political solution" to the debt crisis that many analysts had been looking for. It should further be said, perhaps parenthetically, that the Baker proposal also let the Latin American governments off the hook—although again only partially. Why should they continue to make reforms and sacrifices, they reasoned, if the United States had already indicated that, when the crunch finally came, it was willing to help bail them out?

In this way the United States began inching piecemeal and still only partially toward a "general solution" to the debt crisis, as distinct from its earlier public stand, which was to let the main parties to the dispute (banks and debtor countries) settle the matter by themselves. A further extension of this strategy came in 1987 with a realistic write-down by many U.S. banks of a considerable share of their Latin American loans and with the U.S. government's willingness to underwrite a part of Mexico's loan by means of Treasury bills. Still another extension was announced in 1989 by President Bush's Treasury Secretary Nicholas Brady, who called for partial forgiveness by the banks of some of the debt, the sale of still more debt at discounted prices, and increased assistance by the World Bank and the IDB as a way both of stimulating economic growth and of avoiding the U.S. taxpayer having to absorb the Latin American debt burden directly. At this stage, no one knows precisely what the next steps will be, if there will be a general solution to the debt crisis, what form a general solution to the debt problem will take, when it will be announced, or even (again for political reasons) if there will be anything of a more general solution announced beyond the Baker/Brady plans. But the broad (if there is ever a general solution) outline will probably not be far from the following: (1) the banks will be forced to absorb some of the loss from the unpaid debt, maybe 20–30 percent, but only after they have been given a reasonable time and chance to sell off their debt holdings or roll up some considerable profits; (2) the Latin American governments will continue to be pressured to streamline, modernize, and privatize; (3) the World Bank, the IMF, and the IDB will expand further their loans and assistance to Latin America; (4) further steps will be taken to help the Latin American countries grow out of depression—as they have been doing fairly successfully; and (5) the U.S. government (and that means the U.S. taxpayer) will be forced to absorb a considerable portion of the loss, either in disguised form through inflation, directly in the form of taxes, possibly through a combination of the two, or most likely through some international agency that the U.S. government will fund and support. It is not entirely clear how the taxpayers would respond to all this, but in Washington there is great fear of the backlash that would almost surely come from asking the taxpayers to pick up the tab for the excesses of both the private banks and the Latin American countries.

It is very likely that this is how the debt crisis will finally be "resolved." On the one hand, U.S. officials are very reluctant to get the U.S. government too heavily involved in the crisis for fear that the cure may be worse than the disease and may have unintended side effects that will be damaging to the economy (U.S. and world) as a whole. For that reason we will likely continue to see, at some levels, an ad hoc approach in which general market forces and laissez-faire will continue to operate and, for the most part, the United States will continue to let the banks and the countries affected do most of the negotiating. At the same time, when a major crisis hits, as in Mexico in 1982 and 1987 and Brazil in 1987 (when it suspended its interest payments), it is clear that the United States *will* step in to prevent the country affected from defaulting and an international financial crisis from developing. Meanwhile the Baker Plan, the Treasury plan to underwrite Mexican debt with U.S. paper, the Brady Plan for a measure of debt relief, and other plans still not public or in law indicate a U.S. willingness to provide some general, but still partial, solutions to the debt crisis.

The debt crisis in this way will go through a quasi-disappearing act. Most of the banks will continue to sell off their Latin American loans and thus reduce their vulnerability. They will also have to absorb a part of the debt as uncollectible. The Latin American countries will make some limited reforms, and if present trends continue a number of them will begin to grow out of the debts. The international lending agencies will provide augmented assistance. And the U.S. Treasury will ultimately have to absorb some of the losses. Meanwhile, some countries have reformed their policymaking machinery with good results, the banks have built capital and reduced their exposure, the world economy has remained strong, and the United States has stepped up its assistance and stated its openness to new initiative. In this way the debt will not "disappear" or finally be "resolved"; but it will begin to fade away, become less severe, and it is hoped shade off as an issue of major consciousness and consequences.

If these scenarios prove correct, then the cause of Latin American democracy will also be enormously helped. Historically, as we have repeatedly seen, when the Latin American economies go under, their political systems have usually been swamped as well. That is because of the close relationship between the Latin American "system" as described here (including its institutional weaknesses), economic debility, and the survivability of democracy. The present trends in the region, toward recovery and renewed growth, offer hope that Latin America's new and struggling democracies may be able to survive as well. That will still not solve the long-term economic problems of the area. Nevertheless, gradually, incrementally, and often by fits and starts—not dramatic but not bad either if one values democratic politics[33]—Latin America is moving on a variety of fronts to change its economic structures. These changes include liberalization, diversification, accelerated industrialization, greater productivity, privatization, competitiveness, greater efficiencies, and more exports. Such changes not only help improve the economic performance of the Latin American countries but are important ingredients in their political stability and in the further institutionalization of democracy as well. As explained more fully in the conclusion, these reforms are also critical from a U.S. policy point of view. U.S. efforts need to be directed in large part toward resolving Latin America's economic woes because that is essential to the survival of the area's fledgling democracies and, in turn, to the possibilities for a successful U.S. foreign policy. It is always a delicate balancing act in Latin America between change, survival, and collapse. But in the long run as well as the short term, there *is* a chance that Latin America may make it, both economically and politically. The United States has a powerful interest in ensuring that this occurs.

Notes

1. The figures on Latin America's ongoing economic crisis are available in a variety of places; among the best and most reliable are those of the *Comisión Económica para América Latina y el Caribe* (CEPAL), a United Nations agency that publishes monthly, yearly, and periodic reports; and the Inter-American Development Bank (IDB), whose annual *Social Progress Trust Fund Report* is invaluable.
2. Warren Dean, "Latin American Golpes and Economic Fluctuations, 1823–1966," *Social Science Quarterly* 51 (June 1970): 70–80.
3. See Howard J. Wiarda, *Critical Elections and Critical Coups: State, Society and the Military in the Process of Latin American Development* (Athens: Ohio University Center for International Studies, Latin America Program, 1979).
4. See John J. Johnson, *Political Change in Latin America* (Stanford, Calif.: Stanford University Press, 1958).
5. For example, Edwin Lieuwen, *Arms and Politics in Latin America* (New York: Praeger, 1961); John J. Johnson, *The Military and Society in Latin America* (Stanford, Calif.: Stanford University Press, 1964); and Martin C. Needler, "Political Development and Military Intervention in Latin America," *American Political Science Review,* 60 (September 1966): 616–26.
6. Kalman H. Silvert, *The Conflict Society: Reaction and Revolution in Latin America* (New Orleans: Hauser, 1961), p. 20.
7. Howard J. Wiarda, ed., *Politics and Social Change in Latin America: The Distinct Tradition* (Amherst: University of Massachusetts Press, 1982).
8. For an elaboration of this political process, see Howard J. Wiarda and Harvey F. Kline, *Latin American Politics and Development* (Boulder, Colo.: Westview Press, 1985), Introduction and Conclusion.
9. Charles W. Anderson, "Toward a Theory of Latin American Politics," Occasional Paper no. 2, The Graduate Center for Latin American Studies, Vanderbilt University, Nashville, Tenn., February 1964.
10. Guillermo O'Donnell, *Modernization and Bureaucratic Authoritarianism* (Berkeley: Institute of International Studies, University of California, 1973).
11. See William P. Glade, "Latin America: Options and Non-Options in Contemporary Development Strategy," *Foreign Policy and Defense Review* 5, no. 3 (1985): 5–13; and Joseph Grunwald, "Perspectives on the Latin American Economic Crisis," in Howard J. Wiarda, ed., *The Crisis in Latin America: Strategic, Economic and Political Dimensions* (Washington, D.C.: American Enterprise Institute, 1984).
12. See the various publications of CEPAL, or ECLA (Economic Commission for Latin America) to use its English-language initials.

13. *Washington Business,* February 9, 1987, pp. 6–7.
14. The literature on import substitution is voluminous. For the political implications, see O'Donnell, *Modernization.* A polite but devastating critique of the O'Donnell thesis is David Collier, ed., *The New Authoritarianism in Latin America* (Princeton, N.J.: Princeton University Press, 1979).
15. See especially the chapter by Jiri Valenta and Virginia Valenta, "Soviet Strategies and Policies in the Caribbean Basin," in Howard J. Wiarda and Mark Falcoff, eds., *The Communist Challenge in the Caribbean* (Washington, D.C.: American Enterprise Institute, 1987).
16. Pedro-Pablo Kuczynski, *Latin American Debt* (Baltimore: Johns Hopkins University Press, 1988); and Howard J. Wiarda, *Latin America at the Crossroads: Debt, Development, and the Future* (Boulder, Colo.: Westview Press and American Enterprise Institute, 1987).
17. The waste is described in more detail in Wiarda, *Latin America at the Crossroads.*
18. On the history and functions of Latin American statism and clientelism, see Howard J. Wiarda, "Economic and Political Statism in Latin America," in Michael Novak and Michael P. Jackson, eds., *Latin America: Dependence or Interdependence?* (Washington, D.C.: American Enterprise Institute, 1985), pp. 4–14.
19. Based on interviews by the author among U.S. bank officials and CEOs.
20. W. W. Rostow, *The Stages of Economic Growth* (Cambridge: Cambridge University Press, 1960); Seymour Martin Lipset, *Political Man: The Social Bases of Politics* (New York: Anchor, 1963).
21. Good general discussions of the debt issue include Inter-American Development Bank, *External Debt Crisis and Adjustment* (Washington, D.C.: IDB, 1985); William Cline, *International Debt* (Washington, D.C.: Institute for International Economics, 1984); John H. Makin, *The Global Debt Crisis* (New York: Basic Books, 1984); and Alfred J. Watkins, *Till Debt Do Us Part* (Washington, D.C.: Roosevelt Center for American Policy Studies, 1986).
22. After the phrase in Albert O. Hirschman, *A Bias for Hope: Essays on Economic Development in Latin America* (New Haven: Yale University Press, 1971), chap. 14.
23. For a full discussion see Wiarda, *Latin America at the Crossroads,* chap. 6.
24. Based on extensive field research and interviewing in Central America, Mexico, and South America in 1985 and 1987.
25. Jesús Silva Herzog, First Annual Edward Laroque Tinker Lectureship, American University, Washington, D.C., February 24, 1987.
26. Howard J. Wiarda, "Can the Mice Roar? Small Countries and the Debt Crisis," in Robert Wesson, ed., *Coping with the Latin American Debt* (New York: Praeger for the Hoover Institution, 1988).
27. The question was well stated by Peter Hakim in the discussion that followed the Tinker lectureship cited above.
28. CEPAL, "Preliminary Overview of the Latin American Economy, 1986," *Notas para la economía y el desarrollo,* nos. 438–39 (December 1986).
29. Based on interviews with officials in the international affairs divisions of a large number of the U.S. banks.

30. Based on interviews with U.S. Treasury and Council of Economic Advisers officials responsible for dealing with the debt issue.
31. CEPAL, "Preliminary Overview," p. 13.
32. Based on interviews with U.S. Treasury officials.
33. On incrementalism as a democratic and democratizing approach, see Charles E. Lindblom, *The Policy-Making Process* (Englewood Cliffs, N.J.: Prentice-Hall, 1968).

PART THREE

POLITICAL DIMENSIONS

8

U.S. Relations with Nondemocratic Regimes

Over the years the United States has been moving toward a position, based on both ethical and pragmatic considerations, of support for Latin America's new and often fledgling democracies. But what about the region's still existing and often flagrantly *nondemocratic* regimes? If democracy is such a good thing and we have evolved toward a policy position of supporting it strongly, then should we not also move to nudge nondemocratic or authoritarian regimes toward democracy—and perhaps remove some of them altogether? But that raises all kinds of thorny issues. It is one thing to support democracy where it already exists, but it may be quite another—although we have done so from time to time—to take steps against a sitting and presumably sovereign state to remove its head of government and then to install a new regime—hopefully democratic—in its wake. The issue is complex, but that is all the more reason to consider nondemocratic regimes and what the United States should do about them in this discussion of democracy and U.S. foreign policy in Latin America.

What, then, to do about nondemocratic regimes, regimes often friendly to the United States, that are systematically abusive of human rights, that may be faced with serious guerrilla/communist challenges and yet are unwilling or unable to reach an accommodation with democratic forces and thus avoid the polarization and breakdown that might pave the way for a communist takeover? This is one of the most important and at the same time most difficult foreign policy dilemmas facing the United States.[1]

The fact that the problem had already been faced in Cuba (Batista), the Dominican Republic (Trujillo), Nicaragua (Somoza), Haiti (Duvalier) and—outside the hemisphere—Iran (the shah) and the Philippines (Marcos) did not seem to have raised the issue to the kind of visibility that it deserves. That situation is changing, but so far we still lack the monographic and comparative literature on which to base sound policy judgments. Nor do we seem to have learned from these earlier experiences very many lessons that will help us with the more recent difficult cases: Chile, Panama, Paraguay, and Mexico (not a dictatorship but an authoritarian regime that is badly in need of reform). The quandaries are multiplied if we think not just about right-wing and authoritarian regimes but also about what we should do in a policy sense about such difficult, left-wing dictatorships as Cuba and Nicaragua.

The problem of what to do is twofold: analytic and prescriptive. The first revolves around the question of how we gauge when an authoritarian regime may be susceptible to an overthrow that will be damaging to U.S. interests. Perhaps an even prior question is the moral one of whether the United States should have decent relations with any authoritarian regimes at all—an issue that is addressed in the next section. The second problem is what we do by way of a policy response about authoritarian regimes whose continuation may be damaging to U.S. interests.[2] This chapter explores and offers advice on both of these issues.

The General Problem

Two polar positions have been put forward as to how the United States should respond to authoritarian regimes. The debate over this issue is closely related to the ones examined earlier over human rights and democracy, pitting "idealists" against the apostles of realpolitik. The idealist school would have the United States sever its relations with all such authoritarian regimes.[3] The argument is that the United States, as a special nation, a paragon of democracy, should not be associated with authoritarian regimes. Such regimes violate our standards of acceptable political behavior, and we should distance ourselves from them. They are viewed as repressors of their own people, and therefore they should be punished for their abuses, not cuddled up to and rewarded. To the argument that alliances with such regimes sometimes enhance U.S. security and that we must accept the allies we can get, the idealist school replies that such repressive regimes detract from U.S. security more than they advance it, and that dictatorships, instead of serving as bulwarks against communism, actually prepare the soil in which communism may thrive.[4]

The "realist" school takes the opposite tack. It suggests that the United States should not pay any attention to the internal policies of any regime but should only be concerned with the pragmatic defense of the U.S. national interest.[5] If a regime is friendly to us and opposed to the Soviet Union, we should support it no matter how dictatorial it may be. Such regimes may not be paragons of virtue—and we all recognize that—but they do serve U.S. interests. Cutting ourselves off from such a regime may salve our moral conscience, but it leaves the United States without any handle to influence that regime, hurts our ability to guide the regime in a more demoratic direction, gives us no means to control the postauthoritarian transition, and thus (as in Cuba) may lead to an even worse situation from the point of view of U.S. strategic interests than existed under the old but now ousted regime.

The issue surfaces in a variety of vital areas. South Korea was for some time an authoritarian regime but it held the line against communist expansion from the North. Saudi Arabia is not a democracy, but it has vital oil supplies and a strategic location. Mexico is an authoritarian-corporate state, but it lies right on the southern border of the United States. Taiwan may not be a pure democracy, but it is a strategic outpost and an economic wonder. The South African regime represses blacks, but it has vital strategic minerals and commands major sea-lanes. Jordan is an authoritarian monarchy, but the alternative—control by the Palestine Liberation Organization—seems to be far worse. Iran and Brazil in the 1970s were not democracies, but they were major regional powers that helped protect U.S. interests.

The questions are posed nicely by the Foreign Policy Research Institute in Philadelphia in its study of *Friendly Tyrants*.[6] How do we reconcile the dilemmas in all these cases and arrive at a sensible foreign policy position? Do we emphasize our security interests above all else, or do we stress human rights and morality? Which of these better serves U.S. interests? Do we see authoritarian regimes primarily as allies in the struggle to contain the Soviet Union or as oppressors of their own people? Do we reward such authoritarian regimes for their helpfulness in keeping the lid on potential guerrilla uprisings, or do we punish them for their violations of human rights? Do we accept such regimes as friends and collaborators regardless of the nature of their internal policies, or do we ostracize them, treat them as pariahs, and cast them out from the community of civilized states? These are very difficult questions, and it is hard to strike a balance among the contending arguments. Nonetheless, authoritarian regimes that are also pro-American force both the U.S. public and their officials to make such choices, and there is hardly any foreign policy issue that is as difficult and presents itself so often.

The dilemma—and the opportunity—is that there are two strains in U.S. foreign policy. On the one hand, we want to preserve the nation's security, defend its borders, protect its vital interests, resist Soviet expansionism, preserve and augment our economic well-being, and enhance our own influence. These are perfectly legitimate interests on which virtually all Americans can agree. But on the other, we also wish as a New World and quasi-missionary nation to spread our domestic moral and political values internationally: to support democracy, human rights, freedom, and the rule of law with whatever nations we have relations.

Very often—for example in our dealings with other well-established democracies—our strategic and our ethical concerns pose no problem; the two can be advanced hand in hand. The same applies in reverse to totalitarian regimes: not only is the Soviet Union (and before that Nazi Germany) our principal adversary, but its repression and controls over its own people are also repugnant. In both these cases, whether speaking of our allies or of our enemies, strategic and moral considerations are more or less in congruence; the dilemmas of which we speak here then disappear. The same does not, however, hold for allied authoritarian regimes. The moral and the strategic considerations may and often do conflict. Then we have problems. Then we must draw lines and make distinctions. Then our choices become more difficult.

Both of the polar positions as stated here probably are too extreme. If we sever our ties with all the world's authoritarian regimes, we would be cutting ourselves off from fully two-thirds of the nations of the globe. We cannot give up all our ties to all authoritarian regimes, despite our distaste for their nondemocratic character and human rights abuses, because too many other vital interests are involved. We cannot have a foreign policy that focuses *only* on the human rights/democracy agenda; other matters— diplomatic, economic, strategic, geopolitical—are at stake. The U.S. public clearly wants a foreign policy that *both* protects our security interests *and* works in favor of democracy and human rights. The fact that both desires are strong, and that they are at times contradictory, implies that compromises must be made and balance achieved.

The realpolitik arguments are as problematic as the idealistic ones. The United States cannot be entirely indifferent to the nature of the more nefarious regimes with which we must deal or to the conditions of life of the people who live under them. The realist school would say that we must be indifferent to the plight of the Soviet Jews who wish to emigrate and to

Christians and others who wish only to practice their religions, that we must not be concerned with the situation of South African blacks, that we should ignore the pleas of harassed and often intimidated democratic oppositions trying to operate in authoritarian regimes, or the cries of nuns or peasants in Central America who are brutalized or caught in the cross-fire. In the United States it is not possible to conduct foreign policy without a strong pro–human rights and democracy component—as even the foremost apostles of realpolitik recognize. It therefore becomes necessary to proceed carefully, to draw distinctions, and to blend idealism with realism.

The first fact to recognize is that authoritarian regimes are not all the same. Some are of such overwhelming strategic importance (for example, Saudi Arabia) that we are probably best advised not to tamper with their internal political structure; others (for example, Haiti) have more limited strategic importance. Some authoritarian regimes are fresh and new and full of vim and vigor; others are wobbly and on their last legs, which is usually when such regimes begin surfacing as major concerns to U.S. foreign policy. Some authoritarian regimes, particularly if they are wobbly, are faced with strong communist or guerrilla challenges; plainly they will be of most concern to policymakers.

Authoritarian regimes vary greatly in their character and degree of popular support. Some authoritarian regimes are populist and enjoy wide-spread public backing. It is probably not appropriate, no matter how pure our democratic motives, for the United States to get involved in trying to unseat such populist-authoritarian regimes if to do so would be contrary to the wishes of the people living under those regimes. The fact is, difficult though it is for many Americans to believe, that many authoritarian regimes enjoy genuine popularity. Cultural attitudes toward authority and its practice also vary widely in different parts of the world.[7] Many authoritarian regimes are welcomed and admired because they provide order, coherence, and stability in countries that have long been chronically and pitifully unstable. Such regimes are often at once nationalistic and paternalistic. They may not be our cup of tea, but in their own cultural context they are often admired, even revered. Hence the first step in a rational foreign policy toward authoritarian regimes is to recognize these differences, to distinguish between different types of authoritarianism,[8] and to devise policy accordingly.

Part of this process of understanding will be to use measures derived, for the most part, from local standards to judge such authoritarian regimes and their policies, not simply criteria reflective of U.S. or Western European preferences. Some regimes of course—a Hitler or a Bokassa or an Idi

Amin—are so far beyond the pale that they deserve condemnation from any point of view. But in general with less extreme authoritarian regimes, which in fact constitute the majority of cases, indigenous standards as well as universal ones must be carefully considered. It clearly will not do for us in a policy sense simply to issue a standard and blanket condemnation of all authoritarian regimes as unacceptable to the United States. Degrees of unacceptability must be recognized as well as such criteria as age of the regimes, their wobbliness and potential for losing power, levels of popular support, strategic location, and possibilities for postauthoritarian democracy or, alternatively, a communist takeover.

The second step is to come to grips with the fact that authoritarian regimes change and evolve. They get old, ossified, and out of touch. As they do, they tend to use more and more controls to keep themselves in power beyond their time. The trick is to recognize when a long-reigning authoritarian regime, which had enjoyed considerable popularity, slips over the line toward greater repression, becomes increasingly totalitarian, and finally is no longer acceptable not only by our standards of human rights but by the standards of its own people.

That is the evolution of the most notorious recent authoritarian regimes: Batista, Trujillo, Somoza, the shah, Duvalier, Marcos. All started as authoritarians with considerable popular support, often as populists, or as "saviors" of their country. But they all, similarly, gravitated toward such repression, corruption, and brutality that they became either full-fledged or quasi-totalitarians, controlling more and more areas of their countries' and peoples' existence. As they became more brutal, more totalitarian, and stayed in power too long, they became less and less acceptable to their own populations. And as their base of support dwindled to, typically, a handful of cronies and military officers, the question inevitably arose of how long the United States could continue to support such an unpopular regime, now often challenged by a serious left-wing insurgency, and in a strategically important country.

This is, in a sense, a new twist on the older distinction between authoritarianism and totalitarianism,[9] elevated to foreign policy significance in Jeane Kirkpatrick's writings. Kirkpatrick distinguished between traditional authoritarianism and communist totalitarianism, arguing that from a foreign policy viewpoint (although not necessarily from the point of view of the domestic victims of such regimes) authoritarian regimes may be preferred over totalitarian ones because they (1) tend to be less permanent, (2) may be reformable and even amenable to transitions to democracy, and (3) tend to do less harm to U.S. interests.[10] Here, however, a somewhat different angle on those themes is being suggested. That is, that traditional authoritarianism may evolve in the opposite direction, not toward democracy, but toward full-scale, right-wing totalitarianism—with disastrous consequences both for the country affected and for U.S. policy.[11] That is in fact the route taken by all the most notorious and difficult cases with which we have had lately—and still have—to deal.

Fulgencio Batista was thought of as a populist and a nationalist when he first came to power in the 1930s. Even his coup d'état in 1952 was welcomed by most Cubans as providing order and stability after the corruption and chaos of the previous years. But as Batista became more bloody and repressive from the mid-1950s on, he lost all support. And the United States was unable to control or even influence the post-Batista transition, which produced the Marxist-Leninist regime of Fidel Castro.[12]

The Dominican Republic's Rafael Leonidas Trujillo similarly began with considerable popular support in the 1930s as the "savior" and "benefactor" of his nation. But by the late 1950s his was such a cruel and terroristic regime that it had alienated all its support. Although on several occasions the situation nearly got out of hand, this time the United States did shape and guide the post-Trujillo transition.[13]

Anastasio Somoza, who founded the dynasty in Nicaragua, was an authoritarian and a dictator but not excessively brutal by the standards of his own society. His eldest son, Luís, even accommodated the regime somewhat to the requirements of the Alliance for Progress. It was his second son, Anastasio Jr., who became so corrupt and repressive that he brought the whole house of cards down on his head and, like Batista, paved the way for a Marxist-Leninist takeover.[14]

The shah was similarly popular in his early days. But we failed to recognize how all-pervasive and technologically proficient (a hallmark of rising totalitarianism) his secret police had become and how he had squandered his popularity.[15]

The elder Duvalier, François ("Papa Doc"), had been a country physician who built up a political base by helping his clients, but in office he proved dictatorial, and his son and heir, Jean-Claude ("Baby Doc," not a trained physician like his father), was even worse. Ferdinand Marcos also enjoyed initial popularity by bringing order and coherence to the chaotic Philippine polity, but he became more corrupt and brutal, lost his popular support, and eventually had to flee. Even General Augusto Pinochet was welcomed by many Chileans as providing order and stability after the upheaval of the Allende years, but the mass killings after the coup shocked the country and led to an erosion of his support and to Chile being viewed as a pariah state.[16]

The pattern in all these regimes is clear. A chaotic, corrupt, and disorganized moderate or democratic regime is initially replaced by an authoritarian one that, because it stands for peace and stability, is at first welcomed by the population. As that regime stays in power, however, it gradually loses support and eventually turns to totalitarian terror to keep itself in power and thus loses whatever support it had left. In the most difficult cases, the wobbly and unpopular dictator is faced not just by rising democratic opposition but also by a communist insurgency. The question then becomes: should the United States continue to support and prop up a regime that once was popular and also served as a bastion against communism—in a foreign policy sense, rightly or wrongly, our main preoccupation in that country? Or should we—and how and when—begin to disassociate ourselves from that regime, with all the possibilities for alienating the existing government and for losing control of the situation (and the country) that are implied in such a serious step?

The United States and "Wobbly Authoritarians": How to Judge When to Cut the Ties

In an effort to give more systematic rather than impressionistic responses to this question, a scale was devised to gauge when the United States should disassociate from tired and wobbly authoritarianism.[17] This measure is based on the conclusion that the United States cannot move against all the world's authoritarian regimes; if we tried to do that we would find ourselves in official opposition to some 60 percent of the governments of the world.[18] The problem for U.S. foreign policy is not so much authoritarianism per se (although some of us as individuals and in terms of our own moral and ethical preferences may continue to think so) but rather an authoritarian regime that begins to wobble, verges toward totalitarianism and thus loses virtually all support, and runs the risk of being superseded by a Marxist-Leninist regime allied with the Soviet Union. When that happens or threatens to happen, U.S. security interests are also affected, and then it is time for the United States to get off the boat, to abandon the sinking ship, and to begin thinking about and maybe even moving toward an alternative.

The scale that was devised not only measures authoritarian slippage but also measures movement in the opposite direction, toward democracy. It is a barometer that the author has found useful for research purposes and that may be recommended to the foreign policymaking agencies who must accurately assess and respond to such trends.

The following factors help gauge when more or less tolerable (although not necessarily desirable) authoritarianism passes over that often indistinct line to become not only intolerable to the population of the country but also dangerous from a U.S. foreign policy viewpoint:

- When graft, traditionally in the range of 5–7 percent and constituting more or less acceptable patronage, soars to an unacceptable 25–30 percent and becomes outright and institutionalized bribery.

- When *all* opportunities for legal opposition are snuffed out, for authoritarian regimes typically permit some opposition, but totalitarian regimes permit none.

- When all institutional checks and balances are eliminated, for authoritarian regimes typically retain some limited institutional checks through the congress or the courts; totalitarian regimes do not.

- When free speech, press, and assembly, always under wraps in an authoritarian regime, are wiped out.

- When all self-government at local levels is subordinated to the all-powerful central state.

- When social and political pluralism, always limited in an authoritarian regime,[19] is forcibly erased.

- When terror and technologically proficient torture (as distinct from the traditional techniques of jailings and exile) become institutionalized as state policy and encompass the broader population.

- When economic development and social justice are entirely sacrificed to dictatorial megalomania and the regime's self-enrichment.

- When virtually all human rights are systematically abrogated.

- When a government that was paternalistic and beneficent turns mean-spirited and entirely selfish.

- When all freedom from arbitrary and capricious authority has been sacrificed.

- When the regime has lost entirely its own representative and participatory character—this may involve a system of formal or informal ethnic, functional, or corporative representation and need not necessarily be formalized in a U.S.–style congress.

- When the regime gets old, passé, and starts to wobble.

- When the country is important strategically to the United States.

- When the threat exists of a potential communist or Marxist-Leninist takeover of the country once the dictator goes.

It bears emphasis that these are not necessarily measures of U.S.–style democracy. These criteria are designed especially for Third World countries such as those of Latin America, where the dilemma of dealing with wobbly authoritarianism has been posed most dramatically. The criteria do not presume any one particular set of institutional arrangements. Instead, they are based on the standards by which most Third World people weigh the success (or lack thereof) of their own, often "mixed" political systems.

To complete this exercise, an effort will be made to demonstrate its practical utility. If one assigns a numerical scale, 1 to 10, for each of these criteria—with a score of 10 indicating that the assertion applies to the country under consideration, a score of 1 indicating it does not apply, with

TABLE 8.1
Scale of Unacceptable Authoritarianism

	Arg	Bol	Bra	Chi	Col	CRi	Cub	DRp
Graft	3	7	3	5	4	2	4	4
No legal opposition	1	3	1	8	2	1	9	1
No checks and balances	1	1	1	8	2	1	9	2
No free speech	1	3	1	8	1	1	9	1
No self-government	2	3	2	6	2	2	8	2
No pluralism	1	1	1	7	2	1	9	2
Terror and torture	2	3	2	9	2	1	7	2
No development	2	5	1	2	2	3	5	2
No human rights	1	3	2	8	2	1	8	2
Mean-spirited and selfish	1	2	1	8	2	1	7	2
No freedom	1	2	1	8	1	1	9	1
No representation	2	2	2	8	2	1	9	2
Old, passé	1	3	1	7	2	2	8	3
Strategic importance	7	4	9	7	6	5	6	5
Threat of communist takeover	2	3	2	4	2	1	10	2
TOTALS	28	45	30	103	34	24	117	33
RANK ORDERING	3	9	4	18	8	1	20	5

degrees of more or less in between, it is possible to measure and rank-order different countries. If one then asks a panel of experts (preferably several persons, but the exercise could be done with one analyst alone) to provide their best judgment about the country or countries they know, adds up the totals for all the criteria, and examines the clustering or groupings of countries, some very interesting findings emerge. Such an exercise was carried out in the fall of 1988 and is presented in Table 8.1.[20]

The first thirteen criteria have to do with the internal nature and structure of the regime and how it is perceived domestically. Criteria fourteen and fifteen seek to assess the country's strategic importance and the threat of a potential Marxist-Leninist takeover—that is, how the country is viewed from the perspective of U.S. foreign policy.

Table 8.2 gives the rank ordering that emerged when the scale was

TABLE 8.1
(continued)

Ecu	ElSa	Gua	Hai	Hon	Mex	Nic	Pan	Par	Per	Uru	Ven
5	5	6	5	5	7	5	6	6	5	2	4
1	2	3	4	5	5	8	5	7	3	1	1
1	3	3	4	3	5	8	4	8	3	2	1
1	3	3	2	3	3	8	2	8	3	1	1
2	3	3	4	3	3	5	3	7	3	2	2
2	3	4	3	3	8	8	3	7	3	1	1
2	4	4	3	3	3	7	3	7	3	1	2
2	5	4	5	3	4	5	3	3	4	4	3
2	4	4	4	4	4	8	3	8	3	1	2
2	4	4	3	4	4	7	4	8	4	1	2
1	2	3	4	4	4	7	3	8	3	1	1
2	3	4	4	3	3	7	4	8	4	1	1
3	4	3	4	4	5	5	4	8	3	2	3
4	5	5	3	5	9	5	6	4	5	4	6
3	5	5	3	3	4	10	4	3	5	3	3
33	55	58	55	55	67	103	57	100	54	25	33
5	11	15	11	11	16	18	14	17	10	2	5

214 / POLITICAL DIMENSIONS

applied specifically to Latin America. The rank ordering goes from most authoritarian and dictatorial, verging on totalitarianism, to least authoritarian, or democratic.

TABLE 8.2
*Rank Ordering of Latin American Countries:
from Authoritarian to Democratic*

Rank	Country	Score
1	Cuba	117
2	Nicaragua	103
3	Chile	103
4	Paraguay	100
5	Mexico	67
6	Guatemala	58
7	Panama	57
8	El Salvador	55
9	Haiti	55
10	Honduras	55
11	Peru	54
12	Bolivia	45
13	Colombia	34
14	Dominican Republic	33
15	Ecuador	33
16	Venezuela	33
17	Brazil	30
18	Argentina	28
19	Uruguay	25
20	Costa Rica	24

Now, by clustering these countries whose scores were close together, by assigning categories to the cluster and transposing the order to go from democratic to authoritarian, it is possible to arrive at the following classification, which is approximate and, depending on sometimes daily dynamics, periodically in need of revision:

1. Fully democratic: Costa Rica, Uruguay, Argentina, Brazil, Venezuela, Ecuador, Dominican Republic, Colombia.

2. Mixed and marginal, or en route to democracy: Bolivia, Peru, Haiti, Honduras, El Salvador, Panama, Guatemala, Mexico.

3. Marxist-Leninist: Cuba, Nicaragua.

4. Traditional authoritarian: Paraguay.

5. Pariah state: Chile.

Based on these criteria and measures, it would appear that only one country in Latin America, Paraguay, is still an old-fashioned, traditional, *caudillo*-dominated, authoritarian dictatorship. (This exercise was carried out before dictator Stroessner was overthrown in January 1989.) Such a country is problematic from the point of view of U.S. policy, and it is recommended that in this "precrisis" stage, we should nudge Paraguay toward greater democracy, pluralism, and openness, especially since the dictator is aging and the opposition already senses that the end may be near. But since there is no serious possibility of a Marxist-Leninist take-over in Paraguay, and since our strategic interests in that country are not large, we should probably proceed cautiously and not entirely disassociate ourselves from the regime—at least as yet.

Chile under Pinochet constituted in our survey the single real pariah state. The Chilean regime was a bloody dictatorship, had alienated even its earlier supporters, rested on an exceedingly narrow base, and was close to being fully totalitarian. Chile came to represent a very dangerous situation for U.S. policy, since Pinochet's regime had polarized the population and the possibility existed of the Communist party dominating the opposition. In addition, the dictatorship in Chile had started to wobble. The Paraguayan and Chilean cases are dealt with in more detail later in this chapter; here it simply needs to be indicated that the measures we have used for gauging unacceptable authoritarianism indicate Chile as a real problem area.

The index described above gets us a considerable way toward determining not only the nature and popularity of various authoritarian regimes but also when the United States should begin distancing itself from such regimes and preparing for—maybe even assisting—their end. It will not do, as suggested earlier, for the U.S. to break relations with all authoritarian regimes. Morally and ethically we may wish to distance ourselves, and diplomatically our relations may be limited to a handshake rather than a warm *abrazo*. But the real problem in terms of U.S. interests is not existing authoritarian regimes, but rather what might follow in their wake, and the possibility subsequently of national collapse and disintegration or a takeover by communist elements.

The gauges suggested here help tell us when such traditional authoritarian regimes become entirely unacceptable to their own peoples, when they start to wobble and shake, and when cool and correct relations with the dictator should give way to a more activist opposition stance on the U.S. part. That is precisely the next question: that is, once we have decided a particular regime is on its last legs and represents a danger to U.S. policy, and that a postauthoritarian transition is about to begin, what do we do about it? What is an appropriate U.S. strategy at this stage, how do we deal with an aging but still-in-power dictator, and how do we help shape the transition to a new regime that will be more in accord with U.S. interests? Those are the questions addressed in the next section.

U.S. Strategic Policies

The United States has always been ambivalent about authoritarian regimes. We do not like dictators and much prefer democratic regimes, but at the same time we are reluctant to sever our ties and therefore lose our control over the situation. We have a lurking suspicion that while democracy may be preferable it may not be viable and lasting in most Third World countries; and we also suspect that democrats may be less able or less vigorously willing to deal with communist insurgencies than the autocrats whom they replace. Hence we have usually hedged our bets, temporized, and played both ends against the middle—understandable in the U.S. policymaking context but risky in that it may result in our estrangement from both the regime in power and its opposition. The dilemma for policy was captured nicely by President John F. Kennedy in speaking of the dictator Trujillo and the Dominican Republic: "There are three possibilities in descending order of precedence: a decent democratic regime, a continuation of the Trujillo regime, or a Castro regime. We ought to aim at the first, but we really cannot renounce the second until we are sure that we can avoid the third."[21]

There, in a nutshell, is the challenge for U.S. policy. We prefer democracies but have concluded that right-wing dictators are generally preferable in a policy sense to Marxist-Leninist ones. Moreover, if the democrats are weak and poorly led, we are hesitant about favoring them over the authoritarians, for fear that the resultant instability and political vacuum might lead to a communist *putsch*. Or, that in a "popular-front" strategy aimed at toppling a dictator, the communists will become dominant. Hence we have often opted for what came to be known as the "lesser evil doctrine," the belief that while right-wing tyrants are generally despicable, they represent a lesser evil as compared with the left-wing variety.[22] And when we do eventually move against right-wing dictators, we do so usually with ambivalent feelings and mixed motives, not always from a desire for democracy per se but out of fear that, if the dictator stays in power too long, the result may be, as in Cuba, a full-fledged communist regime that does untold damage to U.S. interests.

There are actually two problems in discussing U.S. strategies and policies toward authoritarian regimes. The first is deciding what the United States *should* do, what U.S. policy *should* be—what the appropriate and most effective levels are. The second is the political one of getting policymakers to pay attention and stimulating the foreign policy bureaucracy and system to move, change course, and formulate effective policies.[23] Here I concentrate on the first problem although without neglecting the importance of the second.

The Range of Responses

The United States has at its command a variety of policy instruments for dealing with authoritarian regimes. In more or less ascending order of escalation, these policy responses include the following:

1. A private letter to the dictator
2. A public statement of concern about the situation
3. Meetings with the U.S. ambassador
4. The dispatch of a personal envoy to the dictator
5. Cutoff of assistance
   a. Economic
   b. Military
6. Cutoff of diplomatic relations
7. Organization of American States and/or other sanctions
   a. Economic
   b. Military
   c. Trade
8. Pressure put on the dictator
   a. To hold fair and honest elections
   b. To share power with a *junta*
   c. To step aside

9. Removal of the dictator
   a. Ushering him onto a waiting U.S. plane
   b. Sponsoring a coup d'état against him
   c. Assassination
   d. Military intervention

Given this range of responses, let us now see how the United States has responded in past cases and should respond in current and future ones.

Batista and Cuba

Fulgencio Batista dominated Cuban politics from 1933, when he helped overthrow the hated dictator Gerardo Machado, until January 1, 1959, when Fidel Castro's revolution came to power. Batista ruled at times through puppet presidents and at times directly. His first period of rule (1934–44) was generally benign, nationalist, and populist. He enacted Cuba's first social security legislation, reformulated the labor code to give greater benefits to workers, and was thought of as a reformer. After a democratic interlude from 1944 to 1952 that was increasingly inefficient, corrupt, and chaotic, Batista staged a coup in 1952 under the banners of peace and order that initially was warmly welcomed by most of the population.[24] His rule this time was less populist, less attuned to the newer Cuban realities, more repressive and corrupt than it had been earlier. As Batista steadily lost popularity, Fidel Castro and the revolutionary elements gained. Eventually Batista was supported by only a handful of cronies and fellow military officers.

The United States was for a long time indifferent to Cuba's political situation, since regime changes there did not seem to portend any grave threats to our interests. We provided some limited military assistance to Batista but eventually cut it off in a move that was more symbolic than substantial. Fidel Castro was viewed as "just another revolutionary" who would surely be bought off, corrupted, and co-opted by the Cuban "system." The Eisenhower administration had no evidence whatsoever that Fidel Castro was or might be a Marxist-Leninist. The administration became sufficiently worried only at the end of 1958, ordering the Department of State to provide a legal brief to evaluate the evidence. The report found nothing conclusive.[25] Ambassador Earl E. T. Smith, a political appointee and founder of the right-wing John Birch Society, was of course convinced all along that Castro was in fact a communist, but he arrived at that conclusion, which proved ultimately to be the correct one, without a shred of evidence.

Toward the end of Batista's rule, the United States moved belatedly to distance itself from the dictator. Military aid had already been terminated. There were private communications with Batista and some public expression of concern about the deteriorating situation. Senator George Smathers and State Department troubleshooter Robert Murphy were dispatched to meet with Batista. They urged him to step aside, to hold fair elections, or to share power with a *junta*. Batista refused all such entreaties, and the United States did not press the issue. Short of sending in the marines either to dispose of Batista or, alternatively, to prop him up, there seemed little more that the United States could do.

Not a great deal of urgency was attached to any of these efforts. The United States was prudently playing it safe, distancing itself from Batista, and trying to provide for a peaceful transition through a more broadly based regime that would ensure U.S. interests were protected no matter who came to power. Castro was viewed as a nationalist and not a Marxist-Leninist; Cuba was not considered high priority. After all, this was still the period *before* the first avowedly communist regime allied with the Soviet Union came to power in Latin America. Therefore, Cuba was not seen as a major crisis requiring immediate and high-level attention. Such attention would only come *after* Castro came to power and declared himself a Marxist-Leninist, and it came in other cases when it was feared that what happened in Cuba was about to be repeated.

The United States had thus determined eventually to move against Batista, but in the absence of a perceived communist threat our efforts were lackadaisical. It was a case of too little too late. Our limited and tardy activities directed toward removing Batista were ineffectual; and, in the absence of a perceived genuine threat to U.S. interests, we did not ratchet up the pressure to a level either to get rid of Batista or to control the post-Batista transition. We thus ended up with the worst possible position, alienated from Batista and despised by the incoming regime as well.

The lessons of the Cuban experience, of the missteps and lack of serious policy, were profound ones. We determined that the Cuban experience would not and could not be repeated. But whereas we did too little in the Cuban case, we did too much in the next case—the Dominican Republic—where it was determined that a "second Cuba" had to be prevented at all costs.

Trujillo and the Dominican Republic

Castro's declaration of Marxism-Leninism in Cuba came just in time to affect U.S. policy toward the aging dictator Rafael Trujillo in the next-door Dominican Republic. The historical context is essential to understand, as is the shift in policy thinking. Heretofore right-wing dictators like Batista and Trujillo were thought to be friendly to the United States and bulwarks against communism. But now, with the Cuban experience fresh in mind, we instead thought of such dictators, because of their repression and opposition to social reform, as preparing the soil in which communism could flourish. The experience of Cuba, Batista, and the transition to Castro could not be allowed to repeat itself.

Trujillo had been, like Batista, popular and a nationalist in his early years, a man who provided much-needed peace and order, the "builder of the nation." But by the 1950s he was old, out of touch, more repressive, increasingly unpopular, a tyrant, and faced with growing opposition—including an exile invasion supported and launched from Castro's Cuba that scared U.S. policymakers stiff.[26]

Even though there was no Communist Party in the Dominican Republic of any size (and certainly not comparable to the Cuban Communist Party before the revolution), no guerrilla movements of any seriousness, and no charismatic leader comparable to Fidel, the U.S. government was exceedingly fearful about the similarities between the two countries and determined to keep another Marxist-Leninist regime from coming to power. Hence we went through the full range of policy responses. We sent private letters, issued public statements, and had the U.S. ambassador meet with Trujillo to get him to clean up his act.[27]

We sent the same "troubleshooters" (Murphy, Smathers) to the Dominican Republic that we had earlier sent to Cuba. Through our lead and that of President Rómulo Betancourt in Venezuela, whom Trujillo had tried to assassinate, we had the OAS impose economic, diplomatic, and military sanctions against the country.[28] We cut off our aid and lowered the level of our diplomatic representation. We put pressure on the dictator to hold fair and honest elections, to share power with a *junta*, and to step aside entirely. We offered a plane, safe conduct, even a stipend.

When these steps all failed to nudge Trujillo from power—as they had earlier failed with Batista—we took the next and ultimate step. The United States became party to a plot to assassinate the dictator. We provided the Dominican conspirators with plans, money, and moral support and—according to some reports—even the arms. On the night of May 31, 1961, Trujillo was gunned down; the U.S. agents involved scrambled for cover or got out of the country fast.[29]

But while the United States had succeeded in getting rid of Trujillo, it could not prevent the dictator's son and heir, Ramfis, from taking over the reins of power. The Trujillo *family* dictatorship thus continued. The U.S.

diplomatic mission, meanwhile, was exceedingly active for the next five months, seeking to build up the centrist democratic opposition and trying alternately to push the Trujillos (1) toward reform; and (2) out. In November 1961, during a crisis within the ruling regime and family, the United States did succeed in ousting the rest of the family. The Atlantic Fleet stood by just over the skyline, with the helicopters and amphibious landing forces at the ready, in case there was any trouble.

The United States thus escalated its activities directed at getting rid of Trujillo to an extent no one had seriously contemplated in the Cuban case. That was because in the wake of the Cuban experience, the United States was determined to prevent another Fidel Castro from coming to power at all costs. Interviews the author has conducted indicate that the United States in 1961 was prepared to go to the lengths of having its troops land and occupy the country if that was necessary. Fortunately it was not—at least not until four years later when the United States did send in twenty-three thousand troops to prevent what was thought to be a Castro-inspired revolution from succeeding.

It is probably a correct conclusion that in Cuba we did too little in the last year of the Batista regime; in the Dominican Republic we overreacted. The Dominican Republic is one of those notorious cases (like South Vietnam in 1963) where the United States went to such extraordinary lengths as to help assassinate a head of state and eventually to occupy the country militarily, all on the basis of mistaken assumptions and false readings of the local situation.

Somoza and Nicaragua

The Somoza regime in Nicaragua was never quite so brutal or repressive as the two regimes just examined. Nor was the United States quite the regime's unabashed bolster and supporter that is often portrayed in the popular accounts. The Somoza regime was authoritarian but not totalitarian, paternalistic but only mildly repressive, dictatorial but not universally hated by the population—until near the end.

Anastasio Somoza was recruited for the Nicaraguan National Guard during a time in the 1920s when the United States was occupying the country; and we helped promote him through the ranks to become commander of the Guard. But in the late 1920s and early 1930s, Presidents Coolidge and Hoover were under considerable domestic pressure to withdraw the U.S. occupation troops from Latin America, including Nicaragua. Once we had withdrawn, we lost interest in the area and followed a policy of "benign neglect," as it would become known in a later era. There is no evidence of U.S. involvement or complicity in the coup that brought Somoza to power.[30]

Nor is it accurate to say that once he was in power the United States unequivocally and consistently supported Somoza. The United States did acquiesce in his rule, provided some limited military assistance, and was grateful for Somoza's support and assistance during World War II and in the cold war. Some U.S. ambassadors and congressmen were supportive of Somoza. But the United States was just as often uneasy about Somoza's dictatorship, tried at times to bolster the democratic opposition, sought to encourage reforms through the Alliance for Progress, and attempted at various times to get the regime to share power more broadly. The United States was, for example, more supportive of Somoza's first son and heir, Luís, who was more liberal than his father; sought to give René Schick, a Somoza puppet who served as president during the 1960s, some greater independence from the family; and rather often (although seldom consistently or effectively) sought to push the family toward greater social and economic development and a political opening.[31]

Preoccupied by Vietnam and Watergate, the United States missed an opportunity in the early 1970s to prod Somoza's second son, Anastasio Jr., toward reform. Instead, the regime became more corrupt, more brutal, and its base of support ever narrower. As the repression and corruption mounted, so too did the opposition, eventually encompassing the middle class, the business community, and the U.S. embassy.

But the United States temporized, followed a contradictory policy, waited too long, and was eventually left with virtually no influence on the incoming Sandinista revolutionaries. We tried, half-heartedly, to get Somoza Jr. to reform the regime, but it was too late and not enough. Again late in the game we tried to get him to hold honest elections, to share power, to leave peacefully. We cajoled and pleaded, sent special emissaries, even promised he could take some of the treasury with him if he left power. To all these supplications, Somoza, like Batista and Trujillo, said no. And again, short of sending in the marines and forcibly removing him from power, the United States was unable to act even against this small Central American country.[32]

Another ingredient was present in our approach to Nicaragua, and that was the Carter administration's reluctance, after Vietnam, to get so involved in the internal affairs of a small Third World country. We knew we had to manipulate Somoza out of power for our own national interest purposes, but many within the administration were reluctant to do so. The Carter administration was divided over how far it should go in pressuring

Somoza; but by waiting until the end of 1978 to do something, it lost the more attractive options that earlier might have produced effective results. It is not that pure idealism (nonintervention) triumphed over pure real-politik; but rather that the ambivalence about intervening postponed needed decisions and led to a disastrous temporizing that rendered U.S. policy ineffective, ruled out decisive action in favor of other alternatives, and enabled the Sandinistas to triumph on their own (with some Latin American assistance) without the United States, even *against* the United States. When finally the United States did act, so much assistance was already in the pipeline that the cutoff had no effect on Somoza; when we resumed our aid after the revolution, it took a long time to get going again, and thus had little effect on the Sandinistas.[33]

At one level the temporizing and indecision over Somoza were reminiscent of the ineffective policy followed twenty years earlier toward Batista. We did too little too late, and in the end could only stand by and watch as the revolution triumphed. The difference is that in the Cuban case there was no evidence that Castro was a Marxist-Leninist and that the outcome of doing so little could be so disastrous. But in the Nicaraguan case the administration *knew* that the Sandinistas were not all freedom-loving social democrats, and yet even with this knowledge could not get its act together sufficiently to carry out an effective policy. That may be partially a product of the new, more immobilized foreign policymaking system of the post-Vietnam era. In any case, the result was a disaster for U.S. foreign policy. We were hated by the right for not supporting Somoza, by the left for not supporting *Sandinismo,* and by the center for being ineffective. And as the Sandinista revolution came more and more under Marxist-Leninist dominance, Nicaragua proved to be a disaster for the United States both on strategic grounds and in terms of supporting democracy.

Duvalier and Haiti

Haiti is the poorest country in the Western Hemisphere, and probably the least developed and institutionalized. Its history has been even more turbulent than that of its neighbors; and years of erosion of its topsoil, pilfering of the public treasury, and neglect of the national economy have left Haiti with little in the way of an economic and social base on which a viable and effective democracy could be based.

Haiti was governed after 1957 by another in the long list of Haitian tyrants, François (Papa Doc) Duvalier. Duvalier had built his political following on the base of his medical practice. He was popular at first, but like the other autocrats considered here, he became over time increasingly brutal and cruel until he had lost virtually all of his popular support. In 1971 Duvalier died peacefully in his bed, and power passed to his son and heir, Jean-Claude (Baby Doc).[34]

For a time it appeared that the young Duvalier would liberalize the regime and provide some needed spurs to the economy. On that basis the United States resumed its aid, which had been suspended in the 1960s. But the political opening closed after a time, and the familiar pattern of corruption, terrorism, human rights abuses, and mismanagement of the public administration reasserted itself.

Duvalier was not an aging tyrant like Batista, Trujillo, and even Somoza Jr. when the end came for him. Nor was there, at least in the short term, the threat—real or perceived by the United States—of a Castro-like revolution and takeover of the country. In these respects the Haitian case is distinct from those previously considered.

At least five special considerations make the Haitian case unique, prompting action from the United States but for reasons different from those that were analyzed in the other cases.[35] First, the plight of the Haitian boat people, risking their lives in makeshift vessels to get to the United States, focused a great deal of unfavorable publicity on the country. Second, the human rights situation in Haiti not only deteriorated badly but became the subject of critical U.S. concern. Third, the Black Caucus in the U.S. Congress focused the spotlight on Haiti and was critical of both the State Department and the White House for not doing more to push for reform.

A fourth factor might be termed the "demonstration effect" of the U.S. opposition to Ferdinand Marcos in the Philippines, which served to focus attention on the Duvalier regime as "next." And fifth, there was the character of Jean-Claude Duvalier himself, who was not as hungry to stay in power as were the other autocrats here discussed. When the showdown finally came, Duvalier did not strenuously resist (although some members of his family did) but instead served champagne at the palace, drove himself to the plane provided by the United States, and went peacefully into exile to enjoy his wealth in the lovely South of France.

The end for Duvalier also came as a result of internal events in Haiti. The Catholic Church had taken up the cudgel of opposition to the regime. The political opposition was growing from other quarters. Riots and demonstrations were spreading. Eventually Duvalier, the United States, and France began a negotiation that resulted in the decision for Duvalier to go, and how, where, and when. The "President for Life" did not put up a fight as the other tyrants had done. Comparatively speaking, while hardly amiable, the negotiations were not rancorous or so confrontational as the others here described. Duvalier in fact made it relatively easy from the point of view of U.S. policy.

While it proved relatively easy to usher Duvalier out of power, achieving democracy in Haiti proved far more problematic. Haiti had almost none of the institutional infrastructure (parties, unions, and so forth) on which a functioning democracy could be built. After a year of violence, bloodshed, and disintegration, elections were held in January 1988. But the military remained the strongest institution in the country; and by mid-1988 the elected president, Leslie Manigat, was out of power, the military was back in, and Haiti slipped back into dictatorial rule.

The moves to help oust Duvalier came as a result chiefly of domestic pressures in the United States—from religious institutions, from the congressional Black Caucus, and from Americans appalled at the events in Haiti. These pressures sometimes had only a limited relationship with the realities of Haiti, most particularly its institutional void. Hence Haiti may yet turn out to be the foreign policy disaster for the United States that the strategy of getting rid of Duvalier was, at least ostensibly, designed to prevent.

Stroessner and Paraguay

In 1985, General Alfredo Stroessner, who came to power in Paraguay in 1954, passed the record of the Dominican Republic's Trujillo as the longest-ruling dictator in the history of Latin America. There is a certain perverse pride among dictators in these matters.

Stroessner's rule was that of a traditional authoritarian in what had been Latin America's "sleepiest," most backward, most nineteenth-century society. Stroessner was the last of the old-fashioned, traditional, man-on-horseback dictators.[36]

But recently things had begun to change, in Paraguay and in the regime. Stroessner was old. The regime was weakening. Sensing that the end might be near, the opposition had become emboldened. At the same time, Paraguay itself was changing in major ways. The considerable economic development of the past several decades had given rise to vast social changes. The society had become far more urban, literate, complex, and differentiated.[37] But as the society became more modern, the means by which Stroessner sought to control it and stay in power also became more complex, even totalitarian. Stroessner's Paraguay was a classic case of the model presented in the first part of this chapter, of a traditional authoritarian whose regime began to wobble, which caused it both to use more totalitarian techniques of control and to lose increasingly its base of popular support.

U.S. policy in Paraguay was directed toward securing an orderly and peaceful transition toward democracy once Stroessner left power. But at the same time, since Paraguay has not faced serious guerrilla challenges and has had only a small Communist party, there was no sense of immediacy to the campaign or of imminent disaster unless we did something.

To that end a succession of U.S. ambassadors—even those who admired the dictator's accomplishments—had put pressure on Stroessner on the human rights issue and urged him to democratize and open up his regime. The U.S. embassy began to distance itself from Stroessner while not threatening to break relations, oust the dictator, or use the other strong methods we used in other cases. U.S. embassy personnel protested against the regime's censorship, met publicly with the opposition, and urged a transition to democracy. The U.S. ambassador backed demands that the dictator lift the state of siege and come out for a free press, urged freedom of assembly and of the rights of independent trade unions, and suggested that political exiles (perhaps 10 percent of the population) be allowed to return home.

These activities did not endear the U.S. embassy to the Stroessner regime. The embassy was accused of interference in Paraguay's internal affairs, and the government threatened to declare the ambassador persona non grata and demand his recall. The United States had to be careful not to overcommit its support to the opposition, or it ran the risk of being booted out of the country and thus losing its capacity to help shape future Paraguayan events altogether.[38]

Although one could continue to quibble about certain individual initiatives of the embassy, the United States pursued a correct policy in Paraguay. The warm *abrazo* had turned into a cold handshake.

We continued to have correct relations with the regime and therefore some influence over it and its future directions. We did not entirely alienate the regime or its important supporters. On the other hand we distanced ourselves from the regime, established ties to the growing opposition, and were thus in a good position to help shape the post-Stroessner transition.

On balance, this measured and careful response on the part of the United States toward events in Paraguay was just about right. In January 1989, Stroessner was ousted and an opening toward democracy seemed in the offing.

Pinochet and Chile

Among the right-wing dictatorships in Latin America, Chile would seem to represent the most dangerous situation.[39] First, Chile is a far more important country to the United States, strategically, politically, and economically, than is Paraguay. Second, because of the long tradition of democracy in Chile, the special U.S. role in aiding the opposition to socialist president Salvador Allende and in supporting the military dictator Augusto Pinochet initially, and all the heavy ideological baggage that this past carries with it—both in Chile and internationally—the problem for U.S. foreign policy is far more complicated, for instance, than it was or is in Paraguay.

Third, the brutality and bloodthirstiness of the Pinochet regime were far greater than that of Stroessner in Paraguay. Chile was not a traditional dictatorship; it verged on the totalitarian excesses which were earlier identified as signaling the turning point between more or less acceptable authoritarianism and unacceptable tyranny. Because of this, Pinochet's popularity had plummeted by 1987 to only 20 percent of the population, and—far more than Stroessner ever was—he was viewed as a pariah (rather like South Africa) in the global community of nations. Although Pinochet was not old by the standards of other long-lived dictators and he could conceivably have stayed in office through 1999, his earlier support had eroded and he had begun to look wobbly—again a telling indicator of the need to shift the U.S. foreign policy posture toward the regime.

Fourth—and again unlike Paraguay—Chile has a strong, experienced, *real* Communist party. The twin dangers exist that the Communist party of Chile might have captured the left opposition to Pinochet, which constitutes some 30–35 percent of the population; or that if Pinochet refused to make any openings to democracy, then the strong democratic center in Chile might become radicalized, in which case the communists would benefit once again.

Yet the United States had limited leverage over Chile. Congress had long since cut off aid to Chile, so we could not very well get effective mileage by eliminating the few programs of humanitarian assistance that did exist. We had earlier ended military sales to the regime, which meant only that the Chileans purchased arms from other suppliers. Our private economic holdings, foreign aid, and number of personnel in Chile were all down, so we had little room for maneuver in these areas either.[40]

Nor is Chile a "banana republic" that we can simply boss around. U.S. government officials recognized the dangers that Chile and the Pinochet regime represented and had tried mightily to do something about them.

228 / POLITICAL DIMENSIONS

But when a U.S. assistant secretary of state for inter-American affairs met in the mid-1980s with Pinochet and in effect told him, "Here are the keys to the Mercedes, here is the number of the Swiss bank account, and here is the plane waiting to carry you away; see you later, *Señor Presidente*," Pinochet all but physically booted him out of his office. Chile is, and thinks of itself, as a mature and sophisticated country; its president cannot be subjected to the same treatment that we in our proconsular role might give to an obscure colonel in Central America.

The Chilean situation is thus a very difficult one, made even harder by the fact that the United States has few levers it can use. That reality is not always appreciated by the Chileans, however, who tend to think that the United States needed only to snap its fingers and Pinochet would be gone. Conversely, while the regime knows it could get along very well without U.S. aid or military sales, it nevertheless wished to have U.S. approval. The result was an anomaly: both the government and the opposition wanted the United States to be involved, but on different sides; and both overestimated the capacity of the United States to shape Chilean events.

Hence a strange stalemate developed in U.S. policy. U.S. officials met repeatedly with Pinochet to get him to improve the human rights situation and to begin a transition to democracy as the other Latin American countries had done, but for a long time the dictator refused to budge. Nor did the United States really have the influence to force Pinochet to do what he was unwilling to do himself. The United States also met with the Chilean armed forces commanders to see if they would either pressure Pinochet to restore democracy or else oust him altogether, but there was little movement from that quarter. There have even been reports (whether true or springing from Pinochet's feverish imagination) that the CIA was again active in Chile, seeking to depose the dictator. If that proves true, it would be a marvelous irony (1) because it is the CIA that is often held responsible for deposing the leftist Allende and bringing Pinochet to power in the first place; and (2) because many of the current protests on U.S. college campuses against the CIA assume that the CIA overthrows only left-wing governments, never right-wing ones.

Chile is an interesting case because it fits virtually all of our criteria of when the United States should not only distance itself from a wobbly tyrant but even move against him for sound political and security reasons. And yet our capacity to act decisively in the Chilean situation was severely circumscribed. Pressure, bribes, blandishments, and gentlemanly understandings were all tried; none worked. Short of sending in the marines to depose Pinochet—an unthinkable and unacceptable act—the U.S. capacity to influence Chile and push it toward democracy was limited. Meanwhile, the domestic dangers in Chile and for U.S. policy continued to mount.

For a long time the United States was frustrated concerning its inability to engineer a democratic opening in Chile. But in 1988 the opportunity came. Pinochet agreed to hold a plebiscite on his regime in which voters could vote yes or no on whether they wished the strongman to continue in office. No alternative parties or candidates were on the ballot, just the up or down vote that Pinochet assumed he would win. The United States had urged Pinochet to hold such a vote; now it assisted in the registration of voters and insisted the votes be counted honestly. To Pinochet's surprise, the no vote won. The vote was not definitive, and at this stage we do not know what the alternative to Pinochet will be. But the referendum at least put in motion a democratic political process that might produce a favorable outcome. The U.S. embassy was heavily involved in all these activities.

Panama

Panama has been a very frustrating case for U.S. policymakers—perhaps the most frustrating of all the cases considered here.

The most powerful force in Panama has long been the National Guard or National Defense Forces (NDF). But Panama has also tried, intermittently, to maintain a democratic facade and to incorporate civilians within the regime. That was the pattern when Nicolás Ardito Barletta was chosen president in 1984, but the NDF under Manuel Noriega remained the ultimate arbiter of national affairs. When Ardito Barletta later ran afoul of Noriega, he was quickly ousted, although a civilian vice president, Eric Arturo Delvalle, helped maintain the thin facade of democracy. Noriega was the main power in the country.

The U.S. had put increasing pressure on Noriega to restore full democracy by holding new elections. Noriega was an embarrassment to U.S. policy in Latin America, which had by now put so many of its eggs in the democracy basket. The issue reached a head when Noriega was indicted by a Miami grand jury for drug-related activities. That elevated the issue in the public consciousness and made Noriega a household name. Some U.S. officials talked brazenly of forcing Noriega to stand trial in the United States, forcing him out of office, and brushing him aside. Such public statements were probably uncalled for; on the other hand, with the drug indictment Noriega had become an issue in U.S. domestic politics—drugs are the most important issue, the polls tell us—and probably could not be dealt with in the quieter way that other "friendly tyrants" had been initially approached. Complicating the situation was the fact that Noriega had long cooperated with and had been on the payroll of the U.S. government.

The U.S. badly underestimated Noriega. While not popular among the urban, educated, middle-class elements, among whose members the U.S. government has most of its contacts, he had widespread popular support in the rural areas. Domestically and to the outside world, he presented himself as "David" against the U.S. "Goliath." Moreover, Noriega proved to be a cunning and very tough *hombre*. Trying to gain mileage out of the anti-Americanism that the U.S. efforts to oust Noriega had generated, Fidel Castro signaled his support and sent reinforcements. Noriega dug in his heels, seemingly outsmarting the U.S. at every turn.

The U.S. efforts to get rid of Noriega merit a book-length analysis. Suffice it to say that we tried *every one* of the methods listed on pp. 217–18— and then some. Since Panama is a commercial center, the U.S. ordered U.S. banks operating there not to pay taxes to the regime. We imposed an economic embargo. We beefed up the U.S. military forces in the Canal Zone, a form of saber-rattling. We threatened to postpone or cancel altogether the Panama Canal Treaties, which provide for the turning over of the Canal to Panama by the year 2000. U.S. political figures made extraordinarily provocative public statements about Panama, apparently hoping to blow Noriega away by sheer bluster. We were even treated to the incredible spectacle of one of Washington's premier *private* law firms, Arnold and Porter, taking on the Panama "case," mobilizing the opposition to Noriega, trying to expand the economic quarantine, and seeking to bring Noriega down. Such "privatization" of U.S. foreign policy had not heretofore been used as a method to get rid of unfriendly dictators—at least since the days of dollar diplomacy.

Most of this spectacle was acted out on U.S. television, including the bloody scenes of an opposition presidential candidate, Guillermo Endara (who presumably had won the election that Noriega tried to rig), being roughed up by pro-Noriega toughs and his presidential running mate, Guillermo Ford, being chased down the street with his shirt soaked in blood. In the Philippine case, such bloody scenes of human rights violations covered on international television had helped usher dictator Marcos from office; but in Panama Noriega survived even the power of television.

The result was an impasse. *Nothing* the U.S. did worked. The Panamanian economy was in ruins but Noriega had managed to survive. The OAS, in an attempt to recapture the decisive role it had once played in the ouster of Trujillo, this time proved ineffectual. The U.S. fumed but Noriega stayed in place. Meanwhile, Panama, along with Iran, became one of the main frustrations and embarrassments of U.S. foreign policy. The U.S. appeared inept, powerless, and a paper tiger. The policy of nudging dictators aside and encouraging democracy proved, in this case, *entirely* ineffective. *Everything* had been tried; *nothing* had worked. Panama did not prove to be an example of dealing with an authoritarian regime whose lessons one would want to apply in other countries.

The key to Panama is patience—not exactly a characteristic of American foreign policy that we are famous for. Noriega could not last forever, especially against all the pressure that had been applied, and there is a Panamanian political process that should have worked to get rid of Noriega. We needed therefore to keep the pressure on, turn down some of our heated and overwrought rhetoric, exercise patience, and not expect instantaneous results. Eventually U.S. patience ran out, however, and the U.S. intervened militarily to remove Noriega.

Mexico

Mexico is a special case and deserves special treatment. The problem is not a tyrant, whether wobbly or otherwise, but a whole *system* of *institutionalized authoritarianism* that has become less and less effective and more and more unacceptable to the Mexican population. An additional special problem with regard to Mexico is that it shares a two-thousand-mile border with the United States, lies on our vulnerable southern flank, and is the last country in the world we would want to see destabilized.

Mexico is governed by a single party, the Institutional Revolutionary Party, that has dominated—one could almost say monopolized—Mexican politics for the past sixty years. The Mexican system is top-down, authoritarian, and closed. It is based on patronage and spoils. Those who understand big-city machine politics in the United States will understand Mexican politics very well, except that in Mexico the machine is national and not just local. In recent years, as Mexico has modernized, this top-down system has become less and less functional. It has become bloated and pervasively corrupt. The various shocks through which the Mexican economy has gone, the devastating earthquake of 1986, and spiraling social problems have added to our worries about Mexico.[41] Mexico is not a dictatorship in the same sense the other regimes discussed here are, but it is an authoritarian regime that many feel to be shaky. Zbigniew Brzezinski has been saying that Mexico may become the "next Iran"—a false and dangerous statement that if repeated often enough could eventually take on the character of a self-fulfilling prophecy. My own belief is that we may well see a gradual, long-term crisis and even some unraveling of the Mexican system, but no general breakdown.[42]

The crisis (really series of crises) in Mexico and the fact that it lies on our border and that it frequently gets entangled in our domestic politics (drugs, immigration, water resources, pollution, investment, and tourism are but some of the ways the United States and Mexico are interconnected) have given rise to the widespread sentiment, in some quarters at least, that *we* should *do something* about Mexico. Plans to do something range from getting rid of Mexican corruption, to reforming the party system by aiding a second competitive party, to making Mexican elections more honest, to privatizing the Mexican economy, to bringing genuine (U.S.–style) pluralism and competitiveness to Mexico, to assisting Mexican local government, to rationalizing and cleaning up the public service.

While many Mexican institutions are badly in need of reform,[43] it is risky for the United States to get too heavily involved in Mexican internal affairs. The United States has limited knowledge of the working of the Mexican system, and it is unlikely *we* can reform it without upsetting the entire applecart. In addition to the nationalistic protests that are certain to vehemently accompany any U.S. efforts to reform Mexico and that would largely render our efforts futile if not self-defeating, we simply lack the knowledge of and empathy with things Mexican and how their system in all its component parts hangs together and "works." One is reminded of Alan Riding's conclusion that, to the degree *we* attempt to democratize Mexico, we run the risk of destabilizing it.[44] And that, recall, is the country of the world we least wish to see destabilized. Nor is Mexico some banana republic that we can easily manipulate.

The Mexicans themselves realize that their system needs to change; and with some sympathy and modest assistance if they wish from us, that is probably the best approach. But the Mexicans are also divided as to what needs to be done. Some want only to tinker very modestly so as to make the present system work a bit better and be acceptable to the United States and the lending agencies. Others want a thorough democratization that would imply some quite radical social and economic restructuring as well as political change. In between are those who would combine some tinkering with some limited structural changes so as to "democratize" the system. This is the more likely scenario, assuming that the system does not break down in the meantime.

But recall that what this in-between group means by "democracy" is not necessarily what is meant in the United States. Here it is important to go back to the discussion at the beginning of this book. If Mexico "democratizes," it will most likely do so in a Rousseauean fashion and not a Lockean one.[45] That means that Mexico will probably remain basically a one-party state, top-down, executive centered, paternalistic, and patronage dominated. But at the same time, some further elements of rationalization, participation, power sharing, and reform will be built into it. That will not make Mexico a Western-style democracy overnight. But realistically, such limited changes may be all we can expect, especially in the short term.

A Summing Up

Because authoritarian regimes in Latin America differ widely as to age, character, and "wobbliness," because some authoritarian regimes are genuinely popular, because there are simply too many of them, and because the alternative may be far worse, it does not seem prudent for the United States to divorce itself from all such regimes. We may wish to put some distance between ourselves and them—the cool handshake—but divorce, no. Too many other factors need to be considered for the United States to follow a pure and idealistic policy of having no contact with the globe's numerous dictatorial regimes. On the other hand, some dictators are so offensive to us that we may wish for both moral and sound political reasons to have nothing to do with them.

On this issue as on others the best position is a centrist one that lies between the pure idealist and the pure realpolitik positions and that also seems to be the most sensible and realistic position for U.S. foreign policy. We cannot seek to unseat all the world's authoritarian governments—neither we nor they will be well served by such a bull-in-the-china-shop approach—but we can perhaps practice an anticipatory policy by nudging them toward democratic openings and greater power sharing. We also need to be alert to when such regimes tip over that fine line that separates permissible authoritarianism by their own country's standards from unacceptable totalitarianism that not only damages them but may represent a danger to U.S. policy as well. It is at this point, as the chart that was devised helps measure, when the U.S. government may wish not only to get off that dictatorial government's bandwagon but also to move for its ouster, both as a way of promoting democracy and as a means of moderating and exercising some control over the postdictatorial transition.

The emphasis here has been on the need to cut our ties with authoritarian regimes once they start to wobble. But it may be that, in some cases, by the time such a regime starts to wobble, it is already too late for

U.S. policy. By that point we may have so antagonized the local population through our support of the dictator that anti-Americanism will already be rampant. Theodore Friend has therefore suggested that in some countries we may wish to practice "thoughtful daring"—that is, to get off the dictator's bandwagon even *before* he starts to wobble. That is a risky strategy, but it may be the one to pursue in certain circumstances. Such decisions will have to be made on a case-by-case basis and cannot become a general, across-the-board policy.

A wide array of instruments and sanctions exist for the United States to help manage this process. These instruments may be arranged in an ascending order of severity—quiet diplomacy, pressure, sanctions, and so on. In a policy sense one may gradually move up the scale, increasing the pressure as one proceeds. In some countries these instruments have been employed successfully. But there are an even larger number of cases where they did not work (Panama, most prominently), where the dictator refused to go along (Cuba), where we lost control of the process (Nicaragua, the Dominican Republic), where the situation degenerated into a dangerous anarchy (Haiti for a time), where our efforts were at first frustrated and unsuccessful (Chile), or where our greater involvement would almost certainly be self-defeating (Mexico).

The many unsuccessful efforts to exercise influence or control should give us pause both about our rushing in pell-mell to unseat very many of the world's authoritarian regimes and about our capacity to build democracy where it had not existed before or to restore it where it had. Our capacities and abilities to say nothing of our comprehension of all these different countries and their political processes are quite limited. As in the chapters on human rights, the National Endowment for Democracy, and economics, the conclusion we reach is for a cautious and careful approach in dealing with dictatorial regimes, especially those that begin to totter. There are things that we can do to influence such regimes and their aftermaths, and to assist democracy, but many others we should not try. Our policy initiatives therefore need to be prudent, realistic, and modest, not wild-eyed, naive, and wishful. On that basis the United States can both advance the cause of Latin American democracy and at the same time best serve its foreign policy interests.

Notes

1. A colleague at the American Enterprise Institute, Mark Falcoff, has helped in the formulation of these issues.
2. The ideas in this introductory section were given preliminary expression in

Howard J. Wiarda, "Introduction: Dealing with Dictators in Decline," presentation made at the Public Policy Week Forum of the American Enterprise Institute, Washington, D.C., December 1985; and published in the special issue of the journal *World Affairs* (Spring 1987) devoted to this topic.

3. See A. M. Rosenthal, "Change of Heart: American Foreign Policy Toward Dictators," *New York Times,* July 26, 1987, p. E25.

4. See the discussion in Barry Rubin, *Modern Dictators* (New York: McGraw-Hill, 1987).

5. The debate between these positions is especially well formulated by Adam Garfinkle, "Conclusion," in Garfinkle and Daniel Pipes, eds., *Friendly Tyrants* (Philadelphia: Foreign Policy Research Institute, 1989).

6. Ibid.; see also Hans Binnendijk, ed., *Authoritarian Regimes in Transition* (Washington, D.C.: Center for the Study of Foreign Affairs, Foreign Service Institute, Department of State, 1987).

7. See the discussion in Douglas Pike's paper on South Vietnam in Garfinkle and Pipes, *Friendly Tyrants.*

8. Juan Linz, "Notes toward a Typology of Authoritarian Regimes," paper delivered at the Annual Meeting of the American Political Science Association, Washington, D.C., September 5–9, 1972.

9. Carl J. Friedrich and Zbigniew Brzezinski, *Totalitarian Dictatorship and Autocracy* (New York: Praeger, 1962).

10. Jeane J. Kirkpatrick, "Dictatorships and Double Standards," *Commentary* 10 (November 1979).

11. Howard J. Wiarda, *Dictatorship and Development* (Gainesville: University of Florida Press, 1968).

12. Hugh Thomas, "Cuba: The United States and Batista, 1952–58," *World Affairs* 149 (Spring 1987): 169–75.

13. Robert D. Crassweller, *Trujillo* (New York: Macmillan, 1966).

14. Richard Millett, *Guardians of the Dynasty* (New York: Orbis, 1977).

15. Gary Sick, *All Fall Down: America's Tragic Encounter with Iran* (New York: Random House, 1985).

16. Pamela Constable, "Pinochet's Grip on Chile," *Current History* 86 (January 1987): 17–20ff.

17. An earlier version of this scale was presented in Howard J. Wiarda, ed., *The Continuing Struggle for Democracy in Latin America* (Boulder, Colo.: Westview Press, 1980), Conclusion.

18. See Roy C. Macridis, *Modern Political Regimes* (Boston: Little, Brown, 1986).

19. On the concept of limited pluralism in authoritarian regimes see Juan Linz, "An Authoritarian Regime: Spain," in E. Allardt and S. Rokkan, eds., *Mass Politics* (New York: Free Press, 1970).

20. The rank ordering presented here, although useful, is still too heavily subjective. It requires a panel of experts rather than the evaluation of just one evaluator. The author's assessments are grounded on long-time study of Latin America and on the country-by-country analysis found in Howard J. Wiarda and Harvey F. Kline, eds., *Latin American Politics and Development* (Boulder, Colo.: Westview Press, 1985; third edition, 1990). But because they are based on one person's evaluations, the tables presented here are treated as examples

of the type of useful analysis that could be presented and not as a basis for the entire analysis that follows.

21. Quoted in Arthur M. Schlesinger, Jr., *A Thousand Days: John F. Kennedy in the White House* (Boston: Houghton Mifflin, 1965), pp. 769–70.

22. Karl Meyer, "The Lesser Evil Doctrine," *The New Leader,* October 14, 1963, p. 8.

23. See the comments of former CIA director and ambassador to Iran Richard Helms at the AEI forum on "Dictators in Decline"; see also the comments of three governmental participants in the Iran crisis—Harold Saunders of the State Department, Gary Sick of the National Security Council, and U.S. Ambassador to Iran William Sullivan, in *World Affairs* (Spring 1987).

24. Ramón Ruiz, *Cuba: The Making of a Revolution* (New York: Norton, 1968).

25. Based on interviews with those State Department officials who prepared the brief. But see also Tad Szulc, *Fidel: A Critical Portrait* (New York: Morrow, 1986).

26. For a full discussion, see Crassweller, *Trujillo;* also Wiarda, *Dictatorship and Development.*

27. Howard J. Wiarda, *Dictatorship, Development and Disintegration: Politics and Social Change in the Dominican Republic* (Ann Arbor: Monograph Series of Xerox University Microfilms, 1975), chap. 11.

28. Jerome Slater, "The United States, the Organization of American States, and the Dominican Republic, 1961–63," *International Organization* 18, no. 2 (1964).

29. Bernard Diederich, *Trujillo: The Death of the Goat* (Boston: Little, Brown, 1978).

30. Millett, *Guardians of the Dynasty.*

31. Mark Falcoff, "Somoza, Sandino, and the United States: What the Past Teaches—and Doesn't," *This World,* no. 6 (Fall 1983).

32. The best account is Shirley Christian, *Nicaragua: Revolution in the Family* (New York: Vintage, 1985); also Robert Pastor, *Condemned to Repetition: The United States and Nicaragua* (Princeton, N.J.: Princeton University Press, 1987).

33. Nicaragua is in fact a good illustration of the ineffectiveness of aid cutoffs and renewals as a means to leverage foreign governments; see *ibid;* also Anthony Lake, *Somoza Falling* (Boston: Houghton Mifflin, 1989).

34. Bernard Diederich and Al Burt, *Papa Doc: The Truth about Haiti Today* (New York: McGraw-Hill, 1969).

35. The best analysis is by Georges Fauriol, "Friendly Haitian Tyrants," in Garfinkle and Pipes, *Friendly Tyrants.*

36. For the context see Howard J. Wiarda, "The Political Systems of Latin America: Developmental Models and a Typology of Regimes," in Jack Hopkins, ed., *Latin America* (New York: Holmes & Meier, 1987), pp. 243–56.

37. Paul H. Lewis, *Paraguay Under Stroessner* (Chapel Hill: University of North Carolina Press, 1980).

38. Ben Wattenberg, "Winds of Change in Paraguay," *Washington Times,* May 7, 1987, p. D1.

39. The analysis here relies on Mark Falcoff, "Chile, The Dilemma for U.S. Policy," *Foreign Affairs* 64 (Spring 1986): 833–48; also Falcoff, "Chile: Pinochet, the Opposition, and the United States," *World Affairs* 149 (Spring 1987).

40. "U.S. Influence in Chile Almost Nil, Envoy Says," *Washington Times,* March 20, 1987.

41. Evelyn Stevens, "Mexico in the 1980s: From Authoritarianism to Power-Sharing?" in Wiarda and Kline, eds., *Latin American Politics and Development,* pp. 403–45.

42. The process by which authoritarian-corporate regimes such as Mexico begin to unravel, fragment, and crumble is given general theoretical treatment in Howard J. Wiarda, "Toward a Framework for the Study of Political Change in the Iberic-Latin Tradition," *World Politics* 25 (January 1973): 206–35; see also Wiarda, "Mexico: The Unraveling of a Corporatist Regime?" *Journal of InterAmerican Studies and World Affairs* 30 (Winter 1988–89): 1–28.

43. Judith Adler Hellman, *Mexico in Crisis,* 2nd ed. (New York: Holmes & Meier, 1983).

44. Alan Riding, *Distant Neighbors: A Portrait of the Mexicans* (New York: Knopf, 1985).

45. That was precisely the argument of Mexican scholar Fernando Pérez Correa, who also served as undersecretary of government, in "The Recent Evolution of Democracy in Mexico," lecture delivered at Harvard University, Cambridge, Mass., April 30, 1986.

9

Democratic Progress—and Its Problems—in Latin America

Let us review the argument presented thus far. A little over a decade ago, the prospects for democracy in Latin America seemed very dismal indeed. Only Costa Rica in Central America and Colombia and Venezuela in South America could be considered to be democracies. The rest of the countries, although varying somewhat in form and direction, were authoritarian, often dictatorial and military regimes. Democracy seemed everywhere in Latin America to be on the wane.[1]

By the criteria of democracy suggested earlier (political competition, participation, civil and political, liberties) countries like Mexico and the Dominican Republic would at that time (1977) have to be considered mixed and marginal at best. The rest of the continent—including approximately 80 percent of its people—was awash in authoritarianism and dictatorship. Not only did democracy appear to be on the decline and authoritarianism, corporatism, and organic-statism appear to be the wave of the future, but the conceptual frameworks and models of interpretation then in vogue seemed to suggest that the development toward authoritarianism was "natural," maybe even "inevitable." The three democracies still extant were viewed as exceptions and oddities whose situations were unique and could not be repeated, or as elite-directed democracies that also exhibited authoritarian-corporatist features. Democracy in Latin America appeared doomed not just because of the political culture, the appalling social conditions, and the economic underdevelopment, but also

238

because the major intellectual constructs that scholars, journalists, and policymakers employ to understand Latin America seemed to have consigned it to the dustbins of history.

Today, that has been considerably turned around. Ninety-one percent of the people of Latin America live under democratic rule. In ten years (1978–1988) ten countries have moved dramatically to establish democracy: Argentina, Bolivia, Brazil, the Dominican Republic, Ecuador, El Salvador, Guatemala, Honduras, Peru, and Uruguay. In several others—Mexico, Haiti, and Panama, and perhaps now Paraguay and Chile—there are powerful forces moving toward democracy. Throughout the continent military presidents have been replaced by elected civilians. Although still problematic in several countries, the situation of human rights—continent-wide—is infinitely better than a decade ago. And at the intellectual level, the preoccupation with authoritarianism and corporatism has been shunted aside in favor of a new preoccupation with transitions to democracy.[2]

While there is reason to hope that these recent democratic advances may mark a turning point between Latin America's sad past and a future of greater freedom, the obstacles in democracy's path are still immense. The authoritarianism and instability so prevalent in Latin America's past and the often unhappy history of U.S. relations with the continent are such as to leave one less than wildly optimistic about either democracy's future in the hemisphere or the possibilities for convergence between U.S. and Latin American interests in these regards. The trends toward convergence, as a quite realistic State Department document recently put it,[3] are real but they are also fragile. The obstacles to democracy in Latin America (discussed in more detail below) include militarism, poverty, horrendous social conditions, and extremisms of various sorts. The barriers to the U.S. overcoming its historic biases, indifference, and condescension toward Latin America, and of assisting the new democratic thrusts, seem almost equally problematic. The questions therefore are whether the Latin American nations can continue to move toward fully consolidated democracies, whether the United States can overcome its historic legacies and assist that process in enlightened ways, and whether in the course of these two movements there is the possibility for some greater harmony of interests between the United States and Latin America. Those are the issues explored in this chapter and the conclusion that follows.

Progress toward Democracy in Latin America

Why is it that democracy has emerged triumphant in so many Latin American countries in the past ten years? What forces are at work that have promoted these changes? Why is it that scholars and others failed to see and predict these changes? Most importantly, is the shift toward democracy in Latin America permanent or ephemeral? Is it likely to last, or is it just another of these periodic turns in Latin America, certain to come full circle, once the euphoria with democracy fades and its failures become apparent, with a return to military rule?[4]

It is to be expected, realistically, that not all of Latin America's new democracies will remain stable and that in some, particularly the more fragmented and uninstitutionalized countries, the lure and attraction of an authoritarian solution will remain present. Nevertheless, we need not conclude, if the military returns to power in some countries, that democracy in Latin America is therefore a failure or that U.S. policy in assisting democratic development is wrong. While there are and will be new pressures for an authoritarian "out," it is also true that some other strong and underlying forces have been at work as well, permanently changing the face of Latin America. These include cultural changes, socioeconomic changes, political-institutional changes, and influences from outside the region, all of which have tended to reduce the influence and strength of the traditional society and to provide the forces of modernization and democratization with a new impetus. This section of the chapter describes and reviews the progressive changes that have occurred and that have led toward democracy and its consolidation; the next describes the obstacles still in the way.

THE EXHAUSTION AND BANKRUPTCY OF OTHER MODELS

By the mid-1970s the wind had clearly gone out of the military regimes that had come to power earlier. Whether of the left "Nasserist" variety in Peru or Panama or of the right "bureaucratic-authoritarian" type in Brazil or Argentina, these military regimes had proven to be just as corrupt and incompetent as the civilians whom they had replaced. This was an especially telling indictment of the military regimes that had always prided themselves on their competence and administrative abilities. But by the middle of the 1970s, the consensus was becoming widespread in numerous countries, even within the military institution itself where thoughtful officers feared the discredit being cast upon the armed forces because of their political and economic mismanagement, that it was time for the military to leave power. Such discrediting and dislike of the officer corps were general, but especially acute in Argentina because economic and political mismanagement had been compounded by disastrous defeat in the Falklands/Malvinas war. By the mid-1970s in some countries and on into the early 1980s in others the authoritarian wave had run its course, and everyone agreed that the military simply had to go. As the armed forces officers themselves came to agree with this assessment, it became simply a matter of time and proper procedures (that would not result in the destruction of the military itself) before the period of dictatorship came to an end.

But the left alternative, in most countries, was equally discredited.[5] Michael Manley's earlier populist regime had been a failure in Jamaica; the Cuban revolution had failed to develop the country economically and its Stalinist-like regime was not attractive politically; and Grenada and Nicaragua demonstrated that a Marxist-Leninist regime yields chiefly chaos, destruction, economic disaster, and bloodshed. Nor was Marxism-Leninism more generally attractive in Latin America: the Soviet Union was not viewed as a very pleasant place, its economic performance was widely known to be terrible, and its invasion of Afghanistan severely damaged its global credibility. Of all the countries in Latin America only Nicaragua—for unique reasons having to do with the special character of the Somoza regime, the history of U.S. interventions and the frustrated nationalism to which this gave rise, and the deftness by which Marxist-Leninist elements within the broader anti-Somoza coalition captured the revolution—opted during this period for a Marxist-Leninist regime. And the results since 1979 have not served to make Nicaragua any more attractive to others.

With the discrediting of both the right-wing solutions and the extreme left-wing ones, centrist democracy emerged as the only viable alternative.

LA MODA

Latin America, as noted in Chapter 3, has always been preoccupied with showing the rest of the world that it too is civilized and advanced. It too wants to be "in style," to keep abreast of and emulate outside tastes and preferences. By the late 1970s and early 1980s it clearly was democracy that was *la moda* globally, as events in Greece, Spain, Portugal, and the Philippines demonstrated. These and other movements, in Poland, China, and perhaps the Soviet Union, bolstered the growing sense that to be for democracy was to be in the vanguard of history. That mood, that sense—however vague and imprecise such notions may be to social scientists—was enormously important in propelling Latin America in a democratic direction. As the movement for democracy and human rights that began in the 1970s grew in the 1980s into a global movement and with global acclaim, the pressures on Latin America to move toward and *remain* in the democratic camp continued and were even stepped up. Democracy's "moment" in Latin America seemed finally to have arrived.

Latin America, in short, has been the beneficiary of a worldwide movement toward democracy that as we enter the 1990s shows no signs of abating.

SOCIOECONOMIC MODERNIZATION

The face of Latin America in the 1990s is quite different from what it was in the early 1960s, when the last great experiment in bringing democracy to Latin America, through the Alliance for Progress, was attempted. This fact is insufficiently recognized by persons who know little of Latin American history and development over the last three decades. Latin America has become far more literate (79 percent versus 55 percent) and educated (primary school enrollments increased from 57 percent in 1960 to 82 percent, secondary enrollment from 35 percent to 63 percent, and university enrollments from 6 percent to 26 percent).[6] An educated, literate population has led to greater awareness, greater participation, expanded opportunities, and growing demands on government for democracy and effective public performance and services.

Latin America also became far more urban, going from 37 percent urban in 1950 to almost 70 percent in 1987. Rapid urbanization led to a more participatory and involved population while simultaneously eroding the base of the traditional wielders of power in the society: the landed oligarchy, the traditional church, and the rural and regionally based men on horseback.

Latin America is moreover far more affluent than it was earlier. This long-term growth has been impressive, despite the more recent economic downturn. Between 1960 and 1980, holding constant for population, real per capita income doubled. There is more money around than there used to be, also more jobs and more opportunities. Not all of this wealth has fled the country for Miami or Geneva or ended up in upper- or middle-class pockets. Some of it has even "trickled down."

In addition, the economic quickening of the past quarter century and the accompanying industrialization, mechanization, and growth have served to erode some of the old class barriers and have stimulated the emergence of an employed working class and of a much larger middle class, which may number 20 to 40 percent of the population now, depending on the country. There remain, of course, immense social and economic gaps in Latin America, and the economic depression of the early 1980s resulted in lowered living standards in many countries. Nevertheless, the overall gains should not be lost sight of. All of the socioeconomic changes of recent years have had a profound and likely irreversible effect on the class structure, the values of the Latin Americans, and their demands for political participation and greater democracy. Cumulatively, these changes made it far harder for the dictatorships of the region to stay in power—or to return.

These trends mean that the scholars who emphasized the presumed permanence of Iberic-Latin corporate-authoritarian regimes had overstated the case and ignored some important change-oriented factors.[7] These scholars had been influenced by studies of Iberia, where the dictatorships of Franco and Salazar proved not only enormously long lived but also, contrary to expectations and a good deal of earlier modernization literature, capable of handling and absorbing a great deal of socioeconomic development without undermining their regimes. The similarly authoritarian-corporate and seemingly long-lived regimes in Brazil, Argentina, and elsewhere on the Latin American continent were thought to be following in the same mold.[8] But the scholars of authoritarianism underestimated the strength of the democratic currents alive and pulsating in these societies, underestimated the effects of the socioeconomic changes, overestimated the strength of the often fragile dictatorships then in power, and failed to take account of the international pressures in favor of democracy that would come to operate.

If the scholarly theorists of authoritarianism-corporatism overestimated that kind of regime's staying power, they underestimated (and indeed had often dismissed) the power—and the literature—of development. The developmentalist school had posited that, once modernization began in societies like those of Latin America, the virtually inevitable and universal outcome would be the growth of moderate, middle-class democracies.[9] Now this school, closely linked to the Alliance for Progress and the earlier U.S. foreign assistance program, had clearly exaggerated its point just as had the authoritarianism-corporatism scholars. In the short run it was clear that the happy, bourgeois, liberal, and democratic regimes that according to the theory were supposed to come to power "universally" and "inevitably" in Latin America were not in fact coming to power.[10] Indeed, as a wave of coups swept the region and bloody, repressive regimes solidified their control, quite the opposite seemed to be occurring, and the theory was assumed to be wrong.

But now, some thirty years later, the ideas of S. M. Lipset, W. W. Rostow, and their school about the quasi-inevitability of social modernization and economic development leading to democratization seem, with certain qualifications, to have been borne out. The process is not "inevitable" or "universal," but there do seem to be important tendencies toward and correlations between socioeconomic growth and democratization. It may well be that we will decide that, while the Rostow thesis of inevitable development under the impact of economic growth relating closely to democracy was wrong in the short run (from the perspective of the late 1960s and 1970s when authoritarianism was in full power), in the longer run (from the perspective of the 1990s) it may have been correct in its main argument after all. In any case, a full reexamination of the thesis, its mistakes as well as its insights, is now due.

POLITICAL AND CULTURAL CHANGES

Modern communications (the transistor radio and television) and transportation grids (jet travel, new highways and farm-to-market roads) have served to break down the traditional isolation of Latin America, particularly its countryside, and to give even previously isolated peasants and Indians access to modern ideas and ways of doing things.

The organizational base and associational life of Latin America have also increased dramatically. Whereas there once were only seven or eight major power contenders (church, army, oligarchy, bureaucracy, industrialists, labor, students, middle class), now there are literally hundreds and sometimes thousands of such associations and interest groups, depending on the size and complexity of the country. The organizational and associational void—the *falta de civilización*—that used to characterize Latin America is now being filled. The number of local associations, grass-roots organizations, church- and community-based interest groups, indeed a vast number of groups for almost all social sectors, has multiplied enormously in recent decades. At the societal and increasingly the political level, Latin America is far more differentiated, complex, and pluralistic than it was a quarter-century ago. These civic movements have propelled more and more people into the political process, made more people aware of their rights and responsibilities in a democratic system, and made it far more difficult for any aspiring future dictatorship to turn the clock back and snuff out all these organizations.

As Latin Americans have become better educated and more mobilized politically, furthermore, they have become more prudent and pragmatic and attracted to centrist candidates. It is no accident that not only has Latin America massively turned to democracy in recent years but the elected presidents may represent the best, most prudent, most able and middle-of-the-road collection of governments Latin America has had in a very long time.

Political development, in short, has begun to keep pace and catch up with socioeconomic change, which was not the case in the 1960s. Moreover, there has been both a demonstration effect and a certain momentum in the democratic process. As more and more countries become democratic, the pressure on their neighbors to democratize becomes overwhelming. And as regular elections and democratic procedures become more institutionalized in individual countries, the pressures for one democratic regime to succeed another become intense. Democracy is gaining momentum and converts. As democratic regimes stay in power longer and as they have become more and more institutionalized, it has become more and more difficult for any would-be dictatorial regime to reverse these trends. It would now require a regime as bloodily harsh as Pinochet's and a full-fledged totalitarian apparatus to go back at this stage to an earlier nonmobilized, nonpluralistic, blatantly undemocratic regime.[11] Too much has happened by now, too many changes have occurred, too many pressures, both domestic and international, are operating. It seems unlikely at this stage, therefore, that we will see very many such full-fledged totalitarian regimes in Latin America in the near future or maybe ever.

INSTITUTIONAL GROWTH

In the twenty-five years between the previous and the current democratic surges in Latin America, the internal changes in the major existing institutions of the area have also been significant. The Catholic Church, we have seen, is far less monolithic, far less conservative, and itself far more pluralistic—and open to pluralism—than was the case before. These developments, plus the phenomenal growth of the various Protestant sects, have led to far greater diversity, openness, and tolerance for other viewpoints, political as well as religious, than had existed earlier.

The universities, or at least some of them, are now more dedicated to serious learning than were the more politicized universities of the early 1960s. The trade unions tend to be more centrist and oriented toward collective bargaining and bread-and-butter issues, as compared with the street demonstrations and highly politicized trade unionism of the past. The bureaucracies are being called upon to provide real goods and services (housing, electricity, water, education, health care, and so forth) instead of only serving as vast sinecure agencies filled with patronage appointments and absentee functionaries.

In Latin America's historically most powerful institutions, the oligarchy and the military, many of the same changes are under way, or at least partially so. The officer corps is better educated and more professional; and while its understanding of human rights and democracy may sometimes be at variance from what most citizens of the United States understand by these terms, the military does understand the message conveyed to them by the Congress as well as members of the administration that, unless they clean up their human rights act, the United States will cut off financial assistance. Similarly the old landed oligarchies dominate very few Latin American countries any more; the elite itself has become more pluralistic, and it no longer can count on the church or the armed forces automatically to back it up.[12]

In brief, at the institutional level as at the social, Latin America has become far more diversified, differentiated, and pluralistic. This has not only provided a stronger basis for democracy than had ever existed before in the region's history, but it has also made it far more difficult for authoritarianism and dictatorship to stage a comeback.

U.S. POLICY

Virtually all the major political openings and democratization in the South American countries, we have seen, were home-grown and at least initially had very little to do with U.S. policy. In fact, U.S. officials as well as scholars were taken by surprise by the strength, breadth, and depth of the democratic currents. Furthermore in the early weeks of the Reagan administration there was a great deal of preoccupation with the cold war, East-West issues, and the strategic implications of the revolutions completed in Nicaragua and under way in El Salvador; but little attention, as we have seen, to democracy issues and considerable disparagement of former president Jimmy Carter's human rights policy.

Later the strategy changed. The Reagan administration elevated its democracy agenda for Latin America into one of the key elements in its foreign policy. The turning point was El Salvador. Faced with a polarized society pitting left-wing guerrillas against a repressive military regime, with collapse predicted, and confronted by the Congress, the administration determined to try to effect a more centrist and democratic regime. It sponsored elections, cajoled, exerted pressure; to make a long story short, a democratic government under José Napóleon Duarte eventually came into existence. In the process the administration discovered not only that democracy was better for El Salvador but that by this policy it could get the public, Congress, the media, the foreign affairs bureaucracies, and even our allies in Western Europe to support U.S. policy, or at least to be less hostile.

As the El Salvador policy proved successful—although the difficulties, too many to even mention here, should not by any means be underestimated—the administration determined to try to apply it elsewhere: not only in Guatemala, Honduras, and Panama but perhaps in Nicaragua and the larger South American countries as well. The democracy agenda proved to be a powerful attraction and a very effective foreign policy tool as well. The administration discovered that standing for democracy not only helped solve its domestic problem (that is, congressional and other opposition) but solved a large number of its foreign policy problems as well: democratic regimes are easier to get along with and cause far fewer problems. Moreover, by standing so strongly for democracy, the United States had an additional lever to use against Cuba and Nicaragua, portraying them as the "odd countries out," isolating them, and painting them as standing against history (an uncomfortable position especially for Marxist regimes) and out of step with the rest of Latin America. To the purist these may not all be the noblest of reasons for supporting democracy in Latin America. But in the highly charged political atmosphere of Washington and to an administration under vigorous attack, they looked like awfully good reasons.[13]

The democracy thrust was so effective in disarming domestic foes, garnering domestic support, and also accomplishing some (limited) reforms in Latin America that the Reagan administration elevated it to the centerpiece of its policy. Moreover, in moving toward a pro-democracy foreign policy agenda, the administration—to the surprise of many and the consternation of some of its extreme right-wing supporters—came remarkably close to the foreign policy of its previously despised predecessor. This new democracy thrust gave analysts hope not only for future increased consensus on foreign policy in the United States but also for greater harmony and convergence between U.S. and Latin American interests.[14]

*   *   *

Democracy in Latin America has been renewed in large part because of a series of coincidences. The military had been discredited, the local elites for various reasons now favor democracy, and the United States had discovered the advantages of coming out in favor of democracy. All these forces came together at one time. In addition, the political-cultural and socioeconomic conditions in Latin America provided a context, really for the first time, in which democracy could be established and maybe even flourish and become permanent. This combination of forces flowing together has made the chances for democracy to survive and thrive better than ever before. Moreover, some of the changes, such as the political-cultural and the socioeconomic ones, can be reversed only with extreme difficulty.

And yet the position of democracy in Latin America, while stronger than before, is still precarious. It could still be upset. The series of coincidences that enabled the transition to democracy to begin and flower could be reversed or go back out of synchronization, causing democracy to falter. There are powerful forces working against democracy as well as for it. Let us review those negative forces now.

Obstacles to Democratic Consolidation

While we are immensely cheered by the progress of democracy in Latin America during the 1980s, we should by no means underestimate the obstacles that democracy still faces. These obstacles in some cases loom very large. Some of the very factors that earlier contributed to democracy's progress might conceivably later plant the seeds for its overthrow. Hence we need not only to celebrate democracy's progress but to analyze carefully its weaknesses as well.

MILITARISM

The military has long been a major force in Latin America, and often a force for dictatorship and repression. That situation is changing. The officer corps is not only better educated and more professional, but in virtually all cases its members are no longer from the upper but from the middle classes and, therefore, less inclined than historically to side with the old oligarchy. The officers tend to be more sophisticated and to have traveled and received advanced training outside their own countries, and thus to have a wider vision of the world—including in many cases a clearer conception of human rights and democracy. In addition, the military was badly burned by its last excursion into politics and is not eager again to make new forays into civilian government, especially if that results in discredit being cast upon the military institution itself.[15]

On the other hand, the Latin American armed forces are, by law as well as tradition, a major force to be reckoned with. In Panama in 1985 the Defense Forces pressured President Nicolás Ardito Barletta into resigning, thus leaving only a thin veneer of democracy and revealing General Manuel Noriega as the de facto ruler of the country; U.S. entreaties to have Noriega step aside and full democracy restored were not very successful. In Ecuador in 1987, in the midst of a coup attempt, President

León Febres Cordero was kidnapped for a period of time by rebellious military officers and thereby suffered some grievous blows to his *machismo* and his political future. Democracy in Central America (Guatemala, Honduras, El Salvador) remains very tenuous, and in the larger and critical countries of Argentina and Brazil the armed forces have expressed strong disagreement (which in Argentina went so far as brief but tense rebellions) with some policies of their civilian governments. In Haiti a tenuous power-sharing arrangement seems to be emerging in which the military exercises authority in some areas and remains the ultimate power in the country, while the civilian leadership also exercises some responsibility. Even in such more strongly institutionalized democracies as Colombia and Venezuela there have been rumblings of discontent from the barracks.

The problem of the military's role in politics in Latin America has to be dealt with on the basis of realism. A new and proper role for the military in civil society and in the political system must be found. For democracy to survive requires not just that the armed forces understand and accept their proper "nonpolitical" role but that civilian regimes act responsibly and effectively. Most coups in Latin America come no longer because the military is eager to seize power but because civilian government has failed. Close military-civilian cooperation on a host of issues—drugs, street demonstrations, anti-insurgency measures, and so on—is therefore absolutely necessary. So is mutual respect. Civilians must recognize the integrity of the military institution and not play politics with the promotions list or, as frequently occurs, seek to drag the military into politics. At the same time, the military must respect the constitution, become better educated about and respect human rights, and administer its own institution in a responsible manner. These injunctions—to *both* groups, civilians and military—are especially important as the memory of past incompetent military rule wanes, as the euphoria of newly established democracy fades and the civilian governments face nearly insuperable political and economic problems, and as the temptations for a new generation of younger officers to exercise power and gain wealth on a grand scale reassert themselves.[16]

In dealing with the military in Latin American politics we must be prepared to accept a series of compromises. Such compromises are necessitated not only by Latin American political traditions and realities, as outlined in Chapter 1, but also by the realization that democracy can only survive that way. For example, in Guatemala it was necessary for the elected government to promise, even before taking office and as a condition for its doing so, that it would not prosecute military officers for past human rights abuses. In that country as well as Honduras, El Salvador, and perhaps Bolivia and Ecuador, it seems advisable—if we wish democracy to survive at all—to recognize a dual power structure, with the military having power in some areas and the civilians in others. These arrangements may not provide an ideal solution, but they may be, for now, in these countries, about the best we can do.

In Argentina and Brazil a major constitutional debate has occurred as to whether the military should be absolutely subordinated to the civilian authority or whether it should be given certain special responsibilities as a "guardian" of public order or as a moderating force among contending (and often contentious) civilian forces, a provision that historically has given the armed forces constitutional entrée and legitimacy for playing a political role. The latter are not ideal solutions, but some compromises on these issues have to be incorporated for the sake of establishing democracy. The compromise may then be adjusted and renegotiated later on as democracy becomes more strongly consolidated.[17]

ECONOMIC DOWNTURN AND THE DEBT PROBLEM

Latin America, as we saw in Chapter 7, has been going through its worst economic crisis since the 1930s. In many countries, standards of living have stagnated or slipped back to 1970s levels; in others the economy has regressed to 1960s levels. Historically, when Latin America has economic problems, political unraveling is usually not very far away. How the parties to these disputes, the banks, the Latin American governments, and the U.S. government have learned to "manage," and maybe even circumvent the debt crisis has been described earlier.[18] While this strategy has all been very clever indeed, it has not solved the problem—in the face of reluctance by banks to loan more to the region or by U.S. and local capital to invest there—of where the money for Latin America's future growth is to come from. The debt problem may be on the way to "resolution" or at least a reduction in its damage potential, but that still leaves Latin America without the capital that it desperately needs for development and to stay afloat politically.

The economies of Latin America have actually been doing fairly well, despite the ongoing problems. Nineteen eighty-five was not a bad year for quite a number of the region's economies, and in 1986 seventeen of the twenty economies showed positive growth[19]—although when adjusted for population the results were not quite so impressive. The growth rate overall for the region in 1987 was 2.6 percent. However, the figures for 1988 showed the region slipping economically once again.

Recognizing the resources, growth potential, and markets of the areas, quite a number of U.S. and other foreign firms and banks have begun to come back into the area. With the slackening of the guerrilla threat and the strong U.S. commitment to the region, local capital is more inclined to stay. The U.S. public assistance program has been considerable, especially in Central America, despite the reluctance of the Congress to fully fund the Kissinger Commission recommendations of a Marshall Plan and a special development agency for that area. The economic difficulties of Latin America, compounded by the pressures for protectionism in the United States that would keep out some of the region's products, are severe; but they are not quite so severe as is sometimes thought. Latin America continues to limp along, to muddle through, with unspectacular performance for the most part but nonetheless with continued growth and, in some countries, real economic dynamism. It remains uncertain as to whether such slow and uneven growth will be sufficient for Latin American democracy to survive.

There is reason to believe that some aspects of the debt crisis may actually have salutary effects on Latin American democracy. For example, Susan Kaufman Purcell argues that the debt has forced Mexico to make necessary economic and political changes that would otherwise have been indefinitely postponed. The changes she sees are toward better candidates being nominated by the ruling PRI, a little greater opening of the current authoritarian system, a little decentralization, and a desire to liberalize somewhat without losing control. But she admits that there have as yet been no major structural changes: no serious reductions in the corrupt, bloated bureaucracy, no serious privatization, no efforts at serious social change, little real democratization, very little opening toward free trade.[20] Much the same applies in such key countries as Argentina and Brazil: some debt-inspired reforms but very little in the way of serious structural reforms. Latin America has clearly learned something from the debt crisis, but the costs of that "learning" may turn out to be its own social, economic, and political disintegration.

The debt/economic crisis continues to be a plague. Democracy may now be ascendant in Latin America, but we could also see a slippery slide down the other side of the slope. In relation to the continued poverty and austerity, people are starting to think: if this is what democracy gives us, maybe military rule (which was in many countries in the 1960s and 1970s accompanied by an economic boom) wasn't so bad after all. There may be some degree of consensus among Latin American elites about the moderate and sensible things needed to help resolve the debt crisis, but among the population at large the resentments stemming from debt and hardship are severe. The rumblings of Peronism in Argentina, riots in Venezuela and elsewhere, the radicalization of Brazil and strong street protests against its democratic government, and widespread discontent are reflections of this growing malaise.

The relations between continuing economic crises and the possible demise of democracy may be indirect and long-term rather than direct or immediate. It seems very possible, for instance, that today's moderate democracies may give way to immoderate populist regimes tomorrow. Argentina's Peronism is again a major example. Populist regimes, if history is any guide (Ecuador's Velasco Ibarra, Brazil's Goulart, Colombia's Rojas Pinilla), are notorious for getting into economic trouble. At that stage a military regime may start to look like an attractive alternative. It is not that anyone is eager to have a new authoritarian government back in power, but to the banks still trying to collect unpaid debts, to the United States worried about demagoguery and possible instability, and to the Latin Americans themselves, such a regime may start to loom as inevitable. Once that conclusion is reached, in the way of a self-fulfilling prophecy, it usually happens. In these ways the debt and the continued economic depression in many areas aggravate the situation of democracy. Economic underdevelopment will not necessarily or directly cause democracy's overthrow, but it certainly makes it more difficult for democracy to survive.[21]

Economic performance is in fact the Achilles' heel of Latin American democracy. Given the weak legitimacy of democratic institutions and the historic tendency for the political system to collapse as the bottom falls out of the economy, continued economic growth is the sine qua non for the survival of democracy. If the U.S. economy should again falter as it did in the early 1980s or if the global economy slips into recession, then the Latin American economies will similarly be in immediate difficulty and so will their democratic governments. To prevent this disaster private investment, U.S. pump-priming, and more foreign assistance are all absolutely necessary for such growth. Without it (and U.S. banks and investors, who have been burned before, as well as the government, are often reluctant to get more deeply involved; the U.S. Congress also seems intent on reducing foreign aid rather than augmenting it) Latin American democracy could quickly be in deep trouble.

One other area deserves mention in this context: drug trafficking. Not a single nation in the Western Hemisphere is unaffected by the production, use, or trafficking in illegal drugs. The political problem comes from the fact that the drug traffickers have often aligned themselves with guerrilla groups and terrorists, both intent on bringing down the decent democratic governments that Latin America now has. Or the narcotics traffickers have sought in some islands of the Caribbean to capture sovereignty for themselves. Or they have used the immense profits from drugs to buy protection from civilian or military officials and thereby, through widespread corruption reaching into high places, undermine democratic legitimacy. The illegal narcotics trade is so big that it now represents a serious threat to several of the region's democratic governments.

CONTINUING SOCIAL PROBLEMS

Latin America remains plagued by immense social problems. These include poverty, illiteracy, malnutrition, poor housing, poor health care, inadequate water supplies, disease, lack of sufficient education facilities; they also include racial and class cleavages and immense gaps between rich and poor. Latin America is socially stratified along oftentimes strict racial, social, and economic lines and has few escalators for upward mobility. The depressed and underdeveloped social conditions make it difficult for democracy generally to survive, let alone thrive in long-range terms.

Democracy may likewise be undermined because of the imbalance between the state and the nation's underlying social forces. Government in Latin America is often weak, of doubtful legitimacy, unable to command large resources or to perform effectively. By contrast such powerful societal groups as the armed forces or the economic elites are often so strong that their power outweighs that of the government, which may get in their way. Or where government is ineffective, the left may be able to mobilize a general strike, a shutdown, or a guerrilla challenge that threatens political stability. Even though there is extensive public ownership and control of vast sectors of the economy in many Latin American countries,[22] that does not at all mean that the government is strong or effective, or has permanent legitimacy. There remain multiple routes to power in Latin America besides elections—coups, general strikes, revolution. Additionally, a major problem in Latin America is often not a government that is too strong (despite the historic authoritarian tradition) but a regime that lacks the strength, legitimacy, and capability of carrying out an effective agenda of social programs in far-flung areas of the country most in need of governmental help.[23]

TRADITIONAL ATTITUDES AND WAYS OF BEHAVING

There can be no doubt that the political culture of Latin America has shifted strongly toward support of democracy in recent years. This has to do with the discrediting of the earlier military regimes, the unacceptability of Marxism-Leninism to most elements in the population, and the support of various elite groups for a democratic opening, as well as strong pressures from the United States, reinforced by the carrot of substantial U.S.

aid if a country becomes democratic. The opinion surveys show that in country after country, 80 to 90 percent of the population favor democracy.[24] That is a remarkable evolution in sentiment from a decade or two ago when Latin American support for democracy was far less widespread.

The problems with these surveys are many, as we saw in Chapter 2, not the least of which is that they fail to show Latin American preference for *strong* government even while choosing the democratic alternative; for democracy's Rousseauean (centralized, organic, top-down, populist) forms as distinct from the Lockean type; for its tolerance of authoritarian "outs" or "emergency measures" in times of genuine national crisis, as well as its lack of positive public backing for those supporting institutions we think of as necessary to democracy: political parties and trade unions. In addition, while Latin American governments have turned recently toward democracy, the area's powerful social institutions—the family, the church, social and class relations, labor relations—are often quite conservative.

Hence we need to ask whether the underlying social institutions are as sufficiently supportive of democratic government as we would like them to be or as they must be if democracy is to survive. Democracy is, after all, more than elections (although that is an awfully good start); democracy is also an entire way of acting, behaving, and relating to one's fellow man that we usually refer to as egalitarianism, civism, and democratic political culture. In Latin America such civism is still weak.

There are, in addition, enormous pressures springing from the traditional political culture that render democracy very difficult to sustain. We are all agreed that Latin America's bureaucracies are too big, bloated, and corrupt to be efficient and responsive; but we need also to recognize that reducing the size of the state too precipitously is likely to result in the destabilization of the very democratic governments we are striving to uphold. Most Latin American regimes, in addition, are shot through with sinecures, patronage, and nepotism; but patronage is often what enables these governments—even democratic governments—to survive and respond to the needs of party hacks and others who may have been waiting for decades (like the *Apristas* in Peru) for their team to come to power. Now they expect to be paid back with jobs and cushy deals for their long years of loyalty and service.

Similarly with corruption: corruption is widespread and virtually endemic in Latin America.[25] While excessive corruption serves to undermine a regime at one level, at modest and manageable levels a present here or a favor there also greases the machinery of government and makes it function; where one draws the line between these is difficult to discern. One worries that by excessive efforts to "clean up" these regimes and make them more "responsible" by our lights, we may inadvertently undermine the very democracies we are dedicated to support. But if corruption becomes too extensive, it may similarly threaten regime stability.

We must ask why it is that Latin America chose to go the democracy route in the 1970s; and despite the encouraging signs from the polls cited earlier not all the answers are exactly the ones that inspire confidence in democracy's future. For example, it is clear that for some reigning military regimes the opening to democracy was dictated not so much by a commit- ment to liberty as by a discrediting of the older bureaucratic-authoritarian model and a desire to step aside and let the civilians have a share of the blame. Such attitudes could fairly quickly be reversed. Second, it is sim- ilarly clear that many civilian elements in Latin America desired a return to democracy because they wanted to inherit the comfortable and often lucrative cabinet, subcabinet, and state enterprises positions that the of- ficers had monopolized for many years.

Third, it must be remembered that it was Latin America's *elites* that determined to go in a democratic direction. The vast mass of the popula- tion was not consulted or involved in this process; and since elite opinion in Latin America is both very unstable and very fickle, such elite-led change does not augur well for democracy in the long run. Fourth, the elites' motives were often mixed at best: democracy enabled them to qualify for U.S. economic aid, democracy enables them to avoid being discredited, "democracy" sometimes is used as a banner to destroy their political foes or to serve other less than glorious purposes. These murky and often poorly understood (by outsiders) motivations in Latin America not only provide a weak basis for democracy but also serve to indicate how easily democracy could be reversed.[26]

The political culture of Latin America is still volatile. It is also chang- ing. Most of the changes are positive but not all of them are in democratic directions. And as in the case of economic development, the political culture has the potential either to be supportive of democracy in the long run or to undermine it in the short term. Neither outcome is inevitable or preordained. We would do well in these areas to be very careful of our actions.

CONTINUING INSTITUTIONAL LAGS

Numerous institutional changes are necessary if Latin America is to achieve a more effective and consolidated democracy. There is a necessity for a judiciary that cannot easily be intimidated so that those who have been implicated in some heinous crimes—in El Salvador and elsewhere— may be brought to justice. There is a need in many Latin American countries to modernize the office of the presidency, as well as the offices of congressmen, mayors, and governors. Public bureaucracies and state-owned enterprises are also in sore need of probity, rationality, and streamlining. Indeed as one goes down the list, it becomes apparent that virtually every institution in the region needs either repair or remodeling.

And that is precisely the trouble. It is doubtful if the United States has the skill, the will, or the resources to carry out successfully such a broad, wide-ranging reconstruction. After all, we are talking about a long-term effort to aid, mend, and *entirely reorient* the system and behavior of Latin American government institutions. Such extensive changes cannot be carried out alone by the Latin Americans, or by the United States; and there are dangers in the United States imposing its preferred solutions and institutions on a society and culture other than our own that we sometimes only weakly comprehend. Nonetheless, there is much that both the United States and Latin America can do to further institutional reform. This theme of what specifically the United States should do is discussed in the final chapter.

EXTREMISM, RIGHT AND LEFT

Political extremism in Latin America is nothing new; it has a long history and it continues today, even in the face of the democratic currents coursing through the area. The problem is especially acute for Latin American democracy and for U.S. policy because the two extremisms, left and right, tend to feed off each other. That is, extremism and dictatorship on the right tend to breed and provide the conditions for extremism to grow and flourish on the left. At the same time, leftist challenges, in the form of general strikes, shutdowns, violence, street demonstrations, insurrections, and outright revolution, tend to make the appeal of a rightist dictatorship that promises order and stability more attractive. Very often in Latin America, moreover, the extreme left and the extreme right join forces in a marriage of convenience to undermine, discredit, and subvert the centrist democrats. Or the left will stake out such an extreme position, or push so hard, that it literally invites a right-wing coup, which may be what the extreme left wanted in the first place, since that will polarize the country and may allow the left to strengthen itself in the process.

The most immediate threat to Latin American democracy is likely to come from the extreme right.[27] For one thing, the authoritarian tradition in Latin America discussed in Chapter 1 is still strong within the military, in the landed oligarchy, and among the nouveaux riches and rising middle class. For another, as the early enthusiasm for democracy has worn off and as a number of the democratic regimes have proven unsuccessful in their economic and political policies, the military option has become possible, maybe even viable, once again. And since political memories in Latin America as elsewhere tend to be short, the inefficiencies, corruption, and brutality of many of the earlier military regimes are being forgotten and the order and economic progress of that period emphasized.

But military regimes tend not to solve any of the nation's problems (except perhaps in the short run); instead they exacerbate them. It is no accident that the strongest guerrilla and Marxist-Leninist challenges have come in those regimes that were most brutal and repressive: Cuba, Nicaragua, Guatemala, El Salvador, and Chile. Hence the *consolidation* of democracy in Latin America, which is the agenda now in most countries as distinct from the earlier *transitions* to democracy, requires not only the further development of democratic institutions and the principle of regular elections but also work on an ongoing and continuous basis toward improving governmental performance. If it is in fact the case that in the new, more participatory and aroused Latin America of today that government must deliver in the areas of goods and services or else, then it is fundamental that we and the Latin American democrats must work to improve output and efficiency and reduce corruption, nepotism, and inefficiency.[28]

But the threat to democracy in Latin America also comes from the radical left. We are in fact in a new era in Latin America in terms of a significantly greater Soviet presence, greater sophistication of tactics and maneuver on the part of Marxist-Leninist elements, and the establishment of Marxist-Leninist bases for training and subversion in Cuba and Nicaragua. The Soviet Union now has normal state-to-state relations with no less than sixteen nations of the region, its trade and commercial ties have increased significantly, it has in Cuba a convenient military base in the region, and its cultural ties and the number of fellowships available for young Latin Americans now outnumber our own. The Soviet Union has cleverly played on Latin American nationalism, anti-Americanism, and frustration to drive wedges between the United States and Latin America; and its influence among some church, labor, student, and intellectual leaders is powerful. The Soviet Union cannot as yet match the local advantage that the United States still enjoys in the region, but its capacity to embarrass the United States and to destabilize Latin American democracies is considerable.[29]

There are in this regard two major, interrelated problems. The first is destruction, terrorism, and subversion by guerrilla movements. In El Salvador, Peru, Guatemala, and elsewhere the guerrillas have been blowing up bridges, dams, highways, electrical stations, and so forth, in an effort not just to subvert the existing (democratic) governments but also to destroy the infrastructure of the country and wreck the economy. Such a strategy harms the poor and the oppressed at least as much as the wealthy. In Colombia and Peru the guerrillas have engaged in indiscriminate and sometimes numbingly brutal terrorism, and have frequently allied themselves with the *narcotraficantes* aimed at sowing terror and brutality and, as in El Salvador, subverting a *democratic* government, not a right-wing or repressive one. The extreme left wants power, it is clear, not reform—even if it has to ruin the country to achieve it.

The second problem relates to the actual foreign policies of the Soviet Union and Cuba, and to a more limited extent Nicaragua. These policies have become more subtle and complex but no less nefarious. So far at least, these strategies have not at all changed under Mikhail Gorbachev, as they have in some other regions. The Soviets and Cubans, and to a lesser extent the Sandinistas in Nicaragua, have provided arms, encouragement, assistance, training in terrorism, and logistics and financial support to the guerrilla forces. The Soviets and Cubans were also responsible for forging the unity among disparate guerrilla groups that enabled the Sandinista (and almost the Salvadoran) revolutionaries to succeed. With regard to the democratic regimes, their strategies have been two-faced. On the one hand, the Soviets and the Cubans maintain cordial relations with most Latin American democratic states, seeking to play on their nationalism to wean them away from the United States. On the other, they secretly aid the guerrilla elements aiming to overthrow these same democratic regimes. It is a two-faced policy terribly destructive of democratic prospects.[30]

The threat is not so much that such subversive guerrilla elements will actually come to power in very many Latin American countries but that they will stimulate a renewed reaction from the extreme right. Even when the perpetrators of antidemocratic actions are not able to seize power for themselves, they nevertheless have the possibilities of producing antidemocratic consequences harmful to both Latin American and U.S. policy.

It is probably hopeless for the United States to try to deal positively and constructively with the hard or communist or guerrilla left in Latin America; they are so unalterably opposed to the United States and to democracy that dialogue would be fruitless. But the cause may not be hopelessly lost among more moderate leftists. These are people who had earlier denounced the "formalities" of democracy (elections, an independent judiciary) and especially its "bourgeois" forms. But in fact some of the most interesting rethinking of the value of democracy in Latin America has been done by people on the left, which of course includes most intellectuals. As the military regimes in Chile, Argentina, Uruguay, and Brazil in the 1960s and 1970s ruled repressively and brutalized their people, many leftist intellectuals began to conclude that maybe "bourgeois liberties" and an independent judiciary were not so bad after all. They were certainly better than the complete absence of same under the military. And as the openings to democracy began in the late 1970s, these same intellectuals also concluded that real choice and elections were also preferable to what went before. Many leftist intellectuals have thus reassessed their own earlier writings and have come to be supporters of democracy. Of course, some of them will continue to push for "more advanced" forms of democracy, an effort that may have the effect of bringing the military back into power; but others may be considered as new recruits to the democratic cause. Even partial victories such as these should be viewed as hopeful signs for Latin American democracy.

THE HEMISPHERIC MOOD

The mood in favor of democracy, which was so strong in Latin America in the early 1980s, is not being sustained. The causes of this changing mood are many and complex, but there is no doubt attitudes have changed. The euphoria that was characteristic a few years ago has in many countries turned to frustration and disappointment.[31]

Popular support for democracy as a *system* remains strong. But unhappiness has grown that the new democracies are not being run well and that the benefits of democracy are not more immediately apparent. Democracy has so far not delivered in the way of social programs and economic growth. There is a lingering fear of repression but at the same time an overall disenchantment with politics. The support for the area's current democratic presidents and institutions has dwindled. Few of the necessary structural changes are yet visible. The new democratic regimes are proving to be as susceptible to corruption and patronage—perhaps more so, since democracies do try to respond to their constituencies—as their military predecessors. The signs of discontent are widespread, the mood is gloomy, and democracy could prove to be among the casualties.

The armed forces are among those most unhappy with democracy's inefficiencies and incapacities. But among persons in the street and even in letters to editors, there are new calls for order, discipline, and military rule. Terrorism helps increase these demands. So do the excesses and flamboyant policies of some democratic leaders. The political parties have not provided the cadres to manage public administration efficiently. The debt and stalemated economies are further agents of broad discouragement.

And with budget constraints from the Gramm-Rudman-Hollings Act plus economic difficulties at home, the United States has not been in a position to increase its assistance. Private investment except in a handful of countries has similarly been scarce. The result is a growing demand from many sectors in Latin America for predictability and a firmer hand.

That may not necessarily mean a new wave of military coups. Latin America does not want that and shudders at the prospect of a new era of authoritarianism. And in several countries efforts are being made to democratize further, to broaden participation, and to create more responsive political institutions. But it does mean that democracy is still tenuous, it is still on trial, it can be reversed in several countries, it requires continuous nurturing, and it cannot, once established, simply be taken for granted. In this area as in others, benign neglect will not do.

Democracy has made great—even amazing—progress in Latin America in recent years, but there remain substantial obstacles to democracy's successful consolidation. The last chapter will focus on the implications of these developments for the United States and for U.S. policy.

Notes

1. Howard J. Wiarda, ed., *The Continuing Struggle for Democracy in Latin America* (Boulder, Colo.: Westview Press, 1980).
2. A spate of new books on transitions to democracy are in the works. Among those already published are Guillermo O'Donnell, Philippe C. Schmitter, and Laurence Whitehead, eds., *Transitions from Authoritarian Rule: Prospects for Democracy* (Baltimore: Johns Hopkins University Press, 1986); Enrique A. Baloyra, *Comparing New Democracies: Transition and Consolidation in Mediterranean Europe and the Southern Cone* (Boulder, Colo.: Westview Press, 1987).
3. *Democracy in Latin America and the Caribbean: The Promise and the Challenge* (Washington, D.C.: Bureau of Public Affairs, Department of State, Special Report no. 158, March 1987). The principle of organization employed in the present chapter in some places runs parallel to that used in this report.
4. See James M. Malloy and Mitchell A. Seligson, eds., *Authoritarians and Democrats: Regime Transition in Latin America* (Pittsburgh: University of Pittsburgh Press, 1987).
5. For a more complete analysis of the bankruptcy of the older models, see Howard J. Wiarda, *Latin America at the Crossroads: Debt, Development and the Future* (Boulder, Colo.: Westview Press, 1986).
6. *Democracy in Latin America;* Inter-American Development Bank, *Economic and Social Progress in Latin America* (Washington, D.C. IDB, yearly).
7. For example, Phillipe C. Schmitter, "Still the Century of Corporatism?" *Review of Politics* 36 (January 1974): 85–131; also Howard J. Wiarda, *Corporatism and National Development in Latin America* (Boulder, Colo.: Westview

Press, 1981), for a parallel view, although less deterministic than that of Schmitter.

8. Guillermo O'Donnell, *Modernization and Bureaucratic-Authoritarianism* (Berkeley: Institute of International Studies, University of California, 1973).

9. W. W. Rostow, *The Stages of Economic Growth* (Cambridge: Cambridge University Press, 1960).

10. See Wiarda, *Corporatism and National Development in Latin America,* chap. 5.

11. Howard J. Wiarda, *Dictatorship and Development* (Gainesville: University of Florida Press, 1968).

12. For a country-by-country survey of all these trends, see Howard J. Wiarda and Harvey F. Kline, eds., *Latin American Politics and Development* (Boulder, Colo.: Westview Press, 1985; 2nd ed., 1990).

13. *Democracy in Latin America;* based also on interviews with Reagan administration officials.

14. *Democracy in Latin America,* p. 7.

15. Luigi Einaudi and Alfred Stepan, *Latin American Institutional Development: Changing Military Perspectives in Peru and Brazil* (Santa Monica, Calif.: Rand Corporation, 1971).

16. *Democracy in Latin America,* p. 10.

17. The issue is dealt with in two recent papers by the author, "Systems of Interest Representation in Latin America: The Alternation between Corporatist and Liberal Forms," chap. 4 in *Finding Our Way? Toward Maturity in U.S.–Latin American Relations* (Washington, D.C.: University Press of America, 1987); and "The Military and Democracy," *Harvard International Review* 8 (May/ June 1986): 4–10.

18. For additional discussions by the author see Howard J. Wiarda, "Can the Mice Roar? Small Countries and the Debt Crisis," in Robert Wesson, ed., *Coping with the Latin American Debt* (Stanford, Calif.: Hoover Institution, 1989); and "The United States, Latin America, and the International Debt: Toward a Resolution?" in James Finn, ed., *The Church and Social Justice in Latin America* (New York: Freedom House, 1989).

19. Economic Commission for Latin America, *Preliminary Overview of the Latin American Economy, 1986* (Washington, D.C.: ECLA, December 1986).

20. Susan Kaufman Purcell, "The Debt Crisis and the Restructuring of Mexico," in Wesson, *Coping with the Latin American Debt.*

21. Latin America scholar Gary Wynia has pointed out these possible scenarios in a private conversation with the author.

22. See Howard J. Wiarda, "Economic and Political Statism in Latin America," in Michael Novak and Michael P. Jackson, eds., *Latin America: Dependency or Interdependence?* (Washington, D.C.: American Enterprise Institute, 1985), pp. 4–14.

23. Samuel P. Huntington, *Political Order in Changing Societies* (New Haven: Yale University Press, 1968); also Linn A. Hammergren, "Corporatism in Latin American Politics," *Comparative Politics* (July 1977).

24. See the various surveys issued by USIA cited in Chapter 2.

25. See the lengthy report in *Wall Street Journal,* September 14, 1987, p. 1.

26. See an earlier analysis by Howard J. Wiarda, "Can Democracy Be Exported?

The Quest for Democracy in U.S. Latin American Policy," in Kevin J. Middlebrook and Carlos Rico, eds., *The United States and Latin America in the 1980s* (Pittsburgh: University of Pittsburgh Press, 1986), pp. 325–52.

27. The analysis here parallels that of *Democracy in Latin America*.

28. Lee C. Fennell, "Leadership and the Failure of Democracy," in Wiarda, *The Continuing Struggle for Democracy*, pp. 201–14.

29. A more extended discussion is in Howard J. Wiarda and Mark Falcoff, *The Communist Challenge in the Caribbean and Central America* (Washington, D.C.: University Press of America, 1987).

30. A more complete analysis is found in Wiarda and Falcoff, *The Communist Challenge*, chap. 4.

31. The analysis here is based on the excellent article of Bradley Graham, "South American Democracy Put to Test," *Washington Post*, October 19, 1987, pp. A15ff; based also on six research trips by the author to Latin America in 1987 and 1988.

10

Implications for U.S. Policy

The trend toward democracy in Latin America—despite the obstacles outlined in the previous chapter—is now more than a decade old. During this decade there have been dramatic and very hopeful transitions from dictatorship and bureaucratic-authoritarianism toward democracy in no less than ten countries, including some of the largest ones (Argentina, Brazil), as well as the most troubled (El Salvador, Guatemala, Bolivia); and even those countries—most prominently Mexico—that have not made a definitive transition to democracy have nonetheless determined they must become more open, more pluralist, and free.[1] These changes enable us to say that over nine-tenths of the population of Latin America now live in nations committed to a future based on democracy or democratic principles. We may still quibble about the precise definition of democracy being used and who therefore should be included in the democratic camp; but even with that reservation the changes in the past ten years, everyone would agree, have been nothing short of remarkable.

There have been dramatic changes in the United States and in U.S. foreign policy during this period as well. It was in the mid- to late 1970s that the United States began a vigorous foreign policy campaign in favor of human rights, and during the 1980s the defense of democracy and freedom became an integral part of U.S. foreign policy. Even those earlier defenders of realpolitik became convinced that the United States cannot have a successful foreign policy unless it contains a strong democracy and human rights component.[2] This sense, strong in both major U.S. political parties, led to a growing bipartisan consensus favoring democracy and human rights. The bipartisan nature of this consensus practically guaran-

263

tees that any future administration in Washington will have to pursue a strong human rights/democracy agenda.[3]

The fact that Latin America has gravitated toward democracy and that, at the same time, human rights and democracy will continue to be integral to U.S. foreign policy offers the possibility for a new era of cooperation between the United States and Latin America. Whereas the discussion in the past has often focused on the growing disparities between the United States and Latin America, on what was called "dependency," on the need to end the "hegemonic presumption," this new convergence around the democracy theme provides new openings and opportunities. There are dangers as well—if Latin America's democratic thrust fails or is allowed to fail, if democracy is subverted by terrorism or extremist groups of left or right, if the United States fails adequately to follow through to help consolidate these new democracies; but for the moment let us focus on the opportunities.

Based on a common democracy agenda it is possible for Latin American development and U.S. foreign policy objectives to be served and go together in relative harmony, not contradiction. U.S. and Latin American development and interests are not necessarily contradictory and incompatible; nor does one go forward only at the expense of the other. Rather they are complementary. Latin America needs the United States economically, politically, and strategically; the United States needs Latin America for the same reasons—although the rank ordering assigned to each of these reasons or their relative weight may be somewhat different in the U.S. view. The correspondence on broad goals is striking. Under prudent and centrist leadership, Latin American development—the sine qua non of that area's desires—can proceed; and at the same time, an *enlightened* U.S. foreign policy, that assists Latin American development and is sympathetic to its aspirations, can both serve U.S. strategic interests and be good for Latin America. The focus on democracy, development, and human rights enables Latin American objectives and U.S. policy interests to be served and advanced at one and the same time.

Three Positions

Three intellectual positions, with strong implications for policy, have been articulated in Washington on the question of democracy in Latin America and the possibilities for U.S. assistance.

The first position argues that Latin America is so endemically and unalterably authoritarian and nondemocratic that it is futile for either us or the Latin Americans to struggle and work for democracy.[4] This argument is strongly rooted in interpretations of Latin American historical political culture: it points to the hierarchy, the elitism, and the highly centralized, top-down system of authority in virtually all Latin American institutions and suggests that these are fundamentally unchanged even at present. Even within such ostensibly democratic regimes as Costa Rica or Venezuela, the argument runs, personalistic leadership, elite rule, and patrimonialist authority remain dominant. If these authoritarian principles, behavior patterns, and institutions are so strong and unchanging, then the present opening to democracy is likely to be only temporary, and it does not make sense for the United States to become closely identified with it. Rather we should remain cool, detached, and prepared for the advent of a new period of authoritarian rule that we should neither applaud nor decry.

This is a strong and by no means trivial argument. But it provides a static picture, not a dynamic one. It ignores the significant changes that have occurred in Latin American political beliefs and institutions over the years, as outlined in Chapters 3 and 9. It presumes an entirely unchanging political culture when in fact there have been many changes. While this viewpoint is correct in forcing us to consider continuity as well as change in Latin America, it considerably overstates the case. In that sense it is a useful corrective but by no means the whole truth. It overlooks much of the vast socioeconomic transformation and with it political and cultural change—including more favorable attitudes toward democracy—that have come to the area. It entirely neglects the incredible and quite real democratizing transitions that have in fact occurred in Latin America in the past decade. And it ignores the imperatives, to be discussed below, that oblige the United States to pursue a policy of assistance to democratizing movements regardless of what some scholars may say on the subject.

The second position, equally extreme and therefore equally objectionable, suggests that Latin America can be entirely remade in the U.S. democratic image. It assumes, condescendingly and patronizingly, that Latin America has no history at all, no culture or institutions worth saving, and therefore that we can simply impose our will and institutions on the area, reconstructing its traditions and culture toward a democratic orientation. It views Latin America as a tabula rasa eagerly awaiting and entirely open to the imprint of U.S. political institutions. It suggests that Latin America is so desirous of democracy that it will literally leap at the chance to ape and emulate U.S. ways and furthermore that the United States has the will, capacity, and resources to carry through a thorough, complete democratization of Latin America. This position is anchored in the "true believer" syndrome, that the United States is a beacon on a hill, a Zion, with the best or maybe only worthwhile political institutions and that these can be readily transferred to Latin America.[5] It would have us rush in pell-mell to reform Latin American trade unions, parties, bureaucracies, electoral machinery, economy, and so forth.

This second position has strong roots in the "missionary" past of U.S. foreign policy. It is often identified with the "idealist" position on U.S. foreign policy. It is a part of the naive and insufficiently realistic Woodrow Wilson school of "making the world safe for democracy." As seen in chapters 5 and 6, it undergirded both President Carter's early statements and policy on human rights and (albeit stemming from a different position on the political spectrum) President Reagan's initial proposals on the democracy agenda. We have already critiqued this position; to me, it seems just as romantic, as extreme, and as divorced from realities—both U.S. and Latin American—as the first position.

This author, some readers might think, should be the last person to denounce a cultural continuity approach, especially since he has written extensively on this theme.[6] In fact, while I have stressed the importance of political culture and its continuity in my writings on Latin America, those writings have been equally informed by an appreciation for the dynamics of change. At the same time, while I have been critical of the missionary approach in U.S. foreign policy, I have also been a "true believer" in democratic development that is wise, prudent, enlightened, and realistic.[7]

The third position, the one taken in this book and in the recommendations for policy that follow, is for a policy of aiding democratic development in Latin America that is informed by a thorough understanding of the area's political culture and institutions, that is based on reasonable prospects for success rather than the romantic and wishful thinking about the area that too often dominates our discussion. Not only do I think that the strongest intellectual arguments can be marshaled for that moderate and centrist position, but I also believe that it is, almost inevitably, where both Latin America and U.S. policy will and must head.

Why Democracy?

The first answer to this question is simply that Latin America wants it. It does not want militarism; it does not want Marxism-Leninism; it wants democracy. It may be something of a marriage of convenience for some groups, but as noted in the previous chapter there are good reasons why the Latin American elites (military and civilian) opted for democracy a few years back and why they are likely, for the most part, to continue on that road. The movement toward democracy in Latin America began as a series of coincidences whose character has not changed fundamentally since then and that may well be maintained. Moreover, the longer the democratic regimes stay in power (*two* transitions to a new government or to the opposition are usually considered a good test of democratic stability), the longer they are likely to remain in power. The simple answer to the question posed at the beginning of this section (and already discussed in Chapter 9) as to "why democracy" is that Latin America wants it, no other system seems acceptable or viable, and there are very powerful forces pushing the region to stay democratic.

A second reason for favoring a strong democracy and human rights policy is that domestic and global opinion demand it. Democracy and human rights have been episodically pursued as foreign policy goals in the past, but since the mid-1970s the demand for these goals as major elements in foreign policy has become widespread. Jimmy Carter undoubtedly touched a global nerve when he began talking about human rights as a foundation for U.S. policy, and Ronald Reagan—after an unfortunate start—continued and expanded the policy. The fact is that democracy and human rights have become part of a global agenda. Public opinion, the media, and diverse groups of people insist on and demand them. No political leader in the West, of whatever party or ideology, can stand against this swelling, universal tide. That is why even hard-nosed proponents of realpolitik have come to acknowledge that, for a successful foreign policy to be carried out, it must have a strong democracy and human rights component.

This third reason is moral and ethical. There was in the 1970s a quantum leap in officially sanctioned and instigated terror, torture, and brutality. Abuses of human rights by both left- and right-wing regimes were widespread. The abuses were perpetrated by authoritarian states seeking to stay in power and by totalitarian movements trying to acquire it. Whatever the sources, there was a rising sense of opprobrium at such terror, violence, and bloodshed and the desire to do something about them. People were simply appalled and morally outraged at the abuses. And they demanded that their governments do something about them.

The fourth reason is developmental. Despite the ups and downs, Latin America has become in the last quarter century more developed, more affluent, more modern, more literate, more middle class. These dynamic factors are pushing Latin America, perhaps inevitably, toward greater social differentiation, pluralism, and institutional growth. Given the lack of popularity and even unacceptability of the main alternatives (Marxism-

Leninism or renewed bureaucratic-authoritarianism), democracy seems to represent the most viable and likely outcome. It is to be emphasized that democracy is not just a matter of preference (although it is that too, overwhelmingly) but the product of a wide range of developmental forces that have provided a strong impetus to the emergence and institutionalization of democratic pluralism.

But this is a chapter on U.S. policy, and hence an equally interesting question is why the U.S. government has come to favor democracy. At one level, of course, one can point to the idealism and the long history of "humanitarian" efforts in the United States to support democracy; and doubtless this factor is important. Such idealism must not be disparaged. But some more subtle, political, and perhaps more interesting factors are at work that go beyond idealism and may in fact provide a policy of supporting democracy with a stronger base than idealism and good will alone.

First, let us listen to former Assistant Secretary of State for Inter-American Affairs Langhorne A. Motley on the reasons for the U.S. support of democracy.[8] Motley argues it is in *our* national security interest to do so. In Motley's words:

> FIRST, democracy's consultative process offers the best means of translating the people's instinctive longing for peace into government policy. Democracy has proven itself in practice a bulwark against the international adventurism so characteristic of dictatorships;
>
> SECOND, democracy offers the surest way to prevent tensions from breaking down into internal violence. The moderating power of effective democracy— based on an open, pluralistic system safeguarded by law—is also the consistent key to respect for human rights and the prevention of internal abuse;
>
> THIRD, as a practical matter of conducting the business of diplomacy, it is far easier to deal with other democratic governments than it is with undemocratic ones. We understand each other. We do not mystify each other when our respective congresses disagree with a chief of state. And we understand the unique power of national consensus when it is achieved in a democratic society;
>
> FOURTH, as a practical political matter, it is easier to mobilize U.S. public support for the foreign policy actions we must take in our own interest when the governments those actions concern are democratic. Americans reject extremism and violence of both the left and the right. They would like to see democracy restored not only in Cuba and Nicaragua but also in Chile, Uruguay, and Guatemala—and defended in Costa Rica and Peru; and
>
> FIFTH, and finally, a functioning democratic system provides the best chance for stability that investors need to plan ahead, confident that the future is less likely to hold arbitrary shifts in government policy or sudden outbursts of civil strife. Democracy provides the flexibility to accommodate change and relieve

internal pressure and the freedom that facilitates enterprise and promotes economic growth.

A more sophisticated and updated version of many of these same arguments was presented in a detailed and path-breaking Department of State analysis of March 1987:[9]

Support for democracy advances U.S. interests in several important ways.

Democracy helps to guarantee U.S. security. Democratic governments, because they must be responsive to their people, tend to be good neighbors. Open and regular political competition lessens political polarization and extreme swings of the pendulum (as happened in Chile, Cuba, and Nicaragua) and makes nations more resistant to subversion. Democratic governments are more reliable as signatories to agreements and treaties because their actions are subject to public scrutiny.

Democracy also advances important U.S. political and economic interests. Democratic countries are more likely to protect human rights and create environments in which people can work to achieve their full potential. Democratic processes are good for business and labor. Once established, political and economic freedoms provide a predictable and equitable basis for economic development.

Democracy helps the United States organize itself to cooperate and get things done internationally. As a people, Americans are more comfortable dealing with democratic governments than with authoritarian regimes. Our common interests are better understood. A foreign policy that supports democracy is capable of garnering broad, enduring public and congressional support. It is much easier for the United States, as a democratic society, to work with civilians like Presidents Alfonsín and Duarte than with the generals that preceded them.

Support for democracy not only embodies American values; it reconciles the conflict that often arises between U.S. strategic interests and the need to give moral substance to whatever policy serves those interests. As a commitment with bipartisan support, it provides the basis for a consistency and continuity in American foreign policy that have long been seen as lacking. Finally, support for democracy enables U.S. foreign policy to match (and exceed) what has been identified as perhaps the strongest element of Soviet foreign policy: an enduring sense of direction.

These new perceptions have particular significance for U.S. policy in Latin America and the Caribbean, where many believe that the United States has sacrificed democratic principles and even encouraged repressive military regimes in the pursuit of containment and stability at any price. This critical view ignores the role that U.S. assistance programs and support for free trade, to take just two examples, have played in the fundamental socioeconomic transformations that have contributed to the democratic transition. Nevertheless, cynicism about U.S. purposes has broad acceptance and contributes to the ambivalence that many people in Latin America and the Caribbean express about relations with the United States. Now that U.S. policy embodies democratic values in an explicit, concrete, and continuing manner, the impact on public opinion will, over time, prove quite substantial.

If one reads these statements carefully, separating the chaff and the rhetoric from the real substance, one finds that there are very solid, unromantic, and quite pragmatic reasons for the United States to favor democracy. In Latin America, we have discovered, democratic regimes seldom get involved in stupid wars (the Falklands/Malvinas conflict between Argentina and Great Britain comes to mind), seldom seek to subvert and destabilize their neighbors, do not invite Soviet missiles and brigades, do not systematically violate the rights of their citizens—all actions that cause endless grief for U.S. foreign policy and policymakers. At the same time (and for many of the same reasons), democratic regimes help solve what might otherwise develop into difficult U.S. security issues, and they have the added advantage of providing, generally, a climate conducive to business and investment.

Even more importantly on the front of U.S. domestic politics (and that is the anvil on which a successful U.S. foreign policy must be hammered out), a U.S. stance in favor of democracy helps get the Congress, the bureaucracy, the media, the public, and elite opinion to back U.S. policy. It helps ameliorate the domestic debate, disarms critics (who could be against democracy?), provides a basis for reconciliation between "realists" and "idealists" (the democracy agenda, if formulated carefully, satisfies both requirements), and enables our citizens better to comprehend and sympathize with U.S. policy. At the same time, the democracy thrust in foreign policy helps get the support of our allies for U.S. policy, demonstrates noble purpose to Latin Americans who are always suspicious of U.S. motives, and gives the United States a clear ideological goal for which to stand and therefore serves as a clear contrast to the strategies pursued by the Soviet Union.

The democracy agenda enables us, additionally, to merge and fudge over some issues that would otherwise be troublesome. It helps bridge the gap between our fundamental geopolitical and strategic interests in Latin America and our need to clothe those security concerns in moralistic language. It enables us also to express our opposition to Soviet intrusions into the area—our prime strategic concern—under a rubric that is acceptable to both right- and left-wing opinion in the United States. The democracy agenda, in short, both is a kind of legitimacy cover for our more basic and bedrock strategic objectives and at the same time serves as a set of practical objectives that enable us to contrast our system to that of

Marxism-Leninism in ways that carry enormous popular appeal. The attractiveness of the democracy/human rights strategy therefore is that it serves all of our objectives, moral, political, and strategic, simultaneously. The difficult questions, of course, arise—as discussed in more detail below—when democratic and strategic objectives, as sometimes occurs, prove *incompatible,* when one must be sacrificed for the sake of the other and we cannot decide which one must go.

In short, whatever the intellectual argument for backing (or opposing) a U.S. policy in support of democracy, the political and strategic reasons for favoring it are overwhelming. And those reasons will predominate whatever any group of intellectuals may think. The fact is that the democracy agenda is irresistible to congressmen and policymakers. They are going to pursue that agenda regardless. To them it offers so many advantages that all reservations are certain to be brushed aside. Furthermore, there is an emerging bipartisan consensus on this issue. Hence we are going to go ahead with a democracy agenda in any case. In my view that is not a bad position for the United States to take; indeed, one could well wax enthusiastic about it. And, more than that, one understands the virtually irresistible political pressures that will oblige any administration to follow this policy direction. The question is not whether to have a foreign policy with a strong democracy and human rights agenda. That has already been decided. It is a given in Washington, D.C., if not in the country at large. The only question left is how to make the democracy thrust realistic, sensible, and amenable to successful implementation.

Democratic Dilemmas

Having decided on the democracy agenda, we should have no illusions that it will be easy to carry out. There will be continued debate and disagreement on specific issues and/or countries. The discussion regarding how much emphasis should be given to democracy/human rights concerns as opposed to other legitimate U.S. interests (economic and trade issues, security and strategic issues, drug matters, political and diplomatic issues) will similarly persist. Various facets of the agenda will be debated. What follows is a list of dilemmas that will have to be wrestled with and resolved.[10] If we can work them out successfully we have a chance of being successful in our policy. If not, we are certain to face continued strife (street demonstrations, deep divisions among policymakers, foreign policy disarray) at home and abroad.

1. There remains the dilemma between our desire for democracy and

our need for security. Very often they are in harmony; but they may become antithetical—for example, if a democratically elected president is overthrown and a repressive military regime comes to power that alone stands against a Marxist-Leninist takeover. We may be forced to support such a regime however it violates our democratic sensibilities. To support such a regime will not be easy. The conflict between idealism and real-politik remains; some tough choices will still lie ahead. Democracy provides a handle, as argued here, to reconcile these moral and security interests; but there will continue to be circumstances when they will not be perfectly reconcilable and when hard decisions and very careful policy planning will have to occur.

2. The democracy we envision still in many of the programs we support looks remarkably and often ethnocentrically just like us. We need a democracy agenda that acknowledges the universals (elections, pluralism, and certain agreed-on political and human rights, for instance) while also allowing adequate leeway for Latin America's own institutions and ways of doing things. We cannot "export" our brand of democracy to the region, but we can certainly aid the process of building Latin America's own democracy. We must recognize and come to grips with the differences between our own and Latin America's sense of democracy— the ethnocentrism problem.[11]

3. There is a fine line between assisting Latin American democracy and unwanted interference in Latin America's domestic affairs. We must generally avoid heavy-handed intervention and proconsularism (dictating to Latin America what to do) and instead work creatively and cooperatively *with* Latin America on these issues.

4. We need to avoid a loud, excessively enthusiastic, and unrealistic *campaign* supportive of democracy in favor of a quieter, gradual, and pragmatic approach. The missionary syndrome needs to be avoided; prudence and realism should be the watchwords.

5. At the same time, we need to be prepared in a policy sense if democracy in some nations should fail. We have been so enthusiastic about the democratic transitions we have recently witnessed that we are unprepared—for example, in Haiti—to deal with the consequences if democracy collapses. These contingencies need to be taken into account; so far I have seen no evidence that much policy planning for the prospect that democracy might be overthrown in some countries—and what we should do about it—has been carried out.

6. Limits must be recognized. U.S. public opinion and the Congress are not enthusiastic about large new foreign aid programs (necessary if Latin American democracy is to survive); the continuing economic de-

pression in Latin America argues ill for democratic survivability; protectionist sentiments in the United States are strong and will further hurt Latin America's capacity to grow out of its crisis; special interests may capture or pervert the democratization effort; and there remain strong doubts about whether we care enough about Latin America to sustain a constructive and enlightened policy. The "new realities" of a lesser U.S. presence in the area coupled with greater Latin American independence and assertiveness also make these plans problematic. Hence we need to know what we can and what we can't accomplish in Latin America, the difference between good intentions and harsh reality.

7. The haunting problem of consistency and double standards still remains. We must be as concerned with democracy and human rights in Cuba and Nicaragua as in Chile or Paraguay. The several human rights lobbies need to be evenhanded in their concerns; otherwise, if they continue to emphasize abuses only on one side, their agendas will be seen as purely political ones.

8. We need to be careful as we reconcile U.S. domestic political considerations with the realities of other nations, for what is advantageous in the former may not work in the latter. Latin America has long been a kind of guinea pig for U.S. social and political experimentation that often produces unforeseen consequences and results harmful to Latin America. We need to avoid imposing our preferred development models on nations where they do not fit or may prove destabilizing (such as a too vigorous privatization campaign applied to Mexico, which could well disrupt and undermine that country's social and political system); and we need to guard against advocating such pristine forms of democracy that we impose a straitjacket on the region that rules out the nuances, mixes, and "crazy-quilt" solutions that are the real world of Latin American politics.

9. We need, relatedly, to exercise patience (not a strong U.S. foreign policy trait) and be prepared to accept compromises and halfway houses on the road to Latin American democracy. If the military still exercises considerable power in Guatemala, Honduras, or El Salvador, that is the price we have to pay for the progress toward democracy that has been made. The cup of democracy may still be half-empty; but it is also half-full, and that is a remarkable evolution from the situation in the late 1970s. Further democratic steps can be negotiated later on.

10. The toughest questions have been reserved for the last. They cannot be completely resolved here but only in the political process. When, for example, our democracy and our security objectives come in conflict—as over the cases of El Salvador, Guatemala, Panama, or Chile at various times in the 1970s and 1980s—which should the United States be

willing to jettison? What if we cannot decide—as in Nicaragua—whether aid to the contras or cutting off such aid will best support our objectives in Central America? Moreover, there also remains a vigorous debate in Washington and throughout the country as to precisely which strategy and which policies are best to follow if our goal is democracy.

*   *   *

It is of course too much to think that all these issues can be resolved quickly and easily, and that we can then have an enlightened policy toward Latin America. On the other hand, by raising them here and elsewhere we contribute to an educational process about Latin America that has been going on in the United States now for some thirty years. Not all mind-sets can be changed, but there is no doubt that we—including many policymakers—are now far better informed about Latin America than in the past. There will continue to be setbacks, but there is a learning process, a learning curve, under way that is slowly producing the kind of more enlightened and empathetic understanding and policy toward Latin America that is called for here.[12]

Strengthening and Consolidating Democracy: What We Should Do

There are many instruments, some old, some new, that the United States has available to it for the strengthening of Latin American democracy.[13] Within the framework of a policy that is restrained, prudent, and above all workable let us review and comment on these instruments.

DIPLOMACY AND POLITICAL PRESSURE

In various cases—the Dominican Republic in 1978,[14] El Salvador in the early 1980s, Ecuador in 1987, Panama in 1985, Haiti for a time in 1987, other countries also—U.S. diplomatic and political pressures and blandishments have been instrumental in establishing democracy, rescuing at least parts of it, or enabling democracy to continue. Often these efforts have been "quiet," involving subtle pressures, diplomacy, and sometimes threats; but the fact is that much of Latin America, despite its nationalism and greater assertiveness recently, is still dependent on the United States and/or frequently willing to follow the U.S. lead. In this way an enlightened and skillful policy—or policies—can help nudge the area toward greater democracy. Such efforts, except in rare cases, cannot be heavy-handed, proconsular, or interventionist; but when employed cleverly and subtly such wielding of U.S. influence can be a very effective tool to support and consolidate democracy.

ECONOMIC ASSISTANCE AND STABILIZATION

U.S. bilateral economic assistance to Latin America, in all categories, totaled $15 billion in 1986. Foreign aid is not a popular item with the electorate or Congress, particularly in an era of budgetary restraint; in fact the aid we have given has been significant. But we need to do much more in the way of providing a Marshall Plan for Latin America, as suggested by the Kissinger Commission.[15] The case needs to be forcefully made domestically that such aid is not just for Latin America; it also serves our strategic interests and is important in stabilizing polities whose destabilization would have a devastating effect on domestic U.S. social programs.

In addition, Latin America is very close to home in ways other global hot spots are not and is interdependent with the United States in all kinds of critical ways—drugs, tourism, immigration, investment, oil supplies, natural gas, water resources, labor supplies, even pollution. Our economy—to say nothing of our politics and social structure—is now intimately affected by what happens in Latin America; Latin American prosperity and stability mean *millions* of U.S. jobs. For these reasons Latin America merits special attention and assistance from the United States in ways that other areas may not, even in an era of budget constraints and intense competition from other deserving causes.

Increasingly, U.S. aid has been going not to development projects but to stabilization programs and debt relief. This is a dangerous step for Latin America's future development, but it may be a necessary one in the current—and continuing—debt crisis. Latin America needs desperately an influx of new capital in almost any form; it requires further steps to get out (as the banks are doing) from under the debt burden, and U.S. currency stabilization programs help provide such relief. But coupled with that must come efforts in the United States to reduce our own trade deficit, to guard against new protectionist legislation, to provide new investment capital, and thus to help Latin America grow out of its crisis. U.S. aid in the form of debt relief is an important instrument in these efforts, but one hopes that stabilization programs prove unnecessary in the long term so that the funds can again be directed toward genuine development projects.

MILITARY ASSISTANCE

The United States needs to increase on a mammoth scale its social and economic assistance to Latin America, but it also requires a program of military aid. When civil war and a strong guerrilla insurrection break out in a country like El Salvador, it is plain that an economic aid program is not enough, or too late, and that assistance must also be provided to combat militarily the guerrilla challenge. Otherwise the entire country may be lost indefinitely for democracy. Such military assistance may not always be our favorite option, but we must recognize that in the conditions outlined above we have no choice but to use it—as a complement to a stepped-up program of socioeconomic assistance.

Military aid, additionally, gives us a handle to help control and reform those armed forces establishments that may be in need of reform and enlightenment. Such aid in certain circumstances also gives a civilian democratic government a means by which to keep its own military contented and thus serves as an added protection for democratic government. There are very good reasons why a limited military aid program, deftly employed, can be a major support for democracy.

CULTURAL EXCHANGES

Our several visitor exchange programs, and our Fulbright and other scholarship programs, have been very successful in Latin America; but we need to do far more. Recently we have begun a new program to combat the even more extensive Soviet activities in these areas, to bring some seven thousand students from lower- and middle-class backgrounds in Central America to the United States for education—another effort that merits support.

We need also a more vigorous program to disseminate U.S. ideas, technological breakthroughs, constitutional precepts, and innovative social science concepts abroad; a vigorous translation and "books abroad" program;[16] expanded scholarly and educational exchanges; a broader fellowship program; more widespread radio broadcasts abroad: expanded cultural exchanges at all levels. We need U.S. aid for U.S.–Latin American conferences on such issues as elections, political parties, interest groups, and the role of the military in a democracy. We need to support research projects on Latin American democracy (particularly its Rousseauean forms), how it may be different from U.S. democracy, and the implications of newer forms and mixed kinds of democracies. After all, if the United States is going to aid Latin American democracy, it had better be pretty sure it knows what Latin America means by that term, so that our policy can be enlightened and not produce the backfires that have been all too prevalent in the past.[17]

THE PEACE CORPS AND THE NATIONAL ENDOWMENT FOR DEMOCRACY

Over the years the Peace Corps has been one of the most successful U.S. initiatives. Its character and orientation have changed over the years; now that the idea of public service is coming back in style the Peace Corps should expand its programs and numbers.

The National Endowment for Democracy (NED) has been controversial from the beginning. We do need a program to provide aid to political parties, trade unions, and other groups with whom we can work. We need to aid Latin American journals, reviews, and study centers. These programs serve our interests as well as those of the groups and individuals assisted. We also need longer-time programs to help build up the democratic idea in Latin America as well as democratic institutions and forces. Such programs must reflect universally agreed-upon criteria of democracy as well as the realities of Latin American institutions and practices and the area's in many ways distinct political-cultural tradition.

Despite the reservations that many have still about its programs and the numerous false starts, the NED is probably the correct agency to do this. Most of its programs have been successful and effective. It has been prudent, responsive, and sensitive to the ethnocentrism charge. It has literally struggled for its budgetary life these first few years; now is the time to release it from its congressional doghouse and give it greater permanence and budgetary support. But its programs, especially those dealing with labor relations abroad, need to be carefully monitored and thoroughly assessed; and the organization of the NED, with its two political party affiliates and a business as well as labor branch, requires a serious reconsideration.

PRIVATE SECTOR ORGANIZATIONS

The U.S. government has long maintained mutually supportive relations with such private sector groups as the Council of the Americas, the AFL-CIO, the "Partners of the Alliance," Caribbean/Central American Action, and so on. The programs of these groups need to be both continued and continuously monitored to ensure their effectiveness and their correspondence to U.S. policy goals.

In the meantime, a great deal in the way of privatization of public sector functions also has gone forward. Congressional testimony, agency budgets, speeches for department heads, planning and programming have been routinely farmed out to private firms rather than done internally by the responsible bureaus. In some cases these "private" agencies are really just fronts for the departments they serve; the agency may prepare a report or a research project that it then gives to the private firm to attach its letterhead to, as if it were really a private activity or initiative. A large number of these quasi-private/quasi-public firms have been involved in Latin American policy without having the experience or personnel to do their assigned jobs responsibly—or with any public oversight. Greater oversight, of this now myriad of activities, which may in fact be quite legitimate and useful, is needed.

OTHER ACTIVITIES

There is a vast range of other areas and other activities in support of democracy on which large numbers of capable people and institutions—some private, some public, some mixed—are working. These include efforts to improve Latin American local government, to regularize electoral institutions, to improve the performance of justice and the judiciary, to better civil-military relations, to strengthen the influence and capacities of legislatures, to modernize bureaucracies, to make the economies dynamic, to lure investment, to clean up corruption and improve governmental performance. These programs deserve our support.

Yet the question remains whether Latin America has the capacity to absorb all these changes at once; and what is the knowledge and sensitivity of the reformers involved. We cannot stop all these Americans from doing "their things," nor, since these are useful programs, would we want to. But in all these activities, in which energetic and well-meaning U.S. citizens are eager to help, we still need the empathy and understanding advocated earlier, to guard against an excess of proselytizing enthusiasm that runs roughshod over local sensitivities and ends up destroying the admirable programs which engage us.

A New Consensus—and a New Convergence?

The United States has often espoused the rhetoric of democracy, but the incorporation of democratic precepts into our foreign policy has been uneven and incomplete. Similarly, Latin America has long had democratic precepts incorporated in its laws and constitutions, but implementation has always lagged behind. Meanwhile, two other sources of discord and divergence require recognition: U.S. foreign policy over the past two decades had become more partisan and divided, and the relations between the United States and Latin America had become more strained.[18]

The emphasis now on democracy offers the promise not only of providing a new consensus domestically for our foreign policy but also of ushering in an era of greater convergence in U.S.–Latin American relations. The opportunity and promise are great.

It seemed for a time that human rights might provide the necessary focus around which a new U.S. bipartisan consensus could be formed. But, as shown in Chapter 5, the human rights policy was implemented irregularly, it was not evenhanded, it sometimes was used as a facade for other political agendas, and it resulted in the alienation of some of our strongest historic allies in Latin America. Bitter discussion surrounded the question of whether our human rights policy may have helped "lose" Iran and Nicaragua. The human rights strategy was often contradictory, and the program as actually implemented (as distinct from the goals) failed either to gain bipartisan support or to serve as the basis for a bond between the United States and Latin America. Moreover, as a State Department report nicely put it, the policy "proved to be an incomplete moral basis for policy because, strictly applied, it treated the problem of political repression without regard to the structure of government [authoritarian rightist or totalitarian leftist] that permits or prevents abuses."[19]

Despite the numerous failures of the Carter human rights policy, the idea that U.S. foreign policy should be grounded in an ethical and moral vision has, as noted earlier, deep historical roots. That the values of the nation should be incorporated in its foreign policy is valid, particularly given the unique U.S. experience. Such a policy is not only valid but, as analyzed here, virtually inescapable.

It is good for the United States and it speaks to the values of our people to base our foreign policy in democratic principles. Moreover, democracy is a broader concept than human rights; it incorporates a strong human rights policy within its larger rubric. It is on the democracy issue, although still disagreeing about particular strategies, that we have been able to forge a new—and doubtlessly lasting—bipartisan consensus. Furthermore, the democracy focus makes it absolutely clear what we stand for as a nation and what the Soviet Union and its allies do not stand for. As the previously quoted State Department report—surely one of the best statements ever prepared by the department—puts it, "Support for democracy, the very essence of American society, is becoming the new organizing principle for American foreign policy."[20]

Not only is there a new consensus in Washington, one that crosses party and ideological grounds, on a strong democracy/human rights agenda, but that same agenda may serve to encourage greater convergence between the United States and Latin America. Shrewd politicians in both the North and South of the Americas, while still disagreeing at times over particulars, have come to see that a prudent, realistic democracy agenda is not only noble and honorable but also enables them to survive and thrive. It brings democratic regimes in the United States and Latin America back into closer proximity. After some earlier romantic episodes our own foreign policy has come back to the mainstream of supporting democracy and human rights. And after similarly earlier flirtations with dependency analysis and various statist, nationalist, and independent positions, a large number of elected, centrist, democratic political leaders in Latin America have also concluded that they must eventually come to grips realistically and make their accommodation with the United States. Western Europe has not come through financially or with aid; the Soviet Union is not an attractive model; and an excessively independent stand (Cuba, Nicaragua) that sacrifices U.S. markets, capital, and technology for the sake of making some ideological point, does not work. Hence, whether they like it or not (and most Latin American politicians as well as citizens, while suspicious of the United States in some particulars, still admire it greatly), the Latin American countries have been forced back into the arms of the United States. But that embrace is now based far more on genuine and mutual interdependence than was ever the case in the past. Democracy is the cement that binds us together.

U.S. policy toward Latin America has long gone through various ups and downs of attention, alternating between neglect—benign or otherwise—or indifference that is later followed by intervention. The new bipartisan consensus on democracy promises a way out of these alternating cycles by providing a constancy, consistency, maturity, and continuity to U.S. policy hitherto lacking.[21] It provides an affirmative and positive basis for policy toward Latin America that has long been absent, and provides a far better strategy than simply crisis-response. At the same time, while Latin America has often been marked by instability in its past, democracy offers the area a way out of these vicious cycles as well. There are very strong social, economic, and political forces, described earlier, that offer the prospect that Latin America may finally achieve democratic stability, or at least that a sufficient number of countries will be able to register a notable change. Many of the same pressures—rising literacy, growing affluence, a broadened middle class—that led to the retreat of the area's dictatorships are also the forces that may enable democracy to last. Such a development would surely be in Latin America's interest and in ours as well.

These trends provide the hope and opportunity not only for a more consistent and enlightened U.S. policy but also for greater cooperation and good relations between the United States and Latin America. That after all had been the dream of Bolívar and of virtually every leading Latin American politician that followed, of a community of democratic states encompassing both North and Latin America. While Bolívar and many others since were pessimistic that such a community of democratic nations would ever come into existence, the prospects now seem better than ever—better even than during the heady days of the Alliance for Progress.

Finally, this democratic foreign policy agenda offers us a way out of the excruciating dilemma posed at the beginning. We have argued here for a sophisticated understanding of Latin American realities, including its meanings of democracy that—derived from Rousseau and others—may at times diverge from our own form of democracy or represent a compromise. And we have argued for a more consistent U.S. policy in Latin America. At some points and in some instances these two positions may not be compatible. But the democracy agenda offers an exit from this dilemma by positing an enlightened and sophisticated U.S. foreign policy—one based on democracy, development, human rights, and mutual understanding—instead of a more narrowly drawn conception of U.S. interests and security. We need, in other words, a broader conception of U.S. security doctrine, one that encompasses democracy and development concerns as well as military/strategic ones. In the democratic agenda we have a way not only of resolving this potential tension but also of formulating a policy by which U.S. interests and those of Latin America can both go forward and in tandem, and not as contradictory.

The democratic accomplishments in Latin America, like those in Spain, Portugal, and elsewhere in the world, are real; with luck and enlightened policies they can be solidified and maybe even made permanent. The democratic revolution throughout the hemisphere is even more impressive because it has been carried out indigenously and on the basis of prudence and realism. The growing sense that democracy forms *the* basis for our own national identity and that Latin America is in parallel fashion moving toward it, a movement that we applaud not only for its own sake but because it also serves our own foreign policy and strategic purposes, has strengthened the emerging consensus over foreign policy goals. If both we and the Latin Americans are enlightened and wise enough, we may find that democracy not only will help resolve our own internal problems of excessive partisanship, deepening divisions, and fragmentation; it may also serve to reforge the close ties between the United States and Latin America.

Notes

1. See the report issued by the Department of State, *Democracy in Latin America and the Caribbean: The Promise and the Challenge* (Washington, D.C.: Bureau of Public Affairs, Department of State, Special Report no. 158, March 1987). The structure of the argument in this chapter is in part based on the analysis presented in this report.
2. Henry Kissinger, "The Realities of Security," 1981 Francis Boyer Lecture on Public Policy, published in *Foreign Policy and Defense Review* 3, no. 6 (1982): 11–16.
3. Howard J. Wiarda, *Finding Our Way? Toward Maturity in U.S.–Latin American Relations* (Washington, D.C.: University Press of America, 1987), Introduction and pt. 4.
4. Glen Dealy, "Pipe Dreams: The Pluralistic Latins," *Foreign Policy* 57 (Winter 1984–85): 108–27.
5. This position, somewhat exaggerated here, was associated with some of the early and excessively enthusiastic supporters of President Reagan's Project Democracy; but as seen in Chapter 6, that position was greatly modified in the actual legislation creating the National Endowment for Democracy.
6. Howard J. Wiarda, ed., *Politics and Social Change in Latin America: The Distinct Tradition* (Amherst: University of Massachusetts Press, 1982).
7. See Howard J. Wiarda, *In Search of Policy: The United States and Latin America* (Washington, D.C.: American Enterprise Institute, 1984).
8. Langhorne A. Motley, "Democracy as a Problem-Solving Mechanism," (Washington, D.C.: Department of State, Bureau of Public Affairs, Current Policy no. 532, December 8, 1983).
9. *Democracy in Latin America*, p. 13.
10. See the discussion in Kevin Middlebrook and Carlos Rico, eds., *The United States and Latin America in the 1980s* (Pittsburgh: University of Pittsburgh Press, 1986), pp. 325–52.
11. Adda B. Bozeman, "American Policy and the Illusion of Congruent Values," *Strategic Review* (Winter 1987): 11–23.
12. See the discussion in Wiarda, *Finding Our Way?*
13. A similar review of these major subject areas is *Democracy in Latin America*. See also George Shultz, "Peace, Democracy and Security in Central America" (Washington, D.C.: Department of State, Bureau of Public Affairs, Current Policy no. 998, September 1987).
14. Michael J. Kryzanek, "The 1978 Election in the Dominican Republic: Opposition Politics, Intervention, and the Carter Administration," *Caribbean Studies* 19 (April–July 1979).
15. *Report of the National Bipartisan Commission on Central America* (New York: Macmillan, 1984).
16. William M. Childs and Donald E. McNeil, eds., *American Books Abroad: Toward a National Policy* (Washington, D.C.: Helen Dwight Reid Educational Foundation, 1986).
17. These recommendations were contained in a report prepared by the author for

the United States Information Agency, "Project Democracy in Latin America: Reservations and Suggestions" (Washington, D.C.: USIA, May 9, 1983).

18. See the discussion in *Democracy in Latin America* for a similar statement.
19. Ibid., p. 13. See also Jeane Kirkpatrick's formulation of this difference in "Dictatorship and Double Standards," *Commentary* (November 1979).
20. *Democracy in Latin America,* p. 13.
21. For elaboration of these themes, see Wiarda, *Finding Our Way?*

Select Bibliography

Abrams, Elliott. "Latin America and the Caribbean: The Paths to Democracy." *Current Policy* (Department of State, Bureau of Public Affairs), no. 982 (1987).

Alexander, Robert J. "Latin America: Human Rights and Democracy." *Freedom at Issue* (January–February 1984): 25–28.

América Latina, La Democracía. San José, Costa Rica: Biblioteca del CEDAL, 1974.

American Political Foundation. *The Commitment to Democracy: A Bipartisan Approach (An Interim Report of the Democracy Program)*. Washington, D.C., April 1983.

Anderson, Charles W. *Politics and Economic Change in Latin America*. New York: Van Nostrand Reinhold, 1967.

Baloyra, Enrique A., ed. *Comparing New Democracies: Transition and Consolidation in Mediterranean Europe and the Southern Cone*. Boulder, Colo.: Westview Press, 1987.

Binnendijk, Hans. *Authoritarian Regimes in Transition*. Washington, D.C.: U.S. Department of State, Foreign Service Institute, 1987.

Blank, David Eugene. "Oil and Democracy in Venezuela." *Current History* (February 1980): 71–75.

Bosch, Juan. *Crisis de la democracía en la República Dominicana*. Mexico: Centro de Estudios y Documentación Sociales, 1964.

Centro de Estudos de Cultura Contemporánea. *A Questão de Democracía*. São Paulo, 1980.

Centro de Investigaciones Sociológicas. *Transición a la Democracía en el sud de Europa y América Latina.* Madrid, 1982.

Chalmers, Douglas A., and Craig H. Robinson, "Why Power Contenders Choose Liberalization: Perspectives from Latin America." Paper presented at the annual meeting of the American Political Science Association, Washington, D.C., August 28–31, 1980.

Cody, Edward. "The Generals Still Run Latin 'Democracies,'" *Washington Post,* November 10, 1985.

Collier, David, ed. *The New Authoritarianism in Latin America.* Princeton, N.J.: Princeton University Press, 1979.

Committee for a Community of Democracies—USA. *Democracy and Cooperation among the Democracies: Latin American–Caribbean Views.* Washington, D.C., 1986.

Constable, Pamela. "South America: A Reawakening of Democracy." *Boston Globe Magazine,* July 14, 1985.

Crahan, Margaret E., ed. *Human Rights and Basic Needs in the Americas.* Washington, D.C.: Georgetown University Press, 1982.

Dahl, Robert. *Polyarchy: Participation and Opposition.* New Haven: Yale University Press, 1971.

Dallas, Roland. "Will Latin American Democracy Last?" *The World Today* 43 (April 1987): 70–73.

Davis, Harold Eugene. *Makers of Democracy in Latin America.* New York: Cooper Square Publishers, 1968.

Dealy, Glen C. "Pipe Dreams: The Pluralistic Latins." *Foreign Policy* 57 (Winter 1984–85): 108–27.

"Democracy in Brazil." *The Center Magazine* 19 (January–February 1986): 40–45.

"Democratic Revival in South America." *Congressional Quarterly* (1984): 839–56.

Diamond, Larry, Seymour Martin Lipset, and Juan Linz, eds. *Democracy in Developing Countries.* 4 vols. Boulder, Colo.: Lynne Rienner Publishers, 1988–89.

Draper, Thomas, ed. *Democracy and Dictatorship in Latin America.* New York: H. W. Wilson Co., 1981.

Einaudi, Luigi. *Beyond Cuba: Latin America Takes Charge of Its Future.* New York: Crane, Russak, 1974.

"Enhancing Hemispheric Democracy." *Department of State Bulletin* 59 (Summer 1985): 183–86.

Falcoff, Mark. "Chile, the Dilemma for U.S. Policy." *Foreign Affairs* 64 (Spring 1986): 833–48.

Frei Montalva, Eduardo. *Latin America: The Hopeful Option.* Maryknoll, N.Y.: Orbis Books, 1978.

Garfinkle, Adam, and Daniel Pipes, eds. *Friendly Tyrants.* 3 vols. Philadelphia: Foreign Policy Research Institute, 1989.

Gastil, Raymond Duncan. "The Past, Present, and Future of Democracy." *Journal of International Affairs* 38, no. 2 (Winter 1985): 161–79.

Gershman, Carl. "Fostering Democracy Abroad: The Role of the National Endowment for Democracy." Paper presented at the annual meeting of the American Political Science Association, Washington, D.C., August 28–31, 1986.

Global Economic Action Institute. *Latin American Democracies—What They Need to Succeed.* New York, 1986.

Goldman, Ralph, and William A. Douglas. *Promoting Democracy.* New York: Praeger, 1988.

González, Luís E. *Transición y Restauración Democrática.* Montevideo: Centro de Informaciones y Estudios del Uruguay, 1985.

Graham, Bradley. "South American Democracy Put to Test." *Washington Post,* October 19, 1987.

Groth, Alexander J. "Democracy, Dictatorship, and Moral Obligations in U.S. Policy." *Global Affairs* 3 (Fall 1988): 31–49.

Hennelly, A., and J. Langan, eds. *Human Rights in the Americas: The Struggle for Consensus.* Washington, D.C.: Georgetown University Press, 1982.

Herman, Donald L., ed. *Democracy in Latin America: Colombia and Venezuela.* New York: Praeger, 1986.

Herz, John H., ed. *From Dictatorship to Democracy.* Westport, Conn.: Greenwood Press, 1982.

Huntington, Samuel P. "Will More Countries Become Democratic?" *Political Science Quarterly* 99, no. 2 (Summer 1984): 193–218.

Jacoby, Tamar. "The Reagan Turnaround on Human Rights." *Foreign Affairs* (Summer 1986): 1066–86.

Johnson, M. Glen. "Human Rights Practices in Divergent Ideological Settings: How Do Political Ideas Influence Policy Choices?" Paper presented at the annual meeting of the American Political Science Association, Washington, D.C., August 28–31, 1986.

Linz, Juan J., and Alfred Stepan. *The Breakdown of Democratic Regimes in Latin America.* Baltimore: Johns Hopkins University Press, 1978.

Lugar, Richard G. "Fostering Democracy Abroad." *Christian Science Monitor,* March 31, 1986.

McGrath, Edward G. *Is American Democracy Exportable?* Beverly Hills, Calif.: Glencoe Press, 1968.

Malloy, James M., and Mitchell A. Seligson, eds. *Authoritarians and Democrats: Regime Transition in Latin America.* Pittsburgh: University of Pittsburgh Press, 1987.

————, and Luís Abugattas. *Redemocratization in Latin America: The Andean Pattern.* Hanover, N.H.: Universities Field Staff International, 1983.

Manion, Christopher, and Ronald R. Nelson, eds. *Will Democracy Perish in Central America?* Washington, D.C.: American Foreign Policy Council, 1985.

Maniruzzaman, Talukder. *Military Withdrawal from Politics: A Comparative Study.* Cambridge, Mass.: Ballinger, 1987.

Manwaring, Scott. *The Consolidation of Democracy in Latin America.* Notre Dame, Ind.: Helen Kellogg Institute for International Studies, University of Notre Dame, 1986.

Middlebrook, Kevin, and Carlos Rico, eds. *The United States and Latin America in the 1980s.* Pittsburgh: University of Pittsburgh Press, 1986.

Migdail, Carl J. "Democracy Blossoms in Latin America." *U.S. News and World Report,* December 10, 1984, p. 36.

Morse, Richard M., "The Challenge of Ideology in Latin America." *Foreign Policy and Defense Review* 5, no. 3 (Winter 1985): 14–22.

Motley, Langhorne A. "Democracy as a Problem-Solving Mechanism." *Current Policy* (Department of State, Bureau of Public Affairs), no. 532 (December 8, 1983).

———. "Democracy in Latin America and the Caribbean." *Department of State Bulletin* 84 (October 1984): 1–15.

Muravchik, Joshua. *The Uncertain Crusade: Jimmy Carter and the Dilemmas of Human Rights Policy.* Lanham, Md.: Hamilton Press, 1986.

National Endowment for Democracy. *The Challenge of Democracy.* Washington, D.C., 1987.

———. *Strengthening Democracy Abroad: The Role of the National Endowment for Democracy: Statement of Principles and Objectives.* Mimeo. Washington, D.C., December 1984.

O'Donnell, Guillermo, Philippe C. Schmitter, and Laurence Whitehead, eds. *Transitions from Authoritarian Rule: Prospects for Democracy.* Baltimore: Johns Hopkins University Press, 1986.

"On Negotiating Democratic Transition." *Third World Quarterly* 7 (April 1985): 7–16.

Oropeza, Luís J. *Tutelary Pluralism: A Critical Approach to Venezuelan Democracy.* Cambridge, Mass.: Harvard University, Center for International Affairs, 1983.

Orrego Vicuna, Claudio. *Basic Human Rights and Political Development: 15 Years of Experience in Latin America.* Washington, D.C.: Wilson Center, 1981.

Packenham, Robert. *Liberal America and the Third World.* Princeton, N.J.: Princeton University Press, 1973.

Paz, Octavio, et al. *Democracy and Dictatorship in Latin America.* New York: Foundation for the Independent Study of Social Ideas, 1982.

Peeler, John A. *Latin American Democracies: Colombia, Costa Rica, Venezuela.* Chapel Hill: University of North Carolina Press, 1985.

Peralta-Ramos, Mónica, and Carlos H. Waisman, eds. *From Military Rule to Liberal Democracy in Argentina.* Boulder, Colo.: Westview Press, 1987.

Plaza Lasso, Galo. *Problems of Democracy in Latin America.* Westport, Conn.: Greenwood Press, 1981.

President's National Bipartisan Commission on Central America. *Report.* New York: Macmillan, 1984.

"Promoting Economic Growth, Strengthening Democracy, Improving Living Standards." *Horizons,* Special Issue (Spring 1986).

Ranis, Peter. "The Dilemmas of Democratization in Argentina." *Current History* 85 (January 1986): 29–33.

Remmer, Karen L. "Redemocratization and the Impact of Authoritarian Rule in Latin America." *Comparative Politics* 17 (April 1985): 253–75.

"The Resurgence of Democracy in Latin America." *Department of State Bulletin* 85 (January 1985): 65–70.

Roett, Riordan. "Democracy and Debt in South America: A Continent's Dilemma." *Foreign Affairs,* Special Issue, no. 62 (1984): 695–720.

———, and S. D. Tollefson. "The Transition to Democracy in Brazil." *Current History* 85 (January 1986): 21–24.

Schwartz, Stephen, ed. *The Transition from Authoritarianism to Democracy in the Hispanic World.* San Francisco: Institute for Contemporary Studies, 1986.

Sharp, Daniel. "A Private Sector View on Democracies in Latin America—What They Need to Succeed." Paper presented at the Inter-American Development Bank seminar, San José, March 24, 1986.

Shepherd, George W., Jr., and Ved P. Nanda. *Human Rights and Third World Development.* Westport, Conn.: Greenwood Press, 1985.

Shipler, David. "Missionaries for Democracy: U.S. Aid for Global Pluralism." *New York Times,* June 1, 1986.

Shultz, George. "Moral Principles and Strategic Interests: The Worldwide Movement toward Democracy." *Current Policy* (Department of State, Bureau of Public Affairs), no. 820 (April 1986).

———. "Peace, Democracy and Security in Central America," *Current Policy* (Department of State, Bureau of Public Affairs), no. 998 (September 1987).

———. *"Project Democracy"—Statement before the Subcommittee on International Operations of the House Foreign Affairs Committee.* Washington, D.C.: Department of State, Bureau of Public Affairs, February 23, 1983.

————. "The Resurgence of Democracy in Latin America." *Department of State Bulletin* 85 (January 1985): 65–70.

Sigmund, Paul E. "Latin America: Debt and Democracy." *Freedom at Issue* (January–February 1985): 25–27.

Smith, Peter H. *Argentina and the Failure of Democracy: Conflict among Political Elites.* Madison: University of Wisconsin Press, 1974.

"The Status of Democracy in the Caribbean." *Caribbean Review,* Special Issue 10, no. 2 (Spring 1981).

Stephens, Evelyne Huber, and John D. Stephens. "Democracy and Authoritarianism in the Caribbean Basin: Domestic and International Determinants." Paper delivered at the Twelfth International Congress of the Caribbean Studies Association, Belize City, Belize, May 26–27, 1987.

Suslow, Leo A. "Democracy in Latin America—U.S. Plan." *Social Science* 26, no. 1 (January 1951): 5–14.

Tocqueville, Alexis de. *Democracy in America.* New York: Knopf, 1955.

Trewhitt, Henry. "Above the Battle, Democracy Gains." *U.S. News and World Report,* July 27, 1987, pp. 26–27.

United States Information Agency. *Conference on Project Democracy.* Washington, D.C., 1983.

U.S. Congress. House. Committee on Foreign Affairs. Subcommittee on Western Hemisphere Affairs Hearings. *Authoritarianism and the Return of Democracy to Latin America.* 98th Cong., 2d sess., 1984.

————. House. Committee on Foreign Affairs. Subcommittee on Western Hemisphere Affairs. *The Status of Democracy in South America.* 98th Cong., 2d sess., 1984.

U.S. Department of State. *Briefing Book: Central American Democracy, Peace and Development Initiative.* Washington, D.C., n.d.

————, Bureau of Public Affairs. *Democracy in Latin America and the Caribbean.* Washington, D.C., August 1984.

————, Bureau of Public Affairs. *Democracy in Latin America and the Caribbean: The Promise and the Challenge.* Special Report no. 158. Washington, D.C., March 1987.

———, and American Enterprise Institute. "Conference on Free Elections." Conference Papers. Washington, D.C., November 4–6, 1982.

Veliz, Claudio. *The Centralist Tradition in Latin America*. Princeton, N.J.: Princeton University Press, 1980.

Viola, Eduardo, and Scott Manwaring. "Transitions to Democracy: Brazil and Argentina in the 1980's." *Journal of International Affairs* 38, no. 2 (Winter 1985): 193–219.

Weinstein, Allen. "The Democratic Faith: New Options in Central America." *The Center Magazine* 27, no. 3 (March–June 1984): 14–20.

Wesson, Robert G. *Democracy in Latin America: Promise and Problems*. New York: Praeger, 1982.

Wiarda, Howard J. "Can Democracy Be Exported? The Quest for Democracy in U.S. Latin American Policy." In *The United States and Latin America in the 1980s,* edited by Kevin Middlebrook and Carlos Rico, pp. 325–52. Pittsburgh: University of Pittsburgh Press, 1986.

———. *Corporatism and National Development in Latin America*. Boulder, Colo.: Westview Press, 1981.

———. "Democracy and Human Rights in Latin America: Toward a New Conceptualization." *Orbis* 22 (Spring 1978): 137–60.

———. "The Dominican Republic: The Mirror Legacies of Democracy and Authoritarianism." In *Democracy in Developing Countries,* edited by Larry Diamond, Juan Linz, and Seymour Martin Lipset. Boulder, Colo.: Lynne Rienner Publishers, 1989.

———. *Ethnocentrism in American Foreign Policy: Can We Understand the Third World?* Washington, D.C.: American Enterprise Institute for Public Policy Research, 1985.

———. *Finding Our Way? Toward Maturity in U.S.–Latin American Relations*. Washington, D.C.: University Press of America, 1987.

———. *Latin America at the Crossroads: Debt, Development, and the Future*. Boulder, Colo.: Westview Press and American Enterprise Institute, 1987.

———. "The Military and Democracy." *Harvard International Review* 8 (May–June, 1986): 4–10.

———. "The Political Systems of Latin America: Developmental Models and a Typology of Regimes." In *Latin America,* edited by Jack Hopkins. New York: Holmes & Meier, 1987.

―――. "Project Democracy in Latin America: Reservations and Suggestions." Paper presented at a United States Information Agency conference on Project Democracy, Washington, D.C., June 1983.

―――, ed. *The Continuing Struggle for Democracy in Latin America.* Boulder, Colo.: Westview Press, 1980.

―――, ed. *Politics and Social Change in Latin America: The Distinct Tradition.* Amherst: University of Massachusetts Press, 1982.

―――, ed. *Rift and Revolution: The Central American Imbroglio.* Washington, D.C.: American Enterprise Institute for Public Policy Research, 1984.

―――, and Harvey F. Kline, eds. *Latin American Politics and Development.* Boulder, Colo.: Westview Press, 1985.

Woodward, Ralph Lee, Jr. "The Rise and Decline of Liberalism in Central America: Historical Perspectives on the Contemporary Crisis." *Journal of Inter-American Studies and World Affairs* 26 (August 1984): 291–312.

Wynia, Gary W. "Democracy in Argentina." *Current History* 84 (February 1985): 53–60.

Zalaquett, José. "From Dictatorship to Democracy." *The New Republic,* December 16, 1985.

Zea, Leopoldo. *The Latin American Mind.* Norman: University of Oklahoma Press, 1963.

Zimbler, B. L. "Debt and Democracy in Brazil." *The New Leader,* June 3–17, 1985, 10–12.

Index

293

Industrialization, 61, 98, 175, 197, 242
Industrial relations, 23, 154–55, 159, 254
Inequality, 8, 21, 44
Institute for Political Education, 106
Intellectuals, 12, 16, 34–35, 146, 159, 238–39, 259, 264–66, 271
Interagency Committee on Human Rights and Foreign Assistance, 127–28
Inter-American Development Bank (IDB), 117, 195, 196
Inter-American Foundation (IAF), 164
International cooperation, 154, 155, 264, 280–81
International Labor Office, 150
International Monetary Fund (IMF), xxii, 116, 184, 185, 186, 187, 191, 192, 193, 196
International Security Assistance and Arms Export Control Act, 117, 118
Interventionism: by the United States, xiv, 85, 97–101, 103, 106, 107, 137, 221, 223, 272
Investment, 181, 251. *See also* Capital flight; Foreign investment
Isabella (queen of Spain), 11–12

Jackson-Vanik Amendment, 115–16
Jamaica, 175, 241
Johnson, Lyndon, 106–7
Jorge Blanco, Salvador, 46
Judeo-Christian tradition, 6–7
Judiciary, 255, 259, 278

Kemble, Eugenia, 148
Kennedy, Edward, 116
Kennedy, John F., 26, 103, 104, 106, 144, 216
Kennedy administration, 105
Kirkland, Lane, 148, 149, 157, 159
Kirkpatrick, Jeane, 131, 132, 149, 208
Kissinger, Henry, 108, 113, 116, 117, 118, 126, 128

Kissinger Commission, 105, 134, 251, 275
Kryzanek, Michael J., 94

La Prensa (newspaper), 162
Latin America: colonization, 13–15; colonial period, 15–16, 92–93; economic conditions, 19, 21–22, 23, 64, 68, 72–73, 169–70, 250–53, 259; foreign relations, 65–66, 264, 275; independence, 16–20, 93–94
Leadership, xviii, xx, 19, 20, 26, 39, 46–47, 186, 190, 257, 265, 280–81; training for, 146, 158, 162. *See also* Dictatorships; Executive power
Lefever, Ernest, 131–32, 133
Legislation, 154; and human rights, 115–18
Legislative power, 35–36
Legitimacy: of democratic governments, xxi, 53, 169, 170; of governments, 32, 45, 47, 49, 50, 172, 253; of military regimes, xii, 70
Liberalism, xiii, xxi, 4, 19–23, 33–34, 60
Liberal Tradition in America, The (Hartz), 5
Lima, Byron Disraeli, 50–51
Lipset, Seymour Martin, 67, 155, 162, 243
Literacy, 19, 43, 242
Living standards, 169, 243, 250
Local government, 12, 18, 35, 37, 211, 278
Locke, John, xx, xxi, 11, 20, 21, 22, 32, 233, 254
Lovestone, Jay, 160
Lower classes, 43, 176, 177, 178, 186
Lusinchi, Jaime, xviii, 46

Machado, Gerardo, 218
Madison, James, 11, 20, 21
Mahan, Alfred Thayer, 98
Maier, J., 21
Manatt, Charles, 148